Politics, Culture, and the Irish American Press

Irish Studies
Kathleen Costello-Sullivan, *Series Editor*

Select Titles in Irish Studies

Fine Meshwork: Philip Roth, Edna O'Brien, and Jewish-Irish Literature
Dan O'Brien

Irish Questions and Jewish Questions: Crossovers in Culture
Aidan Beatty and Dan O'Brien, eds.

Laying Out the Bones: Death and Dying in the Modern Irish Novel
Bridget English

The Rebels and Other Short Fiction
Richard Power; James MacKillop, ed.

Respectability and Reform: Irish American Women's Activism, 1880–1920
Tara M. McCarthy

Science, Technology, and Irish Modernism
Kathryn Conrad, Cóilín Parsons, and Julie McCormick Weng, eds.

Trauma and Recovery in the Twenty-First-Century Irish Novel
Kathleen Costello-Sullivan

For a full list of titles in this series, visit
https://press.syr.edu/supressbook-series/irish-studies/.

Politics, Culture, and the Irish American Press

1784–1963

Edited by
Debra Reddin van Tuyll,
Mark O'Brien, and Marcel Broersma

Syracuse University Press

First Edition 2021

21 22 23 24 25 26 6 5 4 3 2 1

∞ The paper used in this publication meets the minimum requirements of the American National Standard for Information Sciences—Permanence of Paper for Printed Library Materials, ANSI Z39.48-1992.

For a listing of books published and distributed by Syracuse University Press, visit https://press.syr.edu.

ISBN: 978-0-8156-3692-2 (hardcover)
978-0-8156-3694-6 (paperback)
978-0-8156-5504-6 (e-book)

Library of Congress Cataloging-in-Publication Data

Names: Van Tuyll, Debra Reddin, editor. | O'Brien, Mark, 1973– editor. | Broersma, Marcel Jeroen, 1973– editor.
Title: Politics, culture, and the Irish American press, 1784–1963 / edited by Debra Reddin van Tuyll, Mark O'Brien, Marcel Broersma.
Description: Syracuse : Syracuse University Press, 2021. | Series: Irish studies | Includes bibliographical references and index. | Summary: "This book examines the emergence of the Irish-American diaspora press and its contribution to the political and cultural lives of Irish-Americans over the course of the last two centuries"— Provided by publisher.
Identifiers: LCCN 2020007294 (print) | LCCN 2020007295 (ebook) | ISBN 9780815636922 (hardback) | ISBN 9780815636946 (paperback) | ISBN 9780815655046 (ebook)
Subjects: LCSH: Irish-American newspapers—History.
Classification: LCC PN4883.5 .P65 2020 (print) | LCC PN4883.5 (ebook) | DDC 071/.40899162—dc23
LC record available at https://lccn.loc.gov/2020007294
LC ebook record available at https://lccn.loc.gov/2020007295

Manufactured in the United States of America

And so it is that our two nations, divided by distance, have been united by history. No people ever believed more deeply in the cause of Irish freedom than the people of the United States. And no country contributed more to building my own than your sons and daughters.

—President John Fitzgerald Kennedy addressing the Irish Parliament during his state visit to Ireland, June 28, 1963

Contents

Illustrations

Foreword

Daniel Mulhall, Ireland's Ambassador to the United States

I arrived in Washington in August 2017 and have since immersed myself in discharging my responsibilities as Ireland's eighteenth ambassador to the United States. Among those responsibilities is, of course, an active engagement with the phenomenon that is Irish America, by which I mean the thirty-three million Americans who in 2015 identified themselves as Irish American. Those thirty-three million represent 10 percent of the American population and amount to seven times the population of Ireland (4.8 million).[1] This large and diverse Irish American community is a distinct asset to Ireland and a linchpin of our strong contemporary relationship with the United States.

As someone who had not previously served in any of our nine US-located diplomatic missions (although I did spend the summer of 1974 in Kansas City as a J1 student), my exploration of Irish America has been both a revelation and a joy. Although there are those who believe that Irish America is in decline as successive generations feel less of a connection with Ireland, on the contrary I have been buoyed by the continued interest in, and affection for, Ireland on the part of those Irish Americans I have met in the course of my official engagements right across the United States.

A question that has intrigued me is how this Irish heritage has been transferred down the generations so that Americans I meet whose Irish roots are often to be found in the Ireland of the 1840s and 1850s continue to cherish an association with their ancestral homeland. As, I suspect, most Irish people, I have only the dimmest appreciation of my own ancestral background beyond the three grandparents in whose presence my earliest memories were created. By contrast, many Irish Americans can name the Irish counties and even the villages from which their nineteenth-century Irish-born ancestors came.

This book, for which its editors and contributors deserve great credit, goes some way in furnishing an explanation of the durability of Irish identity in the United States. Their work lends credence to the claims of political scientist and historian Benedict Anderson that print culture—and particularly newspapers—are essential to the creation and maintenance of national identity.[2] Hence it was with pleasure and enthusiasm that I have read its diverse, wide-ranging chapters that view the history of Irish America through the lens of journalism, one of the many walks of American life in which Irish immigrants and their offspring have achieved distinction.

It is, of course, true that the degree of identification with Ireland displayed by Americans of Irish descent varies widely from case to case. For most Irish Americans it consists, no doubt, of a fairly passive acknowledgement of an Irish heritage. That is hardly surprising. What impresses me, however, is the number of Americans who feel their Irish heritage quite strongly and for whom it is an important part of their identity. It was an eye-opener for me, for example, to attend the biannual convention of the Ancient Order of Hibernians and Ladies AOH in Louisville, Kentucky, in July 2018 and to meet some of the one-thousand delegates who had taken the trouble to travel from all over the United States to celebrate their Irish heritage.

I have come across a wide range of Irish American organizations, and not just in the well-known strongholds of Irish immigrant settlement—New York, Boston, and Chicago—but everywhere I have been, that keep the flame of Irish identity alight in today's America. My European colleagues in Washington, including those who represent countries from which significant numbers of immigrants came to America in the nineteenth and twentieth centuries, are invariably impressed by the scale and intensity of Irish America's devotion to Ireland.

How to explain this enduring identification with Ireland? In the words of Kevin Kenny, quoted later in this book, the eighteenth- and nineteenth-century Irish found in America a mirror of their homeland, "a nation of immigrants for a nation of emigrants." The scale of nineteenth-century Irish emigration to America is striking and deserves to be called to mind. Between 1841 and 1900, a total of four million Irish people crossed the Atlantic, adding to the almost one million who had arrived in the first four decades of the century. Although other European countries exported people to America in significant numbers, none did so with such demographic impact at home in that Ireland's nineteenth-century population declined sharply on account of the sheer scale of emigration.

A further important point is that from the late eighteenth century onward, the Irish came with a sharp sense of political grievance, from a country wracked with political upheaval to a country that was itself being forged out of the molten material of the American Revolution. It seems to me that Irish America's continued affinity with Ireland has much to do with the particular political makeup of Ireland and America during the nineteenth century. The Irish had a political cause to pursue, and America provided a fruitful setting in which it could be pursued.

I read the book's opening chapter by Debra Reddin van Tuyll with particular interest for it sketches the early history of Irish American journalism, using the experience of three late eighteenth-century figures, Mathew Carey, William Duane, and John Daly Burk, as illustrative of the forty or so Irish immigrants active in printing and publishing during those turbulent, formative years for the new American nation.

Two things strike me about their stories that may be symptomatic of the wider narrative of the Irish in America. I refer to their continued interest in the affairs of Ireland and their immersion in the politics of their new American home. All three featured journalists were sympathetic to the United Irishmen, whose uprising in 1798, by precipitating the Act of Union of 1800 and spawning a tradition of resistance, set the stage for Ireland's unhappy nineteenth century, marked by dissension, defiance, deprivation, and, on the back of the Great Famine, mass emigration.

The three Irish journalists also delved headlong into the maelstrom of American politics, taking sides in the vitriolic debates between John Adams's Federalists and Thomas Jefferson's Democratic-Republican Party. William Duane gets, and deserves, an additional chapter of his own, written by David W. Bulla. Duane's rollicking journalistic career in Britain, India, and America, often under hostile governmental scrutiny, provides a rattling good yarn that culminates in his trials under the Alien and Sedition Acts propagated by the Adams presidency. Carey fought valiantly for press freedom and against a prevailing anti-Irish sentiment rooted in a governmental phobia about the United Irishmen and their alleged infiltration of the American body politic.

In her depiction of the career of Mathew Carey, van Tuyll makes the important point that the Philadelphia Irish were seen by many within the more established community of English descent as "vagabonds and refugees of Ireland [as well as] outlaws, assassins, traitors, and fugitives from justice of every description." Carey argued the case that Irish Americans were loyal to the United States, having proven their loyalty "with their blood during the American Revolution." This points to another reason why an Irish American identity took root and persisted throughout the nineteenth and twentieth centuries. The Irish were America's first significant minority ethnicity and were made to see themselves as an embattled community subjected to periodic hostility from the more established parts of American society. Resentment at anti-Irish and anti-Catholic prejudice helped instill a sense of community cohesion that had an impressive shelf life, and of which there are echoes to the present day.

This collection throws light on another issue that has intrigued me during my first year in the United States. I have in mind the exceptional profile enjoyed by Robert Emmet in the hearts and minds of nineteenth-century Irish Americans. A monument to Emmet stands not far from our embassy in Washington (there is another one in San Francisco) at which an annual commemoration is held in September. It was erected originally in the early twentieth century in the entrance to the Smithsonian Museum (a strikingly prominent location for a statue of someone who never set foot in America, although his brother, Thomas Addis Emmet, did have a distinguished legal and political career in New York) and transferred to its present location in 1966 on the fiftieth anniversary of Ireland's Easter Rising. Emmet, executed in 1803, following a failed, fairly hopeless insurrection, came to epitomize for Irish Americans the spirit of resistance to British rule. In their chapter on the Irish in Savannah, Howard J. Keeley and Steven T. Engel show how the Irish in that southern city were toasting Emmet as early as 1817 as an exemplary Irish patriot whose martyrdom had exposed the reality of tyranny in Ireland, while in later decades he became a source of pride and community cohesion as Savannahans set up a Robert Emmet Association in 1877. Throughout the nineteenth century, the Irish community in Savannah had rallied to the memory of the 1798 uprising, due in large part to its strong connections with County Wexford, which had been at the epicenter of the rebellion.

The other great era of Irish American journalism came in the late nineteenth century when Irish exiles and their descendants exercised significant influence on developments in Ireland. Not only was Irish America an indispensable source of financial support for Irish movements, but Fenianism, especially after the failed uprising of 1867, was very largely an Irish American movement. It was support from across the Atlantic that helped spur this movement's early twentieth-century revival in Ireland, one that helped pave the way for the Easter Rising. There are chapters on Patrick Ford's *Irish World and American Industrial Liberator*, which had a circulation of twenty thousand in Ireland in 1880, and on the *Gaelic American*.

The *Irish World*'s full title brings home the extent to which, like Carey, Duane, and Burk a century before, Ford was both a committed Irish nationalist (he eclectically supported both the Home Rule Party and the Fenian dynamiting campaign in Britain in the late nineteenth century) and an active participant in contemporary American debates. His paper was a proponent of the rights of labor and a staunch advocate of American neutrality, an issue that convulsed US politics in the years prior to America's entry into World War One.

The *Gaelic American*, founded by the Fenian John Devoy and New York lawyer Daniel Cohalan, was a strong supporter of Irish nationalism at a crucial time, in the run-up to, and aftermath of, the Easter Rising. New York–born Cohalan offers an interesting window on the world of Irish American nationalism in the early twentieth century. As Michael Doorley puts it, while "Cohalan prided himself on his Irish nationalism, he also possessed a strong sense of American patriotism and sincerely believed that the British Empire posed as much of a threat to the United States as it did to Ireland." Doorley details Cohalan's disputes with Éamon de Valera, which he says highlight "how the objectives of the paper were fundamentally shaped by American considerations rather than by the perceived needs of the Irish leader." He quotes from a sharp exchange of letters between de Valera and Cohalan in which the latter questioned de Valera's right to dictate policy to Americans and Irish Americans. If de Valera thought he could do so, he was "woefully out of touch with the spirit of the country in which [he was] sojourning." Cohalan stressed that "it was always as an American, and for my countrymen, that I spoke." This exchange brings home a key fact: Irish Americans are Americans, albeit with an impressively strong sense of their Irish heritage and an enduring interest in Ireland sustained by their perception of themselves as the heirs of a dispossessed people who have, in the face of adversity, made it good.

This book provides a wealth of other insights: for example, it offers a view into the controversial career of Young Ireland luminary John Mitchel who became a passionate supporter of the Confederate South in the American Civil War; the achievements of Margaret Sullivan, the most prominent female journalist of her time and a strong Irish republican; and Land League leader Michael Davitt's contributions to William Randolph Hearst's newspaper chain. There is also an account of twentieth-century American influence on Irish journalism in the form of Connecticut-born John J. Harrington's role as general manager of the *Irish Press* during the paper's formative years when he was credited with promoting its forays into investigative journalism.

Irish America has evolved significantly in recent decades. The conflict in Northern Ireland resulted in parts of our community being at odds for a time with the Irish government, which was unstinting in its pursuit of a peaceful solution. At the same time, senior figures in Congress exerted significant influence by encouraging successive US administrations to put their weight behind a political agreement between the parties in Northern Ireland and the Irish and British governments. Today, Irish America is impressively united in its support for Irish government policies with regard to Northern Ireland which are anchored in a deep commitment to the Good Friday Agreement of 1998 and its full implementation. Irish American politicians have long been a source of support for Ireland, especially in the run-up to the Good Friday Agreement, and they continue to take an active interest in our fortunes as a nation.

Irish America is very different today from what it was in the late nineteenth-century heyday of Irish American journalism. It is generationally more remote from Ireland, but perhaps also more knowledgeable about Ireland. Modern communications make it possible for people in America to keep abreast of Irish developments in ways that were not possible in the past. I have been impressed with the extent to which many Irish Americans I meet are relatively well versed in Irish affairs.

With the wide variety of air routes now available between America and Ireland and the more affordable fares that apply, far more Irish Americans now visit Ireland than ever before. A visit to Ireland is no longer necessarily a once-in-a-lifetime, late-in-life experience. I sometimes come across dismissals of Irish America, especially on social media, for being out of touch with the realities of contemporary Ireland. Such criticisms seem to me to be wide of the mark. For one thing, Irish America is a very diverse community, and it would be wrong to typecast it into traditional molds. Furthermore, Irish Americans are not Irish; they are Americans who have an affinity with Ireland. It is not for us to tell them how—and how not—to express their sense of Irishness, which is a product of the American environment in which their community was formed and in which it has evolved.

No book can ever paint a complete picture. This collection does, however, tell a number of important stories and provides invaluable insights about journalism, about Ireland, about America, and about the ethnicity of the Irish in America. In particular, this volume is an important contribution to the understanding of the Irish American experience through history, with its unique, compelling blend of Irish and American elements.

Washington, DC, July 2019

Acknowledgments

From Debra Reddin van Tuyll

No scholar is an island, not even historians, who are among the most hermit-like of the academic species. That is especially true for edited works such as this one. Consequently, we have many to whom thanks are due. First off, I would like to thank my coeditors, Mark O'Brien and Marcel Broersma.

Mark and I met, we think, at a Newspapers and Periodicals History Forum of Ireland conference in Dublin probably close to a decade ago. We started a conversation about the connections between Irish and American journalism at that conference that continued for several years. That conversation culminated in the decision to host two conferences on transnational journalism history, emphasizing the journalistic connections between Ireland and America.

As we were in the planning stages for the second conference, we came across an article by our third editor, Marcel Broersma, that actually defined transnational journalism history and laid out all its parameters and potentials. This appears to have been the first article published on the topic of transnational journalism history, so Mark invited Marcel to be the keynote speaker at the second conference. After meeting Marcel, we invited him to join us on this project. He has been a very welcome addition, and I must thank both of them for agreeing to join me on this journey.

Thanks are due to others as well, including Charles (Skip) Clark, my former dean, and Richard Kenney, my former chair, for supporting and funding the first conference on transnational journalism history, held at what was then Georgia Regents University and is now Augusta

University. I should also thank Shane Stephens, the Irish consul for the southeastern United States. Shane has encouraged this project and even helped arrange for Ireland's ambassador to the United States, Daniel Mulhall, to write the foreword to this book (more on that below). I—and we—are exceedingly grateful to Shane for his support of and interest in this project.

Thanks, too, to Deborah Manion, the acquisitions editor with whom I've had a most enjoyable correspondence as we've worked through the submission, revision, and acceptance processes for this manuscript. I suspect we will owe thanks to others at Syracuse University Press as we work through the production process, so I will thank them even though we haven't yet met.

I would also thank my many colleagues from the ranks of American journalism historians who got behind this project, submitted papers, and attended the conferences—perhaps out of curiosity, but also out of confidence in me, that I was not steering them down a blind alley but down a fruitful new avenue of inquiry. I particularly want to thank a recent Augusta University graduate, Jordan Stenger, for jumping into this project and trusting me as her mentor.

Finally, I must thank my husband, Hubert van Tuyll. An immigrant himself, he has embraced the United States as his home. It is through his eyes that I've been able to get a deeper and more intimate view of what it means to leave one's home and build a new life in America. I have watched Hubert and his parents maintain the connection to their homeland, the Netherlands, through family connections, phone calls, and letters but also through newspapers such as *De Telegraaf* and newsletters such as the *Windmill.* The internet has made this task much easier, of course, but the impetus and the media were there long before the web.

From Mark O'Brien

The history of journalism and the press—their role in forging national identity, shaping politics and culture, and educating the public—has, in recent years, become an ever more prevalent aspect of inquiry. There is a growing awareness among all historians of the importance of "the first draft of history" to every aspect of historical inquiry, with digital newspaper archives making access to this rich research resource ever easier. While national case studies remain important, transnational journalism history adds another layer of complexity and meaning to our understanding of the role and power of journalism and the press. This book grew out of many conversations on this topic with Debbie van Tuyll, and latterly, with Marcel Broersma. Thanks to both for being such amiable colleagues and hosts.

Acknowledgement is also due to Dublin City University's Faculty of Humanities and Social Sciences for funding the second transnational journalism history conference at which Marcel was the keynote speaker and to DCU's School of Communications for funding the index. The editors thank His Excellency, Daniel Mulhall, for writing the foreword, our contributors for their endeavors, and all at Syracuse University Press for bringing this book to fruition.

From Marcel Broersma

For centuries journalism history has been mainly studied within national boundaries. This makes much sense because modern journalism developed in close relation to the rise of the nation state. More recently, however, scholars have acknowledged the intrinsically transnational nature of news and journalism. My interest in this topic was first triggered in 2005 when I organized a conference on "Form and Style in Journalism: European Newspapers and the Representation of News, 1880–2005" at the University of Groningen, and a few years later when I was invited to speak at a workshop in Potsdam, organized by the young scholars of the communication history division of the European Communication Research and Education Association. Later on, Martin Conboy and I directed a project, funded by the Arts and Humanities Research Council and the Nederlandse Organisatie voor Wetenschappelijk Onderzoek (Dutch Research Council), on "Capturing Change in Journalism: Shifting Role Perceptions at the Turn of the 19th and 20th Centuries," in which we embraced a transnational approach to journalism history. Mark O'Brien was part of the second conference we organized and also contributed to the book that came out of this.

Mark and Debbie van Tuyll have been the driving forces behind a series of transnational journalism history conferences that started in 2016. They have brought together scholars from a growing group of countries and continents who have an interest in the topic. I had the great honor to be the keynote speaker at the second conference in Dublin, which offered an inspiring environment to discuss and rethink a transnational approach to journalism history. I want to thank Debbie and Mark for the fruitful discussions we have had ever since and for the opportunity to work with them on this project. I hope there will be many more transnational journalism history conferences and fascinating conversations in the future. Thanks also to the authors of the chapters in this volume and to the helpful and skillful staff at Syracuse University Press. Finally, I would like to thank my colleagues at the Centre for Media and Journalism Studies at the University of Groningen, and Frank Harbers, in particular, for our ongoing dialogue about journalism history and how to study this.

Politics, Culture, and the Irish American Press

1700s

1

Seditionists and Revolutionaries

Planting the Radical Roots of the Irish American Press during the "Reign of Witches"

Debra Reddin van Tuyll

By the end of the eighteenth century, fueled by repression, rebellion, and economics at home, an Irish diaspora spanned the globe.[1] Major surges in Irish emigration to America occurred in the 1720s, the early 1740s, and in the fifteen years before the Revolutionary War. Between 1700 and the beginning of the revolution, somewhere between sixty thousand and one hundred thousand Irish emigrants had arrived in America. The war stemmed immigration for a time, but once it ended, more waves of Irish arrived on American shores. By the end of George Washington's presidency, the Irish represented the largest immigrant group in the United States.[2] As Kevin Kenny, a history professor at Boston University wrote, the Irish flocked to America because they found it to be a sort of mirror of their homeland: "a nation of immigrants for a nation of emigrants."[3]

These early Irish emigrants to America were primarily Protestant workers, tradesmen, professionals, and, in some cases, accused criminals who had been forced to flee Ireland or face imprisonment, exile, or death. Included among those "criminals" were a number of printer/journalists whose crime had been to criticize the government in Ireland or those in its employ. They were generally fleeing an anticipated, if not in hand, indictment for sedition.[4]

More than forty Irish printers and editors are known to have worked in America's printshops and newspapers in the colonial, revolutionary, and very early national (pre-1800) periods. The majority of these men emigrated for reasons other than charges of sedition, or, at least, those few records that exist to document their arrival and work in America show no evidence of their having left Ireland under a cloud.[5] Three of the forty-two stand out, however: Mathew Carey, William Duane, and John Daly Burk. They stand out because they got into enough trouble or had enough political, economic, and/or social influence to make names for themselves and to leave paper trails historians can use to trace their activities and their contributions to the emerging American press. These three, because of their notoriety and influence, can be considered the progenitors of the Irish American press.

Of the three, two are quite well known to historians of the Early Republic: Mathew Carey, the first to arrive in America, and the globe-trotting William Duane, who was born in America to Irish parents but taken back to Ireland as a young teenager following his father's death. The third, John Daly Burk, is not as well known, but he, too, was a United Irishman affiliate who aided in laying the foundation for the Irish American press.[6]

Carey and Duane were printers by training, editors by choice and necessity, as was true of most American journalists of the time. Printers often published newspapers simply as another potential source of revenue to supplement their income from job printing, bookselling, government (usually postmaster) appointments, and government printing contracts. Burk was not a printer. He was the creative among the group.[7] These three would plant the roots of the Irish American press.

Several commonalities connect these three Irish American printer/journalists. First, all three were radicals—leaders of opposition opinion and editors of opposition newspapers in both Ireland and the United States. In the Old World, each would face sedition charges for treasonous acts or publications. Likewise, in America two of the three would be charged with sedition for their support of Thomas Jefferson's Democratic-Republican Party during John Adams's presidency. Carey escaped prosecution, but the Adams government kept him under special scrutiny.

Finally, their devotion to Irish freedom was as profound as their devotion to American democracy, and it informed much of their journalism. Their focus on Irish issues also made them radicals in a period that Thomas Jefferson referred to as "the reign of witches."[8]

This chapter will focus on the contributions of two of these three radical journalists in creating a news presence that served the needs of the burgeoning Irish American population by providing information from home, contextualizing information about their new home through an Irish lens, and also strengthening America's devotion to freedom of the press through their battles over sedition with the Adams administration. Duane's contributions will be considered separately in the next chapter by David W. Bulla, due to his importance to American journalism through his editorship of the leading Democratic-Republican newspaper, the Philadelphia *Aurora*, and his multiple prosecutions for sedition under both common law and the Sedition Act, not to mention his being a constant thorn in the side of the Adams administration.

The American Context

Carey, Duane, and Burk came to the fore of American journalism in the late 1790s. Carey was already a well-known Philadelphia publisher by then. He had arrived in America about a decade before and risen to prominence in Philadelphia, then the capital, as a newspaperman and then pamphleteer, printer, and bookseller. Duane and Burk were the latecomers. Both arrived in America in 1796, the year John Adams was elected second president of the United States, and Thomas Jefferson was elected vice president. This situation was more complicated than it might appear. Adams and Jefferson despised one another. Further, America's first political parties were appearing. The Federalists, who preferred a strong central government, coalesced around Adams and Alexander Hamilton; the Democratic-Republicans, who preferred a weak central government, around Jefferson and James Madison.

Within a year of being elected, Adams faced challenges on both the foreign and the domestic fronts. With regard to foreign affairs, the second president had to deal with a diplomatic incident with France known as the XYZ Affair that escalated into an undeclared war. Domestically, the parties were fighting over who should be America's chief ally: Great Britain (Federalists) or France (Democratic-Republicans).

This already complex situation became even more complicated when Ireland was added into the picture. Ireland, known to have an alliance with France against Great Britain, was exporting thousands of its citizens to America. The Federalists were particularly alarmed by the arrival of those fleeing the United Irishmen rising of 1798. Federalists saw America being overrun by friends of its chief enemy, and, to make matters worse, the majority of Irish who arrived in America tended to support the Democratic-Republicans rather than the Federalists. That diminished Adams's chances of being reelected in the 1800 election.

So, this was the context into which Duane and Burk waded when they arrived in America. Both were thought to be United Irishmen supporters, as was Carey. Both became editors of Democratic-Republican newspapers. Carey no longer edited a newspaper, but he did write pamphlets, and he helped run an aid society for newly arrived Irish. Further, he, too, had been forced to flee Ireland, because of not one but three charges of seditious libel, though his offenses were from much earlier times.[9] From a Federalist perspective, Carey was just as complicit in conspiring against America as were Duane and Burk.

As Democratic-Republicans, Carey, Duane, and Burk were in the political minority at a time when "minority" equaled opposition. This was already a dangerous position for a journalist to be in with a pro-British president in office and a war with France brewing. Both complicated their situations with their journalistic writings. Duane and Burk each wrote editorials that were pro-French, pro–Irish independence, anti-Federalist, and anti-British. These editorials just provoked the Federalists, who already saw being pro-Irish as the equivalent of being pro-French, given that an alliance existed between the United Irishmen and France against Great Britain.

Plagued by an undeclared war with France and cognizant of Ireland's alliance with France in a bid for throwing off British shackles, Adams's rogue of a secretary of state, Timothy Pickering, and his leading press supporters such as William Cobbett and John Fenno, worked to silence and discredit these editors. Carey, perhaps because he had been in the United States longer and had already achieved his success as a journalist and printer, was a bit more sly in his opposition to the constraints on immigrants and journalists imposed by the Alien and Sedition Acts. He had fewer tribulations during "the reign of witches," also in large part because he was out of the news business.[10]

Mathew Carey

Mathew Carey was the first prominent Irish immigrant to make a name for himself in American journalism. Born in 1760, Carey came of age at the time of the American Revolution. Watching as Americans fought for their liberty from Great Britain, Carey developed what might be considered "radical interests." He also became interested in the printing trade, but his father, a former captain in the British Navy and naval contractor, refused to help him find a printing apprenticeship. Christopher Carey perhaps had some idea already of what his son might be capable of and the trouble he could get himself into if he had type, paper, and ink at his disposal. The younger Carey had a fiery temper from childhood, caused in part by bullying he experienced as a youth. Carey was injured as an infant when the family nurse dropped him and injured his foot so badly that he was left with a life-long limp. When other children taunted and teased him about being disabled, he came out fighting.[11]

When his father refused to help him establish a printing career, Carey found his own apprenticeship—with Thomas McDonnell, a pro-American, anti-British bookseller who also contributed to a radical newspaper, the *Hibernian Journal* (Dublin).[12] Carey also began writing for the *Hibernian Journal* and before long took up writing pamphlets. Carey wrote his first pamphlet in the midst of a 1779 rising. It was a screed that called for immediate repeal of Ireland's penal laws. Carey's piece was fairly innocuous, but the ad he created to sell it was not, for it appeared to support armed resistance to British rule. Rather than wait for his son to be arrested, Carey's father shipped him off to France, where he met Benjamin Franklin and went to work in his printshop. Carey also met the Marquis de la Fayette during his year in France. After that year, Carey considered it safe to return to Dublin and the printing trade. He apparently had his father's blessing this time, for the elder Carey funded the venture that made Carey editor of the opposition newspaper, the *Freeman's Journal* (Dublin). He would later open his own newspaper, the *Volunteer's Journal*. The paper was named for and targeted to the Volunteers, an armed militia whose stated purpose was to protect Ireland from invasion by the French but whose real aim was to overthrow the British. The *Volunteer's Journal* was considered the most radical newspaper in Dublin. Carey himself admitted he was not quite skilled enough to operate a newspaper on his own. He wrote that the paper "partook largely of the character of its proprietor and editor. Its career was enthusiastic and violent. It suited the temper of the times; exercised a decided influence on public opinion," and before long, had a circulation greater than that of the *Dublin Evening Post*. For four years, Carey managed to publish his radical journal without provoking British authorities.[13]

All that changed in 1784, however, when the Irish House of Commons issued a warrant for Carey's arrest for sedition for publishing a cartoon portraying the hanging of John Foster, the chair of the Irish Parliament's Committee of Ways and Means. Carey was annoyed with Foster for defeating a protective tariff. Carey also demanded at least once in print that Foster be hanged as a traitor. After evading authorities for some time, Carey made an ill-fated trip to his Abbey Street printing office early on a Sunday morning. A sober and conscientious guardsman who was charged with keeping watch on the printshop apprehended him. Carey successfully argued that only the mayor, not Parliament, had the authority to arrest him on a civil matter. Rather than deal with him then, Parliament shipped the young printer off to prison and left him there until their session ended. The parliamentary recess meant a reprieve for Carey in the form of a temporary release from prison. Rather than await the next session, Carey boarded a ship bound for America in September 1784.[14]

He arrived in Philadelphia almost penniless, but as it happened, Lafayette happened to be visiting the United States and sought out

Carey when he stopped in Philadelphia en route for New York. The young printer told the marquis that he hoped to start a newspaper in Philadelphia, but was penniless because he had not had time to sell his newspaper before fleeing Dublin. The next morning, Carey found an envelope with $400 in it, left for him by the French nobleman. Carey would start a publishing empire with that money that would eventually include bookselling, newspapers, and magazines. Working with a Dublin bookseller, Patrick Byrne, Carey facilitated the flow of information from Ireland to the United States. He got books from Byrne and arranged their distribution with booksellers in virtually every state, thereby creating a transatlantic information network. He would also take an active role in the earliest Irish civic organizations in America—one a society for the relief of Irish immigrants to Philadelphia and the other the United Irishmen. Carey's editorial positions in his magazine, *American Museum*, brought him to the attention and made him a darling of leading Federalists—for a while. He supported many of their policies, including the National Bank, protective tariffs, and the restructuring of the post-Revolution national economy, but by the end of Washington's first term, the party and Carey were moving toward different political philosophies. Carey, an enthusiastic supporter of the French Revolution and its republican ideals, became uncomfortable with the Federalist's pro-British policies. How great a threat the Society of United Irishmen presented for American security was another issue where Carey and the Federalists disagreed.[15]

The United Irishmen and their involvement in American politics would be a major political issue for John Adams's administration. The Society of United Irishmen had its origins in a failed rising in Ireland in 1798, and many Irish emigrated to America either to escape the violence or to avoid prosecution for taking up arms against the British. Irishmen in America formed chapters of the United Irishmen, mostly to support the cause of Irish independence. However, because of the association between the United Irishmen and France, the Federalists viewed anyone connected to the organization with distrust. Also troubling to the Federalists was that so many Irish emigrants affiliated with Jefferson's party. Because the Irish were the largest immigrant group in America at the time, they had the potential to throw future elections to the Democratic-Republicans. Compounding the problem, the American United Irishmen were most active in Philadelphia, then the US capital, and hence worked right under the noses of the Federalist administration.[16]

Meetings of the American United Irishmen focused on reading radical works, many of which Carey likely printed. Members also printed and distributed radical works, such as Thomas Paine's *Age of Reason*. Further, some newspapers linked the United Irishmen with the Free Masons and the Illuminati. In later times, a secret society like the Masons or the United Irishmen would not be cause for concern, but this was early days in America. The US government was yet untried. True, George Washington had given up power to John Adams willingly, but they were both part of the emerging Federalist party. However, Adams had beaten his challenger, Thomas Jefferson, in the Electoral College by only three votes, which was not exactly a ringing endorsement of his presidency.[17] The country, already at war with France, had not yet achieved political stability, creating a situation ripe for suppression of expression. According to Fred Siebert, governments are more likely to clamp down on freedoms of press and speech in times of instability such as that which marked the Adams presidency.[18]

Carey actively worked to overcome the Federalist frenzy over the United Irishmen. By the late 1790s, he had been in America more than a decade, and he was an established and respected businessman. He tried to counter the arguments of the Federalist press that the Philadelphia Irish were "vagabonds and refugees of Ireland [as well as] outlaws, assassins, traitors, and fugitives from justice of every description." In Carey's opinion, Irish Americans were loyal to the United States, and they had proven their loyalty with their blood during the American Revolution.[19]

Though Carey no longer edited either his newspaper or his magazine, he did remain active writing political and economic pamphlets—more so during the debates on the Alien and Sedition Acts—thereby laying the groundwork for the newcomers, Duane and Burk. He began laying the foundation, in large measure, in his earlier publishing days when he took positions that supported American policies that favored relations with the French. Carey wrote little about why his politics shifted toward the Democratic-Republicans, but his Irish heritage and his experience with persecution by British officials must have influenced his political attitudes. His anti-British editorial positions did not have the pro-Irish tinge to them that Duane's and Burk's would have, but Carey's public work on behalf of Irish immigrants and Republican politics spoke clearly of where his loyalties lay.

John Daly Burk

Virtually nothing is known of John Daly Burk's life before he enrolled in Trinity College in 1792. It is thought that he came from Cork, but little else is known of his background. He must have been Protestant, for he started at Trinity a year before Catholics were allowed to attend. It is known that he enrolled at Trinity College as a "sizar." A sizar was a student who had passed a competitive exam and who, having scored high enough to warrant admission, received his education for free in exchange for working at the college. One author concluded this meant he had to have been both extremely bright and from a family of limited means.[20]

Burk was not so different from either Duane or Carey. He was a radical at heart, and his activities while at Trinity got him expelled for deism and republicanism. Burk, like Duane, came to America as a political refugee. He was forced to flee Ireland in 1796 to avoid a sedition charge for his attempt to free a political prisoner on his way to the gallows. Burk was also known to contribute occasionally to an opposition newspaper. According to legend, Burk acquired his middle name, Daly, during his hasty escape from Dublin. He adopted Daly as his middle name to commemorate a young woman who donated a set of her clothing to facilitate his escape dressed as a woman.[21]

Burk's involvement with the United Irishmen predated his emigration. While a student at Trinity, he contributed occasionally to the tri-weekly *Dublin Evening Post*, an antigovernment journal whose owner, John Magee, had spent considerable time in jail for his editorials. That was sufficient to have Burk on the government watch list even without his stunt at the gallows.[22]

Burk arrived in America in late March 1796. He was listed among the new arrivals in the April 2 issue of the Boston, Massachusetts, *Columbian Sentinel.* Rumors of Burk's narrow escape from a sedition charge must have started circulating in Boston soon after his arrival. On April 6, a Boston newspaper carried a story announcing that no reward was being offered for his return to Ireland, for his escape had not been "from prosecution but from persecution." The paper went on to say he was a decent sort whose principles were "rational and republican."[23]

Though a playwright at heart, Burk made his living as a journalist. By October 1796, he and printer Alexander Martin had started Boston's first daily, the *Polar Star and Boston Daily Advertiser.*[24] Burk was a conscientious and able editor. He fact-checked exchanges, translated foreign news into English, and verified geographical locations mentioned in stories. Burk at least initially favored foreign news, though he did devote a column to Congress when it was in session. Further, Burk had ideas about journalistic conduct that were beyond his time. He believed journalists should attribute news to the original source, tell the truth, and be aware that journalists in a democratic country had special responsibilities. Although he was aware of an emerging partisan rivalry between Federalists and Democratic-Republicans, Burk tried to be impartial in his coverage—at least initially.[25] He tended to approve of French ventures abroad—presuming that republicans could never be imperialists.[26] And when he learned of a possible invasion of Ireland by the French, his Irish nationalism came to the fore. He anticipated the liberation of Ireland at last.[27]

The level of newspaper competition in Boston made it difficult for a new start-up paper to succeed, and the *Polar Star* lasted only a few months.[28] Within several months, Burk relocated to New York, where he pursued his playwriting career.[29] He would eventually, however, return to journalism as a member of the staff of the *Time-Piece* in New York.[30] Federalists branded the *Time-Piece*, along with the *Aurora*, as the "most horrible examples of licentiousness" in the press.[31]

The semiweekly *Time-Piece* started publishing slightly more than a week after John Adams was inaugurated president. Its editor was Philip Freneau, formerly of the *National Gazette*. Freneau's editorship was short-lived, however. He retired in March 1798. The paper's second editor was Mathew Davis, who lasted only three months. By the summer of 1798, Burk was hired as the paper's third editor and co-owner. His partner was Dr. James Smith. Like Davis, Burk would last only a few months. He published his last issue in August 1798. Smith's family had a long association with Republican Aaron Burr, and it is likely Burr was the financier of the paper.[32]

Around this time, Burk committed fully to the Democratic-Republican Party, finding its principles to be more in keeping with those of the American and French Revolutions. The behavior of the Federalists during the XYZ Affair and the Quasi-War contributed to "Burk's conversion to full-fledged Republicanism."[33]

The conflict with France made 1798 an inauspicious time to become a Democratic-Republican newspaper editor, particularly if one was of Irish birth. Federalist editors were making all sorts of wild claims about the United Irishmen, including that they had forty thousand members who were plotting "revolution in the United States in favor of France."[34] The Federalists were the power base in New York, but leading Democratic-Republicans such as Burr were building up their party, and they were paying special attention to courting Irish Americans. Just the opposite was true of the Federalists. Federalists presumed most Irish immigrants were supporters, if not members, of the United Irishmen, an organization they believed to be subversive and conspiring with the French against the American government.[35]

The primary Federalist organ in Philadelphia, the *Gazette of the United States*, published a letter to the editor that contended the Illuminati had created a direct communications network with "the usurpers in France, whose aid was readily promised to the United Irishmen."[36] Further, the paper reported, accurately, that the United Irishmen had invited the French to invade Ireland as a stab at ending British rule: "This extensive and dark association of miscreants intended to plunge their weapons of cruel war into the bowels of their mother country. . . . They invited the tyrants of France, brethren in iniquity, as the only power on earth who would promote the scheme of carnage and plunder."[37] The *New Hampshire Gazette* stated flatly, "The Society of United Irishmen has come to America and whatever their intentions, they cannot be good for America."[38]

The New Hampshire paper was partially right. Irish Americans were joining the United Irishmen in droves, but there is no evidence that they were plotting against the United States.[39] Editors such as Burk and Duane exacerbated the problem, though, when they published articles that praised the United Irishmen in Ireland and welcomed the refugees to America. The most spirited defense of the United Irishmen Burk published was a letter to the editor that responded to a *Gazette of the United States* article critical of the United Irishmen and favoring the Sedition Act. The piece argued that anyone who called for the extermination of the United Irishmen was overlooking that they had fled Ireland "to participate in the sweets of Republican liberty, in this asylum of the apprised; not to sap its foundation and fundamental principles, but to support it, if required, against all foreign and domestic traitors." The writer further argued that "if United Irishmen have erred, so have the warriors who effected the independence of America, and the hero of Mount Vernon shall be designated with the title of Arch Rebel."[40]

As editor of the *Time-Piece*, Burk also published announcements of United Irishmen meetings in Philadelphia.[41] Burk was known to have taken a leadership role in the Philadelphia branch of the society. In July 1798, he published a report of a meeting to celebrate the Fourth of July, which he chaired. Some of the toasts given at that meeting should have calmed Federalists' fears. The last of the planned toasts, for example, declared support for "American Independence—Irishmen shed their blood to Achieve it; they will die, if necessary, to defend it." Others would have served only to stir up the Federalists: "The Day; may Americans never be ashamed to celebrate this glorious anniversary, unless they permit their constitution to be violated." This toast was followed shortly by, "The Alien Bill. It must have been intended to operate only against royalists and [unreadable Latin phrase]."[42]

Only the hysterical Federalists, stressed by their undeclared war with France, could read disloyalty into the toasts at that gathering. Of the twelve toasts given that night, "eight . . . dealt with exclusively American problems and only two were to an Irish Republic." This was a gathering of Americans to celebrate Independence Day. Any Irish overtones were slight at best.[43]

As Congress debated the Sedition Act in the summer of 1798, Republican newspapers were scrutinized for any hint of treasonous content. Federalists did not wait for the law to go into effect to go after Burk, however. Arrested on Pickering's orders with a warrant signed by John Adams, Burk was charged with common law seditious libel for calling the president a "mock monarch," and also accusing him of falsifying a letter about government negotiations with France. Burk had also accused Secretary of State Timothy Pickering of being a known associate of a United Irishman.[44]

Burk was released on a $2,000 bond and disappeared for a while after a fight with his partner, who had been charged with libel but not sedition.[45] Without a newspaper to edit, Burk asked his friend Aaron Burr to try to settle his case out of court by getting the federal prosecutor to agree to drop the charges if Burk agreed to leave the United States. His thought was to go to France and work for Irish independence from there. The prosecutor returned with a counterproposal. If Burk would leave the Western Hemisphere, he would drop the charges. Instead, Burk escaped to Virginia, where he remained the rest of his life.[46]

"Wild Irishmen," United Irishmen, and the Press

Americans had been reading about the United Irishmen since the organization's founding in 1792. Originally begun as a civic group, the United Irishmen would quickly turn into the leaders of a rising against British domination and would also support Catholic emancipation. The Irish rising was important for one simple reason: the pro-British Federalists could not conceive that the Irish in America, who tended to be Democratic-Republicans, were not also conspiring with the French against them. Irish Americans posed a threat, Federalists believed, for two reasons: first, there were so very many of them, and second, a substantial portion were affiliated with the United Irishmen. They had numbers, they had ideology, and they had money from wealthy Irish Americans who supported Irish independence.

That Carey, Duane, and Burk were all tainted with the United Irishman brush was compounded by the fact that all three became involved with the Democratic-Republican Party at a particularly tense time in American history. Further, as far as the Federalists were concerned, they were all aliens. Duane, of course, was a native-born American who had spent his childhood and early youth in the United States. However, in the Federalist view, he was as fully Irish as either Carey or Burk.

Britain fanned the fires of partisan divides and immigration fears in America as they mopped up after the failed United Irishman rising. British officials were known to be considering deporting the leaders to the United States. The last thing America needed, in the Federalist perspective, was more rabble-rousing United Irishmen within its borders. American Minister to Great Britain Rufus King stridently objected to the deportation of the United Irishmen leaders to America, and he helped heighten American anxiety with his own panicky dispatches back home. King predicted in a letter to Alexander Hamilton that "France will pursue with us the Plan that she has elsewhere found successful. She will endeavor to overthrow us by the Divisions among ourselves which she will excite and support by all the means of which she is mistress." King also wrote to Pickering about the Irish problem. Federalists were suspicious of the massive Irish immigrant community primarily because of French support for Ireland's revolt against Britain. Federalists believed the Irish in America would join a French invasion of America should one occur. King was especially disturbed at the idea of Irish revolutionary leaders being sent to America. He wrote to Pickering that he could not see how the Irish malcontents could ever be useful American citizens; he feared they would never "become useful citizens of our own." King also fretted that Irish emigrants did not come with pedigrees from their government like those from Scotland, whose churches sent them with certificates that attested to "their honesty, sobriety and generally good character."[47] America was scarcely a decade old and already dealing with multiple crises. The Federalists had a good reason for feeling insecure and needing to "resort[s] for defence [*sic*] to the Sedition law."[48]

This debate and the undeclared war with France gave rise to anti-alien, nativist sentiments that became rampant, particularly among Federalists. Anti-immigrant articles appeared in new party-affiliated newspapers such as Fenno's *Gazette of the United States.* Duane used the *Aurora* to take Fenno to task for his denunciation of Dutch and German immigrants. Fenno, according to the *Aurora*, considered Germans "undermining Illuminati" and the Dutch "dull" and "incorribible [*sic*]."[49]

Earlier in the year, as Philadelphians anticipated the arrival of two ships from Ireland, an Irish ex-pat who signed his letter "An Irishman," felt it necessary to write that he knew several of the families coming on those ships and they were all "honest, peaceable citizens who hold the French in abhorrence." He assured readers that America would have nothing to fear from these new Irish immigrants "who will prove an acquisition to this country."[50]

The reason he had to write this letter was that Americans were particularly suspicious of the growing community of Irish immigrants. At that point, the Irish constituted about a tenth of the American population. That so many potential radicals and potential traitors were floating unchecked around the country, and worse, that they belonged to the party that would try to unseat President Adams in the next presidential election, was nothing less than terrifying for the Federalists.

Add into that mix several prominent newspaper editors who edited national newspapers, who had national influence, and who were writing in opposition to the Adams administration's policies, and the result was a powder keg just waiting to explode. And it would explode within two years of Adams's election. The constant radical carping of the Democratic-Republican press, whose most prestigious and influential newspapers were edited by Irishmen who could not separate themselves editorially from Ireland, and hence from France, was sufficient to frighten the Federalist Congress into adopting the Alien and Sedition Acts. Some seventeen men, many of whom were Irish by birth and several of whom were Irish American journalists, would be prosecuted under the act.[51]

Passage of the laws and then the prosecutions led to even more protests—petition after petition after petition for their repeal was filed with Congress. Riots broke out in the capital city. And Irishmen seemed to be at the heart of each protest. In each letter they wrote to federal prosecutors, Adams and Pickering relished suggesting this journalist, that citizen, that congressman for prosecution. Among their chief targets were Irish journalists, congressmen, and citizens because they were afraid. They had no doubt at all that the Irish were in league with the French both in America and in Ireland; that had to mean the Irish in America would support the French if they decided to invade.

These prosecutions of Irishmen under the Sedition Act actually helped lay the foundation for an Irish American press by forcing Irish Americans to segregate themselves from the mainstream American society. The law punished criticisms of the president, Congress, or government officials—but not the vice president, who was Adams's opponent-in-chief. Irish Americans had faced uncertainty, persecution, and prosecution at the hands of the British back in Ireland. Many were republican in their thinking, and they coalesced into an identifiable immigrant group rather than assimilating as Americans. Irish journalists began writing more and more about issues that would be of interest to an Irish audience, which meant focusing more on Irish issues and espousing uniquely Irish editorial perspectives rather than assimilating American ways of thinking. This constant newspaper barrage of seemingly radical, seemingly treasonous content convinced Federalists they needed to protect the country against such dangerous aliens. This meant enacting repressive legislation that made it much harder to obtain American citizenship and that gave the president power to deport aliens he deemed dangerous—no trial, no judge, no jury, just the president's word was sufficient.

The more the government heaped on abuse, the more Irish Americans came to identify themselves as a subcategory, a special interest group, and the more they flocked to newspapers that represented their interests. By the end of Adams's presidency, the seeds of the Irish American press had been planted. Those seeds were nourished by patronage and government support (to some degree) during Thomas Jefferson's presidency. By the end of Jefferson's presidency in March 1809, the Irish American press was ready to be birthed in the form of the *Observer*, a mostly religious newspaper, and a year later the more general-interest *Shamrock*. Across the next thirty years, at least eighteen more Irish American newspapers would appear in Boston, Philadelphia, New York, and even Charleston, South Carolina.

James Carey rightly argues that the press is a social structure whose cultural identity is a product of the roles and functions assigned to it by its society. Those roles and functions vary with the type and circumstances of the press's home nation, and so, reasonably, most journalism historians seek to understand press role and function within a particular national culture. During the waves of immigration in eighteenth- and nineteenth-century America, however, the concept of "nation" was more fluid, particularly for Irish immigrants whose reasons for leaving home often had less to do with choice and far more with political or economic necessity brought about through the plantation system and penal laws imposed by the British.[52]

The Irish American press demonstrates what is already well known about the function of journalism in a democracy: the press is a social structure that is a product of its society. In a society where there is political discord to the extent of that which existed during Adams's presidency, a strident opposition press will do battle with the establishment press. During Adams's administration, a radical opposition press arose, spurred by anti-Irish sentiment born from fear of Irish collusion with a French invasion and Irish opposition to the established power structure.

Irish immigrants to America shared some characteristics with the denizens of the legendary Avalon. They were both of the new world and of the old world, and they needed something that could help them assimilate as well as keep them apprised of the political struggles and issues from home. This need became particularly acute after the failed rebellion of 1798, when the British treatment of the Irish became even more harsh and restrictive. Irish solidarity in the face of such oppression could scarcely be lost merely through physical relocation necessitated by economic or political exigencies. The growth and expansion of an Irish nationalism that could transcend national borders was an obvious response, for nations are not always the products of geographic boundaries. Nations can be based on shared ideology, ethnicity, or other factors. Benedict Anderson argues that a nation is, in actuality, an imagined political community—imagined because "a nation is always conceived as a deep, horizontal comradeship."[53]

Irish nationalism among immigrants to America, even in the Early Republic period, was based in nostalgia or romanticized notions of home to some degree but also on political exigency and comradeship. To be sustained, the Irish nationalist's need had to be met for news about the political struggles back home and about what other Irish Americans were thinking and doing about the political situation back home. This was the primary role of the early Irish American editors—to provide a forum for continued fellowship and support for those still fighting for Irish emancipation back home. These editors did not publish strictly for an Irish American audience; their journals were directed to those who shared a particular set of political values. That group simply included a large number of Irish immigrants and thus provided a public forum where those immigrants could gather for support and for the sustenance of their community of nationalists—both Irish and American.

Consequently, these early Irish editors did not intentionally perform one of the primary functions that sets a newspaper off as an example of ethnic journalism, namely to help assimilate immigrants into their new society. Yet, their shared political ideals nevertheless addressed this function. The Irish American press would not emerge in the United States until the nineteenth century, but its origins were firmly planted in the eighteenth century by men such as Carey, Duane, and Burk.[54]

2

William Duane

Globe-Trotting Seditionist of the Eighteenth Century

David W. Bulla

American-born Irish journalist William Duane, the globe-trotting seditionist of the eighteenth century, would lead the pack of Democratic-Republican (also known as Republican) newspapers in the United States to ascendency in the political dogfights with the Federalist press during the Adams administration, a period the Democratic-Republicans referred to as the "Reign of Witches." In the process he would face multiple sedition charges, once under the common law and once under the Alien and Sedition Acts, which were specifically aimed at Irish immigrants and Democratic-Republican journalists. He would also get beaten up by Federalist soldiers and be forced into hiding for violating "the legislative privileges of the U.S. Senate." Even such unworthy notables as Secretary of State Timothy Pickering, the chief enforcer of the Alien and Sedition Acts, would denounce Duane as a United Irishman.[1]

Despite his American prosecutions, Duane was never found guilty or silenced by the John Adams administration, which was in a bitter political dispute with Vice President Thomas Jefferson's Democratic-Republicans over the French Revolution and a perceived threat that the French would somehow conquer the United States.

This chapter explores how sedition prosecutions helped propel journalists and journalistic/printing practices and attitudes across the globe, spreading and building journalistic commitment to the notion of freedom of the press. It focuses on Duane's experiences of parrying off seditious libel suits in the United States at the end of the eighteenth century, when America was in its infancy and had just divorced itself from Great Britain.

Duane's Early Life and Career

William Duane was one of the more feisty, spirited, and vitriolic characters in eighteenth-century transnational journalism. Born to Irish parents in what is now St. John's, Newfoundland, he spent his early years in New York (Lake Champlain) before his Catholic mother, Anastasia Sarsfield Duane, moved the family first to Philadelphia and Baltimore and then back home to Ireland after his father, John Duane, a landowner who had read the law, died in 1765 in upstate New York.[2]

Duane came of age during the lead-up to the American Revolution, as did another noted early Irish American journalist, Mathew Carey. Duane, however, was in situ while Carey watched from across the Atlantic in Ireland. Both were teenagers at the time, just the proper age to be inspired by the (imagined) romance and thrill of a revolution founded on a great ideal: freedom from Britain's tyrannical rule. In 1774, two years before the Declaration of Independence was signed, Duane's mother decided to return home to Clonmel in County Tipperary. Her family there were well-to-do Catholics with a long history of resistance to the British.

Despite returning to Ireland, the prewar agitation he had witnessed in America left a huge impression on Duane; it contributed to his life-long belief in individual freedom and liberty, and he would always consider himself an American, despite his Irish parentage and upbringing. By the same token, Duane believed passionately that Ireland should be liberated from British rule. He would spend his career fighting for republican causes. He was active in the Irish Volunteer movement in the 1770s, supported the American Revolution, and, of course, threw his newspaper pages open to all such causes, even as an apprentice at the *Clonmel Gazette*, an opposition newspaper that supported the Irish nationalist Volunteer organization.[3]

Duane became involved in newspaper work not because of his politics, however, but because of romance. He married the daughter of a wealthy Protestant family, Catherine Corcoran, and his very Roman Catholic mother disowned him. He needed a job, and the newspaper offered him an opportunity.[4] Duane's burgeoning radicalism found a salubrious home at the *Gazette*. He began his apprenticeship in 1779, the same year Napper Tandy led demonstrations against British rule in Dublin. Within two years, though, the demonstrations and the Volunteers were in decline, and so were Duane's prospects in Ireland.[5]

Duane moved his family to London to live with his uncle, Matthew Duane, a solicitor who was "very honest, very rich, and a strict Roman Catholic."[6] Matthew Duane had also been something of a rebel himself and worked quite actively for Catholic rights within Ireland and Great Britain.[7] With his Uncle Matthew's help, and that of his uncle's neighbor Horace Walpole, Duane soon had the perfect job: political reporter for the *General Advertiser*, an opposition newspaper whose owner, John Almon, had strong views not just on politics (he published one article that accused British prime minister William Pitt of making £150,000 speculating on how Dutch peace negotiations would go) but also on press freedom. Almon was an influential editor, and he used that influence to effect a change in English libel laws that allowed the English press to report more freely on Parliament. Earlier in his career, Almon was forced to flee England after being convicted of seditious libel against King George III. Almon's offense was publishing a pamphlet titled "Junius's Letter to the King," which was a protest against Crown policy in the American colonies. Almon was an apt tutor to turn Duane into an effective opposition editor.[8]

However, William Duane's international adventures were hardly over with his move to London. Duane worked in London until 1786, the year his uncle died and left his estate to another nephew. Duane was once again disinherited and in need of a more lucrative career, so he looked into moving to America. Unable to book passage, he enlisted in the East India Army, sent his family back to Ireland, and headed to India where he would spend nine years working first as a clerk for the East India Company and then as a journalist.[9]

In 1789 he began publishing the *Bengal Journal*, which had a circulation of only a few hundred.[10] He covered the expatriate community in Calcutta, specializing in trade and British military news. The latter tended to focus on the daily lives of the soldiers in camp and the battles they fought, including Lord Cornwallis's campaigns against Tipu Sultan in Mysore.[11] In one article, Duane criticized French royalists living in India. The English government in India took the side of the royalists against a group of French revolutionaries in India near Calcutta, who had attempted to seize power. Cornwallis provided financial support for the royalists.[12] Duane also criticized the slave trade in his journal and took a dim view of some Hindu rituals. Colonel Canaple, the leader of the French royalists, complained to the British leader in Calcutta that Duane had libeled him. The government official told Duane to tone it down and go visit Canaple to set things straight. Duane had every intention of retracting his story when meeting Canaple at the latter's residence. However, he was made to wait a long time for the French leader, changed his mind, and decided to lecture him on the right of humans to publish as they please. In response to a second complaint from Canaple, the East India Company shut down the *Bengal Journal.* A mob of French royalists also damaged Duane's residence.[13] The British jailed Duane and intended to deport him, but Canaple died unexpectedly, and the new French leader in the Calcutta area was pro-revolutionary and thus sympathetic to Duane. Consequently, the journalist avoided deportation.

Duane started up a second newspaper in Calcutta, titled the *World*, and continued to publish pieces that were sometimes unpopular with the East India Company leadership. He also printed letters to the editor, giving a public forum to his readers. He covered the military closely and hired a soldier to write about camp life. Again, he would take the side of East India Company officers, who wrote anonymous letters to the editor that Duane published. Many of these were critical of the East India Company, particularly its working conditions. In effect, Duane was airing soldier grievances. John Shore, the governor of the East India Company, did not believe the ordinary soldier should ever criticize his superiors. He declared that the *World* contained articles that were improper, intemperate, and licentious. Shore charged Duane with being pro-revolutionary and a supporter of Thomas Paine and ordered Duane to be deported to England.[14] Shore would imprison Duane at Fort William and, in early 1795, would transfer him to the *William Pitt* for the trip back to Portsmouth.[15]

Back in London, Duane sought compensation for his lost newspaper and his home but received nothing. So, he returned to journalism, writing for a newspaper, the *Telegraph*, and eventually became its editor.

The England to which Duane returned was in political chaos. The Whigs were engaged in a battle with radical republicans led by Thomas Paine, whose *Rights of Man* was having tremendous success in convincing readers of the pressing need for equality and liberty for all. Duane, of course, was attracted to this opposition movement and joined its chief progenitor, the London Corresponding Society, the most radical reform group in Britain.[16] Its editorial platform was universal male suffrage and annual meetings of Parliament. After his Indian experience, Duane also wrote pieces criticizing the East India Company.[17] The *Telegraph* also published information coming from the French press. Duane's service as editor of the *Telegraph* during this period was a brave move, given his predisposition and fearlessness. England had been at war with France since 1793 and was cracking down on any opposition. The government had also outlawed seditious publications in 1792, following Thomas Paine's publishing successes.[18]

Duane risked much in this period. His association with the London Corresponding Society, whose usual meeting place was the *Telegraph* office, put him in the center of the radical movement and in the company of like-minded, though perhaps foolhardy, men. Duane lasted as *Telegraph* editor for two years, and then in 1796, he and his family headed to America, where he would eventually put his training and experience as an opposition editor to work for Thomas Jefferson's Democratic-Republicans.[19]

Landing in New York on the Fourth of July, Duane was "in search of a more congenial political atmosphere," according to Kim T. Phillips.[20] Duane, along with several other British editors he had left behind, were sympathetic with the major ideals of the French revolutionaries, especially in the emphasis on press liberty and equality.

A Radical Republican Journalist in America

Duane would find work, off and on, at a variety of newspapers. His first employer was the *Merchants' Daily Advertiser* in Philadelphia. Of course, he almost immediately got involved in the leadership of a republican activist group and became embroiled in the controversy over George Washington's signing of the unpopular and pro-British Jay Treaty. His primary journalistic contribution to the controversy was a pamphlet titled *A Letter to George Washington, President of the United States.* Duane's chief objection to Washington was the "cult of personality that surrounded" the former president. Though the Jay Treaty debate was over by the time this piece was published, the work helped Duane establish a political reputation that would aid him in advancing his editorial career.[21]

A fight with his then employer, Andrew Brown Jr. of the *Philadelphia Gazette*, his second newspaper in Philadelphia, found Duane out of work just as his pregnant wife was dying of cholera and his landlady confiscated the family's belongings to cover unpaid rent. Duane found employment at the Philadelphia *Aurora General Advertiser* (*Aurora*), edited by Benjamin Franklin's grandson, Benjamin Franklin Bache.[22] The position Bache was filling had opened up when James Thomson Callender, Bache's Scottish editorial writer, fled to Virginia to avoid prosecution under the Sedition Act.[23] Duane would spend the remainder of his career at the *Aurora*, and he would assume the editorship after Bache died in 1798.

The two men were well matched. Bache marched to the republican drummer, just as Duane did. His support for France during the Quasi-War made him an easy target for Federalist repression. His house was attacked, Federalists terrorized his family, and John Ward Fenno, son of John Fenno, editor of the Federalist *Gazette of the United States*, physically attacked him. The Federalists would also indict Bache on a charge of common law sedition. Bache's untimely death from yellow fever prevented his prosecution.[24]

Duane, whose timing always seemed to put him at risk, went to work for Philadelphia's leading Democratic-Republican journal just as the Sedition Act was moving through Congress. Federalists argued the law was needed to protect the country from "Jacobin Republicans," including, as Massachusetts congressman Harrison Gray Otis termed them in a letter to his wife, "wild Irishmen."[25] Otis and other Federalists were concerned about the growing United Irishmen movement in America, which had been imported from Ireland in the wake of the 1798 Rising there. Duane, along with Carey and Burk, would be denounced as members of the organization. In Duane's case, the accusation came from no less a personage than Secretary of State Timothy Pickering.[26]

Duane at the *Aurora*

Duane edited the *Philadelphia Aurora*, which was financially independent (it never took government money to sustain its printing costs) and supported the Democratic-Republicans. The *Aurora* was founded by Benjamin Franklin Bache, whose insider information in Philadelphia (then the American capital city) politics helped develop the newspaper's reputation as a leading national political journal. Bache had to work hard to keep his newspaper operating and also spent $20,000 of his own money to keep it solvent.[27] The *Aurora* was effectively the flagship newspaper of the Democratic-Republican press, and editors of that party routinely clipped Bache's pieces and ran them in their own journals.

The upstart Bache began the newspaper when he was only twenty. Bache was not one to back down to anybody, including President George Washington. Bache, for example, brazenly questioned the former general's favoritism toward the English and even his regal style.[28] Bache also admired the French Revolution, and, in the *Aurora*, he cheered on French military victories after the revolution. The Philadelphia editor also excoriated the Federalist-controlled US Senate for holding secret sessions. During Senate debates on the Jay Treaty, Bache obtained copies of secret documents relevant to the treaty and published them. Bache also skewered Adams, calling him senile and a pro-English warmonger. Adams would fight back against Bache and other Democratic-Republican editors with his antipress sedition law, which even his wife, First Lady Abigail Adams, held was necessary to keep the United States from sliding into a civil war.[29]

Even before the Sedition Act passed, Bache and the *Aurora* were under constant attack from Federal editors and politicians. Bache had to face down mobs who intended to ransack his home. Adams's Federalists attempted to try Bache for treason, but he died in 1798 of yellow fever. When Duane married Bache's widow and took control of the *Aurora*, he continued Bache's fight against Adams's Alien and Sedition Acts. Adams and his cronies would charge Duane with libel under the common law, arrest him twice under the Sedition Act, and indict him once under the Alien Act. Duane was one of twenty-six individuals who faced federal indictments under the Sedition Act for words spoken or printed between 1798 and 1801.[30] President Adams considered Duane a libeler due to the journalist's harsh criticisms of the Alien and Sedition Acts of 1798. On the other hand, James Madison, a Democratic-Republican who would become fourth president of the United States, called Duane "a sincere friend of liberty, and ready to make every sacrifice to its cause but that of his passions."[31] Duane's career as a newspaperman offers a singular example of a transnational champion of press freedom in the face of multiple libel prosecutions on three continents.

Federalists Revert to Common Law Tradition

Duane's career played out against the legal backdrop of seditious libel, which originated in British common law. As media law scholars Dwight L. Teeter Jr. and Don R. Le Duc noted, sedition "has a long and bloody history."[32] The common law, according to British jurisprudence scholar William Blackstone in his book *Commentaries*, held that criticism of a government official could constitute seditious libel. However, he also maintained that government could not prevent publication or prior restraint. The injured party would have to sue the journalist after publication and let a court decide whether the offending publication constituted sedition. According to Blackstone, concern that "the direct tendency of these libels is the breach of the public peace, by stirring up the objects of them to revenge, and perhaps to bloodshed" justified the inclusion of seditious libel in the British legal system.[33] Blackstone also noted that whether a publication was true was irrelevant; rather, the issue was the provocation created by printing material. That was what a court should consider in sedition trials.

However, the First Amendment to the US Constitution (ratified in 1791) promoted strong federal protections for the press. It states that Congress can make no law prohibiting, among other rights, the free exercise of speech or press. Yet, when Adams was elected president in 1796, America had not yet tested most of its constitutional law. The first test would come after ratification of the Jay Treaty between the United States and Britain, which took effect in July 1795. Chief Justice John Jay led the American negotiations, and Lord Grenville led the British side. The treaty soothed the relationship between the two nations by resolving some of the issues remaining from the Revolutionary War. Britain agreed to remove its troops from the Northwest Territory and gave the United States trading privileges with England and British colonies in the Caribbean. The treaty also opened the Mississippi River to both countries.

However, the treaty also angered the French, who thought it violated its own accords with the United States, and angered Americans who favored alliance with the new republic rather than the British monarchy. The French navy began attacking American shipping interests in retaliation. America sent three diplomats to negotiate with the French, a mission that failed abysmally. In what became known as the XYZ Affair, the French demanded bribes before they would negotiate. They wanted $250,000 in cash and additional loans. The diplomats were offended by the demands and returned home without any negotiations. President Adams responded by preparing for war, which aroused the Republicans. The antiwar, pro-France stance of Democratic-Republican editors caused Adams and the Federalists to see the opposition party as subversive. The Federalists began to consider legislation that would make it illegal to publicly criticize the president and Congress. In particular, the Federalists targeted immigrants, especially the Irish, who were more attracted to the pro-French Democratic-Republicans.[34]

In the next few years, press freedom would be tested under President Adams and the Federalist-controlled Congress. That is when the Federalists, whose leadership included Alexander Hamilton, went on the attack against the opposition Democratic-Republican press. Even if they had the more appropriate approach to the crisis with France, Adams and Hamilton perverted the Constitution's guarantee of press freedom when they pursued legislation that would guarantee press freedom only for those in power. Their mechanism for squelching the opposition Republican press was the Sedition Act of 1798. The Sedition Act criminalized publishing or uttering "false, scandalous, and malicious criticism of the President, Congress, or the government with the intent to defame them or bring them into disrepute."[35]

Federalists prosecuted at least seventeen cases under the Sedition Act. The first prosecution involved William Durrell, who reprinted words from another newspaper that were critical of Adams. Durrell was found guilty, jailed for four months, and fined fifty dollars.[36] He also had to pay $4,000 in bail.

Another of the early cases under the Sedition Act involved Anthony Haswell, the editor of the pro–Democratic-Republican *Vermont Gazette.* Haswell had defended Democratic-Republican congressman Matthew Lyon, an Irish émigré, who had been also been convicted, jailed, and fined for criticizing Adams. Haswell spent two months in jail and was fined $200.[37]

As media law historian Jeffery A. Smith has observed, the Sedition Act "virtually outlawed criticism of government" and "demonstrated the willingness of some Americans to disregard the Bill of Rights."[38] While the limits of press freedom during wartime have been debated throughout US history, in this case a war never materialized. Diplomatic relations were frayed, but not to the point where France and the United States went to war.

The Feud between Pickering and Duane

In 1799 Secretary of State Timothy Pickering, armed with John Adams's Sedition Act, went on the offensive against pro-Jefferson Republican newspapers. One of his chief targets was initially Bache, and Pickering would add Duane as a target after Bache died in 1798. Pickering was not alone. President Adams, Federalist congressmen such as John Allen of Connecticut, and even Abigail Adams condemned Republican newspapers as lying wretches intent on sowing discord among Americans.[39]

The feud was fueled by a pamphlet Duane and his predecessor at the *Aurora*, Bache, published in 1798, "The Truth Will Out: The Foul Charges of the Tories against the Editor of the Aurora, Repelled by Positive Proof and Plain Truth, and His Base Calumniators Put to Shame." Sold at the time for two cents a copy, "The Truth Will Out" is a twelve-page defense of freedom of the press and a counter to the seditious libel charges pending against Bache in 1798. At that time, Secretary of the Treasury Oliver Wolcott was contemplating an investigation of Bache for treason for having published secret state papers two days before Adams sent them to Congress.[40] The Federalist press began an aggressive anti-*Aurora* campaign, and merchants with Federalist leanings refused to advertise with the Philadelphia newspaper.

In "The Truth Will Out," which included reprints of *Aurora* articles, the authors called a "free press a most formidable engine to tyrants of every description." One of the factors that motivated the editor to compose the booklet was that Speaker of the House Jonathan Dayton had Bache banned from House sessions, thus depriving him of the right to inform the public about the actions of the lower house.[41] Not being able to cover Congress would be a "base dereliction of duty" for a journalist.[42]

The disputes between the *Aurora* and the Federalist government continued even after Bache's death. At that point, Pickering began targeting Duane, the new *Aurora* editor. Duane had been acquitted earlier on a charge of causing a riot when he attempted to get Irishmen in Philadelphia to sign a petition against the anti-immigration Alien Act.

This acquittal stiffened the resolve of the Federalists against Duane, and Pickering was determined to bring down the Republican editor.

On July 26, 1799, Pickering wrote to Adams that Duane "pretends he is an American citizen," noting that the editor had been educated in Ireland. Pickering told the president that Duane had come to the United States in the previous three or four years and that he had "come to this country to stir up sedition and work other mischief." Pickering further wrote that Duane was an alien and "liable to be banished from the United States."[43] The secretary also said Duane would join the French side in case of war against the United States. On that same day, Pickering also wrote to William Rawle, the federal district attorney for Pennsylvania. He encouraged Rawle to prosecute Duane: "If the slander on the American government will justify a prosecution against the Editor or Author, be pleased to have it commenced."[44]

The next day, Pickering again urged Rawle to seek a prosecution of Duane. Adams wrote to Pickering about Duane's newspaper: "Is there anything evil in the regions of actuality or possibility that the Aurora had not suggested of me? . . . I disdain to attempt a vindication of myself against lies of the Aurora, as much as any man concerned in the administration of the affairs of the United States." Adams added that if the prosecutor, Rawle, did not think Duane had been libelous, then he was not "fit for his office." Of the Alien Act, Adams went on to say he was "very willing to try its strength upon him [Duane]."[45]

The type of Duane verbosity that appalled the president and his administration almost always linked Adams with the English. For example, on August 5, 1799, Duane opened his editorial by saying that Jefferson's "all men are created equal" proved American "wisdom" and "virtue," and that those words "scintillated over the whole Universe."[46] He charged Alexander Hamilton with trying to make the American system a monarchy. The *Aurora* editor also criticized the idea of a standing army. Duane also would defend vigorously anyone who supported the Irish, whom he deemed "barbarously oppressed."[47] Later, Duane would write: "From the moment that Britain failed to subject us by arms—she resolved to pursue our humiliation by perfidy—the peace of 1783 was scarcely concluded, when laws calculated to cramp and obstruct our commerce were introduced into the British parliament."[48]

The first federal prosecution of Duane under the Sedition Act was in response to what Pickering called the *Aurora*'s "uninterrupted stream of slander on the American government."[49] The prosecution began in August 1799, based on words in the *Aurora* on July 24 of that year. John Fenno's *Gazette of the United States, & the Philadelphia Daily Advertiser*, a Federalist journal, reported that Duane was brought up before Judge Richard Peters, given bond of $3,000 ($2,000 out of Duane's own pocket and another $1,000 paid by two other men), and assigned a likely trial date of October 1799.[50] Former president Washington was outraged at Duane and wrote Secretary of War James McHenry that he hoped the prosecutor would "probe this matter to the bottom. It will have an unhappy effect on the public if it be not so."

The question was whether Duane had, as he claimed, a letter in President Adams's handwriting that showed the British had influenced the appointment of an officer. In his July 24, 1799, edition, Duane wrote about the British influence, and he upped the ante by adding that, "We have it in the hand-writing of John Adams now President of the United States, that British influence has been employed and with effect."[51] He also claimed to have damning letters in the hands of Robert Liston, the British ambassador to the United States, and American Secretary of State Timothy Pickering. He actually published the letters from Pickering and Liston in that edition.[52]

On August 4, 1799, Duane wrote: "Secretary of State Pickering has instituted proceedings against me for claiming John Adams wrote of British influences in the Washington administration." He called Pickering's vendetta against the press an "Inquest" and said he would answer all indictments against him in the October trial.[53] In late August, Duane announced that it was "prudent to remove" the *Aurora*'s printing office from Philadelphia to Bristol (just northeast of Philadelphia on the Delaware River) because of mob action against the newspaper building.[54] Three times stones had been tossed through the office window, resulting in broken panes. On May 7 and 9, 1798, inebriated Federalists attacked Bache's home. Bache was alone, except for his pregnant wife and children, but a group of Bache's friends drove the attackers away both times.[55]

In October, after Republican Thomas McKean was elected governor of Pennsylvania, Duane appeared in court. In Norristown, Pennsylvania, Judge Richard Peters and US Supreme Court Justice Bushrod Washington presided. Washington was George Washington's nephew. Duane brought the letter that substantiated his claim that Adams had written about British influence on the executive branch under Washington. Duane's attorney, Alexander James Dallas, argued that the letter was admissible, as the Sedition Act, in opposition to the tradition of the common law, allowed for truth as a defense. The letter would show that Adams did in fact write that the Washington administration had British influence. First, the judges postponed the proceedings, and then the prosecutor dropped the matter. Duane speculated in the *Aurora* that bringing the letter into open court would have given Adams unfavorable publicity.[56] He also agreed to a gag order that he would not give "copies of the indicts" or a report of the arguments in the court to the public.[57]

Next, Duane published a bill, introduced by Federalist senator James Ross (who had lost the Pennsylvania governor's race to Democratic-Republican Thomas McKean in 1799), which would create a committee to handle presidential elections. Because of anticipated close elections, the Federalists no longer had faith in the Electoral College system. The Electoral College would still exist, but the committee would do the decisive work. It would consist of six senators, six congressmen, and the chief justice of the Supreme Court. Its decision on the presidential election would be final, with no opportunity for appeal.[58] Duane commented on Ross's bill: "The truth is that this bill was calculated in its birth to set aside the public voice and to place in the hands of a few men—and we know what a few men in the Senate are capable of—the nomination of the chief magistrate" (which is what the president was called at that time).[59] The committee would decide which Electoral College votes counted and which did not. At that time, both branches of Congress had Federalist majorities, and all members of the Supreme Court were Federalists. Duane observed that this committee was outside the Constitution—that there was no provision for it in the founding document.

Printing a copy of Ross's bill, along with a critical editorial, in the *Aurora* in February 1800 was perhaps Duane's most significant work in his long journalism career. He wrote the Ross legislation was designed to "influence and affect" the upcoming presidential election. Duane, who did not have every fact exactly right in his reporting on the Ross legislation, stated that the Federalists behind the bill were "opponents of independence and republican government."[60] He also told his readers that seventeen senators had met in a Philadelphia house in the summer of 1798 and agreed to vote as a bloc on certain measures in the full Senate, and that this was the precedent for the proposed Ross committee on elections. The journalist went on to write the "bill is an offspring of this spirit of faction secretly working; and it will be found to be in perfect accord with the outrageous proceedings of the same party in our state legislature."[61]

His words did not go unnoticed. The majority-Federalist Senate claimed Duane had criticized them and therefore had libeled the institution. Two-thirds of the senators had voted in favor of deliberating in secret. The Federalist senators also claimed the *Aurora* editor had no right to publish what they considered secret deliberations, begging questions of transparency in this new experiment in representative government. Connecticut senator Uriah Tracy claimed nobody had the right to question this secrecy.[62] President Adams instructed federal prosecutors to indict Duane under the Sedition Act. Adams wrote that Duane, in the *Aurora*, had printed "certain false, defamatory, scandalous, and malicious publications in the said newspaper of the February 19 law last, tending to defame the Senate of the United States and bring them into contempt and disrepute."[63]

Perhaps the Federalist senators were keen to prosecute Duane because they had failed to prosecute his predecessor Bache, who died before he could be tried for common law sedition. The Senate, presided over by Vice President Jefferson, ordered Duane's arrest for contempt, but the editor could not be found, although his newspaper continued to be published.[64] Next, the Senate censured Duane by resolution and asked the Philadelphia editor to appear before that body to answer charges. There was no due process; he was just told to appear. Despite Republican opposition, Duane was to be charged for printing "false, scandalous, and malicious assertions" that defamed the Senate.[65]

Duane made his appearance as ordered but immediately asked if he could hire attorneys to help with his defense. This privilege was granted, and the session ended. Duane was allowed to leave, and he sent letters to attorneys Alexander James Dallas and Thomas Cooper (a scientist, journalist, college professor and president, and defender of press freedom), who declined to accept the case because they believed the Senate had already decided Duane's fate and could not possibly be unbiased. Furthermore, the attorneys would not be allowed to defend Duane with free-press arguments, nor could they argue that the Senate had no jurisdiction to try the journalist.[66] Next, Duane sent a letter to Jefferson, who was president of the Senate, saying his counsel refused to serve and that he, too, would not attend the proceedings himself.[67] Of course, Duane published the correspondence in the *Aurora*. Consequently, the Senate charged the *Aurora* editor with contempt, and Jefferson signed the arrest warrant. Duane evaded the warrant for several weeks until Congress recessed. Meanwhile, Duane's friends circulated a petition asking the Senate to reconsider the charge against the journalist. The vote to read the petition was a tie. Jefferson's vote to have the petition read broke the tie.[68]

Although the Senate heard the petition, members did not drop the indictment. The US attorney general charged Duane with libel under the Sedition Act despite the objections of Republican senators. Those same senators reminded the majority that the pro-Federalist *Gazette of the United States* routinely criticized Republican senators, who, of course, should have been exempt from any criticism under the Sedition Act. However, the case turned into a procedural marathon and would not be resolved until after the election of 1800, which Adams lost. The new president, Jefferson, allowed the indictment to proceed, but a grand jury refused to indict.[69] Duane was in the clear. Furthermore, the Ross bill, while it passed in the full Senate, failed in the House of Representatives and never became law. Thus, victories for Duane all around.

In 1800 Jefferson won the presidential election over incumbent Adams with more than 60 percent of the popular vote. However, the vote in the Electoral College was much closer; Jefferson won only 73–65. Adams won all of New England, while Jefferson won all states from New York to the South. Jefferson ran successfully against the Alien and Sedition Acts. The new president flatly said Duane's *Aurora* had been a "rallying point" for his party during the election. Likewise, Adams said that Duane was one of the handful of people responsible for the incumbent's defeat.[70]

Jefferson was an avowed Francophile who had lived for a time in Paris. He certainly sided with the French in their rivalry with Great Britain. He well remembered that France had supported the upstart patriots in the War of Independence against the Crown. Jefferson and his ilk were appalled by the excessive bloodshed in the French Revolution, but they did not believe that nullified the basic principles behind the revolt or the right of the oppressed to throw off their chains from their monarchial oppressors. Opposing revolution, as the Federalists were doing in their support of Great Britain, meant going against the progressive element of the Enlightenment. These Federalist counterrevolutionaries were squashing equality, liberty, and democracy, including freedom of the press, according to the Republican editors.

The Republicans, led by Jefferson, Cooper, John Madison, St. George Tucker, and their editors, made strong arguments in favor of press freedom, using John Locke's natural law principles for their arguments. Freedom of speech and press are essential to a self-governing society, they argued. Madison held that both prior restraint and post-publication punishment would limit freedom of the press. He believed that if no laws should be made to abridge press freedom, as the First Amendment stated, then no laws should be made fettering the press.[71] The right of the individual to discuss public affairs was inviolate. Indeed, Cooper also opposed "political restrictions on the liberty of the press."[72] The Republican press often quoted or reprinted from *Cato's Letters*, and the *Time-Piece* of New York printed the Bill of Rights to remind its readers of their civil rights.[73]

The American people seemed to buy the Democratic-Republicans' arguments, as Jefferson won the popular vote in 1800 overwhelmingly. The Republican argument for freedom of the press was a state's rights argument. In this formulation, the Democratic-Republicans saw the federal law as a threat to the freedom of expression (speech, religion, and press) that was enshrined in state constitutions. The federal attempt to supersede these state laws showed a centralized government that had—unconstitutionally, in Democratic-Republican eyes—overstepped its boundaries. The Democratic-Republicans, in fact, held that only the state governments could abridge basic rights involving human expression and communication.

Other Cases of Seditious Libel under the Sedition Act

Perhaps in retaliation for Duane not being prosecuted, Cooper, editor of the *Sunbury and Northumberland Gazette* in Pennsylvania, was tried for seditious libel in April 1800 for words he had written in the fall of 1799 on a handbill. The handbill included an attack on Adams for assembling both a standing army and permanent naval fleet. In Philadelphia, Justice Samuel Chase stated that Cooper had "poisoned the minds of the people" with his remarks about Adams and had "excited hatred of the good people of the United States" against the president.[74] Cooper, a scientist who would go on to be the first president of the University of South Carolina, argued truth as a defense to his publication (i.e., that President Adams had said the words for which Cooper criticized him). However, truth at that point was not a reliable defense to sedition, and Cooper lost his case. He had to pay a fine of $400 and spend six months in jail. Adding injury to insult, Cooper's wife died while he was in jail.[75]

While incarcerated, Cooper sent Duane a letter to be published in the *Aurora*. It stated Cooper would not accept clemency from Adams. At that time, several of Cooper's friends were agitating for his early release.[76] Cooper had taken meticulous notes during the trial and had them published after the trial. He wrote: "The Citizens of this

Country may learn some useful lessons from the trial; and principally, that if they mean to consult their own peace and quiet, they will hold their tongues, and restrain their pens, on the subject of politics."[77] After Cooper's release, Governor McKean would appoint him deputy attorney general of Northumberland County. Cooper also made the argument that Alexander Hamilton should have been tried for sedition because he too criticized Adams in the former's "Letter from Alexander Hamilton, Concerning the Public Conduct and Character of John Adams, Esq., President of the United States," which stated that Adams did not have the talent to be president.[78]

Other journalists tried under the Sedition Act included Scottish immigrant James Thomson Callender, jailed for six months and fined $900, and Irish-born Vermont congressman Matthew Lyon, imprisoned for criticizing Adams in his magazine *Lyon's Republican Magazine* (later changed to *The Scourge of Aristocracy*) and in a letter that he sent to a newspaper. Callender wrote for five Democratic-Republican newspapers, including the *Richmond Examiner*. He also wrote a diatribe against Adams and the Federalists titled *The Prospect before Us*. In it, he called Adams a "strange compound of ignorance and ferocity, of deceit and weakness."[79] Callender's trial was a farce, as his attorneys were constantly interrupted by Judge Samuel Chase, and the lawyers quit the case. The trial lasted only a single day, outraging Jefferson, who had told James Madison that Callender deserved to "be substantially defended."[80] Accordingly, Democratic-Republican newspapers printed transcripts of the trial in the lead-up to the fall 1800 election. Jail time did little to blunt Callender's pen, however. In the second volume of *The Prospect before Us*, he called Adams "an unprincipled oppressor."[81]

Lyon undertook his journal because his local Federalist newspaper, the *Rutland Herald*, refused to print his responses during his reelection campaign. He actually wrote the offending letter, which claimed that Adams had an "unbounded thirst for ridiculous pomp, foolish adulation, and selfish avarice," before the Sedition Act took effect, but it was published after enactment.[82] Lyon's letter, published in the *Vermont Journal*, also claimed that President Adams had corrupted Christianity by being a warmonger. The indictment also accused Lyon of seditious libel because he published a letter by Joel Barrow, a poet, which blamed Adams and the Senate for the international crisis with France.[83] In trial, Lyon argued that the congressional act was unconstitutional, that his comments were true, and that his letter was not malicious. However, the judge claimed by merely printing it, Lyon was being malicious. Judge William Paterson told the jury: "You have nothing whatever to do with the constitutionality or unconstitutionality of the sedition law."[84] Still, the jury convicted.[85] Judge Paterson sentenced Lyon to four months in jail and fined him $1,000. Paterson thought Lyon deserved a strong sentence because he was a member of Congress, and the judge wanted to make an example of the Vermonter.[86] However, the public seemed to take pity on Lyon, who won reelection to his House seat while in prison. Lyon's case was one of seven seditious libel trials in Vermont, which was staunchly pro-Federalist. Later, the Vermont circuit court asked that Lyon be arrested for letters he had written in jail that criticized his harsh penalty. In May 1800 the marshal gave up on looking for Lyon, who had left Vermont and settled in Kentucky, where he would also serve in the US House of Representatives for four terms. In 1840 Congress granted his heirs' request to refund the fine, plus the prosecution costs Paterson forced him to pay, with interest.[87]

The British Press and Restraints on Duane's Press

Meanwhile, the British press cheered on the attempt to squelch Duane and his Democratic-Republican colleagues. The *Cambridge Intelligencer* stated that Duane had libeled the Senate and that his attorneys had "insulted" the Senate by refusing to appear when the editor was ordered to defend himself in that body.[88] In August 1801, the *Hampshire Chronicle* (Winchester, UK) reported that Duane had been ruled a noncitizen of the United States, even though he had been born in the country but prior to independence. Because Duane had subsequently lived abroad in India and Great Britain, he was no longer entitled to American citizenship and was therefore considered an alien "and a subject of the King of England."[89] Thus, Duane's vitriol in the *Aurora* and his somewhat complicated national identity made him a main candidate for Pickering's anti-Republican press campaign.

The British press was intrigued by Duane, in part because he was at least culturally and ethnically Irish but also because he obviously made waves in the American political system. Often the British press took a dim view of Duane, largely because of his pro-France stance. The *Times* of London hinted that Duane and the *Aurora* were "in the pay of France."[90] The *Kentish Gazette* (Canterbury, Kent), in May 1800, published pieces about his Senate trial for federal libel, including a letter saying that he would leave his case up to his counsel.[91] The *Times* approved of the Adams administration and Congress pursuing seditious libel prosecutions against Duane. The *Times* editors wrote when the "liberty of the press degenerates into licentiousness," then the people deserved to be protected by "restrictions" on the press from the government.[92] The *Oxford Journal* had a critical tone as it reported that the Senate was trying Duane for several libels against "that body." The *Journal* snarled at Duane for failing to appear at the trial.[93]

After the sedition cases, the British press continued to report on Duane. In 1807 the *Belfast Commercial Chronicle* noted that Duane, "Editor of the American newspaper the *Aurora*," had been nominated to stand for a state senate seat in Pennsylvania.[94] In 1808, when it was announced that Duane had been made a lieutenant colonel in the US First Regiment of Riflemen by President Jefferson, the *Manchester Mercury* criticized Duane for "endeavouring to involve his country in a war on the side of France against Great Britain." The *Mercury* labeled Duane "an infamous, French printer mercenary."[95]

Conclusion

After the libel cases flittered away under Jefferson, the third president would grow close to the Philadelphia editor. Jefferson named Duane a lieutenant colonel, and during the War of 1812 the former journalist was an adjutant general. Duane, who continued on with the *Aurora* until 1822, died in Philadelphia in 1835. His son, William J. Duane, would serve as secretary of the treasury under Andrew Jackson. The younger Duane also edited the *Aurora* for a time, along with James Wilson, Woodrow Wilson's grandfather.

The Sedition Act of 1798 set a precedent for federal constraints on the press in certain circumstances. Adams would refer to the likes of Duane as "foreign liars" in justifying his fettering of a press that he believed had too much foreign influence. The Southern states would use much the same arguments in the antebellum period to defend their creation of antiabolitionist laws that were aimed at Northern newspaper editors who wanted to see slavery ended. The abolitionist editors were essentially "foreign" creatures on the American political scene and had no right to print their attacks of the Southern economic system. Free (white) men were entitled to freely possess (nonwhite) men as free laborers, and others had no right to castigate those who took part in this domestic practice—or the institution itself.

Then, in World War I, President Woodrow Wilson would get Congress to pass the Espionage Act of 1917, to which was attached an amendment in 1918 that outlawed sedition of the federal government. Almost two thousand people were prosecuted for seditious speech and perhaps one hundred for printed words they had written. German-language newspapers in particular were targeted.

For his part, William Duane was the globe-trotter who had a view of his profession that was not tied to a single nation, its journalistic customs, and its laws. His personal experiences took him to British North America (Canada), the United States, Ireland, England, and India. He was also a product of the Enlightenment. He thought truth came from reason, not God or king. He believed in republicanism and thought it should not be limited to one country. Rather, it was an international political philosophy, and freedom of the press was one of its bedrock principles. His international background made him easy prey for Federalists bent on making the early United States more British in its cultural and political tone than internationalist or French revolutionary. His support of the French Revolution in his Calcutta newspaper the *World* established him as being at odds with Parliament, the Crown, and the East India Company. After his deportation from India, he returned to London and found English politics too stifling.

America beckoned, a land where freedom had been enshrined in the Constitution, and he believed he would be able to speak and write as he pleased about politics—and anything else. That was the case up until the Federalists, led by President John Adams, passed their antipress legislation in 1798. Then, Duane had to fight for his right to publish as he pleased in the court of law while continuing to ply his trade as a journalist, even with threats of mob violence and the loss of advertising swirling around him. Indeed, he helped turned the tide against the Federalists and made a lasting case for press freedom in the United States. Thomas Jefferson narrowly defeated John Adams for the presidency in 1800, and the new president allowed the Alien and Sedition Acts to die a natural death. The *Aurora* continued to publish until 1824, as Duane passed the journalistic torch to his son. At the end of the eighteenth and the beginning of the nineteenth century, the man who returned to North America for political and journalistic freedom had secured the rights of man for posterity—and, for Duane, those rights were universal.

1800s

3

A "Respectable Body of New Comers"

Transnational Journalistic Perspectives on the Wexford, Ireland, Diaspora in Savannah, Georgia

Howard J. Keeley and Steven T. Engel

An Irish citizen, a global scholar, and the celebrated author of *Imagined Communities: Reflections on the Origin and Spread of Nationalism* (1983), Benedict R. O'Gorman Anderson counted as a great-great grandfather Nicholas Purcell O'Gorman, an activist in the Society of the United Irishmen. Inspired by the American and French Revolutions, that organization spearheaded a significant but unsuccessful revolution in Ireland in 1798.[1] Because the so-called '98 Rebellion (or, simply, '98) imagined Ireland as an innovative, modern community—specifically, a sovereign republic characterized by religious tolerance—and because it produced thousands of rebel and civilian deaths, its commemoration became an essential touchstone of Irish nationalism. British government angst over the rebellion precipitated the Act of Union, which dissolved the Irish Parliament, replacing it, from January 1, 1801, with direct rule from London under a new national entity: the United Kingdom of Great Britain and Ireland.

Throughout the nineteenth century, the lore of '98 was polemically rehearsed, both nationally and internationally, not least by newspapers. Building on analysis in Jürgen Habermas's *The Structural Transformation of the Public Sphere* (1962),[2] Anderson's *Imagined Communities* deems newspapers—or print capitalism[3]—historically central to the coalescence of identity groups. Attention in the Irish nationalist press, both at home and among the Irish diaspora, allowed the event and its martyrs to dwell, generally with revered status, in the Irish political imaginary. The rebellion's fifty-year (1848) and centenary commemorations in particular stoked Irish nationalists at home and abroad.

The Young Ireland organization inherited some of the United Irishman mantle and produced a newspaper, the *Nation*, whose April 1, 1843, edition featured a ballad of anonymous authorship, the first line of which threw down a rhetorical gauntlet: "Who Fears to Speak of '98?"[4] In a way, the publication venue answered the question: newspapers like the *Nation* were not afraid to speak of the event and to shape and sustain its legacies, from the Shannon River to Sydney, Australia, to Savannah, Georgia.

As this chapter shows, by 1860, the Atlantic port city of Savannah, Georgia, was home to a significant population of Irish emigrants—sufficient, certainly, for the city's principal retail newsagent, Estill's News Depot, to advertise in the *Savannah Morning News* of August 7, 1875, that its stock of newspapers included the *Nation* (Dublin), the Young Ireland mouthpiece (which published, with some gaps, from 1842 to 1900).[5] Other Irish-diaspora titles from New York and Boston were also offered at Estill's agency, including *Irish World* (New York), *Irish American* (New York), *Celtic National* (New York), *Freeman's Journal* (Dublin), and *Boston Pilot*.[6]

Clearly, both the *Nation* and the Irish American press had a distinct interest in what Louis Althusser calls nationalist interpolation: that is, the deliberate shaping of consumers—in this case, readers—into human subjects who think, propagandize, vote, and otherwise act to advance the national or group cause. Very explicitly, in its *Prospectus* of 1842, authored by Thomas Davis, the *Nation* announced the newspaper's intention "to direct the popular mind and sympathies of educated men of all parties to the great end of . . . a[n Irish] Nationality which may embrace Protestant, Catholic, and Dissenter."[7]

While Savannah newspapers presented no such overriding Irish-nationalist agenda, Ireland and its diaspora did feature in their pages in a variety of ways. The longest-lived Savannah paper of the period was the Savannah *Daily Morning News*. Debuting on January 15, 1850, as one of the South's first penny newspapers, and claiming "neutrality" and "independence" as guiding principles, the *Daily Morning News* enjoyed a fourteen-year run, folding only when Union forces captured the city during the American Civil War. In its first issue, the *Daily Morning News* presents an Irish discourse in the form of advertisements by Savannah bookshops for new (1849) works by Irish authors: Charles Lever's novel *Confessions of Con Cregan, the Irish Gil Blas* and a five-volume set, *The Works of the Right Reverend John England, First Bishop of Charleston.*

Lever's text includes references to the 1798 Rebellion, the bloodiest year in Irish history. With close to thirty thousand conflict-related deaths, '98 directly impacted all parts of Ireland. Under British colonial rule, the country had developed multiple mercantile, agrarian, and ethno-religious anxieties. The Society of the United Irishmen posited republican democracy as a solution. By March 1798 the authorities were cracking down on the society, a policy that precipitated armed clashes between the state and rebels, the first of which occurred in Dublin on May 23. Tensions accelerated quickly so that June saw gory warfare. Certain regions, such as County Wexford, were especially affected, typically due to local grievances and larger national aims.

In 1829 Charles Gidden Haines's book, *Memoir of Thomas Addis Emmet*, was advertised for sale in Savannah, permitting citizens there to read the opinion that "[no] thing in the atrocities of French history . . . exceed[ed] in cruelty what happened in Ireland [in 1798]. Massacres in cold blood—house burnings—military executions—whole districts depopulated—tortures—flagellations, submersions, and imprisonments."[8]

Of Ireland's traditional thirty-two counties, none experienced greater violence than Wexford, a maritime county in the island's southeast. Estimates vary, but it is plausible that as much as a fifth of Wexford's population perished during '98.[9] In connection with the bicentennial commemoration, the development of the National 1798 Center in Enniscorthy, a town in the center of the county, constituted recognition of Wexford's special relationship to the rebellion and its trauma. But that relationship should also be factored into studies of the Wexford diaspora, whose link to the United States is particularly strong in Savannah.[10] An inquiry into when and how '98 has been present in Savannah by virtue of its Wexford population seems apposite, not least because such work responds to Adrian Mulligan's contention that scholars "problematize the spatial framing" when "theoriz[ing]" the "development of [Irish] nationalism."[11] Consideration of Wexfordians in Savannah helps broaden the Irish American historiographical purview, so long invested in the big three of Boston, New York, and Chicago.

In the 1860 US federal census, Wexford had become the leading Irish county-of-origin in Savannah. Nearly one in four among the nonslave Savannah population had been born in Ireland.[12] If any Irish county was going to export recollections of '98, it was Wexford, two of whose ports—Wexford Town in the east of the county and New Ross in the west—provided direct, winter-season sailings to Savannah for around a decade, beginning in 1845.[13] According to Edward Shoemaker, between 1848 and 1852, "the peak [five] years of Irish arrivals" into Savannah, 56.1 percent of "direct arrivals . . . identified Wexford as their point of origin."[14]

Savannah-bound emigrants leaving Ross (as it was popularly called) in the early 1850s would likely have had more than the ballad version of "Who Fears to Speak of '98?" in their heads, for the Battle of Ross on June 5, 1798, yielded approximately three thousand fatalities, a one-day death toll comparable to that of September 11, 2001, in the United States. County Wexford was also the scene of the rebellion's defining engagement: the Battle of Vinegar Hill, an Irish loss on midsummer's day. Named for a prominence just outside Enniscorthy, that fight became a synecdoche for the larger complex of 1798 engagements. Thus, in Ireland's most popular novel of the late-nineteenth and early-twentieth centuries, Charles J. Kickham's *Knocknagow* (1873), one female character, "old Mrs. Donovan," who witnessed the traumatic period in girlhood, explains '98 as "the year uv [of] the hill, an' the hangin' an' the floggin' an' all."[15] Addressing a veteran of the conflict, another character (a male, likely in his middle to late twenties), alludes to the rebel weapon that became iconic: "I'd like to see that old pike of yours taken from the thatch [the roofing of a house] for a manly fight like that you fought in '98."[16]

This chapter examines aspects of how mainstream newspapers in nineteenth-century Savannah reflected the greater reminiscence of '98. By regularly associating Savannah's Irish immigrants with the memorialization of the rebellion, its paraphernalia, and its protagonists, those publications effectively assisted in the production of an imagined community that functioned distinctively within the city: the Irish—but, specifically, the Irish as defined by republican aspirations and atavistic pride. As Savannah's Wexford-heavy Irish diaspora pushed upward socioeconomically and politically, newspapers captured its activities, such as the formation, in 1877, of the Robert Emmet Association, a cultural organization whose name honored the United Irishman leader who, through an unsuccessful uprising in Dublin on July 3, 1803, attempted to reignite physical-force Irish republicanism a mere five years after the tragedy of '98.

Whether Irish or not, a given reader in nineteenth-century Savannah could link an instance of (fairly extended) local-newspaper coverage of a Robert Emmet Association event—an anniversary dinner, a fundraising excursion, a celebratory parade—with another piece of reporting, one not focused on the association but nevertheless either implicitly or explicitly conscious of 1798 and its legacies. A compelling example of the latter is a feature in the "Things Laconically Noted" column of the January 31, 1879, *Savannah Morning News* about a pike. The paper details "an Irish pike, which was used in the Irish rebellion of '98 and which was brought from Ireland by an Irish lady, now a resident of this city." That artifact, the paper continues, may be viewed "on the Sisters' table"—that is, a stand operated by the Sisters of Mercy—at the upcoming Catholic Fair. Clearly, for the nineteenth-century newspaper reader, potential existed to shape a larger narrative about collective memory, priorities, and values among the Irish in Savannah. As Anderson acknowledges in *Imagined Communities*, the consumption of press content across days and months can produce coherent discourses around certain topics or themes, for readers respond to newspapers' "novelistic format."[17]

The next section expands on how, in nineteenth-century Savannah, the novelistic effect of local newspapers helped produce a discourse on Irishness infused with the memory of '98 and Robert Emmet's follow-on uprising. It also argues that, from the 1840s, newspapers introduced into that "plot" a distinctive new "character," namely the Wexford immigrant, and did so in a manner contrary to the common framing: "No Irish Need Apply." A second, briefer section considers aspects of how the midcentury Wexford press inscribed Savannah, an effort that included some engagement with Savannah newspapers. Overall, the contention is that print capitalism on both sides of the Atlantic proved crucial in integrating a significantly Wexfordian Irish Catholic diaspora into Savannah, a largely Protestant Southern city (founded in 1733) in the decade-and-a-half prior to the American Civil War.

Savannah Newspapers, 1798, and Wexford

As well as the de facto narrative about Irishness that they offered general readers, Savannah newspapers provided the city's Irish with plot-points about themselves. Across the nineteenth century, that community constituted a gradually coalescing ethnic coterie, some of whose formative experiences in Savannah encompassed not only labor as domestic, healthcare, railway, dock, foundry, and municipal-service workers but also weathering major yellow-fever outbreaks (in 1820, 1854, 1876), enduring the Civil War, and building up (from 1850) a Savannah-based Catholic diocese.

Before Wexford vessels made Savannah a regular destination, the memory of the 1798 Rebellion had, by virtue of local press coverage, already started to become a marker of Irish identity in the city. Until the early eighteen teens, "Irish" in Savannah connoted primarily Irish-born Scots-Irish Presbyterian merchants, such as John Cumming, an Edinburgh-trained physician-turned-Savannah factor. Cumming would serve for three years as the first president of the Hibernian

Society of Savannah, founded on March 17, 1812, as an ecumenical body dedicated to "tender[ing] the aid of a delicate charity"[18] to a new facet of Irishness then forming in Savannah: poor and needy, mainly Catholic Irish, some of whom included unemployed veterans of the Napoleonic wars. Thereafter, more "digger" and "ditcher" Irish arrived, many in response to various large-scale construction projects. Timothy Lockley has demonstrated that Georgia "low country canal and railroad" jobs attracted Irish laborers "during the 1820s and 1830s." Additionally, he has analyzed how advertisements appearing in newspapers in "Northern states" caused Irish immigrants there to "[flock]" into Savannah to help rebuild after a January 11, 1820, fire "destroyed more than a quarter of the city."[19]

As early as March 29, 1817, the *Savannah Republican* aided in constructing the cultural milieu, the sociopolitical, and the moral predilections of Savannah's Hibernian Society. Specifically, the newspaper reported in detail on toasts that concluded the Hibernians' "elegant [anniversary] dinner" each St. Patrick's Day. First among the eighteen official toasts was "The Day"; second was "The United States of America"; and third was "The Emerald Isle." The fifteenth toast, "Naturalization," lauded the "glorious constitutional privilege" of obtaining citizenship merely by "identifying with . . . America"—a matter exemplary of the United Irish principle that national affiliation should eschew the traditional calculus of blood, birth, and sect in favor of voluntarily and designedly embracing republican equality. Following the scheduled toasts, sixteen volunteer toasts were offered, the second and third of which invoked United Irish heroes: "*By the Vice-President*—The memory of . . . Robert Emmet"; "*By the Treasurer*—The memory of Lord Edward Fitzgerald."[20]

Applying Anderson's notion of the newspaper's role in creating nations, it is easy to recognize how the Savannah *Georgian* of March 19, 1825, contributed to further elaboration of (what might be termed) the '98 plot. In that edition, it enumerated, across a column and a third, the Hibernian Society's toasts during that year's "festival of St. Patrick." Relocating '98 and its attachments to a more central position within the newspaper's coverage of notably more pluralistic Savannah, the report records that two United Irish champions—Robert Emmet and Theobald Wolfe Tone, both Protestants—were included in the official, as opposed to the voluntary, toasts. Further, a long-term reader of the Savannah press might well have remarked that Emmet received considerable elaboration as a protagonist, by contrast with the simple invocation of his name eight years earlier, in 1817. With a paragraph of sorts now attaching to him, Emmet, sixth among the thirteen scheduled toasts, could, in 1825, be seen as analogous to a character making a second appearance in a novel because he had gained critical importance to the narrative: "*Robert Emmet*—The *Patriot* who would have freed his country—The *Martyr* whose death established the truth, that Tyranny reigned over the land."[21]

The twelfth official toast concerned Tone, the middle-class Dublin barrister who served as the ideological leader, as well as a military leader, of the antisectarian Society of United Irishmen. Thanks to that day's Savannah *Georgian*, city residents read that Tone shared American political values: "Theobald Wolfe Tone—He lived a Republican—He died a Hero."[22] As to the forty-two volunteer toasts the newspaper recorded, two privileged Emmet, while one, from John Cumming, the Hibernians' founding president, associated "firmness of purpose, patience in suffering, and fortitude in death" with an individual identified only as "*Byrne*." This likely was a reference to William Michael Byrne, a United Irishman from the minor Catholic gentry of County Wicklow. That Byrne accepted a death sentence for high treason rather than implicate a fellow rebel, Lord Edward Fitzgerald. Clearly, Savannah's daily newspapers of the second two decades of the nineteenth century were invested in a sophisticated rehearsal of United Irish lore that advanced a desirable Irish type: resolutely principled and selflessly patriotic. The coincidence of that effort with the arrival into Savannah of more and more poor Irish may be sociopolitically significant. Conceivably, the regular iteration in newspapers of such estimable '98-related characters as Emmet, Tone, and Byrne engendered some degree of receptivity on the part of white Savannahians toward the Irish newcomers, thus opening the possibility of a tolerant host society.[23]

Shoemaker's research has identified the late 1840s and early 1850s as prime time for Irish migrant entry into Savannah. More than half of direct arrivals in Savannah during the period disembarked from vessels out of County Wexford. Shoemaker quantifies the bigger picture by noting that "by 1860," the year prior to the outbreak of the Civil War, 14.7 percent of "the city's Irish natives" were Wexfordians: "more than were born in any other single county."[24] But even as it was relating such specifics as the landing of eighty-three women and men from Wexford Town on January 10, 1850, the Savannah press continued to attend to the '98-inflected discourse on Irishness.

When reporting on the Hibernian Society's 1850 "Festival . . . in honor of St. Patrick's Day," the March 20, 1850, issue of the *Savannah Morning News* quoted a (volunteer) toast to Robert Emmet's memory,[25] but it also acknowledged tributes to phenomena closer to the moment. The seventh official toast recalled "*The Irish Patriots of '48*"—that is, the Young Ireland rebels of the small-scale, one-day uprising of July 29, 1848. The tenth such toast lauded "*Father Mathew*," the Irish Capuchin priest who had administered the total abstinence pledge to over a thousand Savannahians in the city's St. John the Baptist church on January 27, 1850.[26]

The above example demonstrates that, as the nineteenth century reached its halfway mark, Savannah's newspapers did not forsake their well-established, encomiastic "narrative" about United Irish personages, especially Emmet, but instead allowed it to cohabitate with and, thus, color newer developments, such as Young Ireland's modest but ambitious uprising and Father Mathew's big and successful campaign. Bearing in mind Anderson's claim that newspaper content creates a "novelistic" effect—in individual issues as well as across multiple issues and titles—it is possible to consider that midcentury readers in Savannah might have imaginatively processed coverage of Wexford immigrants in such a way that at least some details became imbricated with the press-fostered plotline about the moral righteousness of both 1798 itself and Emmet's 1803 coda to that series of events.

Particularly because of the despair associated with Ireland's Great Hunger (1845–49)—a calamity that prompted the formation of a relief committee in Savannah—there was likely openness among Savannahians to countenance postfamine Irish characters with energy and drive comparable to Emmet's, Tone's, and William Michael Byrne's. And, in fact, by contrast with narratives elsewhere about emaciated, diseased, helpless, and sometimes even feckless Irish famine refugees, robustness and ability are qualities regularly highlighted in press treatment in Savannah during the early 1850s of newcomers from Wexford.

The Great Hunger crucially informed Robin Cohen's decision to place the Irish under the classification "victim diaspora" when he delineated a five-category typology of diasporas in his 1997 book, *Global Diasporas: An Introduction*. However, Wexford migrants to Savannah in the immediate postfamine period are perhaps better deemed a "labor, service diaspora," per Cohen's influential schema.[27] While the Great Hunger affected Wexford, the deleterious impact there was less than in almost any other Irish county. Boasting the moniker Model County (or *Exemplar Hiberniae*), Wexford was agriculturally progressive and diverse, with malting barley and beans among the crops that lessened dependence on the blight-vulnerable potato. Thus, during both "the pre- and post-Famine decades . . . the [population] outflow from [Wexford] was modest compared to that from most parts of Ireland."[28] Newspaper evidence points to Wexford vessels carrying to Savannah healthy, skilled individuals.

If engaging with the *Savannah Republican* on January 12, 1850, citizens of Savannah could, immediately below the masthead, encounter "83 emigrants of the better class of Irish peasantry" who, two days earlier, had "arrived from Wexford [Town], Ireland" on the "barque Menapia."[29] Arguably, several Savannah press inscriptions of newcomers from Wexford set them apart, almost as if they constituted a tribe distinguished by economic value. Essentially editorializing, the January 12 *Republican* underscored that the males among the eighty-three steerage passengers included "some valuable mechanics, blacksmiths, carpenters, &c." Shifting to the females, the newspaper deployed descriptive conventions typical of many novels. It averred, "The women were decently dressed, full of health and spirits, and seemed to attract attention." That attention resulted in full employment as "servants"—that is, domestics—for "stout rosy cheeked girls."[30] Echoing perhaps the approbatory discourse on the Irish with which, across decades in Savannah, newspaper consumers of Hibernian toasts would have become familiar, the piece, as its closing rhetorical move, highlights ethos or character. Specifically, it invokes the "very creditable account of the demeanor of his passengers" provided by the *Menapia*'s captain, a man with the distinctively Wexford family name of Rossiter.

Clearly, this socioeconomic narrative unsettles the popular "Green Atlantic" perception of famine-era Irish emigration as a matter of overcrowded "coffin ships." Undoubtedly, truth inheres in that assertion, for "the rate of [transit] deaths in the Famine's worst year [1847] was 20 percent out of 214,000 Irish emigrants" bound for North America;[31] however, the tale of Wexfordians in Savannah progresses differently. The following sailing season, the winter of 1850–51, saw another Allen barque, the *Brothers*, captained by Rossiter's associate Lawrence English, dock in Savannah on December 5, 1850, directly from Wexford Town. The next day, the *Savannah Morning News*, which competed with the *Republican*, offered comments about the "125 emigrants" the vessel carried. Explicitly identifying them as being "from Wexford," the paper declared, "rarely do we see a more respectable body of new comers from any portion of Europe . . . who we learn design settling in Savannah."[32]

Here, a self-proclaimed authority—"Largest Circulation in the City"!—colors a particular cadre of Irish, namely, Wexfordians, for absorption into Savannah's mainstream white consciousness. Not only does the *Morning News* end the piece with the sentiment, "May they realize their brightest anticipations, of prosperity and happiness in their new home," but four days later it provides new intelligence. Redeploying the notion of uprightness—this time via the phrase, "respectable body of emigrants"—it reveals that the arrivals "from Wexford, Ireland" had "presented to Capt. ENGLISH a handsome Silver Cup, in testimony of their esteem for him as an amiable and kind hearted gentleman and accomplished commander."[33]

One speculates that the infusion into Savannah of a significant number of men and women from Wexford had the effect of further stimulating what might be deemed the city's United Irish or Tone-Emmet sensibility: an ethics of bold action and mutual solidarity whose apotheosis, arguably, was the conversion, in 1902, of a downtown open space, informally known as Irish Green, into a city-maintained park named Emmet Park. Certainly, as the Wexford settlers integrated into Savannah, the general description "from Wexford" would mature in the city's newspaper-informed consciousness so that the county registered with the public not just as a discrete societal coterie but also as specific individuals—for example, Michael Cash, a "highly esteemed [Savannah] citizen and well known contractor," whose obituary in the *Savannah Morning News* of August 18, 1880, identified "Blackwater, county Wexford" as his place of nativity. "About fifty years of age" at his death, Cash had, after arriving in Savannah "about twenty-five years" earlier, "accumulated" in the city "a handsome [professional] competency" and "made many friends among all classes of our people."[34]

According to his multiparagraph obituary in the *Morning News*, Cash's affiliations included two benevolent (or fraternal life-insurance) societies of Irish American provenance, each committed to furnishing aid to any physically and/or fiscally compromised members, as well as the wives and children of deceased members. Founded in 1847, one, the Irish Union Society, was indigenous to Savannah.[35] The other was a Savannah branch of the Catholic Knights of America.[36] The two societies signaled pragmatic unity among Irishmen, and their emergence, like that of other essentially Irish organizations in nineteenth-century Savannah, was symptomatic of the city's increasingly large, coherent, and confident Irish community. While some of the new entities privileged the well-being of working families, others espoused temperance and yet others the moral and financial support of domestic Irish causes (such as the Repeal Association and the Land League). Whether a given organization was identified with one or more Wexfordians, its portrayal in the Savannah press was, from at least 1850, enhanced by the press's positive editorial depictions of Irish competence and their descriptions of Wexford immigrants as a supremely "respectable body of new comers."

In fact, Wexford personages regularly featured in press elaborations on socially, fiscally, and/or morally responsible Irishness in Savannah, especially as demonstrated in the creation and operation of various kinds of societies.[37] In an era when the New York–based *Harper's Weekly* occasionally printed Thomas Nast cartoons showing the Irish as uncouth simians, white Protestant Savannahians must have derived some comfort in the newspaper-delivered intelligence that two benevolent societies—one explicitly Irish, the other explicitly Catholic—would "render" a "last tribute of respect" at the 1880 funeral of the "highly esteemed . . . and well known" Wexfordian Michael Cash.[38]

Arguably, small anecdotes, such as the above, amass to produce the didactic moral core of many a nineteenth-century novel. In the case of a serialized novel, that accumulation requires weeks or months of reading, a practice eminently comparable to the sequential consumption of newspapers. Across the 1880s, as in other decades after the Wexford-to-Savannah migration, regular readers of the Savannah press could develop fairly detailed knowledge about certain Wexfordians, often in connection with their steering or otherwise advancing endeavors that enhanced the Irish in Savannah, the Irish back home, or the larger Savannah scene. At that time, a rising star in and beyond the city's Irish community was P. J. O'Connor (1859–1908), the Savannah-born son of two Wexford immigrants. Newspaper "capture" of O'Connor, a Georgetown-educated lawyer, during the 1880s included, but was by no means limited to, his keynote oration at a July 4, 1881, assembly at Savannah's beach resort, Tybee Island, in support of the Irish National Land League, and his acting as secretary and treasurer, in early 1884, to a committee representing the seven "Irish societies" then cooperating to arrange "the celebration of St. Patrick's day" in the city.[39] When O'Connor's father, Daniel, died in 1887, the *Savannah Morning News* obituary (on February 16) noted that, four years earlier, the son had succeeded the father as a member of Savannah's Board of Aldermen.

As if recapitulating the Savannah press narrative about Wexford respectability and economic worth, first articulated almost forty years earlier, the *Morning News* underscored that Daniel, "born in Wexford,

Ireland," had built his business into Savannah's largest wheelwrighting, blacksmithing, and wagon-making operation. That immigrant success facilitated P.J.'s Georgetown law degree and Savannah law practice, but Daniel in his own right became "one of Savannah's most prominent Irish citizens," a man "prominently identified with public affairs [in Savannah]," and a charitable donor "to all objects worthy of support."[40]

Regardless of his father's exemplary munificence, however, in 1899, the year after the centenary of the United Irish Rebellion, P. J. O'Connor declined to offer financial support to a Dublin memorial to the Irish nationalist politician Charles Stewart Parnell, "insisting instead that a statue to Wolfe Tone and the 'heroes of '98' should be first in order."[41] This intransigence confirms the allure of the United Irish narrative for a man so proudly Savannahian that he headed much correspondence with the locution, "Office of National President, A.O.H. of America. Savannah, Ga.," during the four years that he held the top slot in the Ancient Order of Hibernians, America's oldest and largest Irish-Catholic fraternal organization.[42] In assessing P. J. O'Connor, David Gleeson and Brendan Buttimer assert that "he undoubtedly grew up [in Savannah] hearing the lore of 1798," and one assumes that that narrative was particularized by his parents to reflect Wexford's trauma during that year.[43]

Broadly speaking, the "heroes of '98" circulated among unreconstructed Irish nationalists in Savannah as a shorthand for their aspirations. After the establishment, in 1858, of the Fenian Brotherhood—an American organization committed to supporting Irish physical-force nationalism—a Savannah branch emerged, calling itself the Wolfe Tone Circle. Whether intentionally or not, newspapers imbue facts with drama, and the perhaps novelistic denouement of a minor crisis associated with the circle was reflected in Savannah's *Daily News and Herald* of December 13, 1866. Specifically, readers discovered that the Savannah City Council had, on the previous evening, heard from its Committee on Public Buildings about the settlement of what, in essence, was the (potentially contentious) double-booking of a municipal "room" on Exchange Row by the Wolfe Tone Circle and the Irish

Union Society.[44] This society opposed the principles espoused by the circle; while the circle worked for Irish home rule, the society opposed it. Consequently, when members of the circle arrived to find the space already occupied by the society, violence could have resulted. Conceivably, readers of the *Daily News* could create in their minds a symbolic interpretation of the incident; namely, that the exigencies of their working lives and, thus, material stability in the adopted city had, for the Savannah Irish, partially shut out an effort to support precisely what Wolfe Tone had espoused: paramilitary activism to attain Irish independence.

Certainly, just over a decade later, Savannah newspapers bore witness to a redeployment—or at least significant nudging—of a United Irish figure, Emmet, away from the domain of physical-force nationalism toward that of cultural nationalism. An internal initiative on the part of some among the Savannah Irish, the Robert Emmet Association arose in 1877 as perhaps what could have been the city's first organization primarily dedicated to a broad-spectrum Irish cultural agendum rather than a specific cause such as philanthropic assistance (the Hibernian Society), an insurance fund (the Irish Union Society), or a political end (the Wolfe Tone Circle). The association met monthly, and a sense of its priorities may be gleaned from the title of the lecture given at its November 1878 gathering. "The Early History of Ireland."

The kind of right-feeling personal and social morality advanced by certain nineteenth-century realist novels (what Henry James called "moralized fable[s]")[45] seems implicit in much of the *Savannah Morning News* coverage of the Robert Emmet Association. Readers could intuit a positive moral valence in such reports as that of the singing of "an old familiar and patriotic song" by the eighty or so members of the association gathered in Savannah's Metropolitan Hall on March 4, 1879, to commemorate the 101st anniversary of Emmet's birth. The song occurred just prior to "the good byes," and the greater gathering configured, according to the paper, as a "pleasant occasion" that was "marked by conviviality and genial humor": "Jokes were told, sentiments given and anecdotes related, and thus the hours wore on in most social and convivial style."[46] In essence, the Irish patriotism expressed never became threatening, the crowd mob-like, nor the mood unpleasant.

The report quoted from a speech at the gathering was optimistic about Ireland's future, not least because the country's contemporary populace included such types as "the earnest student of the pages of . . . Banim," almost undoubtedly a reference to John Banim (1798–1842), the better-known of two brothers whose novels established Ireland's Catholic middle class as a subject for fiction. The descriptive mode of much middle-class fiction perhaps informs how, later the same year (specifically, on August 7, 1879), the *Morning News* presented a story about a recent "grand picnic" at Tybee Beach, organized by "the Emmets," that attracted around 250 "excursionists" in support of a construction project at a Savannah female orphanage. In this instance of Irish-Savannahian activity, the center of gravity is not the memorialization of the radical Irish past but, instead, participation (with "a marked absence of everything like drunkenness or disorder") in a distinctly American present: "surf bathing," dancing to "the Mechanics Brass Band and a string band," and more. In effect, the newspaper resituated the name of Emmet so—in Savannah, on the cusp of the 1880s—it could connote "charmingly delightful" sociability rather than the bloodshed endured by the Society of United Irishmen.[47] Emmet may have been a recurring character in the tale of Irishness conveyed, somewhat novelistically, by the Savannah press; however, what he represented did not remain static.

Always dynamic, the production of Irish American identity in nineteenth-century Savannah resulted from multiple factors, one of which was the impact of an appreciable Wexford diaspora, present from around the midcentury. When communicating to the broader white population aspects of how the Irish immigrant community *in* Savannah became increasingly *of* Savannah, local newspapers could be explicit about Wexfordians, either as a "body" or as discrete individuals. The bourgeoisification of much of the Irish community may have been accelerated by virtue of the Wexfordians' possession of skills and health upon their arrival in Savannah, conditions acknowledged by the contemporary print media. Furthermore, the perpetuation in Savannah papers of a discourse on the 1798 Rebellion and the United Irish martyrs would certainly have had special resonance for Wexford-born residents of the city and their offspring due to the distress experienced in Wexford during the Year of the Hill.

Wexford Newspapers and Savannah

Contemporary Savannah newspapers furnish some hermeneutic precision-tools for elaborating scholarly understanding of nineteenth-century Irish, especially Wexfordian, emigration to—and integration into—Savannah, Georgia. But if such titles as the *Savannah Morning News* and the *Savannah Republican* had the effect of inscribing Wexford as a peculiar component of the city's über-narrative of Irishness, then the twice-weekly *Wexford Independent* must have played a comparable role in conveying Savannah—or Savannagh, as the paper sometimes spelled the name[48]—as a distinctive dimension of Ireland's footprint in the United States. Recurring across multiple issues of the *Wexford Independent* during the early fall of 1853, a Graves & Co. advertisement for its "First-Class Superior Packet-Ship" *Dunbrody* explicitly privileges Savannah over New York by insisting that the "winter" Atlantic passage from Ireland to the former city was "safe and comparatively easy," as contrasted with the "long and dangerous" New York sailing at that time of year.

Thanks primarily to the *Independent*, from around 1849, Savannah, a theretofore largely unknown quantity, entered both the reasoning and fantasizing spaces of the Wexford mind as an American space—one open to and suitable for new arrivals.[49] The fundamental form of that message was advertisements taken out by the three shipping companies that developed the nonstop, winter-season Wexford-to-Savannah emigration route: Howlett & Co., the larger Graves & Son of New Ross, and R., M., & R. Allen of Wexford Town. Graves extended its advertising of Savannah to the *Kilkenny Journal* and the *Waterford Mail*, the leading newspapers in the largest cities in two neighboring counties. According to letters written by captains in the employ of Graves (documents now housed in the National Archives of Ireland), the Wexford vessels—most of them barques—skirted the Azores and Barbados before anchoring in the Savannah River at the Savannah city wharfs.

Initially, a local firm, Andrew Low & Co., the city's largest factorage, handled most Savannah logistics for the Wexford vessels, from receiving them at the port to procuring supplies for return voyages to honoring hospital invoices for sick crew members. However, in 1849, William Graves, patriarch of Graves & Son, replaced his commission-based relationship with Low & Co. by installing one of his adult sons, James Palmer Graves, in Savannah. The Wexfordian J. P. Graves arrived there in October 1849, and on December 8 of that year, the *Savannah Daily Republican* included his business in a list of over seventy "factors and commission merchants," almost all of them based on Bay Street.

As if a protagonist in a novel, "Mr. J. P. GRAVES" appears as the opening gambit in the second paragraph of an advertisement, placed by his father's company in the September 20, 1851, *Waterford Mail.* Occupying a striking position—the top of the first column on the newspaper's front page—the piece explains that J. P. Graves "will receive the Passengers on landing" in Savannah should they avail of the service being promoted: an emigrant voyage, scheduled for October 1, of a Graves vessel, the "Splendid First-Class Packet Ship 'GLENLYON,'" from New Ross to "the chief City of Georgia, (one of the most prosperous States in the American Union)." Implicit in the parenthetical data is awareness that readers in Waterford were generally unfamiliar with Georgia, let alone Savannah, a city that the text elsewhere conveys as desirable by virtue of its offering "in the winter season . . . full employment for a large number of tradesmen and labourers." However, the advertisement registers some anxiety that Savannah may not be fully compelling to its readers, for prior to discussing labor conditions there, it presents the city as a springboard for rail and steamboat travel "to the interior States and Cities, and to the Valley of the Mississippi."

The great majority of advertisements for Wexford-to-Savannah sailings appeared in the Wexford press, and in the *Wexford Independent* of September 18, 1852 (just under a year after the notice discussed above), the Graves enterprise presented a new opportunity for "Emigration from Ross to Savannah" aboard the *Glenlyon*. Conceivably, this 1852 advertisement rehearses material garnered from Savannah newspapers when it asserts that "the Cotton and Corn Crops are reported to be this year unusually large." That contextual scenario established, the advertisement proceeds to more personal concerns on the part of prospective emigrants by insisting, "There is every reason to expect full Employment, at good Wages, for both Artizans and Labourers."[50] Of note in these Savannah-focused Irish artifacts from the early 1850s is their invocations of skilled professions: "tradesmen," "Artizans." In a way, they are shaping before the fact the Wexford community in Savannah, whose debut in that city's white press would be as a "respectable body of new comers."

While the Wexford diaspora was forming in mid-nineteenth-century Savannah, the *Wexford Independent* occasionally printed nonadvertisement data about Wexford people and interests in the Southern US city. Consider, for example, how the paper's January 1, 1851, edition offered a brief confirmation—obtained from the "master" of the Allen brothers' barque *Brothers*—of the "abundant employment" available in Savannah.[51] He was commenting on the aftermath of his recent, forty-two-day Wexford-to-Savannah sailing, the one whose 125 steerage passengers the *Savannah Morning News* of December 6, 1850, had deemed "respectable." Importantly, the piece coexisted with almost three columns of coverage of agricultural issues—primarily activism, much of it in Wexford, for tenant-farmers' rights, a source of anxiety and, thus, a push factor for emigration. For readers across County Wexford on New Year's Day 1851, the *Independent*'s choice to print the master's words made advertising claims about Savannah more credible. Suddenly, due to the salience attaching to the paper as a reporting (as opposed to an advertising) entity, Savannah gained a new panache that would be further enhanced on March 29, 1851, when the *Independent*, speaking as the editorial "we," declared "great pleasure in giving [i.e., presenting in print] . . . extracts of a letter, just received by Mr. McLaughlin of this town [Wexford Town], from his son."[52]

During the 1850–51 sailing season, the *Brothers* departed for Savannah in October 1850, while its sibling Allen vessel, the *Menapia*, embarked in December of that year, with McLaughlin Junior as one of the passengers. The selection of his correspondence offered by the *Independent* pronounces that "every passenger was engaged before he left the vessel," which docked in Savannah on February 13, 1851.[53] Adding an affective timbre to the greater presentation, the letter writer concludes by declaring, "This is the finest city I was ever in." In a way, Savannah, so meticulously explained to Wexfordians across multiple advertisements, here becomes a familiar, intimate notion: a "This" that perhaps could be contemplated as an extension of, as well as an alternative to, Wexford.

However, Savannah deepened in the minds and imaginations of Wexford residents not just because the *Independent*'s editors curated it publicly, now and then, in their pages. Likely, emigrants mailed full copies of Savannah newspapers to their natal county. Within the "extracts" of his letter quoted by the *Independent*, McLaughlin Junior promises, "I will often send . . . some of the United States papers," the most affordable and ready-to-hand of which would have been Savannah's daily titles.[54] One imagines a scene in a Wexford kitchen or parlor similar to one presented in Kickham's *Knocknagow*, a novel alluded to earlier. In one of the edifices identified by that work's subtitle, *The Homes of Tipperary* (a county in south-central Ireland), a literate male character—a tailor by profession—declares, "'Tis an American paper I'm afthr gettin' the lend of." Indicating that class of artifact to be familiar in the rural hamlet of Knocknagow, the man continues, "I can't see much in id that we hadn't before," beyond a speech by the Irish-born Bishop John J. Hughes of New York, probably the American city best known across the island of Ireland during the nineteenth century.[55] By contrast, at least from the 1840s, Savannah, Georgia, was for newspaper readers in Ireland something to "see . . . that we hadn't before."

To advance greater specificity (indeed, truth) in how we comprehend the Irish-US emigration narrative, the interrogation of local newspapers in linked locales on either side of the Atlantic can be productive. In this case, Wexford and Savannah have been considered, not least because the relationship between the two places has received scant attention in Irish migration or diaspora studies to date. Benedict Anderson's notion that "reading a newspaper is like reading a novel whose author has abandoned any thought of a coherent plot"[56] is useful, for it allows one to see that over days, weeks, months, or even years of consumption, a given newspaper reader—an individual at liberty to shape an abundance of information—could identify a set of more or less related data points and conjoin them into a plausible plot.

From the multiple local, regional, national, and international stories on offer across the pages of, say, the *Morning News*, a local reader in nineteenth-century Savannah could discern and inventory printed facts and opinions pertaining to the city's Irish community. During and after the middle of the century, it became possible, perhaps even unavoidable, for such a reader to situate Wexfordians—a new but distinctive and ineluctable Irish subgroup—within a preexisting values discourse that the press had underscored as being predicated on the memorialization of the pike, Tone, Emmet, and other dimensions of '98 and its immediate aftermath. For her or his part, a mid-nineteenth-century consumer of the *Wexford Independent* in, say, the town of Gorey, in the north of County Wexford, could enter into a consciousness of Savannah, Georgia, not only as an accessible locale (Allen company advertisements indicated an agent, Thomas Harvey, in Gorey), but also as a font of good employment, as verified by other Wexfordians.

Newspapers mark time; however, they also transcend it in so far as any newspaper reader can select temporally disparate elements from within their pages and then assemble them into a coherent and perhaps even revelatory whole. Things come together, yielding a kind of epistemic immediacy. Extracted from their sequential presentation in Savannah newspapers and contemplated retrospectively as a novelistic storyline, data about Wexfordian newcomers—in part because following on from recurring coverage of United Irish phenomena—likely contributed to the largely successful emplacement of Irishness within the communal life of nineteenth-century Savannah. Furthermore, Savannah likely became attractive to at least some prospective Wexford emigrants as a result of their imaginatively synthesizing the various ways in which the Wexford press presented that Southern US city.

4

"Good American Citizens"

Boston's Pilot *and Social Reform*

Ian Kenneally

The last decades of the eighteenth century and the first decades of the nineteenth century saw the rise and rapid demise of a number of Catholic newspapers in the United States of America. One of the most resilient of these early journals, the *Catholic Miscellany*, was founded in Charleston, South Carolina, in June 1822 under the guidance of Cork-born bishop John England. According to the paper's prospectus, it was to have a twofold purpose: to provide the members of the local diocese with a means of communication and to defend the Catholic Church against external criticisms from the dominant Protestant society.[1]

The *Pilot*, as detailed below, would be similarly inspired. Bishop England had once been a director of the *Cork Mercantile Chronicle* in Ireland, but, despite this journalistic background, he struggled to make the *Miscellany* financially viable. Indeed, shortly after founding the *Miscellany*, the bishop explained in a letter to a local businessman that the paper was struggling to gain the three hundred subscribers that it needed to break even.[2] Nevertheless, the paper limped on under constant financial strain until a fire destroyed its offices in 1861. Yet, the *Miscellany* had an enduring legacy in that it inspired a number of similar papers, especially in New York and Boston. Among these papers was one which would eventually become known as the *Pilot*.

This chapter examines the *Pilot* newspaper, its development throughout the nineteenth century, and its attitude toward various social reforms, particularly from the 1860s to the 1890s. During those decades the *Pilot* was at the height of its popularity, and to better understand its editorial output, we will examine the careers and ideologies of those who owned and edited the paper.

Patrick Donahoe's Paper

In Boston, spurred on by the steady growth of the city's Catholic population, Bishop Benedict Fenwick launched the *Jesuit or Catholic Sentinel* on September 5, 1829. The paper's prospectus promised that the new publication would benefit Catholics in the region through "the good effect it will provide, especially on the minds of the Protestants."[3] This desire for respectability—to integrate Catholics into wider society—was a leitmotif for the paper throughout the nineteenth century. A related goal was the defense of Catholicism, as can be seen in the prospectus: "We are fully aware of the crying calumnies, and gross misrepresentations, which in this section of our country have been so long, so unsparingly, so cruelly heaped upon that church which alone influenced and directed the world for sixteen centuries . . . we deeply regret that even at the present day the various sectarian presses groan under the oppressive indecorous calumnies of virulence and abuse."[4]

The paper was renamed the *United States Catholic Intelligencer* in October 1831 before returning to its original title in January 1833. It had yet another name in 1835, the *Literary and Catholic Sentinel* before becoming the *Pilot* in 1836. All these name changes are a demonstration of the financial problems facing the paper during its early years. The difficulties in gaining subscribers were, perhaps, partly a result of the product itself and the manner in which it was presented. Each edition was densely packed with theological arguments and admonishments toward critics. There was little in the way of news and little around which a community of readers could be built. The paper's difficulties culminated in April 1837 when it was forced to cease publication. Its story would have ended at that point were it not for the efforts of businessman Patrick Donahoe. He purchased the *Pilot* and relaunched it on January 27, 1838. Donahoe saw a commercial opportunity in the *Pilot*, but he also claimed to be providing a service to the

Irish in the United States, as was declared in one editorial: "We were convinced that such a paper was needed—that the laboring Irish and the stranger needed someone to speak for him."[5]

Donahoe had been born in County Cavan, Ireland, on Saint Patrick's Day 1811.[6] Around ten years later, he traveled with his family to begin a new life in the United States, attending school in Boston, where he so often fought back against other children who mocked his Catholicism that he remembered his childhood as "the days of the discoloured eyes and the swollen lips."[7] Aged fourteen, he was forced to leave school because of his family's financial difficulties, taking an apprenticeship as a printer with the *Columbian Sentinel.* It was through such work that he developed the skills necessary to publish a newspaper, skills that he employed after taking over and then relaunching the *Pilot* in 1838. At that time, the *Pilot* claimed to have a circulation of only six hundred subscribers, concentrated in New England, but six years later this figure had increased to seven thousand readers, located across the United States.[8] Donahoe credited this larger circulation to his policy of printing regular news from Ireland, particularly his coverage of figures such as Daniel O'Connell and the campaign to repeal the Act of Union, which had tethered Ireland to Britain in 1801.[9]

From 1838, and over subsequent decades, Donahoe's *Pilot* played an important role for immigrants, linking their old society to their new one. The paper, as with other immigrant papers, sought to maintain the self-esteem of the new arrivals and offered advice on the political, social, and economic environment that now surrounded them. The *Pilot* also printed notices from freshly arrived immigrants who sought information on the whereabouts of family members who had preceded them to the United States.[10] Donahoe was well aware of the potentially vital power of newspapers, and he was especially keen to fight the sense of defeat that afflicted so many Irish immigrants as well as what one *Pilot* editorial described as their tendency to "assume the air and action of inferiors."[11]

In so doing, the paper provided a sense of community and sanctuary to Irish immigrants, a service that was vitally important in those early years and especially in the face of the anti-immigrant and anti-Catholic nativism of the 1840s and 1850s. This nativism was most infamously encapsulated in the form of the "Know Nothings," a political grouping that often resorted to violence against Catholic immigrants. The historian Francis Robert Walsh has well described the *Pilot* during this time as a sort of "fortress" that "reflected the insecurity of the Irish in the years before the Civil War."[12] This insecurity, so exacerbated by the anti-immigrant sections of US society, deepened the sense of group identity among the Irish, as can be seen in the pages of the *Pilot* throughout the middle decades of the nineteenth century. In an attempt to counter racist and sectarian propaganda that claimed the Irish were a threat to the United States, the paper lost no opportunity to highlight and frequently embellish the role of Irish immigrants in the early development of the nation. This aspect of the paper's reportage, acting as "guardian of the good name of the Irish," would continue throughout the nineteenth century.[13]

As the number of Irish immigrants to the United States soared during the 1840s, the market for such Irish American newspapers greatly expanded. The *Pilot*'s circulation rose to meet this demand, and by the 1860s the paper was long free of its early financial fragility. Donahoe had flourished along with his paper. His flagship business, the *Pilot*, was housed in lavish headquarters on Franklin Street, and he had used his accumulated wealth to expand his business interests. These included two banks: he was cofounder of the Union Institution for Savings in 1865 and founder of the Emigrant Savings Bank in 1870.[14] He was also a steamship agent, and by 1870 he was estimated to be worth around $500,000 and was making a $40,000 annual profit from the *Pilot* alone.[15] Donahoe used a portion of this money to help others and to further his reputation. He was involved in many charitable causes and had sponsored Irish regiments in the Union Army during the American Civil War.

A Change of Ownership

Donahoe had a reputation for hiring talented young journalists and, in 1870, he hired a man with whom the *Pilot* has become inextricably linked, John Boyle O'Reilly from County Meath in Ireland.[16] A year earlier, O'Reilly had arrived in the United States as an Irish American sensation, having escaped from the penal colony of Western Australia, where he had been incarcerated by the British government for his activities as a member of the Irish Republican Brotherhood. Born in 1844, O'Reilly had worked as a printer in Drogheda and as a reporter in the English town of Preston, before joining the British army in 1863.

O'Reilly had enlisted in the British army at a time when the Irish Republican Brotherhood (which would become popularly known as the Fenians or Fenian Brotherhood) was steadily gaining popularity, partly through the efforts of its widely distributed newspaper, the *Irish People*.[17] This paper was, as R. V. Comerford has written, "largely responsible for transforming [the] movement into a major phenomenon in Irish public life in the mid-1860s."[18] As the Brotherhood's popularity increased, it began to prepare for a rebellion in Ireland. O'Reilly was keen to take part in this rebellion and, in September 1865, he took the Brotherhood's oath by pledging "allegiance to the Irish Republic now virtually established."[19] During the following six months, O'Reilly attempted to undermine the British army through recruiting fellow soldiers into the Brotherhood. This was dangerous work, and an informer betrayed O'Reilly, who was arrested and imprisoned. He was subsequently court-martialed, found guilty of treason against the British Crown, and sentenced to twenty years penal servitude. He spent time in various Irish and English prisons before being transported to Australia in late 1867. A little over a year after his arrival in Western Australia, however, O'Reilly escaped aboard an American whaling ship.

The ex-convict was talented, hardworking, and ambitious. He was also determined to forge a career in journalism, and Donahoe had little trouble persuading O'Reilly to join the *Pilot*. Within a year O'Reilly had become editor, and the paper's continued success seemed certain. However, a scarcely believable series of events soon threatened to destroy Donahoe's financial and media empires. In November 1872 the buildings housing the *Pilot* and the Emigrant Savings Bank were consumed by the Great Boston Fire, which devastated much of the city center.[20] The *Pilot* moved to a temporary office nearby, which was destroyed by a fire only weeks later. The paper then established a new headquarters on Washington Street, but this too was destroyed six months later in a fire that spread across a small section of the city center. Finally, Donahoe moved production of the *Pilot* to a building on Boylston Street, which would serve as the paper's new headquarters.[21]

Patrick Donahoe had been put under unbearable financial strain as a result of the fires that had consumed his businesses.[22] When the *Pilot* moved to its new head office on Boylston Street, Donahoe was forced to take out mortgages on a number of his properties, including his own home.[23] His businesses were put under further strain as result of the financial panic of 1873 and the depression which subsequently hit the US economy. As an immediate consequence of that panic, there had been a series of bank failures resulting from widespread reckless real estate lending and grossly inflated property values. The Massachusetts economy was not spared the turmoil, and Donahoe's commercial empire steadily lost the ability to maintain itself.[24]

By March 1876 Donahoe was $569,000 in debt, and his creditors filed an involuntary petition for bankruptcy against him. Donahoe's estate was taken over by these creditors, who assigned control of his business interests to a group headed by the politician Patrick Collins.[25] The businessman's one performing asset was the *Pilot* and, in this, O'Reilly saw an opportunity.[26] O'Reilly could not afford to buy the *Pilot* but he put a proposal to the archbishop of Boston, John J. Williams, that the Diocese of Boston take part ownership of the paper.

The archbishop was a Boston native, and he was eager to see such a renowned Catholic paper remain in publication. From that basis the two men were able to forge an agreement whereby they purchased the *Pilot* and its offices for $28,000, with Williams contributing $21,000 and O'Reilly $7,000.[27] The deal was closed on April 15, 1876. Editorial policy would henceforth remain completely in the hands of O'Reilly, who would receive an annual salary of $5,200 (the average salary of "non-farm employees" in the United States during 1876 was $403).[28]

O'Reilly's Voice

Under Donahoe's ownership the *Pilot* had been a supporter of the Democratic Party, and O'Reilly retained this policy. As O'Reilly explained in an 1884 speech, he regarded the Democrats as historically more kindly disposed to the Irish in the United States. The Republicans, he declared, were not only antagonistic to the Irish but were also inextricably wedded to the political elites and the maintenance of the status quo.[29] This analysis was unlikely to have upset any of the *Pilot*'s readers. The Irish and the Democratic Party had become intertwined over the preceding decades. As O'Reilly explained, the Irish had originally joined the party to gain a measure of protection from hostile groups such as the Know-Nothings of the 1850s. In return for votes the Democrats gave the Irish access to opportunities for social and political advancement that they would otherwise have been denied. Membership in the Democratic Party also, as Kerby Miller has shown, gave the Irish "a sense of belonging to a powerful *American* institution."[30]

By the 1870s, in the words of Thomas O'Connor, the previous "docility of the Irish in political matters was fast becoming a thing of the past."[31] O'Reilly was fully attuned to this development, and he continued what had long been the *Pilot*'s policy of involvement in American politics. In 1877 O'Reilly noted that "there is not one Irish person in 10,000 who will ever return to live in Ireland. . . . Is it right to tell these people . . . that they must live solely for that country's politics, and that until she is free they must not become good citizens of this country? Is it not plainly the duty of the 9,999 to become good American citizens?"[32] Consequently, O'Reilly devoted much of his paper's reportage to the social and economic turmoil that he witnessed all around him. Over the remainder of this chapter, we examine the *Pilot*'s attitudes toward workers' rights and the campaign for female suffrage, though we do not have space to discuss O'Reilly's support for African American civil rights during the Reconstruction period and afterward.[33]

The improvement of workers' rights was a topic on which the *Pilot* regularly editorialized, especially in the aftermath of the financial crisis that began in 1873. Throughout its earlier existence, the *Pilot* had an ambivalent, often antagonistic, attitude toward trade unions, but under O'Reilly's editorship the paper would become a consistent proponent of workers' rights. Nevertheless, O'Reilly would often equivocate on the role that unions and strikers should play in the promotion of those rights. During 1871 he contributed a piece to the *Pilot* in support of Pennsylvania miners who were then on strike: "It must be remembered that the miners have interests to protect as well as the owners, and the only effective way for the worker to protect his interests is by association."[34] Two years later, the *Pilot* reversed this position, using an editorial to warn that any worker who joined a union "throws away the great gift of individuality which God has given to him."[35] The same editorial deplored the use of strikes, concluding that "the idea of working men protecting their interests by strikes is a blind and suicidal one."[36] However, the depression that hit the United States after 1873 made such tidy assumptions less easy to maintain and caused O'Reilly to modify his thoughts on this matter, and he came to believe that his hostility to unions was untenable.

One of his original reasons for opposing unions was that many of those organizations were secret societies, and since leaving the Irish Republican Brotherhood in 1870, O'Reilly had followed the Catholic Church's line on such organizations.[37] Yet, as workers across the United States saw their attempts to unionize quelled by intimidation from bosses and company owners, O'Reilly realized that many unions were being forced to operate secretly. As the economy of the United States grew increasingly turbulent, O'Reilly became convinced that workers across the country, of all ethnic backgrounds, were being exploited by railroad companies, factory owners, mining companies, and industrialists. According to O'Reilly it was employers, acting in concert to preserve their mutual interests, who were driving down the worker. They had used the ongoing economic crisis as pretext to cut wages to "starvation levels."[38] Therefore workers had every right to group together in furtherance of their own interests and to protect themselves from the owners and industrialists who employed them.

The *Pilot*'s changing attitude to strikes could be seen in April 1876, when hundreds of Irish workers in Newton, near Boston, began a strike against their pay and conditions. Each week, the workers at the Newtown water-works construction site saw two-thirds of their pay packet deducted by the contractor. This deduction was supposedly to pay for food and board, but the workers were provided with "the cheapest and coarsest fare, and lodgings in the rudest shanties."[39] The *Pilot* took up their cause stating that: "No wonder the poor men should strike when ground by such rascally extortion. Herded like cattle and worked like slaves, the men have been driven to rebellion to save their manhood."[40] However, the legal advantage in such disputes lay with the bosses rather than the workers: the contractor, one Mr. Moore, publicly stated that "not another Irishman will be employed on the Newton water-works while we control their construction."[41] Within a few days of the strike beginning, Moore had arranged for the transportation from New York of 250 Italians as strikebreakers.

The *Pilot* deplored the use of strikebreakers although, in such cases, it laid the blame with the contractors rather than the workers who took the jobs of strikers. In the above instance, the Italians who had replaced the Irish workers were to suffer just as badly as their Irish forerunners and so followed them on strike. In June 1876 the *Pilot* reported gleefully that Moore had lost his contract and that a new employer had taken control of the project: the striking laborers, "most of them Irish," were back to work.[42] In O'Reilly's eyes this episode was a lesson on how a strike could be effective in righting a wrong. It also demonstrated how he could use the *Pilot* to publicize the cause of maltreated workers.

By the mid-1870s strikebreaking was just one of the tactics that industrial companies used against discontented employees. Rail and mining companies, for example, deployed hired militias against their workers. Indeed, Pennsylvania had passed legislation in 1865 and 1866 that allowed companies to form private police forces. These "Coal and Iron Police" were supposed to operate as guards for the mines, but by the 1870s they were being engaged by rail and mining companies as paramilitary forces against workers.

One example of such conflict could be seen in the anthracite coal fields of northeastern Pennsylvania, which had been wracked by violence since the 1860s as miners protested against their low pay and extremely dangerous working conditions. On one occasion, in September 1869, a fire in a mine killed over one hundred people. A manifestation of this unrest was a group called the Molly Maguires, which was comprised almost entirely of Irish Catholic miners. It was not a trade union but a secret society that had sprung from the tradition of Irish agrarian groups such as the Whiteboys and Ribbonmen. Those groups had routinely used violence against their enemies and, displaying a similar mode of operation, the Molly Maguires had been responsible for a number of assassinations of mining company officials over the previous years.

In 1873 the Philadelphia and Reading Railroad Company hired the Pinkerton Detective Agency to combat the Molly Maguires. The Pinkerton Agency was not just a detective service; it also supplied private militias to its clients. In Pennsylvania, the Pinkertons would use undercover agents to infiltrate the Molly Maguires, while the agency also supplied the names of suspected Molly Maguires to vigilantes in the pay of the mining companies. Through this combination of infiltration and intimidation they were able, over the subsequent years, to bring a number of Molly Maguires to trial, facing charges of murder.

In 1877 O'Reilly offered an editorial defense of the Molly Maguires. The editor did not justify their actions but, perhaps remembering his own court martial in 1866, deplored the use of paid informers against the defendants. Following the hanging of ten leaders of the group in June of that year, he argued that the real criminals were the mine owners: "The Corporations of Pennsylvania first drove the miners into Molly Maguirism and murder, and then virtuously hounded them to the scaffold. The same Corporations have caused the present strikes and have dragged down on themselves the fire of their burning wealth and the blood of many victims."[43] O'Reilly was one of relatively few commentators to offer any defense of the condemned men. Press commentary, which mostly emanated from the point of view of "corporate capital or American middle-class society," was overwhelmingly hostile to the strikers and had applauded the executions of the Molly Maguires.[44] The Molly Maguires, according to the historian Kevin Kenny, were "also shunned and condemned by the clergy and hierarchy of the Catholic Church to which most of them belonged."[45]

By 1880 O'Reilly's *Pilot* had reversed its earlier opposition to strikes. It now concluded that not only were strikes "a necessity" but that "when wisely managed their effect is almost invariably good."[46] From this premise, O'Reilly became a supporter of the Knights of Labor, at that time the most prominent labor organization in the United States. The *Pilot* also regularly targeted business owners such as Jay Gould and Franklin B. Gowen, the president of the Philadelphia and Reading Railroad Company, declaring on one occasion that those men and others like them "believe that nature has selected them to do the governing, while the only right of the common people is to be governed."[47] O'Reilly concluded, although reluctantly, that the federal government had to intervene to combat the growing power of such industrialists and their monopolizing of the economic landscape.[48]

Aside from O'Reilly's belief in human rights and concern for the underprivileged, his analysis of the conflict between laborers and industrialists was, according to the historian Arthur Mann, "socialist in spirit and source."[49] It is necessary, however, to examine what socialism meant to O'Reilly. As Francis G. McManamin has pointed out, O'Reilly was often kindly disposed even to those social reformers with whom, ultimately, he disagreed.[50] O'Reilly did have much sympathy with the claims of socialist thinkers that selfish, materialistic, and acquisitive behaviors among people were the products of a culture that encouraged such behavior rather than an inherent feature of humanity. Even so, O'Reilly had many reservations about socialism, especially among those thinkers who attacked religion. Socialism, as O'Reilly understood it, meant a more equal society and a higher level of protection for workers amid the laissez-faire ethos of the time. He recognized that this would necessitate some level of government involvement in labor disputes but, in general, O'Reilly was opposed to state intervention on a large scale unless it was absolutely unavoidable. Nor did he support any reformer who called for the abolition of private property or the forcible appropriation of land.

Despite his policy of reviewing works such as Edward Bellamy's *Looking Backward*, a novel set in a socialist utopia, O'Reilly was wary of what he considered to be radical solutions to the problems he described. The *Pilot* was at its most caustic when attacking a target, especially some corrupt politician or greedy corporate figure, but was far less assured when it came to providing answers to the societal problems that he described. O'Reilly's personality was that of a natural mediator whose instinct, at least with regard to workers' rights and economic issues, was toward piecemeal progress. Throughout O'Reilly's editorship of the *Pilot*, he regularly lauded himself and the paper's readers as being "calm," "rational," and "respectable." Whereas Karl Marx had castigated those who had sought only to interpret the world rather than to change it, O'Reilly confined his role to that of critic, stubbornly exposing the tribulations afflicting society. "The first duty of the social reformer," he later wrote "is to teach—not to do."[51]

For example, O'Reilly was an advocate of cooperative movements whereby workers would group together and take control of a business and divide the profits among themselves. He advised: "Instead of a strike let the dissatisfied workmen start a shop or a store of their own and meet the masters on their own ground by becoming masters themselves."[52] This was also a policy embraced by Terence Powderly, the Irish American head of the Knights of Labor. Cooperation appealed to O'Reilly and many of the Knights "precisely because it aimed to ameliorate specific labor problems such as low wages, insecure employment, and declining craft control."[53]

One of the editor's clearest ideas was his advocacy of arbitration as a means of dealing with labor disputes. O'Reilly's proposal, which he had adopted in the 1870s, was that the government could provide an independent mechanism whereby workers and industrialists would meet and undergo a process of mediation. This should be done, he argued, through "a constitutional law."[54] He believed that this would have the benefit of protecting the workers by affording them an opportunity to openly and legally air their grievances. Thereby, it could save them from a prolonged struggle such as a strike through which they would lose their only means of income. O'Reilly was willing to let the government legislate for a system of compulsory arbitration if corporations refused to enter the process. As an addendum to his arbitration idea, O'Reilly urged the government to legislate to protect workers' wages: "Mathematicians can tell us the point where strength ends and weakness begins in a beam; so should the legislators find out and fix the market point at which profits should cease and wages begin."[55]

Women's Suffrage

Despite the *Pilot*'s advocacy on behalf of workers, the paper would play a different role in the long-running campaign to obtain voting rights for women, since O'Reilly was a vehement and consistent opponent of female suffrage. In his resistance to this reform, O'Reilly was very much in line with the views of the Catholic hierarchy. The traditional Catholic stance on this issue was that each sex had its distinct spheres of activity. The woman's duties revolved around her role as the center of the family and as the mother of children. It was a system, in the words of one historian, "designed by God, revealed by a Pauline interpretation of scripture and/or the natural law, re-enforced by biological differences, and supported by a historical tradition which proclaimed the political supremacy of man."[56] This "natural law" could be rent asunder by any attempts to alter the traditional roles of men and women.

Opposition to female suffrage was not merely a Catholic phenomenon, and it was a common occurrence to see preachers of various faiths working in concert to prevent the enfranchisement of women. They marshaled a variety of justifications to aid their cause, other than that of "natural law." A commonly stated view was that women were intellectually inferior to men and so it was futile to provide them with a vote. Others argued that women were hamstrung by their supposedly capricious and irrational natures. Women, in this argument, would prove an unstable element in the political compound and could not be trusted with the ability to use the vote wisely. O'Reilly did not subscribe to the assertion that women were intellectually inferior to men, but he was a firm believer that a woman's place as, to use a popular phrase of the time, "queen of the household," would be destroyed by any grant of suffrage. This belief manifested itself in the *Pilot* on many occasions over the 1870s and into the 1880s. A lady, it once opined, "will be gentle and modest, mistress of temper and curiosity. . . . She will know and honor her own place in the social order, as the divinely appointed moulder, teacher, and refiner of men and out of this beautiful and noble place she will not seek to move."[57] The perfect lady, in other words, would provide an example to other women by knowing her place and keeping to it.

Unsurprisingly, Archbishop Williams, the *Pilot*'s co-owner, was in full agreement with O'Reilly. In 1885 Williams gave an interview with the *Boston Advertiser*, in which he declared that there was "no general movement among Catholic women towards voting." He suggested that the whole idea was being pushed forward by a noisy minority, adding that: "I do not think that women ought to take part in politics; they can be much better employed."[58] Williams was correct in stating that there were many women who opposed female suffrage. This was especially true among Irish Catholics. However, their antagonism toward suffrage, as the historian Hasia Diner notes, was not merely a result of the Catholic Church's attitude to this reform. She lists many issues, such as involvement in trade-unionism and attendance at public schools, in which Irish women ignored church directives.[59] Their ambivalence toward suffrage was more a consequence of the economic and cultural divisions that separated immigrant women from the middle- and upper-class Protestants who dominated the prosuffrage movement. Those Irish women who were active trade-unionists, for example, were far more upset by the vast economic disparities in the United States rather than what they perceived as a misguided focus on inequality between the sexes.

The gulf that separated many Irish women and the female suffrage movement was further widened by a strong strain of anti-Catholic and anti-Irish prejudice that ran through the movement and which gave the clear indication that some women were more suited to equality than others. It is likely that neither Williams nor O'Reilly were interested in these complex reasons behind Irish women's attitudes to suffrage campaigns. O'Reilly, in particular and as can be seen below, had very specific justifications for his aversion to female participation in the political process. However, the archbishop and the newspaper editor would use the lack of enthusiasm displayed by Irish Catholic women toward this reform as a means with which to attack the concept of female suffrage.

In 1886 O'Reilly made one of his rare forays into direct political action as part of an antisuffrage lobby group. This group, headed by the transcendentalist Octavius Brooks Frothingham, was roused to action by prosuffrage attempts to put a suffrage motion before the Massachusetts state legislature. Frothingham organized a group of journalists, politicians, and religious figures to compose a pamphlet that outlined their position under the succinct title: *Woman Suffrage—Unnatural and Inexpedient.* O'Reilly contributed a lengthy article:

> To compel women to vote is to excite the brutal in men, and to engender disregard for law. Women cannot enforce an ideal equity, when they have enacted it. The physical weakness of woman is her strength when it appeals to the spirit of man; but let it attempt to control or obstruct his physical or intellectual movement, he will push it aside or trample on it. Ideal statutes openly disregarded is barbarism and anarchy, the rule of the stronger appetite. It would be no more deplorable to see an angel harnessed to a machine than to see a woman voting politically, giving up her divine intuition for a vulgar material compromise. It is not fair to let women make laws they cannot enforce.[60]

The logic of O'Reilly's contribution, if carried to its end, is chilling. It is clear from his writings in the *Pilot* and elsewhere that O'Reilly believed civilization was ultimately underpinned by force; that society was a fragile blend of competing interests, each of which was backed by men willing and able to fight for what they believed. "Moral force," he stated, "has always a threat in reserve."[61] It was those competing interests that were the driving force of history, and if the disparate groups that formed the social order failed to compromise, then violence was the inevitable result. According to O'Reilly, the delicate balance of society would be skewed by female suffrage. His reasoning was that women are physically the weaker sex, so it was worse than futile to give women the vote. They would never be able to protect their interests through force and would be trampled upon by men. The ensuing disregard for law would set a brutal and dangerous precedent that would spread anarchy throughout the land. "A vote, like a law," he wrote in the *Pilot*, "is no good unless there is an arm behind it; it cannot be enforced. This is a shameful truth, perhaps, but it is true."[62] The same editorial added that "women ought to be fully guarded by law in all rights of property, labor, profession, etc." but concluded by arguing that "roughly stated, the voting population ought to represent the fighting population."[63]

O'Reilly's *Pilot* never wavered in its opposition to female suffrage. Many of the paper's articles on the topic resorted to listing virtues and characteristics that O'Reilly believed were inherent to women and which made them perfectly suited to their historical mission as "queen of the household." For O'Reilly they often seemed to be wholly defined by these supposed characteristics:

> We want no contest with women; they are higher, truer, nobler, smaller, meaner, more faithful, more frail, gentler, more envious, less philosophic, more merciful—oh, far more merciful and kind and lovable and good than men are. Those of them that are Catholics, are better Catholics than their husbands and sons; those who are Protestants are better Christians than theirs. Women have all the necessary qualities to make good men; but they must give their time and attention to it while the men are boys.[64]

O'Reilly's attitude would persist in the pages of the *Pilot* long into the future. James Jeffrey Roche, who joined the paper in 1883 and who became editor after O'Reilly's death, revered his friend and former boss. Roche followed his hero's line on many issues, including female suffrage. Indeed, he considered the above passage from O'Reilly as "one of the best ever" responses to the supporters of that reform.[65] O'Reilly, Roche, and the *Pilot* remained unmoved by the arguments of women who sought to climb down from their pedestal and who refused to let such lists be the limits of their lives.

Donahoe's Return

By 1890 O'Reilly was famous across the United States, admired as a journalist and as a poet.[66] The *Pilot* was similarly successful and had increased its circulation to over seventy-two thousand copies per edition.[67] However, O'Reilly died suddenly in August 1890, after which Archbishop Williams offered Patrick Donahoe the opportunity to repurchase the *Pilot*.[68] By January 1891 Donahoe had bought Williams's shares as well as those of Mary Murphy, O'Reilly's spouse, thereby assuming complete control of the paper.

In the first edition after his return, Donahoe informed his readers of how the *Pilot* would proceed into the future: "In American politics our principle has been and will continue to be; Country first; Party afterwards. . . . Our policy is the same in the matters affecting the welfare of Ireland. He who serves his country best shall have our support."[69] It was these ideals that Donahoe continued to espouse through the remainder of the 1890s, although his failing health at the end of the decade meant that he was less involved in the paper's daily management. After his death in March 1901, the many obituaries rightly concentrated on Donahoe's career with the *Pilot*, a newspaper that he had saved and then transformed into one of the leading immigrant newspapers in the United States.

5

The Story without a Source

A Tale of Irish Death in New Orleans

Nancy McKenzie Dupont

Memories bind communities together, but the accuracy of those memories matter less than stories recounted, especially if the stories are told over and over again. "Memory, being a phenomenon of motion and magic, accommodates only those facts that suit it."[1]

When communities preserve the memory, perhaps even add to it, they bring memories into the present.[2] In New Orleans, one such communal memory is the fate of Irish immigrant laborers who dug the New Basin Canal. Theirs is a story, a memory, of disease and death, numbers of deaths that seem—and perhaps are—unreal. But communal memory in New Orleans says otherwise. Indeed, the story has been told so often, in novels, newspapers, and song, that it scarcely matters whether it is true or what its source might have been.

In the early nineteenth century, New Orleans was on the verge of being the largest city in the southern United States and the third largest city in the nation. People were drawn to New Orleans because of its port, which allowed access from the lower Mississippi River into the Gulf of Mexico. New Orleans had distinct disadvantages, too. Surrounded by water, it was prone to disease—cholera, which thrives in wet climates, and mosquito-borne diseases such as yellow fever were the most common.

Epidemics ravaged the city's population every few years during the 1800s, and the inadequate medical system was unable to do anything to stop the outbreaks. Living in close quarters in unsanitary conditions rendered people susceptible.

Irish immigrants fleeing political persecution and famine made their way to New Orleans even before the Louisiana Purchase in 1803. The Irish took up several occupations, such as running shops, restaurants and bars, banking, journalism, and teaching. A few became wealthy, among them Maunsell White, who arrived penniless in New Orleans in 1801 from County Tipperary. White went into buying and selling commodities and soon owned his own business. He fought at the Battle of New Orleans in the War of 1812, establishing himself as a military hero as well as a business leader, and he was wealthy enough to build a mansion in the 1820s. He was part of the group that organized the first New Orleans St. Patrick's Day celebration in 1809, and he became first lieutenant of the Hibernian Society. Though the Irish were not part of the group that had achieved hegemony in New Orleans, like the French-speaking Creoles who descended from the original French and Spanish settlers, they mingled among them and encountered no social stigma because of their Irish heritage.[3]

Maunsell White would figure into a renowned New Orleans myth regarding the city's Irish American population, one that became so pervasive and so much a part of the city's fabric, that when historians researched the story and found it to be implausible, New Orleanians had a hard time coming to terms with the findings. In the 1830s White was one of the owners of a company that built a second New Orleans canal. This one ran from the Mississippi River to Lake Pontchartrain, a distance of six miles. The canal came to be known as the New Basin Canal. In the days before power tools and pumps, the workers had to dig painstakingly through the swamps with hand shovels, which was backbreaking work.

> The freshly dug areas were continuously pumped throughout the process to keep them from refilling with water. Pilings were driven to support the sides by placing large rocks on top of them until they sank into the muck.[4]

According to the legend, White's company used Irish workers for the canal construction because slaves were too valuable; if a slave was killed or died of disease, the owner stood lose a healthy amount of money. Poor Irish immigrants were expendable and replaceable.[5]

Sometime in the twentieth century, the legend intensified as new claims arose that between eight thousand and thirty thousand Irish workers had died of disease during the construction and were buried near where they fell on the banks of the canal. Journalists, some of them very well respected, perpetuated the story. A prolific New Orleans writer told the story often, as did members of the New Orleans Irish Cultural Society and two Irish folk song composers.

While there is documentation of the brutality of the company employing the immigrants and a few newspaper articles about complaints of the workers, little information exists about the actual digging of the canal. Laura D. Kelley, who wrote *The Irish in New Orleans*, is one of the historians who considers the story implausible.

> If we consider what we know about Irish immigrants, submissive behavior was not part of their collective character. Images of men dropping like flies, their bodies left rotting alongside the canal, don't follow the Irish's history of action.[6]

The Story

Classifying the story within the realm of narrative theory is difficult. The story has some characteristics of a myth, which, according to the Oxford Dictionary, is defined as a "widely held but false belief or idea." A myth may be exaggerated or fictitious, but it generally has a purpose in the culture and some relation to the truth, even if only peripheral. The Irish have a rich tradition of folk tales, legends, and myths passed orally and aurally through the generations. Any purpose to the story of the New Basin Canal would have to be mere speculation. For the story to be a legend, it would have to have details not outside of the possible and never really doubted. At a certain point, the story of the New Basin Canal tragedy was doubted, so much so that it changed a campaign by the New Orleans Irish Cultural Society.

The story of the tragedy of the New Basin Canal likely began within this oral tradition among the New Orleans Irish community.

5.1. The New Basin Canal in 1915. Wikimedia Commons/Library of Congress.

By then, the tale had been memorialized not only in myth but also in song. It would also become part of the printed record, which gave the story more permanence.

There are few records of the beginning of the New Basin Canal project, and it was rarely mentioned in New Orleans newspapers. What is known is that prominent businessmen, White among them, formed the New Orleans Canal and Banking Company in 1831. These men had the idea that a second canal from the Mississippi River to the south and Lake Pontchartrain to the north would break the monopoly of the company that owned the original canal that was built in 1794. These canals were valuable to shipping; vessels anchored in the lake, accessible from the Gulf of Mexico, waited for flatboats to bring goods from the Port of New Orleans, eliminating the need to navigate the Mississippi River. The new company hired Simon Cameron of Philadelphia as engineer. Cameron, who would become a member of Abraham Lincoln's cabinet, recruited 136 Philadelphia Irish to travel to New Orleans to work on the canal; Cameron offered them room and board, passage to and from New Orleans, and twenty dollars salary a month.[7]

Many more men would be needed to build the canal, and historians estimate that Irish immigration to New Orleans was robust from 1830 through 1860. However, these new arrivals faced discrimination early Irish immigrants had not endured. The newer immigrants were considered less intelligent and less educated than those who arrived in the early nineteenth century. "The Irish of the present day, whom we see landing on our levees seem to be a different race of the Irish of ten, 15, or 20 years since," according to one New Orleans newspaper.[8]

Almost immediately, the Irish laborers Cameron brought from Pennsylvania became discontent. The *Louisiana Advertiser* noted that, among other things, they had been sold as indentured servants, the company store prices were too high, and they had no medical care. They claimed that when they refused to work under unacceptable conditions, the company boarded their sleeping rooms and stopped feeding them.[9] These 136 were the only workers complaining about conditions on the New Basin Canal in 1830, but there would be more objections later.

The Irish stage actor Tyrone Power, an ancestor to the twentieth-century American film actor by the same name, made a tour of America in the 1830s and observed the digging of the New Basin Canal. He described the Irish laborers as industrious, civil, and courteous, but their job was unimaginably difficult.

> [They labored] amidst a pestilent swamp whose exhalations were fetid to a degree scarcely endurable even for a few moments; wading amongst stumps of trees, mid-deep in black mud, clearing the spaces pumped out by the powerful steam-engines; wheeling, digging, hewing, or bearing burdens it made one's shoulders ache to look upon.[10]

Power described the lives of the laborers as mere existence, nothing more.

> [They are] holding life as a tenure as uncertain as does the leader of a forlorn hope; excluded from all the advantages of civilization, often at the mercy of a hard contractor, who wrings his profits from their blood; and all this for a pittance that merely enables them to exist, with little power to save, or a hope beyond the continuance of the like exertion.[11]

He described the Irish immigrant, just landed in the "long-sighed-for-shores," only to have his spirit broken by the "spirit-sinking" labor he'd have to do. Power described disease and the incredible toll it took on the laborers, but he made no mention of epidemics or where the victims would be buried. "They are worse lodged than the cattle of the field," Power wrote, and the priest was the only comfort for the men, the only one who told them that they had not been forgotten.[12]

Power had nothing but contempt for the New Basin Canal project financiers. He observed that

> Christian charity and justice alike suggest that the labourers ought to be provided with decent quarters, the [*sic*] sufficient medical aid should always be at hand, and above all, that the brutalizing, accursed practice of extorting extra labour by the stimulus off corn spirit should be wholly forbidden.[13]

It should not have been surprising, then, that harsh conditions and extremely hard labor should create such frustration that it boiled over into violence. In early 1834 a sugar refinery wanted a canal dug and encouraged underbidding by groups of Irish diggers. A riot broke out when Irish laborers from the New Basin Canal attacked another Irish labor group; four men were killed.[14] New Orleans newspapers called for swift police action. Another newspaper condemned the violence, but pleaded for mercy for the Irishmen. "Have we the peculiar right to hunt down these men, because indeed they crave our hospitality, because they are poor and ignorant, because oppression has made them wild—are these reasons to track them down as the fallow beast? Certainly not," the editors wrote.[15]

The Epidemic of 1833

In the fall of 1833, New Orleans experienced its worst yellow fever epidemic in recorded history. Every summer, mosquitos bore the disease through the population (though doctors did not yet realize that mosquitos were the cause). Edward H. Barton, MD, made the official report to the Charity Hospital of New Orleans of how the disease spread and intensified through the year. Barton noted that there had been a cholera outbreak in the winter months of 1833, but as the temperatures turned warmer, yellow fever became the scourge. The treatment for yellow fever was painful and ineffective; leeches would be placed on the patient or cuts to the veins would be made. Barton reported that the total mortality of the epidemic was 2,631 persons, roughly 5 percent of the city's population. Barton reported burials in the city's Catholic and Protestant cemeteries, with breakdowns by gender and race, but nowhere in his report does he mention those who died from disease being buried outside cemeteries.[16]

Origins of the Tragedy Story

More than a hundred years after the New Basin Canal opened to barge traffic, newspapers began printing the story of the Irish immigrant diggers and their sacrifices. On July 18, 1937, Meigs O. Frost, with a Pulitzer Prize under his belt, published an article in the New Orleans *Times-Picayune* with the headline, "Deaths of 10,000 Irishmen Digging New Basin Canal is Recalled by Refilling Ditch." The story was a report on the partial closing of the canal to prepare it for being filled with dirt and bricks.[17] Most notable in the article were the lyrics to a song that were to be cited over and over again for the next fifty years.

> Ten thousand Micks, they swung their picks,
> To dig th' New Canawl.
> But the choreray was stronger'n they,
> An' twice it killed them awl.[18]

Frost made no reference to when the song or poem was written. The remainder of the article was as poorly referenced as the ditty, with Frost claiming that the construction company's records had been burned. He detailed the horrible existence that the Irish diggers had endured, which was supported by Power's diary, but he added a new detail: that the bodies of the workers were buried in the canal.

> Hopes of a free life in a New World that ended in tragic death for thousands of sweating human beings rest buried in the mud and water of that New Basin canal. . . . Craft and greed and written Records mysteriously destroyed are part of the canal's story.[19]

Frost accurately described the work and conditions the Irish laborers endured; they worked in waist-deep water under a hot sun, they ate poor food, all the while living in overcrowded construction camps. Then, admitting that the story was amazing, he described the burials of the men.

> Some 20,000 Irishmen died of the cholera that broke out among them, and . . . some 8000 survived who drove that ditch through the muck amid the dying, and buried the dead in the "back dumps" by covering them with the wheelbarrow loads of muck they shoved up slanting planks out of the big ditch.[20]

Frost claimed that the owners of the canal company were watching international affairs and picked Ireland as a place to recruit workers.

> Ireland and hell were synonymous in those times. Irishmen were fighting mad over what they called the oppression of absentee British landlords, who milked their Irish properties of the last farthing agents could squeeze from them, and lived in London or abroad. Family stalked the fields of Erin, with a black blight on the potato crop. And the only answer England knew to "Irish malcontents" was the noose . . . or the cell.[21]

In 1950 reporter Diane Farrell wrote a story on the city's disappearing canals: "New Orleans' Canals Go Underground." She repeated the lyrics of the song published in 1937, claiming the Irish diggers sang the refrain as they worked. She also wrote, without citing a reference, that workers were buried on the banks of the canal: "The greatest mass of human life ever swallowed by a New Orleans canal at any one period was gulped down by the New Basin project in the 1830s. Over 10,000 immigrants died of cholera while digging it."[22]

Frost had actually claimed that twenty thousand had died of disease while digging the canal, though the headline on his story claimed the number was ten thousand. Farrell claimed the number was ten thousand, even though she reprinted the lyrics that claimed ten thousand workers were twice killed by disease, making the number twenty thousand.

For a time the *Times-Picayune* newspaper settled on ten thousand as to the number of Irish workers felled by disease but did not include the details of the grizzly burial that had been chronicled in the past. In 1950 the Union Passenger Terminal was built over the filled-in New Basin Canal, and as part of a report of the new facility, the writer crafted a ghost story. He painted a picture of elegant trains riding over the ghosts of the New Basin Canal.

> The route of the canal was swampland, and swampland meant unhealthy working conditions. . . . So the immigrants—most of them Irish—signed up as laborers, came to New Orleans and early in 1832 took pick and shovel in hand and set to work in the stumps, until cholera and yellow fever struck the city, claiming the lives of 10,000 immigrant laborers.[23]

The estimated number of the Irish laborers who died digging New Basin remained at ten thousand in a report of the New Orleans government taking over what was left of the filled-in canal belonging to the state. The writer assumed local residents did not remember what the canal had been, much less its history.

> In terms of human life, it was probably the most Expensive public project ever completed in the Crescent City. . . . The route of the New Basin Canal was swampland and this meant unhealthy working conditions . . . more than 10,000 immigrant laborers, mostly Irish, were claimed by cholera and yellow fever.[24]

Excavators found bodies and coffins at the six-to-eight-foot level at Canal Street and Claiborne Avenue in 1967. At first the city believed the remains were from the St. Louis Cemetery number 2 in a little-used part of the graveyard that was owned by the city, not the Catholic Church. The discovery led the *Times-Picayune* to speculate that there were hastily buried yellow fever and cholera victims among the dead, and perhaps some Irish immigrants. "Who knows but that some of the remains are those of the immigrant excavators of the vanished New Basin Canal, who fell in the great cholera epidemic of 1832–33?"[25] the newspaper asked. There was no speculation in this article as to how many Irish workers died.

The number did not stay at ten thousand; soon it doubled again. A report by United Press International done in advance of a 1979 visit to New Orleans by Irish prime minister Jack Lynch claimed that twenty thousand Irish ditchdiggers were buried in the banks of the New Basin Canal.[26] The reporter did not mention what the laborers died from, only that they died at their shovels and were promptly buried, and their widows were given fifty cents for their husbands' working a half day. The descendants of those immigrants were preparing to show the prime minister an out-of-season St. Patrick's Day parade in the Irish Channel, the neighborhood where immigrants made their first homes.[27]

Suddenly, the newspaper estimates of the number who died of disease digging the canal fell to eight thousand and stayed there, largely, throughout a campaign to memorialize the workers. A genealogy column printed in the *Times-Picayune* in 1983 lowered the estimate, but the writer made a curious claim. The reporter wrote that, "Records show that they worked for $1 a day, and slave owners preferred that the Irish do the job since they were worth less than slaves."[28] The writer also noted that construction of the New Basin Canal was the magnet that drew the Irish to New Orleans.

For fifty years the *Times-Picayune*, New Orleans's newspaper of record, reported various versions of the tragedy that befell the Irish laborers working on the New Basin Canal. Sourcing was always flimsy. The inability to present a consistent set of facts may signal that the story entered an oral tradition, where information gets reported with no respect for facts. It is significant that the story survived as a tragedy for more than 150 years.

Mary Lou Widmer

No author has written more about the Irish immigrants who came to New Orleans than historian Mary Lou Widmer who, through a series of novels and nonfiction books, has chronicled the first Irish citizens of the city. In 1988 the Irish Cultural Society of New Orleans gave Widmer the Caomhnoir (Preserver) Award for making a significant contribution to "fostering of traditional Irish culture"[29] in the city. Just two weeks before she was honored, Widmer wrote an article in an American magazine with new details of how the disease victims of the New Basin Canal were buried.

> Men began falling dead with yellow fever as they dug the canal, and as the months went on, the numbers multiplied. Each day, the death wagons passed to pick up bodies of whose who died during the night.[30]

She claimed most of the victims were buried in a potters' field near the canal, and she wrote that some bodies had been found.

> A year ago, when Canal Boulevard was being widened, many bones of Irishmen who had been buried in common graves were found, reminding New Orleanians once again of the tragedy of the 1830s.[31]

Three years earlier Widmer had written *Lace Curtain*, a fictional account of an Irish immigrant family from Skibbereen in County Cork, with two brothers who worked on the New Basin Canal. She chose as the name of her central character Danny Callahan; the only person ever named by the newspapers in the 1834 Irish violence was "Allahan," probably Callahan.[32] Included in the novel is at least one nonfictional character, Maunsell White, who improbably becomes a friend of the immigrant family, helping them to achieve the status of "lace curtain" Irish; that is, more affluent and respectable—able to afford lace curtains for their windows. In the book Callahan leads the New Basin Canal laborers in a strike, finds charity for them when their huts are burned, takes their case to White, and wins concessions. He goes into business with White and is elected to the city council. In negotiating for better conditions for the laborers, Callahan explains to the company why digging the canal is taking so long.

> They did not count on the heat an' the faever takin' its toll, an' the water running up to our ankles after every shovelful of mud. . . . More pumps are needed. More men are needed. The work is harder. It takes longer. And it's going t'get worse as we go along. I think you'll do well t'face the fact that the canal is goin' to cost a whole lot more than you thought.[33]

While campaigning for office, Callahan makes the claim that ten thousand died and were buried where they fell.

> Fer six long years an' six endless summers, hundreds of men braved the heat and the yellow faever to shovel dirt from the belly of that canal. Ten thousand men died of the cholera and yellow fever epidemics of '32 and '33, and were buried on the banks of the canal.[34]

In a curious narrative, Widmer has Callahan make a hopeful campaign speech, reminding the Irish immigrants that their lives were better after the work on the New Basin Canal was finished. "Silence fell and the faces looking up at Danny became confused and disgruntled. They didn't know if they liked the prosperity Danny had just imposed on them. They loved suffering and having the world to know about it."[35] Widmer may have presented a theory about why the story of the suffering in the New Basin Canal has endured for so long.

Widmer continued the story of the Callahans with the novel *Twin Oaks* in 2012, following Danny's daughter through marriage and the Civil War.

The Story in Song

Danny O'Flaherty grew up on the Aran Islands off the coast of County Galway. The son of accomplished musicians, he learned the songs of his native land early in life. His first language was Irish Gaelic, learned in his parents' cottage on Inis Mhór. In 1968 he left Ireland for Chicago. In 1989 he and his brother established O'Flaherty's Irish Channel Pub in the French Quarter of New Orleans; Danny and other performers played Celtic music and shared the history of the Celtic nations every evening. As happened with many New Orleans businesses, the tragedy of Hurricane Katrina in 2005 closed the pub for good.[36]

An Evening at O'Flaherty's, an album released in 1991, contained a song called "New Basin Canal." The lyrics tell the story of ten thousand Irish immigrants who went to New Orleans in 1832 to dig a canal. The chorus is, "There was nothing for him at home / Only a dream across the sea / But the Irish Navvy's labor / Made that dream come true for me." By the end of the song, the canal is gone but "St. Patrick's Church still proudly stands to remind us of those navvies' lives."

"This is a story of both sides of the ocean," O'Flaherty said. "The Irish were skinned to the bone (by the British agents). There were smaller famines before the Great Famine in 1845, and the penal laws were so severe that there were no options to feed a family. . . . When you tell a whole tribe that they're inferior, they begin to believe that 'they are my masters' and it gets in the DNA to accept any treatment."[37] O'Flaherty believes the history of Ireland is important to the understanding of the New Basin Canal and the Irish in America. "This mistreatment in Ireland happened in the 1830s, the 1730s, the 1630s, the 1530s; it happened again and again."[38]

To O'Flaherty, it does not matter how many Irish died digging the New Basin Canal; that even one laborer died is an outrage to him. The lyrics of his song recall how the Irish were picked to be the diggers.

> The bayou heat and steaming rain
> Were much too risky for their slaves
> So the city fathers send abroad
> For Erin's sons to dig their graves . . .
> They dug with only pick and spade
> The fever felled them in their tracks
> They worked in hell and died in pain
> Yet this canal got built on Irish backs.

"How many died? Why go there?" O'Flaherty asked. "If eight thousand died, or eight hundred, or eight, or even one, it shouldn't have happened. Humanity shouldn't do that to humanity." In the end, O'Flaherty said he believes the song is a story of Irish resilience. "How did they survive? The accomplishments of the Irish, the spirit of the Irish, are just remarkable."

Tributes

In the late 1980s, the New Orleans Irish Cultural Society began raising money for a memorial to the Irishmen who died digging the canal—at least, that was what supporters talked about when they spoke about the proposed monument. The memorial was to be a Celtic cross made in Ireland with an inscription in English and Irish Gaelic. It was to be erected over the neutral ground (a term New Orleanians use for a street median). There was a fundraising event and a poster was created, a limited edition silkscreen scene of Ireland that sold for forty dollars. Stephen Dooley, a descendant of an Irish immigrant to Canada, was the artist.[39]

Dooley told the *Times-Picayune* that he understood the neutral ground to be a cemetery because many of the Irish laborers who died were buried on the banks of the canal. "No one knows the exact number—records were not kept—but over eight thousand Irish immigrants died digging the New Basin Canal," Dooley told the newspaper. The president of the Irish Cultural Society, Dr. Rodney Jung said, "We need a monument in honor of those who sacrificed their lives digging that canal."[40] The newspaper supported the fundraising effort with an editorial.

> Historians' estimates of the number of diggers who died of the yellow fever and cholera outbreaks common in that day vary from 3,000 to 30,000. For a day of primitive medicine, lack of sanitation and a pestilential tropical climate, the larger figure is quite credible.[41]

The editorial writer praised the project for its contribution to the prosperity of the city, and likewise praised the Irish descendants who contributed to the wealth of New Orleans.

> But the prosperous results and the financial cost [of the canal] pale against its human cost, and the nameless, vanished thousands who died building this now vanished canal should be given an honored place among the others we hold in our collective memory.[42]

On November 4, 1990, Padraic N. MacKernan, the Irish ambassador to the United States, was among those gathered to witness the dedication of the monument in the green space that is known locally as New Basin Canal Park. The more than seven-foot-tall Celtic cross had been made in Ireland—just as the Irish Cultural Society promised—of Kilkenny stone. And as the Irish Cultural Society had also promised, it contains a plaque in both English and Irish Gaelic.[43] The plaque read:

IN MEMORY OF THE IRISH IMMIGRANTS
WHO DUG THE NEW BASIN CANAL 1832–1838
THIS CELTIC CROSS CARVED IN IRELAND HAS BEEN ERECTED
BY THE IRISH CULTURAL SOCIETY OF NEW ORLEANS,
DEDICATED NOV. 4, 1990.[44]

There was no mention of disease, no mention of the number of men who allegedly died, no mention of the men being buried underneath on the banks of the canal. The Irish Cultural Society has never made a public statement about the wording of the plaque, but one must conclude that there is no conclusion on the facts of the story.

Members of the Irish Cultural Society, however, remember it as a memorial to the Irish immigrants who died and were buried below the monument. Hurricane Katrina caused several levees to fail in New Orleans, causing flooding and devastation. The US Federal Emergency Management Agency used the New Basin Canal Park as a dumping ground for debris, but an unidentified person roped off the memorial before it could be crushed. An article published in *Irish America* in 2007 recounted the saving of the monument and repeated an estimate of the number of workers who died:

> A mere stone's throw from one of the major levee failures in the Lakeview neighborhood rests a monument erected by the Irish Cultural Society. . . . it was built to honor the estimated 8,000 to 20,000 Irish immigrants who died during the construction of the New Basin Canal beginning in 1832.[45]

The article included a quote from a wife of a late president of the Irish Cultural Society, who repeated the story of the workers being buried on the canal banks.

> These men who were working for an incredibly low wage and maybe a shot of whiskey, would die and then were simply and unceremoniously buried in the levees along the banks of the canal they were building.[46]

The Republic of Ireland sets its annual commemoration of the Great Famine at different locations every year, and in 2014 it had international locations in Atlanta, Georgia, and New Orleans. During the visit of Heather Humphreys, the minister of arts, heritage and Gaeltacht, both the *Irish Times* newspaper and a news release from the Irish government called the monument a memorial to Irish immigrants who died building the canal. The news release called them "many Irish emigrants"[47] and the newspaper referred to the deaths in the "thousands."[48] Humphreys honored the Irish immigrants to New Orleans, saying that by 1860 the Irish were one-sixth of the city's population. The minister led the blessing of the neutral ground space known as the New Basin Canal Park, now renamed Hibernian Park, dedicating it to Irish immigrants. The now four-acre park contains the Celtic cross memorial.

Faubourg St. Mary, 1830s

While the New Basin Canal was being built, New Orleans was split into three municipalities, each with its own laws and taxes. They were the Vieux Carré (French Quarter), the Faubourg Marigny, and the Faubourg St. Marie (Faubourg is the French word meaning "suburb"). Many of the Irish immigrants working on the New Basin Canal were housed in a strip of land by the Mississippi River which came to be known as the Irish Channel. During 1833 St. Patrick's Catholic Church was built on Camp Street in the Faubourg St. Marie, primarily to serve Irish immigrants.[49] And in 1836, the woman who would become New Orleans's most influential Irish immigrant arrived in town with a life of tragedy and service in front of her. When she died, she would be given a state funeral, and a statue would be erected to her memory just a few years later.

Margaret Gaffney came as child with her family to the United States from Ireland. Both of her parents and her youngest sister died in a yellow fever epidemic in Baltimore when she was nine. She lost track of a brother when he was taken in by a Protestant woman, and she never learned to read and write. She married another Irish immigrant, Charles Haughery, but he became sick, and a doctor suggested they move to New Orleans, a warmer climate. The couple had a baby girl named Frances. As Charles grew even sicker, he wanted to return to Ireland. Charles survived the trip but died in Ireland. Most tragically, Frances died when she was less than a year old. A priest suggested that Margaret find a job and volunteer at an orphanage.[50]

Margaret took a job as a laundress and began to volunteer. She eventually established a dairy and a bakery, turning over her profits to the orphanage. Before her death, she established four orphanages. Her funeral in 1882 was attended by the New Orleans mayor, the governor of Louisiana, a former governor, a former mayor, and all city councilmen. Stores and city offices were closed all day.[51] A statue to Margaret was dedicated two years later, the second statue of a woman in the United States.[52] It still stands today on Camp Street, down the street from St. Patrick's Church.

Today, just like most American cities, the St. Patrick's Day parade in New Orleans draws hundreds of marchers and thousands of spectators. The Irish Channel is filled that day with people celebrating. St. Patrick's Catholic Church is considered one of the most beautiful churches in New Orleans for its stained glass and interior design. The Margaret statue still stands and is a tourist attraction. Irish heritage is on display around the city, especially in the historical sections.

But the story of the Irish men who died in New Basin Canal, a story without an obvious source, endures also. Since it is part of the cultural heritage of New Orleans, it may never be disputed, even if people are presented with the fact that no one can prove that ten thousand to thirty thousand died. It may be that it tells the story of immigrant hardship so the descendants can feel proud of what their forebears did. As O'Flaherty's song says, "But the Irish Navvy's labor / Made that dream come true for me."

Conclusion

In her ongoing research, Janice Hume has examined how newspaper reports encouraged Americans to identify with their new county after the revolution. In much the same way, newspapers could have helped Irish immigrants think of New Orleans as their new home. There is no evidence that happened. So it's curious that beginning in the 1950s, the stories about the New Basin Canal causing so many Irish deaths began appearing in newspaper accounts, which led to the story being retold in novels and folk songs. Hume argues that some newspaper accounts were meant to be inspirational, becoming both journalism and history.[53] There are those who argue for the story of the New Basin Canal, as well as those who argue against its truthfulness, and both are involved in the memory of the Irish immigrants who came in the early nineteenth century to New Orleans.

6

Kindred Spirits

An Unlikely Friendship Born Out of Mutual Suffering

Jordan Stenger

The dark cloud of the Indian Removal Act cast its shadow on the Choctaw tribe in 1831 as they were forced to relocate to a reservation in Oklahoma.[1] The survivors of this forced removal never forgot their struggle, and perhaps that is why in 1847 they gave $170 to the Irish during the height of the famine.[2] This gift is significant because it came only sixteen years after the Choctaw were forced off their lands by the US government and suffered a great loss of life and traditions. Today, near Cork, Ireland, a monument, an empty bowl made of feathers, symbolizes the gratitude of the Irish people to the Choctaw and represents kindness transcending tragedy.[3]

An examination of the newspaper coverage of the 1847 gift and the 2017 erection of the monument offers insight into the connection forged between the Choctaw and Irish by sacrifice and gratitude. This study delves into the struggles both peoples faced in the nineteenth century and the news coverage of the building of the monument. The newspapers of both eras and nations offer a glimpse into the mindsets of each era and how they have changed, and it also demonstrates that there is a connection of media beyond national borders.

The Choctaw people believed that their ancestors had migrated to the area that now makes up the state of Mississippi from western North America, "a place they called 'the Land of Death.'"[4] The story of this migration is a tale of weary travelers marching east, toward a better life. The story maintains:

> The years passed; the People walked on. Babies were born, the young grew old, the aged passed away. Their bones were added to the packs. The burdens of the ancestral bones increased with each passing year. Forty-three long years passed in this manner, with thousands of living Choctaws bearing their ever-increasing sacred burdens.[5]

Finally, the Choctaw reached their final home, known to them as Nanih Waiya. After traveling with their ancestors' bones, they laid them down and, "then to manifest their respect for the spirits of the dead, everyone carried earth to cover the bones until a great mound was built."[6] "The Great Mother Mound" is now known as the state of Mississippi.[7]

After living peacefully in Mississippi for generations, the early to mid-nineteenth century brought a series of hardships. President Andrew Jackson, during the 1830s, instituted his "Indian Removal" policy.[8] This plan was a "thinly veiled" attempt at forcibly removing Native Americans from their lands for "very little compensation, and no apologies were offered to the Indian people" for this act of thievery.[9] "Ironically, the man who forced them off their lands was . . . the son of Irish immigrants," who some claim came to America when they were forced out of Ireland to make way for wealthy English landowners to lay claim to Ulster's fertile land. Others surmise the Jacksons emigrated to escape persecution as non-Anglican Protestants (Presbyterians) or that perhaps a French invasion in 1760 that had French troops marching through their land to assault Carrickfergus Castle "had a last straw effect."[10]

The Unites States acted swiftly, and, "within a mere half century . . . would use its laws to force Native people to appear to willingly dispossess themselves, an amazing accomplishment in and of itself."[11] The American press was instrumental in pushing the idea that the Indians were willing and excited to leave their ancestral homeland for land west of the Mississippi. "Jackson and the American agents painted a picture in the press and Congress of a Choctaw majority who *wanted* to move west but were restrained from doing so by the efforts of the intermarried whites and 'mixed bloods,' who wanted to remain where they were because of their financial interests, of which, of course, the average Choctaw had none."[12]

In 1829 the *Boston Recorder* published a speech, translated from Choctaw, that the Choctaw are "a small people; who do not know much" and are "like an infant *so high*, who has just begun to walk."[13] This speech was almost self-deprecating, as the Choctaw perhaps expected the white people to see them. However, it did call out the hypocrisy of the American government, stating, "The American people say that they love liberty." If that was true, then "Why will they take it from the red man?"[14] This speech was obviously tailored to white Americans with its references to the inferior Choctaw, but it also called for Americans to question the morality of their reasoning behind seizing Choctaw land. The last statement of the speech is telling: "Here we have lived and here we wish to live. But whatever the white man wishes to do with us, he will do. If he shall will us to stay here, we shall stay. If he wishes us to go, then we shall go."[15] This statement seems to foreshadow the tragedy that was to befall the Choctaw people in 1831.

A poignant letter published in 1830 in the *Cherokee Phoenix and Indian's Advocate* (New Town, GA) disputes the claim that the Choctaw were excited to leave, a claim President Jackson and his cronies were making, and takes a firmer tone than the speech published in 1829 in the *Boston Recorder*. The letter from the Choctaw to the US government shows that the Choctaw were well informed about how the US government worked, and their worries were spelled out in this letter:

> Will not the great American people, who are men of truth, and love justice, still love us Choctaw red men? Surely we think they will love us. And although there are new thoughts about red people, and new language held out to them we cannot think that the American government will turn away from us and not even look on us. We have no expectation that if we should remove west of the Mississippi, any treaties would be made with us, that could secure greater benefit to us and our children, than those already made. The red people are of the opinion, that, in a few years the Americans will also wish

> to possess the land west of the Mississippi. Should we remove, we should again be removed by white men. We have no wish to remove to one that is not fertile and good, wherever situated.[16]

The Choctaw knew that if they accepted a treaty to remove west, it was likely nothing would stop the US government from asking them to move further west in time. The letter further explains that their refusal to remove was not simply because their land was fertile. They stood firm: "But here is our home, our dwelling places, our fields, and our schools, and all our friends; and under us are the dust and bones of our forefathers. This land is dearer to us than any other."[17] This emotionally charged and insightful letter shows how the Choctaw referred back to their story of coming out of the Land of Death into Mississippi. This land was not just their home physically, it was also their spiritual and ancestral home, one they could not fathom breaking away from.

On September 15, 1830, the US government got what it so desperately wanted. The Treaty of Dancing Rabbit Creek ceded the Choctaw's ancestral lands to the United States of America.[18] The treaty was published in the *Statesmen and Gazette* (Natchez, MS) and gave the Choctaw land west of the Mississippi. The treaty required the Choctaw to start removal in the fall of 1831. It was stipulated that the US government would pay the Choctaw Nation $20,000 over a span of twenty years.[19] To put this in proper perspective, the *United States Telegraph* (Washington, DC) reported the Treaty of Dancing Rabbit Creek, and one with the Chickasaw tribe, gave the United States "seventeen millions of acres" and "the Choctaw and Chickasaw lands will net to the government, when disposed of, thirty millions of dollars."[20] This was obviously more advantageous for the United States than it was for the Choctaw Nation. However, there is more to this treaty than what was published in the newspapers.

One historian has claimed that "the treaty of Dancing Rabbit Creek was procured with the rankest sort of dishonesty and foul play on the part of the U.S. government negotiators."[21] No friends of the Choctaw were present, "whiskey vendors" were invited by the US government, and negotiations were postponed to ensure intoxication of the Choctaw.[22] When the negotiations began, the Choctaw were told "that the U.S. government wanted them to remove from their lands and sell them or give all lands east of the Mississippi to the government and not one Choctaw was in favor of such a treaty."[23] The Choctaw "reminded the American negotiators" that they had always been a friend and ally to the United States, and "they called upon the United States to honor its treaty promises and allow the Choctaws to remain on their homeland in peace."[24] Secretary of War John H. Eaton threatened the Choctaw with military retribution and told them "the president, in twenty days, would march into their country—build forts in all parts of their hunting grounds" and "their lands would be forcibly seized on as the property of the enemy and the Choctaws would be forcibly removed west of the Mississippi."[25]

The Choctaw stood firm and refused to sign a treaty they did not agree with. Eaton ended negotiations, but when the Choctaw had left, he told the "few Choctaws who had been bought by the U.S." to sign the treaty. So, "in the absence of the great majority of the Nation . . . John H. Eaton, secretary of war of the United States, fraudulently obtained a few signatures of the Choctaws who were not empowered or authorized to negotiate by the Choctaw National council."[26] Once the ratification of the treaty had reached the public, newspapers such as the *United States Telegraph* published that the "Indians were delighted with the prospect before them, and are anxious to move, west of the Mississippi, as soon as arrangements can possibly be made for that purpose."[27] The *Farmers Cabinet* (Amherst, NH) published in 1831 that the Choctaw had explored west of the Mississippi and found it abundant with natural resources, and that "the Indians expressed themselves highly delighted with the country and are anxious to remove immediately."[28] The letter in the *Cherokee Phoenix and Indians Advocate* in 1830 disputed this claim, as the Choctaw expressed in the letter that they did not wish to move to land that was not fertile.[29]

In 1832 many Choctaw were hastily forced off their homeland and embarked on what would become known as the Trail of Tears. "Their faces grimly set against the wind . . . miles of Indians on horseback, on foot, and in wagons with an escort of shouting 'conductors' in army blue."[30] Many died on the road west and left a gaping hole in the social fabric of the Choctaw Nation.[31] After arriving in their new lands, they tried to rebuild their lives, but nature was against them. In 1833 "the Arkansas river overflowed its banks in one of the greatest floods in its history."[32] Rushing water took with it food, homes, lives, providing yet another devastating blow to the disheartened yet resilient Choctaw. "Many families went hungry and almost starved, waiting for relief from the U.S. government."[33]

The Choctaw Nation suffered horrific blows, one after another in the early to mid-nineteenth century. Just as they would recover from one disaster, another would strike. This cycle of suffering seemed endless and perhaps that is why, when news spread of suffering in Europe, they stretched out their hand to help another group of people who also had suffered with their experience of colonialism.

Across the Atlantic, the English oppressed the Irish for centuries before they wielded power over the American colonies and Native peoples. The English justified their unethical treatment of the Irish with the perspective that the Irish were savage and unworthy of fair and just treatment.[34] Colonization of Ireland was grounded in the same behaviors and beliefs used later to justify the poor treatment of Native Americans.

The culture of Ireland was similar to that of Native Americans in some ways. "History for Irish and Indians alike was essentially genealogical, an account based on memory, of the succession of kin and friends."[35] The Irish, like the Indians of America, were tribal and loyalty was supremely important.[36] "Both the Irish and Indians were ruled by tribal/clan chiefs or chieftains,"[37] and one of the most important aspects of similarity was the lack of a concept of private property in a way that was familiar to the English. "Neither the Irish nor Indians had developed any sense of private property." This was especially true of "land that was used communally and for which there were no titles or anything resembling them."[38]

Before the famine, the Poor Law Act of 1838 was passed in Ireland to provide a safety net for the millions of poor Irish people.[39]

Newspapers such as the *Belfast Newsletter* reported on the potential Irish poor laws. It stated:

> A system of poor laws, if established in Ireland, must not be expected to work miracles. It would not immediately give employment or capital; but it would, I think, serve to help the country through what may be called its transition period; and in time, with the aid of other circumstances, would effect a material improvement in the condition of the Irish people.[40]

The article continued, "It is, I think, a circumstance favourable to the establishment of poor laws, that there is so much land lying waste and uncultivated in Ireland."[41] The Poor Law established workhouses to provide a place for the poorest in society to work and live—and open up the land for more English landowners. However, "The Irish people feared the workhouse, with its harsh and degrading conditions."[42] Like the reservation conditions the Choctaw were experiencing, the conditions of workhouses were almost unbearable. "The paupers, as the poor were called, were badly treated," and the food was hardly palatable.[43] The Irish workhouse was not unlike the reservations set aside for the Native Americans who were removed to the west. Workhouses provided a similar, small-scale "reservation" from which residents were not allowed to leave without permission.[44]

In 1845 disaster struck, and for millions of Irish, their conditions deteriorated to an unimaginable state when "a mysterious blight attacked the potato crops, destroying the only real food of Ireland's rural population."[45] Over the course of the famine, one million people died due to starvation, and two million fled their country.[46] Like many disasters of this magnitude, the famine became increasingly political, and the English debated just how serious the situation was in Ireland. "The letters and reports about the crop failure poured into the British government, but the British leaders remained cautious and skeptical."[47] The *Kerry Evening Post* (Tralee, Ireland) reported that the failure of the potato crop was concerning; however, "The alarm, we are told, is somewhat abated; 'still under the most favourable circumstances, and allowing for every exaggeration, there will be a lamentable deficiency of the crop, which will be far under an average one'"—yet optimistically reported that some of the crop may be salvageable.[48] The *Belfast Newsletter* also reported on the blight, but the majority of its article focused on the crop failures in England and on the European continent. It briefly mentioned the Irish potato blight, stating that "in Ireland, the failure has been only partial, and far more insignificant than the failures of former years."[49]

In 1846, as the suffering of the Irish people increased, newspapers began to cover the story with a sense of urgency that would only strengthen as the famine dragged on. The *Nation* reported that "the ravages of the blight by which the potato crop is likely to be utterly consumed are now felt in every county in Ireland."[50] It continued, saying that "the result of the fog on the growing crops is most appalling, cabbages and other vegetables having been attacked with a disease similar to that in potatoes. Throughout the entire county the potato fields look as withered as they would be in the month of November."[51] Some newspapers, such as the *Tuam Herald*, published articles questioning English morals, asking if they "would quietly submit to the destitution and privation which the poor but honest, virtuous, and loyal peasantry of this country are now enduring."[52]

Another subject that newspapers focused on during the famine was the case of the Anglo-Irish landlords and their relationship with their tenants. In the years preceding the famine, British prejudices against the Irish, in addition to religious prejudices, included reasons such as "the Irish didn't work hard enough to improve their lives," and the Irish married too young, had too many children, and depended overwhelmingly on the potato.[53] After the potato blight began, "one Kerry landlord even called the potato destruction 'a blessing to Ireland,' while others claimed it was an act of God, designed to reduce the Irish population to realistic levels."[54] For landlords, the famine created an opportunity for them to "consolidate their land and lower their poor rate."[55]

This was strikingly similar to the forced migration of the Choctaw and other tribes from their traditional homelands so as to free up land for whites. One landlord's agent "calculated that it would cost the major [client] £11,534 per annum to keep his tenants in the local workhouse, twice the cost of transporting the tenants to Canada (£5,768)."[56] The statement "a Celtic Irishman will be as rare in Connemara as is the Red Indian on the shore of Manhattan" shows how possible it was to draw similarities between the Irish emigration and the removal of Native Americans.[57]

This issue of the landlord was reported on in Ireland and the United States in further demonstration of the similarities between the Choctaw and Irish. The *Irish Examiner* (Cork) published in 1847 "A Picture of Irish Landlords."[58] The article reports that:

> To Irish landlords, as a class, are all the evils of Ireland mainly attributable. To Irish landlords is the famine which has so desolated the land solely attributable. . . . These same Irish landlords, how clamorous too they are for "a bill to facilitate emigration!" Of course, in pure charity for the poor and not at all to enable themselves to "clear their estates."[59]

The article continues to say that "if the clearance of 1846–7 will not satisfy them [landlords], I know what can, Emigration! How many thousands have emigrated to the—grave?"[60] In America, newspapers such as the *Wisconsin Democrat* (Madison) reported that "the parchment of an Irish Landlord should drip with blood" and that "the naked truth is that it would be more in accordance with justice that every Irish landlord should die of hunger than one of the poor, plundered peasantry of Ireland should starve."[61]

The similarities between the Choctaw displacement and the Irish emigration are evident. Like the Choctaw, for the Irish "many evictions occurred under the guise of voluntary surrender."[62] The tenants were "under threat of eviction" to abandon their homes for "a small cash handout."[63] "Although not strictly speaking evicted, they often had little choice but to leave when faced with a landlord who made up his mind to take the land."[64] Both "the British and the Americans who arranged for the relocations did so in the name of kindness" and unsurprisingly "both sets of Natives saw their removal as an act of unspeakable cruelty—and were condemned as ungrateful as a result."[65] American newspapers of the time seem to have been quick to accuse the Anglo-Irish landlords and the English of cruelty without turning the lens of scrutiny upon themselves and drawing similarities between the evictions of Native Americans and the Irish poor.

At the height of the famine in 1847, the Irish press boldly showed its displeasure at relief attempts by the English, and the *Kerry Evening Post* was no exception. It published an article titled, "English Legislature and Irish Suffering" that stated that while Irish aid measures were postponed for two weeks, "The fat, contented English members, whose easy indolence has been insolently disturbed by the death-shrieks of contemptable Irish thousands, may sip their claret in quiet for two happy weeks."[66] This seems to mirror the tragedy the Choctaw faced when the Arkansas river flooded its banks and government aid was slow.

In America, the *Wisconsin Democrat* reported in 1847 that "some of the recitals before coroners' juries in Ireland are too horrible for publication."[67] In another article, the same newspaper wrote that "amid our own excitements it is not well for us to forget that one million of our fellow-creatures, separated from us by a distance of only 15 days, are dying of hunger and pestilence."[68] The *New England Puritan* (Boston, MA) in 1847 reported on the lawlessness in Ireland fueled by hunger and desperation, as well as reporting the aid from America, saying they "have been slow in their operations" due to the magnitude of this disaster.[69]

As the Irish were suffering through the famine, the Choctaw Nation was trying to establish a semblance of normal life on their new land in Oklahoma. Hearing of the Irish plight and remembering the recent apocalypse of their way of life and traditions, the Choctaw decided to send a portion of what little they had to the Irish. The gift of $170 was reported in both Irish and American newspapers. The *Belfast Newsletter* published that "the Choctaw tribe of North American Indians have contributed a sum of 170 dollars for the relief of the distressed Irish."[70] The *Arkansas Intelligencer* described the gift as "the poor Indian giving his mite to the poor Irish."[71]

The gift was an act of great compassion by the Choctaw. The fact that it was reported on in both Ireland and America is remarkable in a way, especially since in the United States, Americans used the idea that the Native Americans were savages, incapable of charity and civilized behavior, to remove them from their homeland just over a decade before. The gift, although small, was monumental in displaying the kindness of the Choctaw. "The Choctaw . . . had every reason to turn their backs on a European country that, despite its own colonization, was contributing to the colonization of North America."[72] Instead, they showed true compassion for a people suffering in similar ways they had.

The Choctaw Nation, 150 years after the gift, received recognition for the extraordinary monetary gift to the Irish: a commemorative monument titled *Kindred Spirits* only a few miles outside of Cork in the town of Middleton. *Kindred Spirits* was unveiled in June 2017 in the presence of a Choctaw delegation.[73] The sculpture, created by Alex Pentek, is a circle of "6m tall feathers, all unique 'as a sign of respect'" to resemble the feathers the Choctaw use in ceremonies.[74] Shaped like an empty bowl it "symbolizes the hunger suffered by Irish people in the famine."[75] Gary Batton, chief of the Choctaw Nation, said at the unveiling ceremony, "Your story is our story. . . . This was money pulled from our pockets. We had gone through the biggest tragedy we could endure, and saw what was happening in Ireland and just felt compelled to help."[76]

The Irish relationship to the Choctaw has also been covered in Native American news. *Indian Country Today* published an article that said, "What is amazing is that the generosity came from a people who a decade earlier had been driven from their homes at a terrible cost in lives."[77] A Choctaw Nation press release also detailed the dedication of the *Kindred Spirits* monument. "The Mayor of the County of Cork, Councilor Seamus McGrath said, 'We have a shared past as people who experienced unwelcome intrusion, and a shared sense of injustice.'"[78] The recurring theme in these articles is that the selfless act of generosity to strangers across the ocean stemmed from a mutual understanding of great suffering and has finally received the recognition it deserves.

The dedication of the monument to the Choctaw was not the first time the Irish and Choctaw recognized one another's sorrows. "In 1990, Choctaw leaders travelled to [County] Mayo to take part in a re-enactment of an 1848 protest."[79] In 1992 "Irish leaders took part in a trek from Oklahoma to Mississippi," and the former Irish president Mary Robinson was named "an honorary Choctaw chief."[80] *Irish Central* reported that "thanks to the work of Irish activists such as Don Mullan and Choctaw leader Gary White Deer, the Choctaw gift has been recognized in Ireland."[81]

For the future the Choctaw and Irish look to strengthen and build upon the unlikely friendship that started in the 1840s. In March 2018 "history was made for the Choctaw Nation . . . when Prime Minister of Ireland Leo Varadkar arrived in Durant [Oklahoma]."[82] Chief Gary Batton said, "We consider it a great honor" to have the prime minister visit the Choctaw reservation; "we have a kindred spirit."[83] The biggest news came when "Taoiseach Varadkar stunned and elated those present with the announcement that Ireland is starting a scholarship program for young Choctaws to study in Ireland."[84] This program began in autumn 2019.

The American government in the nineteenth century trampled the Choctaw, dehumanized them, accused them of savagery, and eventually ripped them from their homeland to create opportunities for white settlers. The Choctaw lost their homeland, traditional way of life, and thousands of their people, but President Andrew Jackson and other Americans could not stamp out their generosity, kindness, and compassion. The gift of $170 to the Irish was a gesture that flies in the face of all the politicians and American citizens who claimed that the Choctaw were a savage, juvenile people not worthy of respect.

Not wanting others to suffer as they had, the Choctaw showed great compassion to destitute strangers across the Atlantic. Who knew then that that simple act of kindness would lead to a close and continued friendship, promise of future educational opportunities, and shared interactions of culture and gratitude. After hundreds of years of pain at the hands of colonialism, famines, disease, and displacement, human kindness proved resilient. Compassion of one people for another has not only survived a tragic history, it has thrived in the aftermath, and continues to create new opportunities for the descendants of those who suffered immense tragedy on both sides of the Atlantic. "The Irish Choctaw link . . . brimmed with solidarity like an arrow shot through time, waiting to land for almost 150 years."[85] Finally it did, and out of great pain and suffering, the Choctaw and Irish emerged stronger, as kindred spirits.

7

John Mitchel

Transnational Journalist

Debra Reddin van Tuyll

Irish-born journalist John Mitchel was not a moderate man.[1] When he took up a cause, he took it up with passion and commitment—in at least one case, a lifelong commitment that "made his name a household word in the hearts of his [Irish] countrymen."[2] Unfortunately for Mitchel, he lived in a time and place where only certain passions and commitments were acceptable, and because he espoused opposition notions, he would find himself exiled from his beloved homeland at the age of thirty-three under a law written specifically to ensure his conviction for treason. As a result of his exile, Mitchel would spend the rest of his life traversing the globe before returning to Ireland in time to die. He covered many different stories, but he always covered them through emerald-colored lenses.

Mitchel's career offers an excellent case study in "how individual life histories influence journalists' understanding of their work."[3] Mitchel, like most journalists in democratic countries, functioned as both a news conduit and a news gatekeeper. As he picked and chose which facts to include and which facts to exclude from his stories, he created frames for those stories that indicated to readers how they should think about the issues he was covering. A nineteenth-century journalist had none of the prohibitions against including opinion in his stories; Mitchel labored in a period of personal journalism when an individual journalist's personal perspective was almost always the basis of his (and occasionally, her) stories.

Mitchel's work—for the *Nation* in Dublin, the *Citizen* in New York City, the *Southern Citizen* in Knoxville, Tennessee, and Washington, DC, the *Charleston Mercury* in France, the *Richmond Examiner* and *Richmond Enquirer* in Virginia, and finally the *Irish Citizen* back in New York—fits easily within Gaye Tuckman's theory that journalists tend to choose stories and facts for inclusion in those stories based on certain patterns. Tuchman focused more on twentieth-century influences—sources, beats, organizational resources and requirements—but this was no less true in the nineteenth century.[4] The primary difference was the nature of those influences, and in the nineteenth century, they were most likely the individual journalist's perspectives, experiences, and histories. These perspectives, experiences, and histories would be composed of the same four influences Michael Schudson has identified for twentieth-century journalists: economics, politics, general culture, and news culture.[5] Journalists in the nineteenth century were free to reveal the ways in which these influences affected their work. That was the nature of the personal journalism that was so prevalent at the time.

Mitchel amassed a richly diverse journalistic history through his world travels—voluntary and otherwise. He edited at least seven newspapers in two different countries and corresponded for at least another six from three different continents. He was acquainted with news audiences, practices, and routines in Ireland, Australia, America, and France. He crafted content for audiences in Ireland and America, and for a divided America during the antebellum and Civil War eras. In each of those places, through his political activities as well as his journalism, Mitchel's career exemplifies how a journalist's individual experience and global movements can transfer ideas, as well as professional practices, from one place to another and thereby contribute to the creation of a type of journalism that transcends national borders: transnational journalism.

Through his career, Mitchel would also become a transnational symbol of what was both right and wrong about nationalism. Whether he was corresponding for American newspapers from France, Irish newspapers from Australia, or writing for American newspapers in

America, Mitchel always had an agenda: freedom for Ireland, even if it required a violent uprising. Mitchel's early stories for the *Nation* would probe the boundaries of the definition of freedom for Ireland, something a lot of people in a lot of places were doing around the world in 1848 when Mitchel was at the apex of his career in Irish journalism. He would continue to write about the nature of freedom in America, but his stories always carried a tint of emerald as he compared the lot of Irish peasants to that of American slaves.

Mitchel's work was unquestionably influential. It got him tried for treason in Ireland and admired in America, especially in the South. Southerners shared Mitchel's version of radical conservatism; theirs may have been spoken with a hint of moonlight and magnolias while Mitchel's was heavy on the Irish brogue, but the essence of the thought was similar. Mitchel's journalistic explorations of the meaning of freedom would help shape Southern ideas about and justifications for secession.

This chapter examines Mitchel's journalistic history and experience through the framework of transnational journalism history. It demonstrates that Mitchel was a quintessential transnational journalist in the nineteenth century.

While transnational journalism is sometimes defined as non-state journalism, better definitions are offered by Marcel Broersma and Kevin Grieves. Broersma defines transnational journalism as an "interwoven picture" that focuses on "journalistic routines and textual forms" so that it can overcome national histories. In other words, transnational journalism history deals with "norms, practices, and forms. . . . It emphasizes transnational contacts, networks and patterns, and underlines intertwining national and transnational developments." Grieves's definition is similar. He sees transnational journalism as journalism "with a strong national connection but a global reach," journalism that is "active across and whose content deals with matters across nation-state borders."[6]

National events were intertwining in 1848, the "Spring of Nations," when Mitchel started his journalistic career. Some fifty rebellions raged that year against old feudal systems. These rebellions were a step along the way to the creation of new nation-states. Some countries, including the United States, had been to the brink of civil war and backed down. However, even in America, the pot was still simmering as abolitionists stoked the scarcely contained Southern fire-eaters—radical secessionists whose solution for each sectional crisis of the antebellum period was disunion. Mitchel's political activism with a group that would come to be called the Young Irelanders and his early journalism may have dealt specifically with freedom for Ireland, but both carried messages that resonated internationally. Irish nationalists' conflict with England was not so different from Polish nationalists' conflict with Prussia, Cuban nationalists' conflict with Spain, the South's conflict with the North. His journalism transcended national borders because his issue—freedom for his homeland—was not contained to Ireland. It was a global issue that did, indeed, cross nation-state borders, just like the newspapers he worked for.[7]

As Broersma argued, history, including journalism history, tends to follow national contours. Studies of press history typically examine some component of the role, history, or regulation of the press within a nation-state "without structurally considering international developments and cross-border influences."[8] Yet those influences existed, even if historians did not notice them, and they extended to newspapers. The *Nation*, the first newspaper Mitchel worked for after getting involved with the Young Irelanders, circulated in America. So did the *United Irishman*, the newspaper he founded when he broke with the more moderate Irish nationalist group. Mitchel already was a known quantity in America in the 1840s. Americans read newspaper accounts of Mitchel's treason trial—as well as those of Meagher, O'Brien, and Martin. They read about the monster meetings occurring around Ireland, and they followed Mitchel into exile to Bermuda and then Australia thanks to stories picked up from Irish and English newspapers.[9]

Americans read that Mitchel was convicted under a new treason law for writing he was "not 'loyal'" to the queen, for "the time is long past when Jehovah anointed Kings . . . there is no divine right now but the sovereign people." But the *Lafayette Daily Journal* (Indiana) proclaimed: "No foreign fugitive ever crossed the ocean to seek rest in this country under circumstances of so much interest as John Mitchel. Toward no other outcast was American sympathy ever more deeply excited, nor the arms of welcome so widely opened."[10] They also read that Mitchel believed the source of the Irish famine in 1847–48 was the diversion of food from Ireland by the British. And, they read his injunction to his fellow Irishmen, "Will you not gird up your loins for this great national struggle, & stand with your countrymen for life and land?"[11] Such words would ring true to the sons and grandsons of the Revolutionary War generation.

Americans would read about responses to Mitchel's arrival in the country. They would read about speeches Mitchel gave after he arrived in America. The *Baltimore Sun* quoted the *New York Times*'s observation, after one speech, that Mitchel "rehearses with his usual eloquence and ability, the wrongs Ireland has suffered from the British Government."[12] They would read several years later, after Mitchel's daring escape from exile in Australia and arrival in America, that the Irish patriot had been invited to speak at the University of Virginia graduation ceremony in 1854. "This is a distinction which has never been conferred upon any but the most eminent men of the country," the *Alexandria Gazette* (Virginia) commented. "The personal character of Mr. Mitchel is worthy of all respect and admiration."[13]

Mitchel not only labored as a transnational journalist, he became a transnational story—a symbol of what happens to one who challenges power and loses—and that was a powerful story in the America where citizens still celebrated their fresh, new democracy, born of revolution against England.[14] Mitchel's experience was especially poignant in the South, where slave owners feared the same loss of power if they lost control over the national political system.[15] In the 1850s Jefferson Davis, then a US senator, explained that the South believed Northerners were looking for ways to weaken the political power of the South so as to advantage New England industry at the expense of Southern industry. To be fair to Davis, even some prominent abolitionists such as Wendell Phillips and Stephen Foster believed their movement was more an attack on Southern power than the region's peculiar labor system.[16] To Southerners who believed their rights as citizens, livelihoods, and way of life were under attack by a more powerful adversary's, Mitchel's defiance of England was an appealing story, for it was the sort of story of which many Southerners were fond: that of a valiant hero defending his country against a power-hungry foe.

Even on the issue of slavery, Mitchel was caught in that nether land of transnationalism. Mitchel has been criticized for a piece he wrote for his New York newspaper, the *Citizen*. In the article, he wrote that he "wished he had a good plantation well-stocked with healthy negroes in Alabama." The comment was made in reply to a letter written to Mitchel's partner in the newspaper and former Young Irelander comrade, Thomas Francis Meagher. The author of the letter was Dubliner James Haughton, who also served as a contributor to William Lloyd Garrison's *Liberator*. Not only was Haughton an abolitionist, he was also allied with O'Connell's Home Rulers, who had kicked Mitchel, Meagher, and their Young Irelander comrades out of their organization for their extremist views on Irish home rule. The younger group had also disagreed with O'Connell on the issue of whether to return donations to the Irish repeal movement from American slaveholders.[17] Haughton had written to Meagher to chide him about American attitudes toward slavery and urge him—and Mitchel—to "distinguish yourself as an American citizen—as the friend of freedom—freedom for all."[18]

In truth, Mitchel did not so much support slavery as he opposed abolitionism. His primary objection was the movement's attachment to progressivism. He, like Southerners of the time, believed progress, as conceived of by nineteenth-century reform groups, was not necessarily a good thing for society. Mitchel's view of slavery was colored by his experience with the famine in Ireland and the treatment of Irish workers. Mitchel believed that the paternalistic slave system was a far better labor system, for it provided cradle-to-grave care for the worker while Ireland's industrial and agricultural workers were left to fend for themselves. His statement of support for slavery was grounded in his concern for Irish workers, and, as historians have pointed out, it has been taken out of context. Bryan McGovern, author of one of the several twentieth-century Mitchel biographies, has pointed out that, while some historians—and other Irish writers as well—condemn Mitchel as a racist and "traitor to humanity,"[19] others have taken a more nuanced look at his actual views and come away thinking of him more as an enigma than an apologist or polemicist for slavery.[20]

It is perhaps difficult to comprehend how Mitchel could simultaneously support liberty for Ireland and slavery in America. To consider Mitchel a bigot is, McGovern believes, "simplistic." Mitchel and his thoughts were much more complex than many presume. Neither he nor his wife ever owned or even really wanted to own slaves. Mitchel's wish for a plantation and slaves in his response to Haughton has the feel of having been written in a fit of pique—an exaggeration written expressly to shock and annoy Haughton. Mitchel's support of slavery and the Confederacy was the product of his ideals that created a blend of "ecumenical nationalism," which was very similar to Southern thinking at the time in that it allowed him to be both culturally conservative and a revolutionary at the same time.[21] Mitchel's response to Haughton illustrated the distinct differences he saw between American slaves and Irish peasants and explained why he believed slavery was more humane:

> This is enough. Mr. Haughton has written at least one thousand letters, all to this precise effect; and especially six or seven years ago, while the doomed white slaves of his own country were in the very crisis of their agony, we well remember that this worthy gentleman was seized with a paroxysm of violent sympathy with fat negroes in America. He was in the midst of the most hideous and ignominious slavery that ever deformed the world. "Slave-drivers" were living in Eccles street, around his very gates: slaves were crowding the poorhouse gaols, within sight of him, or dying like dogs, surplus-slaves, they were, in the charnel-garrets of the Liberty. *Slaves* [emphasis his] we say, with no more rights, social or political, than Alabama negroes, the difference being that an Alabama negro is of value to

> his mater, and that prudent men will actually pay certain dollars for one, and feed and clothe him afterwards; but the poor white soul was not only of no value to his born owner, but was found to be "surplus" and money was paid to chase him, kill him, make away with him off the face of the earth. Mr. Haughton knew it well; but those poor creatures labored under two fatal disqualifications for the sympathy of so benevolent a man—they were white, and they were at his own door. His heart was in Africa.[22]

Mitchel got himself into deeper trouble when he went on to state unequivocally that he was not an abolitionist, that he did not believe it was a crime to buy or sell slaves, that it was acceptable to beat slaves when necessary. Haughton had warned Meagher, and by reference Mitchel, not to remain quiet on the issue of slavery. Mitchel replied that he had no intention of remaining quiet when words needed to be spoken, and that was when he made his wish for an Alabama plantation. When properly contextualized, this editorial is less about slavery in America than it is about the treatment of the working classes and poor in Ireland. Mitchel conflates the two in the piece. As far as he was concerned, the question of the treatment of nonelites by those in power was neither an Irish question nor an American question. It was a question that transcended borders. It was a transnational question. Mitchel's work, if read carefully, very clearly demonstrates that to call for action on one while ignoring the other is both inhumanly cruel and shortsighted. Further, his response was a response to Haughton, and that is how it must be read—not as a far-ranging, grand-theory policy statement regarding slavery in America.

Mitchel's foreign correspondence ranged from typical international journalism to occasional transnational stories. For example, he functioned as both when he corresponded for the *Charleston Mercury* (South Carolina) while in Paris in 1860 and 1861. As the *Mercury*'s correspondent, he wrote several stories about how secession was perceived in France. He told the *Mercury*'s readers, "You flatter yourselves of late years that you are beginning to be pretty well known in Europe. . . . You were never more deceived in your lives." Mitchel referred to an article in *La Patrie* which claimed the North "fed" the South; that is, without Northern industry, the South would have nothing. He wrote that the paper demanded to know, "If you [the South] alienate the North, who will bake your bread and butter it? Who will put hay in your horses' mangers? Who will put ice in your juleps?" Another paper, *L'Opinion nationale*, opined that the South should "remain calm and quiet" because they were "entirely at the mercy of their Northern brethren."[23] This is the usual fodder of foreign or international correspondence.

However, Mitchel took more of a transnational approach when commenting on censorship of Northern newspapers during the Civil War, likely a tender topic for him in any circumstance. He opened a November 8, 1861, story with the comment, "Three New York newspapers suppressed and without so much as an advertisement! *Habeas Corpus* suspended, and not even by the British method of a special Act of Parliament, but by the will of a soldier! [emphasis his]." In another article, Mitchel compared the discrimination against the Irish in America with that of the Irish who were fighting in Italy "to crush the Romagna." Mitchel complained that Irish soldiers in the Union army were used for the worst sort of manual labor—digging—"in the cause of nasal Yankees, who have burned their convents, dishonored their military companies, and made laws to keep them out of their rights as citizens."[24]

Nor did Mitchel let the Confederates off the hook, although that was the side with which he sympathized and for which he sacrificed two sons as well as his own labor, journalistic and otherwise.[25] Mitchel spent the first few years of the war in France, working for the *Charleston Mercury* and the *Dublin Irishman*. He returned to New York but soon decamped to the Confederacy and settled in Richmond, where he first went to work for Jefferson Davis's organ, the *Richmond Enquirer*, and then later, when he began questioning Davis's conduct of the war, the *Richmond Examiner*.[26]

Mitchel's editorials and leaders for that paper and others supported the Confederacy, but, as one would anticipate, he also wrote frequently about Ireland—so much so that William Holden, editor of the *Raleigh Standard* (North Carolina), actually questioned Mitchel's loyalty to the Confederacy.[27] Holden's annoyance with Mitchel—to the point that he even threatened to cane the Irishman—was based on articles such as the one the Irishman wrote for the Dublin *Nation* regarding his escape to the South from New York City when he returned from France in 1862.[28] After briefly describing his escape from New York and the Confederate sympathies he found in Maryland, he turned to the topic of the Irish in the Confederate army. Mitchel explained that some forty thousand Irish served among the Confederate troops, but they were dispersed among all the units and had never formed an Irish brigade, which Mitchel applauded. He wrote, "They [the Irish Confederates] do no pretend to fight this American quarrel as Irishmen, nor do they desecrate the name nor prostitute the flag of Ireland at all."[29]

With regard to the Northern Irish Brigade, commanded by Mitchel's old Young Irelander comrade Thomas Francis Meagher, he had little good to say. He wrote, "As for the Northern Irish, [they] seem to have got themselves persuaded that the enfrenchisment [*sic*] of Ireland is, somehow, to result from the subjugation of the South, and that the repeal of one Union in Europe depends on the enforcement of another Union in America." The Southern Irish objected heartily to the Irish Brigade's use of Irish symbols and considered them merely "Yankee insignia." Mitchel applauded this perspective. He wrote, "In all this I agree with them entirely. Nobody has the right to unfurl the colors of Ireland in a war of invasion and plunder and coercion."[30]

Mitchel did conclude his article with the prediction that the Confederacy would win the war. Still, for Holden, who up to that point was a loyal Confederate himself (if something of an iconoclast—another story for another day), the story of the day was not one to be considered from the broader transnational perspective of the struggle for national independence but from the specific perspective of removing the South from a perfidious and noxious union with the North.[31]

When the war ended, Richmond was in tatters, and so was Mitchel's work life. As Confederate troops pulled out, they set fire to warehouses in the city to keep their contents from falling into Union hands. The fire spread to the *Examiner* office and destroyed both building and content. John Daniel, editor of the *Richmond Examiner*, had died only a few days before the fall of the capital city from wounds received in a duel. Without a means of earning a living, Mitchel returned to New York to work as editor of the *New York Daily News*, a pro-Southern paper edited by Benjamin Wood.[32]

Only a few weeks into his new job, Mitchel was arrested for his pro-Southern editorials and jailed at Fort Monroe in a cell next to Jefferson Davis. Mitchel was fifty at the time of his arrest, no longer a young man whose constitution could endure prison conditions as easily as when he was in his thirties. He left prison a changed man. His health declined as he developed tuberculosis, and he became even more skeptical about government. By 1867 Mitchel decided, despite his ill health, to start a new newspaper, the *Irish Citizen*, and to pursue his real passion: independence for Ireland. His work at this paper, as was true of his earlier work, was still transnational in nature. He covered Ireland and Irish independence as a timely, immediate, and proximate story of significant magnitude for an audience that lived in America—many of whom were likely naturalized American citizens—but who also felt an allegiance to their homeland and its struggle against British rule. Mitchel ran the newspaper for about five years before his declining health forced him to put the paper to bed for the last time on July 28, 1872, though he continued writing for other Irish American newspapers. His most common topic for those newspapers, as always, was Irish independence.[33]

The Quintessential Transnational Journalist

On the two hundredth anniversary of his birth, the *Irish Times* called Mitchel "the contentious patriot." According to the paper, Irish historian and former Trinity College provost F. S. L. Lyons considered Mitchel to be among the "most forceful and effective journalists to write for Irish newspapers during the 19th century."[34] He was admired by Pearse and de Valera, and at one time considered as important a historical figure as Wolfe Tone. Yet, the two hundredth anniversary of Mitchel's death went relatively unnoticed in Ireland, largely because of his supposed support for slavery during the American Civil War.[35] His position on slavery, however, was shaped as much by his life in Ireland as it was by his experience in America.

Mitchel was one of those bothersome, busybody journalist types common in the nineteenth century who just would not shut up once his passions were aroused, and aroused they were in the 1840s when Europe and the Americas were erupting with revolution after revolution—some fifty in all across the globe. And worse, he took the wrong side on the issues. O'Connell, the patron saint of Home Rule, wanted a peaceful transition to Ireland being governed by the Irish. Once Mitchel's passions were enflamed on this issue, nothing short of militant and military action would do to overthrow the English usurpers who had grown fat and happy on Ireland's back. He is still paying for his support of slavery in America. As the bicentennial of Mitchel's birth approached, the National Famine Commemoration Conference was to meet in his hometown, Newry. Mitchel's militancy was in large part influenced by what he saw of the famine-ravaged west of Ireland in 1848, and if his pen had dripped vitriol before that trip, poison flowed from it afterward. Still, the Famine Conference was reluctant to use Mitchel as the theme of their conference because of his association with slavery.[36]

Mitchel's background makes him the quintessential transnational journalist. Mitchel was born an Irishman, but he died an American who had just been elected to the British Parliament for County Tipperary.[37] He certainly threw his heart and soul into America's greatest conflict, choosing to support the least popular side among Irishmen of his day (and today) because of his belief in national independence and self-determination. Mitchel spent almost as much of his life outside of Ireland as he did inside. He lived on three continents, and, more to the point, he edited newspapers in two countries and corresponded for fifteen newspapers from three countries. He edited newspapers in Ireland, in the American North, and the American South. He corresponded for American and Irish newspapers from France and Australia, and his writings were influential because of the reputation he developed as a hero of the 1848 Rising in Ireland. When John Mitchel wrote, readers read. His work—his journalism—contributed to the spread of ideas about the nature of empire, the meaning of nation, the value of revolution, and the rightness of slavery. This is what makes him a true transnational journalist.

Mitchel's work for the *Nation* helped spread ideas of what freedom meant—and while his thoughts were not in accord with twenty-first-century thinking, at least in America, they resonated with American Southerners of his own time and offered them an outside voice that could be held up in defense of their peculiar labor system. Southern newspapers reprinted Mitchel's speeches, letters, and editorials, and, once Mitchel began his own newspaper in America, hawked subscriptions on his behalf.[38] Mitchel's Irish writings on the transnational topic of the nature of revolutions and the relationships between citizens and government caught the attention of Americans, especially Southerners, long before he immigrated to the United States. Initially considered a hero of Irish nationalism and independence, Mitchel was held up as a role model for republicans (with a lower case *r*) across the globe.[39]

Mitchel's personal politics put him squarely in the most radical faction of Southerners, the so-called "fire-eaters." Like the Young Irelanders, the fire-eaters wanted immediate action. Unlike the Young Irelanders, the fire-eaters did not advocate war, mostly because they did not expect any resistance from the North. Their reading of the Constitution was that states came into the Union voluntarily; hence they could leave voluntarily as well. But, in both cases the Young Irelanders and the fire-eaters had lost patience with the peaceful, let's-work-things-out approach.[40]

However, as he waded in on debate on slavery after his arrival in America, Mitchel's status changed. In both the North and the South, other journalists used him and his own writing as symbols of the wrongheadedness of proslavery advocates and as a warning about foreigners who had the audacity to wade in on American issues that were none of their concern.

William "Parson" Brownlow of the *Knoxville Whig* (Tennessee) did not offer Mitchel the same warm welcome when he moved south that other editors in that region did. The good parson, a strict Unionist who would be thrown out of the Confederacy as a traitor, had this to say when Mitchel showed up in Knoxville in 1854:

> We know Mitchel well. He is the concentrated embodiment of all that is arrogant, vile, mean and rebellious—of all that is treason and fiendish by nature—the Irish brute. This depraved tool of a rotten but dying despotism, this representative of an English prison, this representative of hell in the garb of a man, this blink-eyed insulter of decency, this sponger of traitors for a living, this defunct patriot, this censorious incarnation of all that is damnable, this beast John Mitchel is not able at home or abroad to damage any man by his tongue or pen.[41]

Brownlow was offended by the parallels Mitchel drew between the Irish nationalist movement and Southern secessionists. Brownlow was a nativist as well as a Unionist at heart, so there was no good in Mitchel at all from his perspective, and he represented Mitchel as a scourge upon the South.[42]

In his lifetime, John Mitchel was many things to many people. To the British and to American Northerners, he was a traitor. To the Irish Nationalists and to American Southerners, he was a hero; when he died in 1875, New York, San Francisco, and New Orleans all held memorial services in his honor.[43] He lost two sons in America's bloodiest war, and he himself served as an effective opposition journalist during that war. Above all, though, Mitchel was an Irishman. His gaze was always toward the Emerald Isle.

Mitchel's place in history is complicated, in large measure because of its transnational nature. He was both Irish and American. He was entangled with each country's struggle to achieve freedom for all. That was the overarching theme of his life and his work—struggling to help readers understand the essential, and transnational, natures of freedom, nationhood, and citizenship.

At best, Mitchel was an enigma.[44] Historians have tried to pigeonhole his beliefs, and they have concluded, alternatively, that he had no coherent political theory directing his actions and opinions, that he did have a coherent political theory, that he was a libertarian, that he was about as close to being a socialist as one can get and not be a socialist, and that he was a conservative with revolutionary ideals.[45] In the end, the newspaper where Mitchel started his long career, the Dublin *Nation*, probably best captured who Mitchel was in a story about his death and that of his best friend and brother-in-law, John Martin, who died within the same week as Mitchel. According to the *Nation*: "In the death of John Mitchel men saw the loss of the ablest pen, the boldest tongue, the keenest intellect that ever waged war scornful and victorious against the enemies of our race."[46]

Mitchel was indeed all those things—perhaps a more natural writer than speaker. His Young Irelander colleague Thomas Francis Meagher easily beat out the rest of his comrades when it came to oration. Certainly, Mitchel was bold, brilliant, and passionate. He must have loved America. He did, after all, sacrifice two sons for his adopted country, he served in the Richmond, Virginia, ambulance corps (being too old to join the Confederate army), and he turned that mighty pen of his first in support of Confederate president Jefferson Davis, but then against when Davis's policies took a turn toward the sort of state making that smacked too much of what England had done to Ireland. In the end, though, he loved Ireland more, eagerly returning home, but leaving his wife and children back in America, to claim the seat in Parliament to which he had been elected. All his globe-trotting aside, Ireland came first for Mitchel. Always and forever. Ireland was a story that transcended national borders, for it really was not a story solely about British domination. It was a story about humankind's longing for freedom and self-determination—a story that is as poignant and relevant across the globe today as it was in Mitchel's time.

8

Gilded Age Humor as a Moral Force

Representations of the Irish and Irish Americans in Texas Siftings

Mary M. Cronin

The September 8, 1883, issue of *Texas Siftings*, the widest-circulating American humor magazine of the late nineteenth century, featured a story called "John Bull's Irish Relations" that opened with an anecdotal account of a forlorn restaurant owner who was on the verge of tears because several "gentlemen" dined, then absconded, before paying the bill. The unexpected circumstance forced the proprietor to take the price of the meals out of the headwaiter's salary. The owner told a customer that he could stand his own unhappiness about the situation, but it upset him that the waiter's wife and numerous children would suffer from the reduced paycheck.

The magazine's editors then imparted the moral of the story:

> This little story very neatly illustrates the present relations between England and Ireland. John Bull is weeping because the condition of Ireland is so pitiable. A large number of landlords obtain possession of the rents and spend the money abroad. John Bull grieves over absenteeism, but it cheers him up to know that he can make up the deficit from the poor Irish who rent the land. It never occurs to him to put his hand in his pocket and pay up. Pat has to stand the damage."[1]

The editorial commentary was unusual by American humor publication standards. Although it used recognizable stereotypes (i.e., the threatening and uncaring British "John Bull" and the victimized

Irishman "Pat"), the article used those stereotypes to highlight the political and moral inequalities in Ireland.[2] The short sketch also portrayed Ireland's working-class population sympathetically. The other major American comic magazines of the era, *Judge*, *Life*, and *Puck*, as well as the popular illustrated magazines (e.g., *Harper's Weekly* and *Frank Leslie's Illustrated News*), exhibited a variety of stereotyped portrayals of the Irish, but those portrayals were used either to poke fun at the Irish and Irish immigrants or to deride them. As Kerry Soper has found, nineteenth-century portrayals of Irish stereotypes varied, depending upon the creator's meanings and uses. Complex patterns of "identification, sympathy, and denigration" existed side by side. Changes in images and meaning also occurred over time.[3]

Some late nineteenth-century publications depicted the Irish immigrants to America as mostly harmless, ignorant, peasants who were out of place as urban dwellers. In these representations, the men often were portrayed as enjoying drink and a good fight and as emotional, rather than rational, creatures who were "eternally hostile" to England. Such portrayals usually depicted the Irish peasant's morals as uncertain. Readers were led to believe the Irish were willing to lie or engage in acts of minor thievery, when they felt it warranted.[4]

Other publications, editors, and illustrators imagined the Irish as more nefarious, threatening figures. The Irish physiognomic characters popularized by *Punch* magazine in England found a receptive audience in the United States because many white, native-born Americans shared similar cultural and racial beliefs in Anglo superiority.[5] Thomas Nast, a leading editorial cartoonist of the late nineteenth century who worked for *Harper's* magazine, regularly used physiognomic illustrations to depict the Irish as simian in appearance in order to demonstrate they were untrustworthy and an unassimilable "other." Nast's Irish were quick to anger, willing to riot (frequently while drunk), and devoted to a religion that he believed would undermine America's Protestant ideals of liberty and equality.[6]

The Irish were not alone in being seen as undesirable. The producers of print and other popular culture materials represented African Americans and a host of non-Protestant immigrant groups, including the Chinese, Eastern European Jews, Italian Catholics, and Mexicans, in simplistic and often demeaning fashion.[7] Ethnic humor, with its pejorative, stereotypical portrayals, was used by white, often native-born members of society against supposedly "inferior" newcomers and nonwhites as a tool of social control. Such humor reassured the established classes against perceived threats and differences from growing numbers of politically powerful immigrants and minorities.[8]

Disparaging portrayals of certain immigrant groups often increased when members of those groups did not acculturate themselves with the rapidity that was expected. While many native-born Americans would have preferred to close America's gates to immigrants, persistent labor shortages throughout the nineteenth century kept politicians from doing so.[9] Such ethnic humor demonstrated native-born, white Americans' feelings of superiority and revealed their racial antagonisms and fears about the nation's seemingly unrestrained immigration and the country's recently emancipated African Americans.[10] Humor also was useful as a device from which fearful Americans could question the worthiness of certain immigrant groups for citizenship. While the majority of immigrants and African Americans at the time lived segregated lives, humor was used to reiterate social and spatial distance by its use of stigmas and stereotypes that presented the native-born Anglo Protestant population as superior intellectually, educationally, socially, and, often, morally.[11]

Many of the late nineteenth century's comic magazines found audiences on both sides of the Atlantic, a reality that allowed editors to shape readers' perceptions of African Americans and immigrants beyond the boundaries of the United States. Beginning in 1887, one humor periodical, *Texas Siftings*, took a transnational approach to its comedy by reprinting its magazine for European and English readers out of a London office. The editors also produced three compilations of their articles in book form during the 1880s that were sold in the United States, England, and Germany.[12]

Although *Texas Siftings* was rife with portrayals and editorial commentary about all immigrant groups, this research focuses on the

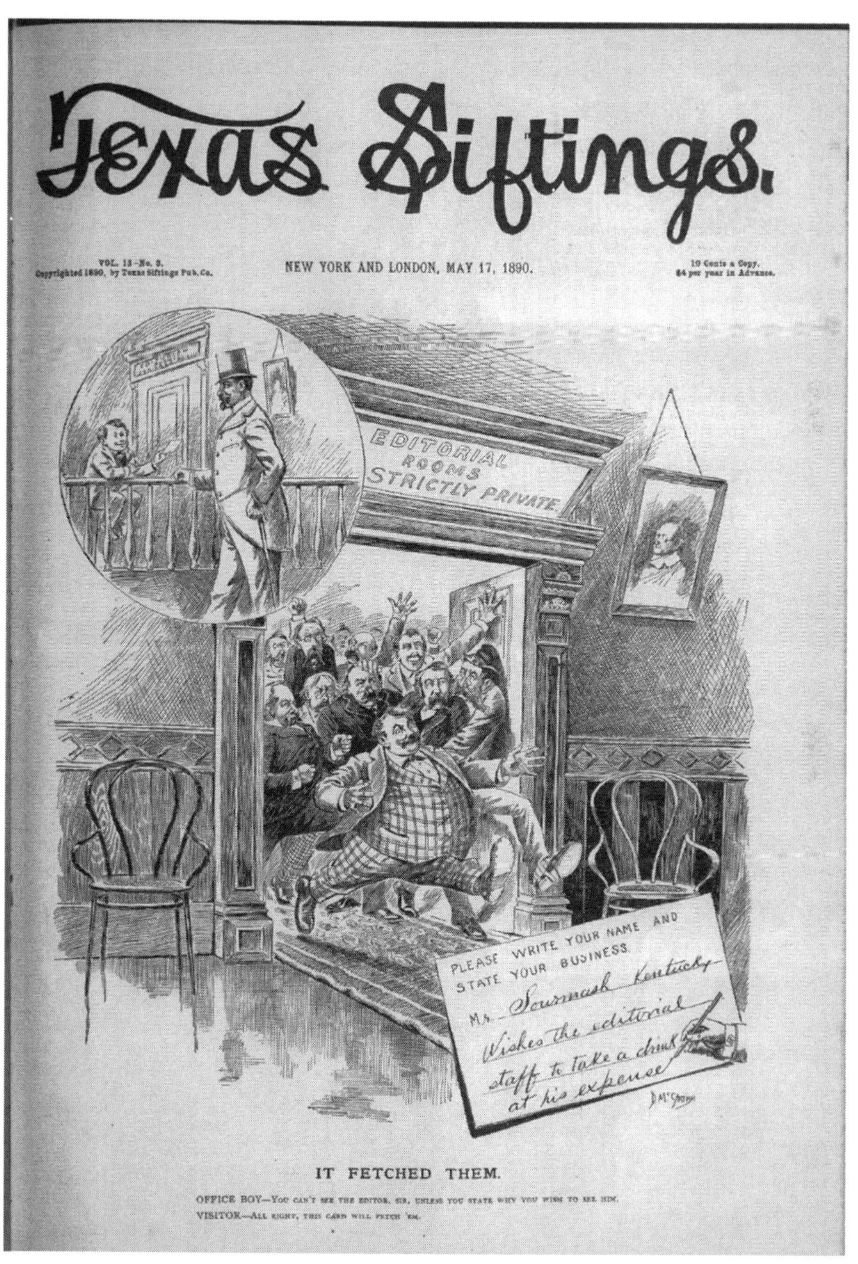

8.1. A *Texas Siftings* cartoon from the March 8, 1890, edition that perpetuated the simian image of the Irish.

magazine's representations of one specific group: the Irish, during a period when the Irish nationalist movement flourished and American antagonism against Catholic newcomers often was virulent. The research argues that editors John Armoy Knox and Alex E. Sweet offered readers an often-sympathetic portrayal of the Irish in part because the editors were immigrants themselves.[13] Sweet was a Canadian by birth and Knox was the son of a flax and grain mill owner from Ulster. But, Sweet's and Knox's personal editorial stance also led them to make use of commonly held stereotypes of the Irish and other immigrant groups for other purposes—namely, to illuminate political and social hypocrisies of the time, as well as to highlight what the editors believed were the correct behaviors expected of immigrants and native-born Americans. The proud, the vain, the ultramoralists, the drunks, the teetotalers, the ruthless social climbers, and those putting on airs all received their comeuppance within the pages of *Texas Siftings*. As will be shown, the two "sifters," as they called themselves, relied on gentle mockery and, at times, more vicious satire, but stayed away from the more insidious portrayals of the Irish as so often was put forth by their brethren of the quill.

Texas Siftings also serves as an important case study of how changes in editorial personnel can lead to changes in content. In 1885 Knox gave up most of his editorial duties to become the publication's business manager. A. Minor Griswold, a well-known American journalistic humorist from Ohio, assumed coeditorship of the magazine. Although the magazine continued a policy of supporting the Irish against their English oppressors, the comic illustrations of the Irish often depicted the immigrants with simian, physiognomic features, although the publication continued to support justice for the Irish and never denigrated Irish immigrants' Catholic religious beliefs.

Before examining how and why the Irish were portrayed within the pages of *Texas Siftings*, an examination of Knox's and Sweet's backgrounds, as well as some background on the role and importance of humor magazines in late nineteenth-century America, are necessary to provide some context.

Nineteenth-Century American Humor Magazines and the Rise of *Texas Siftings*

Americans' love of humor is evident in popular-culture materials that date back to the country's colonial origins. Almanacs, songs, theatrical presentations, books, magazines, and newspapers all offered the public a variety of humorous forms, from gentle satires to full-on mockery, much of which centered on political issues or social concerns. Foreign visitors pronounced humor to be ingrained in the nation's character from its outset.[14] Much of what passed for humor in the late 1700s and into the early 1800s was not unique, but instead was borrowed from English popular culture and adapted to American audiences.[15]

By the mid- to late 1800s, magazines were the most popular vehicle from which to spread humor to mass audiences.[16] The popularity and financial success of three publications in particular—*Life*, *Puck*, and *Judge*—led to dozens of national and regional imitators in the 1880s and 1890s, including *Truth*, the *Philadelphia Jester*, the *Chicago Figaro*, and the *Arkansas Thomas Cat*.[17] An anonymous writer from the mid-1890s noted in the *Hamilton Literary Monthly* that no library or reading room was complete if it did not subscribe to humor publications.[18] A host of factors during the late nineteenth century, including rising literacy rates, a growing middle class with access to disposable income, improved printing presses, reduced printing costs, and improvements in transportation networks allowed the periodic press to become a crucial disseminator of news, information, and entertainment.[19]

America's comic periodicals usually were the creation of individual editors. Readers received a mix of original humor writing, exclusive contributions from local and national wits, and humorous pieces reprinted from other publications. More financially solvent journals were illustrated. Humorous stories, sketches, comic paragraphs, verses, puns, and two-line dialogues—what editors referred to as "short stuff"—filled the magazines' pages.[20] Satire and lampoon dominated, with most humorous barbs focusing on social and political issues.[21]

Many of the nation's comic publications hailed from the major urban publishing centers, but sectional writing also flourished following the US Civil War. So-called "local colorists" proliferated. These regional writers often sentimentalized folk culture, and many continued a number of the antebellum humor traditions, including the use of tall tales, character types (including drunks, dandies, and rogues), and specific topics (including rituals, sports, and elections).[22]

Texas Siftings debuted into this periodical milieu in 1881. The product of Sweet, a nationally known newspaper humor columnist from Texas, and Knox, an Irish immigrant journalist, the publication found a receptive audience from its inception. The magazine's popularity was grounded in large measure in the notoriety of Sweet's work but also because a substantial portion of the humor in the publication's first three years focused on the American West.[23] By the end of its first year, *Texas Siftings* was selling twenty thousand copies weekly. By 1884 the publication's success led Sweet and Knox to move their office to New York City, although they kept an office in Austin. A European edition produced in London debuted in 1887.[24]

Sweet and Knox were both acute observers of human behavior and iconoclasts. No social norms, established practices, cherished beliefs, or longstanding values were left unquestioned by the editors, and many such beliefs and norms were rejected in humorous fashion. The two men frequently included themselves as characters in sketches, especially in the first four years of the publication, but always as wry, detached observers who were knowledgeable enough to comprehend what was happening but able to stay above and apart from most situations and concerns.[25]

Today Sweet, Knox, and their publication are largely forgotten. Only a few academic journal articles, a book chapter, and one modern compilation of their writings exist.[26] Neither went on the lecture circuit, as was common for nineteenth-century humorists, nor did they expand their talents into comic novels, which might have made the two more memorable to future generations.[27]

But, in the last three decades of the nineteenth century, Sweet's and Knox's names loomed large. Sweet's often-satirical *Galveston News*

8.2. Alexander E. Sweet and J. Armoy Knox. Published in Thomas E. Hill, *Hill's Album of Biography and Art: Containing Portraits and Pen-sketches of Many Persons Who Have Been and Are Prominent* [. . .]. (Chicago: Hill Standard, 1887), 241.

columns that poked fun at western life and institutions were reprinted in dozens of publications across the country, as well as several international newspapers. Not surprisingly, when Sweet began *Texas Siftings* in May 1881 with Knox, the eight-page journal quickly gained a national audience.[28]

The men were part of a pop-culture humor phenomenon, a group of journalists turned comic writers whom historians have dubbed the "literary comedians." Although the humor produced by this group drew upon some traditions, topics, and stylistic elements of antebellum humor, these Civil War–era and postwar comics largely rejected the prewar practice of explicitly linking violence and laughter.[29] These humorists, which included Charles Farrar Browne (Artemus Ward), Henry Wheeler Shaw (Josh Billings), George Horatio Derby (Squibob and John Phoenix), David Ross Locke (Petroleum Vesuvius

Nasby), Robert H. Newell (Orpheus C. Kerr), Charles Henry Smith (Bill Arp), James M. Bailey (the Danbury News Man), Edgar Wilson Nye (Bill Nye), and Finley Peter Dunne (Mr. Dooley), created personas that allowed them a degree of anonymity from which they could undertake their often piercing social criticism.

A writer for the *Vancouver Independent* (British Columbia) labeled Sweet "a Canadian by birth, an American by adoption, and a paragrapher and funny man by instinct."[30] Sweet was the son of Charlotte James, the belle of a wealthy Canadian family, and James Sweet, a man of modest upbringing who was known as "a delightful witty fellow." James Sweet moved his family, including eight-year-old Alex, to San Antonio, Texas, after suffering financial difficulties at his business in Saint John, New Brunswick. Whether because of his wife's family's money, help from influential friends who also immigrated from Canada to Texas, or his own abilities, James Sweet became a successful merchant, alderman, and, eventually, mayor of San Antonio.[31]

Although the Sweet family became established in Texas, young Alex spent only eight years of his childhood in the state. At age sixteen, the rambunctious future humorist was packed off to College Hill Collegiate Institute, in Poughkeepsie, New York. After graduation, he finished his education at a technical school in Carlsruhe, Germany. In 1861 he married a young German woman, Marie Zittel, and the two of them made a precarious trip back to Texas in 1863 that involved running the US Navy's federal blockade of southern ports. Sweet served under his father in the 33rd Texas Cavalry, Confederate States of America, as a private, but saw only limited action in east Texas.[32]

Following the war, Alex Sweet briefly worked as a store clerk, read law, and was admitted to the bar in 1868. He practiced law for several years, including serving as city attorney for San Antonio, but discovered his real passion and his power to right wrongs came from journalism. Sweet eventually would work for three San Antonio newspapers, including the San Antonio *Express*, where he wrote under the nom de plume of "Prickly Pear" or "PP." When Sweet became a political columnist for the Austin *State Journal* in 1873, he took the pen name with him.[33] His fame as a wry observer of politics and as a humorist grew throughout the 1870s and into the early 1880s as editors across Texas, the United States, and a variety of foreign countries, including England, Germany, and Australia, began clipping and reprinting his columns. A harsh critic of political patronage, ineptitude, graft, and incompetence, his editorial stance often put him at odds with editors who were trying to boost Texas in the postwar era.[34]

Sweet's coeditor, John Armoy Knox, seems, at first glance, an unlikely scribbler of American humor. Born in 1851 in the town of Armoy in what is today Northern Ireland, he was the son of a successful merchant. His father, Thomas Knox, and his uncle ran the Armoy Flax and Grain Mills. Biographical information about Knox is slim. He wrote little about himself, including information concerning his life in Ulster prior to immigrating to America.

The biographical sketches that exist relate that Knox immigrated at the age of twenty in search of a healthier climate, but offer no details about what maladies he may have had. He settled in Texas in 1874.[35] An obituary from the Belfast *Evening Telegram* notes that he spent three years as an "official" at the Ulster Bank before leaving his home country. His brother, the Rev. D. B. Knox, was editor of the Belfast-based *Irish Presbyterian*, a position that may have inspired John Knox.[36] After settling in Austin, Texas, he worked as a reporter and as a sewing-machine salesman before meeting Sweet and establishing *Texas Siftings* in 1881.[37]

Knox's decision to immigrate to Texas was not an unusual choice for an Irish immigrant. Although a large proportion of the millions of Irish that settled in America established themselves in the northeastern and midwestern states, Texas also lured the Irish. The nearby city of New Orleans proved a convenient port of entry for ships from Liverpool and Europe.[38] As early as the 1820s, when it was still a Spanish colony, opportunistic Irish seeking land began arriving in Texas.[39] Irish migration to Texas was steady throughout the nineteenth century. By 1850, 1,403 Irish were living in Texas. A decade later, that number had jumped to 3,480.[40] By the late 1870s, approximately 215 Irish, including Knox, lived in Austin, a growing, multiethnic city that boasted 4,428 residents in 1870. By 1880, with the arrival of railroads and manufacturing, more than 11,000 people called Austin their home.[41] Whites, African Americans, Mexicans, and immigrants from Sweden, Ireland, Mexico, Poland, China, France, Germany, and Italy all lived side by side in Texas's capital city the 1870s.[42]

Although Sweet wrote more of *Texas Siftings*' original content than did Knox, the Irish humorist produced many of the journal's early sketches that satirized the frontier and its immigrants and native-born inhabitants. He continued writing after he became the publication's business manager, penning a regular column. He also expanded his talents into a second career as a playwright and had several successful shows to his credit. He cowrote a theatrical farce, *A Stuffed Dog*, with Edwin Atwell in 1889, produced a comic musical with an Irish theme, *Shane-na-lawn*, in 1884, and cowrote two other plays, *Harley's Wife* and *Marcel*, in the late 1800s.[43]

The date of Sweet and Knox's first meeting is unclear, although the two men were part of a group of journalists who were invited to witness the May 1878 hanging of Brown Bowen, an associate of Texas outlaw John Wesley Hardin.[44] What is known is that Sweet left his position at the *Galveston News* in 1881 and began *Texas Siftings* with Knox after the men purchased the *Austin Weekly Review* and turned that publication into *Texas Siftings*. The first edition of their eight-page weekly appeared in May 1881. Sweet and Knox initially offered readers a mix of news and humor in a format that resembled a newspaper. The men hired two associate editors, Franklin P. Holland, a Galveston resident who later founded *Texas Farm and Ranch* magazine, and William O'Leary, who later became a city editor for the *Dallas Morning News*. Because illustrated periodicals attracted wide readership, Civil War veteran Major William Henderson Caskie served as illustrator.

Texas Siftings was selling 70,000 copies weekly by 1883.[45] By 1888 the journal's circulation stood at 110,000 copies weekly.[46] The magazine reached the zenith of its circulation in 1890, selling 150,000 issues per week. It was the best-selling humor magazine of the time in the United States.[47] By contrast, the second-largest circulating humor magazine, *Puck*, was selling 89,700 copies per issue while *Judge* averaged 67,000 to 70,000 copies per issue. *Life*'s circulation stood at 40,000 in 1888, but increased to 55,000 by 1890.[48] Two book-length anthologies, *Sketches from Texas Siftings* (1882) and *On a Mexican Mustang through Texas* (1883), saw multiple reprints in the United States, England, and Germany.[49] A third book of assorted sketches, *Three Dozen Good Stories from Texas Siftings*, was issued in 1887.

The magazine personnel and content changed upon its move New York in 1883, but its popularity continued. Knox moved comfortably into the position of business manager, while associate editors Holland and O'Leary remained in Texas. A new associate editor, A. Minor Griswold, joined Sweet and Knox in New York after purchasing a share of the business. Griswold already was a noted humorist in his own right, having achieved fame at the *Cincinnati Commercial* and with his own publication, the *Cincinnati Saturday Night*, under the pen name of "the Fat Contributor" (a reference to the number of articles he penned). The *Siftings*' original artist, W. H. Caskie, left the magazine, and three new artists, Thomas Worth, T. Ramsden, and Frank Bellew, were hired.[50]

Sweet, Knox, and Griswold reduced the magazine's physical size from a tabloid to a quarto to make it more in line with other magazines of the time but increased the publication to sixteen pages. Sketches and jokes about the American frontier and Texas declined in favor of news and humorous barbs centered on national and international issues. The editors also skewered the rollicking world of New York City's political scene, as well as members of the city's high society. Although Sweet, Griswold, and, to a lesser extent, Knox, wrote many of the magazine's sketches, jokes, and puns, they did not write all of the original material. A number of regular contributors submitted poetry, stories, and humorous pieces, including the Houston (Texas) *Telegraph*'s former humorist, R. R. Gilbert, and nationally known humorists Opie Read, Bill Nye, Frank Bellew, Bill Art, H. C. Lukens, and W. H. H. Murray. Poets Joaquin Miller and James Whitcomb

Riley also submitted pieces. Reprints of humorous sketches from publications in the United States, England, and Germany also appeared within the magazine's pages.[51]

Sweet and Knox shared a number of commonalities with their fellow literary comedians. Both men were more urbane and educated than they let on in their writing and, like many of their fellow humorists, both worked as journalists before turning to satire.[52] But their writing was more approachable for middle-class readers because it was not filled with constant literary references, as was the norm with many of their fellow literary comedians. Although a few common literary references, including to Shakespeare's works, were evident, the two "sifters" chose instead to use satire and lampoon and spoof the day's politics and cultural conventions—topics with which most readers would have a passing familiarity.[53]

Sweet and Knox provided their audience with standard types of late nineteenth-century humorous fare. "Short stuff," including tongue-in-cheek sketches, comic narratives, racist and gender-based humor, comic illustrations, and a solid dose of political and social satire filled the journal's pages. Sweet's and Knox's powers of observation led them, in the words of one historian, to comment "on virtually everything," including immigration, marital relations, race relations, social conventions, politics, urban and rural life, professions, sports, the theater, natural phenomena, and various "types" of individuals, including the Dude, the trickster, and the gullible eastern greenhorn.[54] A writer for the *New York Journal* noted in that publication's April 16, 1881, issue that Sweet was "second to no living writer in freshness, originality, sparkling wit, and refined humor."[55]

Portrayals of the Irish in Late Nineteenth-Century Humor Magazines

Every issue of *Texas Siftings* offered readers news and humor that skewed heavily toward the subject of immigrants and the political and social scenes from which they hailed. With more than 25 million foreigners descending upon America's shores from 1860 to 1900, Sweet, Knox, and Griswold worked in an immigrant landscape. While these new citizens came from all corners of the globe, the greatest numbers, proportionally, came from Ireland and Germany.[56]

The Irish were not new arrivals. They had been coming to America since the 1700s. Historians estimate that as many as 250,000 Irish immigrated to the United States during the 1700s, most of whom were Protestants from Ulster, a migration that continued steadily until 1830. Statistics show approximately two-thirds of the Irish immigrants prior to 1830 identified themselves as Protestants. Largely Presbyterian and Anglican, they hailed from a variety of classes and professions. Port officials in 1820 recorded that 27 percent of the Irish were farmers, 22 percent identified themselves as artisans, 21 percent were poor laborers, and 10 percent identified themselves as tradesmen and professionals.[57]

As political and religious conflicts between Catholics and Protestants in Ireland increased, and later as famine took hold, Catholic immigrants began outnumbering Protestants, a reality that created fears among native-born Anglo-Americans.[58] German immigrants found themselves accepted far more quickly among native-born Americans than the Irish because the majority of Germans were Protestant and thus were considered easier to assimilate. Catholics, by contrast, were viewed with suspicion and often portrayed in American popular culture as a nefarious "other" whose allegiance to Rome gave rise to nativist suspicions that they would not support America's democratic government.[59]

Nineteenth-century American Protestants, particularly Methodists, envisioned a nation that was evangelical and Anglo-American at its core.[60] They believed their faith brought "order, morality, and civilization" to the United States' diverse population.[61] Most Protestant denominations also believed that Catholic traditions did not "harmonize easily" with American concepts of individuality and freedom. Protestant Americans saw the Catholic Church's authoritarian nature and its long association with European monarchies as being in opposition to political liberty.[62] Protestant Americans felt politically and socially besieged by the millions of Irish Catholics who poured into the country.[63]

Both the nation's serious magazines and popular comic publications discussed and debated immigration and assimilation during the last three decades of the nineteenth century. While the serious magazines focused on analysis, the humor publications relied upon verbal and visual stereotypes of immigrants to provoke laughter. They also used their humorous barbs to question the fitness of non-Protestant immigrants for citizenship.

Gilded Age humor publications drew upon and, in some cases, modified existing ethnic caricatures, many of which had been around for several hundred years and were of English origin.[64] These stereotypes, which centered on differences in race, religion, and class, were used to shape the English public's identification of the Irish.[65] American publications as far back as the early 1700s borrowed the often-pejorative images.[66] Such stereotypes were used to stress the "otherness" of the Irish, while providing native-born Americans with a sense of superiority and cohesion.[67] These colonial-era portrayals often presented the Irish as fools or tricksters, and sometimes as victims of "absurd misunderstandings." More negative portrayals also emerged, with the Irish represented as lawless, "pugnacious," fortune hunters.[68]

The nation's humor magazines used caricatures, which were not based upon close observation of real people, because their creators and readers often believed that such portrayals, especially those that were physiognomic, contained at least a kernel of truth about their subjects' characters and behavior.[69] *Puck*'s editor, a German Protestant immigrant named Joseph Keppler, regularly ridiculed the Irish with stereotyped portrayals of violent drunkards. Keppler's stereotypes in *Puck* evinced the Anglo majority's fears that unchecked immigration would lead to the undoing of American institutions and to the dilution of the Anglo-Protestant work ethic.[70]

Such stereotypes and exaggerated representations (via physical features, expressions, gestures, and poses) helped readers navigate an increasingly changing social landscape. The public recognized the caricatures' features, styles of dress, and poses, and that they served "as components for a normative description of society that classified individuals into a range of 'social types' bearing predictable and predetermined characteristics."[71] Such portrayals remained popular in American culture in part because of the "psychic needs of audiences" who presumably recognized and found satisfaction, humor, and "at least a grain of truth in the caricatures."[72]

The stereotyped Irish male in late nineteenth-century American magazines was usually called "Pat." He usually was depicted as filthy and often idle, with a clay pipe sticking out of his mouth and a bowler hat on his head. When the Irish were shown as working, most were depicted as unskilled laborers. The stereotyped Irish woman, named "Bridget," was portrayed as the worker of the family. A devout Catholic who often tried, but failed, to improve her husband, Bridget also had her own personal failings. She often was presented as a domineering domestic servant whose lack of respect for her upper-class employers showed that she was unwilling to recognize her station in life. And, her lower level of intelligence often left her vulnerable to the schemes and machinations of her husband who, as John J. Appel found, was "prepared to send his and Bridget's hard-earned dollars to support lazy relatives or harebrained, landlord-murdering, dynamite-happy compatriots in the Emerald Isle or the United States."[73]

Throughout the 1880s, native-born Americans "continued to laugh at the Irish, but their jokes became somewhat more abusive, and their laughter was interjected with a distinct note of fear" as Irish immigrants increasingly gained political power.[74] By the 1890s, as the Irish began moving up the economic ladder and Eastern European immigrants began taking their place as the new immigrant "other," some of the extant Irish stereotypes began to soften.[75] Other publications depicted the Irish as sinister and predatory. These caricatures, James H. Dormon notes, "become wholly unappealing, animalistic, even threatening to bourgeois society. Irish laborers became lazy parasites."[76]

Although anecdotal evidence demonstrates that the subjects of the humor occasionally wrote letters to the editors of these humor publications denouncing the stereotyped representations (especially when they were particularly pejorative),[77] two things are clear. First, the majority of the readers of these publications were not the subjects of the humor; they were part of the emerging native-born middle class. Second, pejorative humor sold. Circulation figures demonstrate the comic magazines' readers were clearly delighted by and fascinated with such depictions.

Irish Representations in *Texas Siftings*

Comic portrayals and editorial discussions of the Irish both in their home country and as immigrants appeared with regularity in *Texas Siftings*. While an occasional issue contained no representations of the Irish, most issues had two to four examples in editorials, news items, humorous pieces, or comic illustrations.

An examination of the news items and comic pieces in *Texas Siftings* demonstrates that Knox and Sweet opposed repressive laws against the Irish, decried absentee British landlords, and supported Irish nationalist aims generally; however, they did not support the growing violence (i.e., assassinations and bombings) that was occurring in the 1880s in England and Ireland.[78] A March 29, 1884, article noted that another railway station in London had been blown up, then wryly noted that the Fenians were causing destruction, but not obtaining their nationalist objective:

> These wild searchers after Irish liberty seemed determined to free their country from the cruel oppression of the despot's heel, if they have to blow up all the railway stations in London. It is funny how it works though. Instead of Ireland being "unchained, unshackled, disenthralled," somebody generally gets put in jail for manslaughter.[79]

Previously, in December 1882, at the end of a tumultuous year for Ireland that saw the release of Irish Nationalist leader Charles Stewart Parnell from prison, the resignation of W. E. Forster, the hardline chief secretary of Ireland, and the murders of two British officials, the "sifters" lampooned John Spencer, the fifth Earl Spencer, when his attempts to pacify Ireland resulted in the destruction of several secret societies and the hanging of Myles Joyce, who had been convicted of murder, but whose hanging brought international condemnation.[80] The editors of *Texas Siftings* noted: "The English are having a harder time of it than ever in trying to conciliate the Irish. The only thing they have not mismanaged in 800 years was the recent hanging of a malefactor; and the only encouragement they get for not blundering it is that the Fenians have promised Marwood, the public executioner, he will be assassinated, if he again ventures into Ireland."[81]

Although much of the money raised for the Fenians came from America, Sweet and Knox attempted to clarify for readers that not all Irish nationalists in America were dynamite-happy assassins. "Instead of invading Ireland, the New York Fenians went up the Hudson river on an excursion, with a brass band and other provisions," the magazine noted in the June 16, 1883, issue about a large Irish gathering.

As serious as the nationalist cause was, the two "sifters" willingly lampooned an unnamed Irish American newspaper editor for publishing unproven accusations that some of the best-known Fenians in America were traitors. The ongoing violence abroad also allowed Sweet and Knox to evince some sympathy for the British government: "The New York Irish papers intimate that O'Donovan Rossa and Tynan are in the pay of the English government. It seems that there is nothing too vile for the New York Irish to say about the English government."[82]

More common in the pages of *Texas Siftings* were comic jabs against the British government's policies that used an unexpected twist to provide laughter. For example, a January 23, 1886, sketch, "Justice to Ireland," made use of an imaginary family, the Fizzletops. On the possibility of justice for the Irish, Sweet opined the following:

> All the justice that Ireland gets from England will not amount to much if it is voluntarily given. It will be spread as thin as the butter is on the bread in the Fizzletop family.
>
> "Johnny, do you want butter on your bread?" asked Mrs. Fizzletop.
>
> "Just suit yourself, ma. You spread it so thin that I don't get the bad taste of it in my mouth anyhow."[83]

The editors also allowed guest writers to lobby for Irish justice, and some did so via recognizable, although not severely pejorative, stereotypes. For example, John Knox's brother, the Rev. D. B. Knox, suggested that some stereotypes about the Irish had a grain of truth to them, but that events, rather than the perceived character of a race, needed to be examined. It is true, he wrote,

> that the Ulsterman is shrewd, far sighted, and practical, takes good value out of his days and weeks, and seizes a better hat if he can't find his own. It is also true that the southern Irishman is warm-hearted, generous, improvident, is apt to live on hope and potatoes without beef, and to complain that having to work between meals is killing him, but the causes of the success of the Scotchman and the failures of the Celt must be sought in other circumstances than in the character of the people.

He then discussed how British policies drove many Irish from their homes and "cruel penal laws" deprived the Irish of rights and liberties.[84]

Unlike other comic and illustrated publications of the time, the editors of *Texas Siftings* never portrayed Catholicism or Irish Catholics as sinister, but Sweet, Knox, and Griswold delighted in unmasking the hypocrisy and seemingly bad behaviors of religious figures through both humorous pieces and editorials. One such humorous jab, from December 16, 1882, used wordplay to criticize the pope: "The Pope is indisposed again. This time he is indisposed to put up with the decision of the Italian Supreme Court, which gives the Italian government jurisdiction inside the walls of the Vatican."[85]

In an era when the majority of ethnic humor was based on lampooning immigrants' character, speech, and dress, most late nineteenth-century comic publications portrayed newcomers to America as foolish, illogical, uneducated—clearly not the equals of native-born white Americans.[86] By contrast, Knox, Sweet, and Griswold did not single out specific immigrant groups, including the Irish, to deride simply to obtain a laugh. Instead, the "sifters" used humor as a vehicle to lampoon and rebuke the follies and foibles of many individuals, both American and foreign born.

Through the use of humorous, but not malicious, "types" in sketches, the readers of *Texas Siftings* were able to recognize and laugh at the exploits of many common characters of the era, including bragging young professionals desperate for attention, traveling salespeople who thought themselves smarter than their rural customers (but whose clientele got the upper hand in transactions), religious figures who always seemed ready to fleece their flock, social-climbing women who used false modesty to get ahead, and haughty hotel clerks who believed themselves better than their surroundings and the customers. The subjects of these types included all races and immigrant groups to demonstrate that good and bad behaviors were not the province of one ethnicity, culture, or nation.[87]

Irish characters sometimes were portrayed as tricksters within the pages of *Texas Siftings*, but their cleverness was shown as being put to good use against those who deserved it.[88] For example, the January 6, 1883, issue included a lengthy comic piece about an attorney in Ireland who needed to serve a writ to a magistrate but was unable to present the paperwork because the man kept to his house, except when he was in court, and the neighborhood in which he lived was dangerous. So the attorney, who was a member of Parliament, hired one of his tenants, a "very shrewd fellow" named Tom MacNamara, to get the job done. Tom managed to get himself arrested for appearing suspicious in order to be brought before the judge. When taken in front of the magistrate, Tom claimed his arrest was a case of mistaken identity and that he was, in actuality, a poor yet honest laboring man who could provide proof of his character via a letter written by a parish priest. When asked for the "letter," Tom handed the writ to the magistrate, who realized he'd been served.

> "Take the rascal out of my sight," exclaimed the magistrate. "He is more rogue than fool."
>
> "Do you mean to acquit him, sir?" enquired the constables, who had not yet comprehended the affair.
>
> "Of course," said the magistrate; "don't you perceive that he has been playing a trick on us in order to serve me with a writ?"
>
> "Service acknowledged, your honor," said Tom.[89]

The successful Irish trickster was a staple feature of *Texas Siftings* for much of the magazine's existence. Illustrations with two-line dialogue captions brought humor via the trickster's ability to gain the verbal upper hand in many situations, including with overbearing mothers-in-law and difficult employers. Such characters were shown as intelligent but not deceitful, a character trait attributed to the Irish by many other publications at the time.[90] The publication often portrayed their Bridget and Pat stereotypes as domestics and common laborers.[91]

Some humor praised Irish cunning, while tweaking the English. In the April 2, 1887, issue, a Miss Murphy married a landlord. Her aunt, a Mrs. O'Raherty, tells a visitor that her niece has "done as well for herself as if she married a real English lord."[92]

More pejorative images of the Irish began appearing after Knox became business manager and A. Minor Griswold took over the joint editorial duties with Sweet. The harsh caricatures were more in line with those produced by other publications that used them as a means of social control and to establish racial rankings.[93] Illustrations within the pages of *Texas Siftings* more frequently featured physiognomic portrayals of simian Irish, drunken Irishmen were the butt of an increasing number of jokes, and more class-based humor occurred. For example, in the April 28, 1888, issue, a cartoon by F. M. Howarth shows a poor Irishman, possibly a hod carrier, smoking a pipe and wearing his bowler hat. He finds a silver dollar on the ground that has a hole drilled into it and tosses it away, thinking that it is only worth "nointy cents."[94] The image of Pat's counterpart, Bridget, also evolved while Griswold was coeditor. While never threatening in nature, the household domestic became more social climbing and arrogant. She also began being portrayed as simian in appearance, and her intelligence dropped in direct proportion to her scheming and laziness.[95]

By the late 1880s, *Texas Siftings* was also lampooning social-climbing Irish immigrants. "A Just Rebuke," a cartoon reprinted from *Puck* magazine, shows a drunken husband named Dicey McShake who mortifies his wife by bringing a live turkey home instead of a dressed one for the family's holiday meal. The wife, Kathleen, rebukes her husband before going through a series of machinations trying to save the family from disgrace.[96]

Such stereotypes may have angered, but the subjects of the jokes may not have been readers. Regardless of the ethics of *Texas Siftings*' turn toward denigrating ethnic humor, those representations clearly attracted a wide audience. The editors noted on page sixteen of their December 22, 1888, issue, that their regular circulation was 120,000 copies.

Conclusion

Although America's late nineteenth-century humor magazines provided readers with a continuum of Irish characters' portrayals that shifted from benign fools and tricksters to social climbers and nefarious Catholic "others" who lacked the ability to assimilate, *Texas Siftings* used ethnic humor for different ends. In its early years, while an Irish immigrant served as coeditor, the Irish were not shown to be one amorphous ethnicity, but instead were shown to be individuals with varying beliefs and values. Irish nationalism was given a sympathetic hearing, but its adherents who advocated or participated in violence were not.

Sweet and Knox parted ways in 1895 after disagreeing about the magazine's finances and selling the publication to Robert E. Morgan. Sweet returned to Texas and attempted to start a new magazine, the *Texas Sifter*. It was short lived. Sweet soon returned to New York and took a position on the *Tammany Times*. He continued to pen political and satirical pieces, including letters from Bill Snort, until his death in 1901. Knox spent two years (1892–94) as the editor and manager of the *Atlanta Herald* before also returning to New York, where he freelanced humor pieces for newspapers and magazines. He also penned several plays, two nonfiction books, *All About the Klondike Gold Mines* (1897), which provided readers with factual information about the gold rush taken from news accounts, and *A Devil of a Trip; or the Log of the Yacht Champlain* (1888), an account of sailing his yacht through the Saint Lawrence River to the Atlantic and down to New York.[97] In December 1906 Knox died suddenly of heart disease at his home, located at 203 West 108th Street in New York, at age fifty-six.[98]

9

Presidents, Protection, and Politics

Political Cartoons in the Irish World and American Industrial Liberator, *1890–1913*

Úna Ní Bhroiméil

In the ferment of newspapers that proliferated in late nineteenth- and early twentieth-century New York, the ethnic Irish American newspaper, the *Irish World and American Industrial Liberator*, plied its trade and jostled for position. Using the journalistic genre of political cartoons to command attention and to communicate its editorial opinion, its editor, Patrick Ford, decided and defined the relevant issues for his readers whether Irish or American.

The period 1890–1913 is an interesting era for the newspaper as it is sometimes regarded as a politically "quiet" time in Irish political history—"after" Parnell and "before" Home Rule. For an ethnic newspaper in New York, this, then, is an ideal period in which to investigate the paper's focus on American politics and policies. This chapter will examine and probe the political cartoons published in the *Irish World* from 1890 to 1913 to reveal the disposition of the paper, the temper of its readers, and the ambiance of the era in the United States.

The *Irish World*

Patrick Ford's *Irish World*, and from 1878, *Irish World and American Industrial Liberator*, was the highest circulation Irish American paper in the United States during the period 1890–1913. Its circulation rose from 35,000 copies in 1876 to 100,000 in 1884, with a readership of

20,000 in Ireland in 1880.[1] By 1900 its circulation had increased to 125,000, and although this number declined to around 60,000 in 1914, its publication in New York had the advantage of being in the center and hotbed of American newspaper publishing at the turn of the century.[2] The title of the newspaper attests to its interest in encapsulating the Irish world in its entirety. Whether it existed in Ireland, America, or elsewhere, the *Irish World* reported on it and stated on its masthead that it was "committed to the Irish race throughout the world."[3] But, it was not simply an Irish paper *in* America. Its secondary title, *American Industrial Liberator*, demonstrated the support of the editor, Patrick Ford, until his death in 1913, for labor in the United States. David Brundage points out that Ford "drew parallels between the land struggle in Ireland and the labour struggle in the United States,"[4] and his paper supported the policies of Henry George in the 1880s as well as the Land League in Ireland.[5] Published on Saturdays as a weekly paper, it supported Irish nationalism, and Home Rule in particular, until 1914 when it broke with John Redmond because of his support for Britain in the Great War.[6] Ford's paper was consistently anti-imperialist and heralded the British empire as the root of all evil, not merely in Ireland but around the world. On that basis the *Irish World* supported O'Donovan Rossa's dynamiting campaign of British cities in the 1880s, the Boers against the British at the beginning of the twentieth century, and espoused a strong campaign of United States' neutrality on the outbreak of World War I in 1914 while being anti-British and pro-German at the same time. Under the Espionage Act of 1917, the paper was banned from the US mail because of its anti-British sentiments.[7]

In its editorials, the *Irish World* stressed that it was nonpartisan in American politics and that it did not automatically support one political party no matter who the candidates or what the platform.[8] It was, however, "political" in that its editors believed in shaping the political debate and influencing voters. One of the ways in which it transmitted its views to readers was through publishing "political" cartoons that commented on contemporary national and international affairs. Political cartoons had initially found a place in illustrated journals such as *Harper's Weekly*, which had carried Thomas Nast's powerful cartoons since 1862, and in other publications such as *Frank Leslie's Illustrated Journal* and the New York *Daily Graphic*.[9] The 1884 presidential election displayed the clout of the political cartoon in electoral terms when a cartoon published by Pulitzer's *World* linked candidate James G. Blaine with corruption and the moneyed classes and was credited with his loss of New York State by 110 votes and, consequently, the presidency.[10]

This graphic journalism became a fundamental feature of what became known as "New Journalism," and in the late nineteenth and early twentieth centuries, newspaper editors and publishers hired editorial cartoonists to improve their circulations and enhance their reputations. The potential of the political cartoon to expose those in public life was demonstrated by the effort of Republican political boss and New York senator Thomas Platt to present an anticartoon bill to the New York State Legislature in 1897.[11]

This formidable tool of pictorial journalism was one that the *Irish World* used to great effect in the period 1890–1913. While an in-house editorial cartoonist was expensive and many immigrant newspapers could not afford one, the *Irish World* used cartoons accredited to other newspapers regularly from the 1880s on and, from 1900, carried a front-page cartoon directly under the masthead. In 1901 the front-page cartoons were mostly taken from and accredited to other newspapers. However, Charles Pickett drew a number of cartoons for the paper from 1901 to 1904, and from 1904 on, the paper had a cartoonist, Thomas J. Fleming, who drew a weekly cartoon for the front page.[12] The political cartoonist had, therefore, a strategic opportunity to convey in one single panel an editorial position. He was most likely hired for his political alignment with the paper and his ability to convey the editorial viewpoint succinctly through visual expression, encapsulating "a complex of political and social ideas, distilling them into one illustration with accompanying caption."[13]

Political Cartoons

As Edwards and Ware have stated political cartoons function as "windows to the political world."[14] Because they are time based, drawn in response to contemporary events, and focused on a particular "critical discourse moment,"[15] they are not always easy to interpret when looking back at them from the present. Indeed, Elisabeth El Rafaie has pointed out that even current cartoons can be difficult for readers to understand as they require "a broad knowledge of past and current events, a familiarity with the cartoon genre, a vast repertoire of cultural symbols, and experience of thinking analytically about real-world events and circumstances."[16] But this historical hurdle can be mitigated by placing the cartoon in its original context and into the framework of the newspaper in which it was published. The *Irish World*, by printing its primary political cartoon consistently on its front page, drew readers' attention in a visual way to the editorial position of the paper. Joel Wiener maintains that many editorials in American newspapers went unread,[17] and so the sight of a one-panel cartoon that could be taken in quickly and in a single scan would "entrap the eye" and draw readers in more readily than multiple columns of gray text. Both, however, were facets of the New Journalism.[18] The cartoon, though, was, in essence, a "kind of shorthand."[19]

The ability of political cartoons to shape and influence the opinions of its reading public is a contested one. The persuasion of readers fits with what Wiid, Pitt, and Engstrom term the "strong" theory of political cartoons in that they can mold "public attitudes, intentions and behaviors."[20] Medhurst and DeSousa describe cartooning as a form of persuasive communication. They argue that through "dispositional forms" such as contrast, contradiction, and commentary, as well as the "use of line and form, exaggeration of physiognomical features, placement within the frame, relative size of objects, relation of text to visual imagery, and rhythmic montage," the cartoonist can reveal some "truth" about the character or situation and thus literally draw the attention of readers to what they want them to see.[21] Scrutinizing political cartoons for all or some of these "signs" can provide insight into what a cartoonist intended to convey to readers of a particular newspaper, although it is difficult to gauge what the impact of the cartoon actually was on the reading public at any given moment.[22] Nonetheless, the editor of the *Irish World*, by employing a regular cartoonist after 1904, clearly expected to influence his readers on specific issues whether they related to national or international events. The consistency of the artistry of the cartoonist, the symbols he used, and the placement of the cartoon gave readers of the *Irish World* a familiarity with the cartoons and a better chance of interpretation than with random cartoons seen out of context.

Many scholars have pointed to the "weak" theory model that political cartoons reflect contemporary public attitudes,[23] and Fischer states unequivocally that they rely and build upon the "a priori beliefs, values and prejudices" of readers.[24] Without some recognition by readers of the symbols, referents, and allusions used in the cartoon, it would fail and would therefore be pointless. This use or exploitation of conventions which Fischer states are in "fundamental harmony with the cultural literacy of the public"[25] are devices used by the cartoonist to tap into the prevailing attitudes and beliefs of the readership of the newspaper so that the cartoon will ultimately "work." Recurring visual cues allowed the reader to participate in constructing a political position or identity for themselves and allowed readers to participate in a democratic manner in political debate.[26] Decoding the cartoons, therefore, allows the historian to discern traces of the views of the readership at various times in the life of a newspaper. They are for this reason a potent and powerful tool in the historian's armory as this is one of the few methods of tracking the remnants of contemporary public attitudes in the past.

Range of Cartoons and Selection of Themes

For the purposes of this chapter, all the weekly editions of the *Irish World* published between 1890 and 1920 were examined, and all the front-page cartoons were collected. Cartoons were also collected from elsewhere in the paper in the period before 1904 when Fleming became the paper's regular cartoonist. The aim was to capture a wide range of cartoons and to allow specific categories and themes to emerge from the data.[27] Putting aside all those cartoons that dealt solely with Ireland, this study focused on cartoons that dealt with events in America or about America. This was done in order to determine the engagement of the paper and its readership with American politics and policies and to identify the positions Irish Americans took in relation to national events in particular during this period. Four key themes came into view: presidents and their personalities and records, the economic policy of protection and tariffs, the threat that Japan posed to America internally and externally, and the overall influence of Britain on America and Americans, and the threat that it posed to America.

Presidents

Six men served as president of the United States during the period 1890 to 1913: Benjamin Harrison (Republican) 1889–93; Grover Cleveland (Democrat) 1893–97; William McKinley (Republican) 1897–1901, assassinated; Theodore Roosevelt (Republican) 1901–09; William Howard Taft (Republican) 1909–13; and Woodrow Wilson (Democrat) 1913–21. The *Irish World* published no cartoons of Benjamin Harrison and only one each of Grover Cleveland and William Howard Taft. The majority of the *Irish World* front page and other political cartoons focused on the presidency of William McKinley and on his foreign policy during the period of the Spanish-American-Cuban War, 1898–1903. The *Irish World* was ideologically opposed to what it termed the United States' policy of imperialism and castigated McKinley's policy of "benevolent assimilation" and the "civilization" of the Filipino people. Although Press has noted that, during a national crisis, there is normally a "rally effect" where newspapers, and especially cartoonists, rally around a president and his policies in a burst of national patriotism, this was not the case with the cartoons carried in the *Irish World*.[28] In his Cuban message to Congress, which brought the United States into the war with Spain, McKinley controversially stopped short of recognizing the Cuban republic as he believed that Cubans were incapable of self-government.[29] The Philippine Republic, newly declared by revolutionary leader Emilio Aguinaldo in June 1898, was not recognized by the US government either. In February 1899, the United States annexed the island under its treaty with Spain enforcing, as Paul Kramer points out, "its 'sovereignty' in the Philippines against a newly internal 'insurrection.'"[30] The ensuing Philippine-American War and the McKinley Philippine policy of benevolent assimilation toward "our little brown brothers" drew the ire of the *Irish World*, and much newsprint was given over to the wrongs McKinley was perpetrating on the Philippines with his imperial mindset. It is the cartoons, however, that bring the position of the *Irish World* into sharp focus. By devoting a series of cartoons over time to a regular and growing readership, there was the opportunity to communicate to readers what might have been ignored or lost in long and textual editorials or columns.

In many of the cartoons, McKinley is seen as acting contrary to the values of the United States. In a cartoon taken from the *New York Herald* and printed on the front page of the *Irish World* on August 5, 1899, McKinley and General Otis, the military governor of the Philippines, conspire to censor reports and accounts of United States' atrocities in the war.

Whispering into Otis's ear, the darkly drawn McKinley conveys an air of secrecy and scheming and an effort to keep the truth from the American people as represented by Uncle Sam. Standing sidelined with a pencil and blank paper under his arm, Uncle Sam looks askance at the actions of McKinley, even as he clearly sees the gravestones and prone figures lying on the ground. While Otis was being condemned by newspaper correspondents for his censorship regime, in which he threatened to charge any correspondent with espionage if he sent reports of what was actually happening in the Philippines home rather than the manipulated and censored "facts" that Otis deemed "advisable," his size in the cartoon makes it clear that he was subordinate to McKinley and a mere minion in this collusion.[31] This view was reinforced by the text, especially by the quotation from Otis added by the *Irish World* to the original cartoon and which stated that Otis was in fact under instructions from McKinley to act as he did. The placement of the cartoon on the front page of the newspaper was a deliberate act by the editor to point the finger of accusation directly at McKinley and at presidential policy and was a very provocative act in time of war.

9.1. *Irish World*, August 5, 1899.

But the war was popular in the United States, and the opposition to it was generally fragmented and fruitless.[32] McKinley ran on a platform of prosperity and victory in the presidential election of 1900, and this led to a renewed focus on McKinley as the architect of the rush to imperialism. On October 13, 1900, the *Irish World* printed its own front-page cartoon of McKinley as a bloated figure after expansion, supported by financiers and industrialist donations through his campaign manager Mark Hanna,[33] denoted by the prominent dollar sign on his shirt, and poised to win the presidency for the second time.

9.2. *Irish World*, October 13, 1900.

In attempting to persuade its readers not to vote for him, the cartoon's text compared McKinley to Shakespeare's Macbeth before seizing the Scottish throne, when he stated "bring forth men children only" to his wife. This quote in the play commends the manly characteristics of force, violence, and ruthlessness displayed by Lady Macbeth, and as used in the cartoon, suggests McKinley's affinity for these qualities. Even if the readers were not familiar with the exact meaning of the literary quotation, it clearly taps into the debates in the United States between imperialists and anti-imperialists, particularly during the election of 1900.[34] The nation, according to imperialists, was becoming more manly—it was youthful, vigorous, and male, expanding in the world to fulfill its manly destiny, and was leaving behind the domestic space occupied by women where it would become passive and frail. The anti-imperialists were portrayed as old and musty and as women. The prevalence of this "national manhood metaphor"—that the United States had become a man—is reflected in this cartoon and is immersed in the contemporary conversations around manhood and manliness.[35] McKinley, previously accused of having no backbone and thus of not being "manly" enough to use force before the declaration of war against Spain, is now portrayed as so in thrall to bellicose manliness that he has no time for women or girls.[36]

Anti-imperialists also portrayed American mothers as strongly opposed to the war, and this is captured in the cartoon in the second section of text below the image. Using a Mr. Dooley quotation, the cartoonist focuses on the need for boys as American soldiers and on the possibility that they will be maimed or killed in the war. This brings the eye back to McKinley's disdainful treatment of the mother and daughters in the cartoon, fearful and pleading and dressed shabbily, with one girl barefoot. If their husbands and fathers and brothers are to be destroyed by war, what will become of them? The cartoon suggests that McKinley will not be the person to approach for help in that event. While McKinley looms large in the cartoon and is without doubt the prime mover in the continuation of the war, in the top left-hand corner is a small, horse-riding figure shooting a gun in the air, having broken through a fence. He rides alongside a sea, a rising sun behind him and the cloud of imperialism above him. This is likely a reference to Theodore R. Roosevelt and his "Rough Riders" cavalry. Roosevelt, as McKinley's vice president, was eager for imperialism and vociferous in his support for vigorous, manly pursuits such as war. These scenes—an uncontrolled war, a loss of male citizens, and contempt for the women left behind and for their characteristics—are therefore ones that the voters should expect to encounter if McKinley won the presidency.

McKinley did, winning 51.6 percent of the popular vote. The *Irish World*'s voice, as with many of the anti-imperialist opposition, could not detract from the popularity of McKinley and the Republican campaign in 1900. What the cartoons demonstrate, however, is the condensed message of the paper's columns of newsprint at a given historical moment. Those columns reveal the complex interplay of contemporary debates and discussions and the concentrated effort to communicate the paper's position to its readers. Janis Edwards suggests that the "stories" cartoons tell about their subjects can be more revealing than any one cartoon by itself. The story depicted in the twelve cartoons featuring McKinley as a central character in the *Irish World*, from the first one in 1899 to the last in November 1900, just prior to the election, was that he was the driver of the imperial policy of the United States, careless about the knowledge and welfare of the citizens of the republic, and therefore a destructive force.

None of the antagonism displayed so clearly by the *Irish World* toward McKinley was directed at Theodore R. Roosevelt, his vice president and successor upon his assassination in 1901. On the contrary, although the *Irish World* printed two anti-imperial cartoons on July 5, 1902, and December 19, 1903, neither of them featured Roosevelt. The 1902 cartoon featured contrasting images of the crest of the Rochambeau Monument that had been dedicated in Washington, DC, that year representing Lady Liberty protecting the American eagle from the British lion and a threatening American eagle attacking a helpless Filipino.[37] The 1903 cartoon, taken from the *Columbia Daily Express*, saw an overwhelmed Uncle Sam in military dress dealing with the problems of being a world power as Columbia gently asked him if they had been happier in their old (isolationist) home. Both cartoons appeared on the front page of the paper and marked the continuing ideological opposition of the *Irish World* to the trajectory of American foreign policy. The villain in these cartoons was not personalized as it had been with McKinley, however. The policy of imperialism was presented through emblematic American symbols and not as the figure of the president representing the nation. In fact, as the 1904 presidential election approached, the *Irish World* printed a flattering lifelike line drawing of Roosevelt above a wide and lengthy column listing his labor record and his "favourable action on labour legislation." In the aftermath of Roosevelt's victory, the paper celebrated the result by printing many pages containing congratulatory messages from other newspapers on its "potent influence" in bringing about the "overwhelming victory of Roosevelt."[38] By March 1905 the paper was extolling the honesty of Roosevelt in recognizing Irish American contributions to the American Revolutionary War and Civil War as well as his statement that pride of race did not lessen patriotism.[39] The only cartoon featuring Roosevelt in the *Irish World* appeared on the front page on September 8, 1906, after Roosevelt signed an executive order in August mandating the use of the Simplified Spelling Board's list of "American" spellings of English words.[40]

Picturing a horrified John Bull defending a spelling book of "obsolete words," "cockneyisms," and "dropped *h*'s," Roosevelt presents him with a book entitled the "President's American" instead of the "King's English." A delighted Uncle Sam looks on. This separation and setting apart of the American version of the English language was the subject of another front-page cartoon on September 22, 1906, when Roosevelt's name appeared on the primer in the schoolroom. Glorying in the appalled reaction of the British press to Roosevelt's decision, the *Irish World* cheered visually and applauded Roosevelt's action.

But it is the absence of Roosevelt from political cartoons in the *Irish World* that signifies the paper's support for him as president during this period and the benign way in which the paper regarded him. This is telling as it provides an insight into how the paper saw the

9.3. *Irish World*, September 8, 1906.

political cartoon at the time as a weapon to punish and to identify the object of derision of the paper and of its readership. "The power of the political cartoon is not in its direct, persuasive effects, which are contestable, but in the way it frames and defines what is at issue," according to Edwards.[41] The political cartoons during the tenures of McKinley and Roosevelt all identified the imperial policy of the United

States as what was at issue but, as Greenberg states, the cartoon also frames a contemporary political issue by "diagnosing causes, making moral judgments, and suggesting remedies."[42] Though McKinley and Roosevelt were both Republicans, and both were expansionists, the *Irish World* identified one as the problem, marked him as a purveyor of censorship, violence, and disregard for the American people and their values, and suggested rejection by the electorate. His vice president on the other hand, associated with the same policies and outcomes, was supported and celebrated. Ideologically and politically, this seems to make no sense at first glance.

The support for the Republican Party is interesting in the *Irish World*. By the nineteenth and early twentieth centuries, Irish Americans were more usually associated with the Democratic Party and the city boss system in the United States.[43] One of the reasons the *Irish World* was pro-Republican was because of its stance on protective tariffs for American industries. The *Irish World* had supported the Republican James G. Blaine throughout the 1890s on this issue.[44] The Republicans supported economic nationalism through governmental control of trade, mostly through protective tariffs and import restrictions so as to protect the national market from international competition.[45] This, ironically, was encapsulated most obviously in the McKinley Tariff of 1890, though while the *Irish World* printed a full "protection issue" before the election of that year, its front-page cartoon focused on the British threat to the United States from the free-trade plank of the "Anglo Democratic support" and of the "Anglo Mugwump support" rather than on the "true" Republican protection policy.[46] There was no sign of McKinley in the image. Throughout the 1890s, the Democrats under Grover Cleveland reduced the tariffs and the Republicans under McKinley raised them.[47] Marc-William Palen argues that Cleveland's free-trade policies were anti-imperial in that the Democratic Party wanted to extend free trade to avoid having to annex territory. The imperial acquisitions of the Republican administrations, however, allowed the United States to practice protection at home but to have the advantage of reciprocal treaties and foreign markets abroad.[48] This suggests, therefore, that the editor and readers

The "Trojan - Horse" Game Wont Work this Time.

9.4. *Irish World*, September 24, 1904.

of the *Irish World*, in supporting protectionism and tariffs, were economic Republicans but foreign policy Democrats. This could account for the paper's antagonism toward McKinley for his Philippine policy.

The cartoons published in the paper until 1909 featured the Democratic donkey[49] prominently—as a "horse" needing to be broken,[50] as a Trojan "horse,"[51] and as a "horse" wearing a Belmont bridle.[52] Contemporary readers in 1904 would have easily recognized the reference to the racehorse owner, breeder, and builder of the Belmont race track in New York, August Belmont, the son of August P. Belmont, who had been chairman of the Democratic Party.

He was also identifiable in the cartoon as one of the wealthy financiers backing the free-trade Trojan "horse" in attempting to gain entry to America's "Fort Protection." Both he and the Democratic candidate

Alton B. Parker, who had been a judge in the New York Court of Appeals and who had declared the eight-hour law unconstitutional, were portrayed climbing up a ladder into the Trojan horse.[53] Etched on the wooden body of the Democrat donkey were the initials "A.B." and a dollar sign as well as the words "free trade." All these elements together conveyed a message of wealthy investors and antilabor candidates literally inside the Democratic Party, scheming to bring in free trade and usurp one of America's core protectionist values. The fort, a symbol of protection in itself, clearly houses factories within its walls as can be seen from the smoke coming from the industrial chimneys on the factory buildings. In dedicating four cartoons to the protection issue in the month leading up to the 1904 presidential election, the *Irish World* staked its claim to supporting tariffs and the Republican candidate Roosevelt and opposing the Democrats and their candidate Parker. There was no sign in any cartoon of the Socialist candidate Eugene Debs.

The cartoonist used the full range of a bank of images in relation to the protection and tariffs issue. The Trojan horse cartoon referenced Virgil's *Aeneid* and the commonplace phrase "to look a gift horse in the mouth" in the accompanying text. The cartoon published on October 29 referenced the biblical story of Samson and Delilah, with "Miss Democracy" holding a free-trade scissors to cut Uncle Sam(son's) hair.[54] Rebuffing her, Uncle Sam refuses the haircut and maintains his strength. While both of these cartoons reference the past and assume an education or a familiarity with the Bible on the part of the paper's readers, the cartoon published on October 22 showed a modified image of a gramophone with the Democratic donkey instead of a dog, referencing the Victor Talking Machine's logo while the text mimicked its catchphrase "his master's voice." This allusion to contemporary life in the United States is supplemented by the text underneath the Trojan Horse cartoon. Referring to an era of "search lights and x rays," the cartoon text makes the point that a Trojan horse would not fool people on this occasion because of new technological advances. In using these contemporary cultural references, the cartoonist related the image to readers' lives and experiences and also suggested that Americans were too advanced to be taken in by such old-fashioned scams as a Trojan horse.

The later cartoons in 1909 and 1911 draw on the idea of a tariff wall made of bricks that can be built up or taken apart brick by brick, as suggested by the *Irish World* in the case of the Payne-Aldrich Tariff Act of 1909 or friendly neighbors talking over a wall in the case of Canada's and the United States' reciprocity treaty of 1911.[55] The most iconic image used by the cartoonist was that of George Washington stalling a woodcutter congressman's hand (Payne) in cutting down the protection of American industries tree in 1911 and relating the protection issue to a founding principle and to an honest and virtuous politician. The cherry tree myth was well known to all Americans and was carried in the McGuffey readers used in American schools.[56]

These tropes of American life and symbols of American cultural literacy were offset by the consistent appearance in these cartoons of John Bull representing the British Empire. The *Irish World* was implacably opposed to the British Empire because of its treatment of Ireland and captured the essence of its opposition in a cartoon published on April 22, 1905, entitled "What We Hate—Why We Hate," featuring the convict John Bull in stocks and a list of his high crimes against Ireland.[57]

The appearance of John Bull in *Irish World* cartoons was therefore well established and would have been familiar to readers of the *Irish World* as a threatening, sly, and untrustworthy figure in relation to Irish affairs. Including this symbol in cartoons that dealt specifically with American issues was designed to evoke emotions and connotations with previous representations, and this symbol's interocularity conveyed the same message to readers in the American context as it did in the context of Ireland. The very presence of the John Bull symbol in a cartoon signified menace and intimidation even if the character did not appear himself to be dangerous.

There was in America at the turn of the century what Stephen Tuffnell terms "a discourse of Anglophobia" that came to the fore as the United States became more commercially prosperous and industrially powerful at the end of the nineteenth century, and which became

9.5. *Irish World*, April 22, 1905.

a cipher and a "negative referent in the expression of a positive sense of American nationality."[58] At the same time, there was a discourse of Anglo-Saxonism celebrating racial exceptionalism and the civilization of the race, particularly in relation to overseas conquests and the advent of an American imperialism after 1898. This led to an era of rapprochement between Britain and the United States, especially after 1910.[59] This trend of celebrating Anglo-Saxonism was anathema to the *Irish World* and was to be resisted and rejected at every opportunity. Part of this resistance included highlighting the machinations of Britain to influence American policy or to ingratiate itself with Americans. This Anglophobia as manifested in the *Irish World* certainly had its origins in Irish American hatred of England, but the paper also exploited the wariness of Americans toward Britain, its attempts to set its own course, define its own identity, and determine its own interests at home and abroad. Sensitive to the perils of exclusion in the United States as an immigrant group, and still insecure about their own status within society, Irish Americans strove to be *of* the nation and not just *in* it at the beginning of the twentieth century. A core aspect of a separate American identity was economic nationalism, and this is what the *Irish World* espoused and promoted in the face of increased pressure from Britain for free trade. Because the Democratic Party was associated with the policy of free trade, it was therefore regarded as being hand in glove with Britain during this period.

This linking of the Democrats with treacherous British influence on trade had its origins in the American Civil War and became associated with the administrations of Grover Cleveland in 1888 and in 1894 as the Republicans questioned his patriotism and accused him of being prepared to put Britain first in the matter of free trade.[60] This led to a front-page cartoon of the "Cleveland Band" rehearsing a rendition of "God Save the Queen" under the conductor Grover Cleveland in December 1893, while the text stated that "Hail Columbia" and "The Star Spangled Banner" were "vulgar airs."[61] Based on the proposed reinstatement of Queen Lili'uokalani to the throne in Hawaii by Cleveland in 1894, the cartoon's underlying message emphasized Cleveland's and the Democratic Party's fascination with the British policy of free trade.[62] This was much more openly conveyed in the 1904 election campaign as is clear from the Trojan horse and the gramophone cartoons. John Bull directs Belmont and Parker up the ladder into the wooden horse which bears the inscription "Made in England" on its base.[63] The gramophone in the later cartoon belongs to John Bull and "his master's voice" bellows free-trade orders at the Democratic candidate.[64] Cheap English goods and manufactures carried by a delighted John Bull make their way into the United States in 1909 through the gap created in the tariff wall by the Payne-Aldrich Tariff Act as the threat to American wages of the dismantling protection is made clear.[65] This, then, is the broad and expansive environment in which the *Irish World* conveyed its views on protectionism encompassing opposition to free trade, the Democratic Party program, the influence of the British on American policy, and its support for the protection of labor and wages in the United States. This led the paper to support Republican candidates such as Roosevelt for the presidency in 1904.

John Bull and Japan

The signing of the Anglo-Japanese Alliance on January 20, 1902, was not marked by a cartoon in the *Irish World*, but the Russo-Japanese War, which began in February 1904, spawned a series of anti-Japanese cartoons published between September 1905 (after the war's end) up to May 1913. The notion of a "yellow peril," associated with Chinese migration to California in particular, was already prevalent in the United States, where white citizens saw Chinese emigrants as competitors for jobs. This "threat" had been exploited by Irishman and labor activist, Denis Kearney, in San Francisco in the 1870s and 1880s and led to the Chinese Exclusion Act of 1882.[66] The term was also commonly used in Europe, particularly by Kaiser Wilhelm II of Germany, to justify colonial acquisitions in China and to encourage Russia to curb the ambitions of Japan in the east. An editorial in the *Irish World* in September 1904 accused the Japanese of aiming for an overlordship of the Pacific if they were successful in the war against Russia and of "attempting to enact the role England once played in world affairs . . . [to] become the robber nation of the twentieth century."[67] The cartoon

9.6. *Irish World*, September 16, 1905.

published in September of the following year, after Japan had won the war, juxtaposed the encouragement of the Japanese in their imperialist ambitions by John Bull through the Anglo-Japanese alliance and the threat of the "yellow peril" to the United States.[68]

This threat was compounded by the anger of the Japanese at what they perceived to be the unfair terms of the Treaty of Portsmouth, which was mediated by President Roosevelt.[69] A rabble of Japanese identified by stereotypical eyes, dress, and hair cast rocks at Uncle Sam and carried threatening clubs, while in the background, more Japanese made their way with smoking torches toward him. The nature of the Japanese threat is interestingly portrayed as being almost medieval in this instance as the cartoonist appeared to suggest that in spite of their win over Russia, the Japanese and their "weapons" as portrayed here would be no match for the United States. Uncle Sam, holding the Russo-Japanese Treaty disinterestedly, walks away, but John Bull slyly peeps out from behind the wall holding the Anglo-Japanese Alliance. The word "foretaste" in the text of the cartoon suggested that the threat to the United States was only beginning from the Japanese and British together, and this was compounded by a front-page cartoon the following month showing John Bull and Japan, arm in arm clutching a club each on which was inscribed "the bully of the west" and "the bully of the east," respectively.

Captioned "Looking for Trouble," the absent Uncle Sam had only to be imagined in the middle, across the Atlantic from Britain and across the Pacific from Japan.[70] While the smaller Japan personification in the cartoon could be explained by the smaller stature of the Japanese more generally, size in cartoons normally refers to a discrepancy in power relations.[71] The continuing portrayal of Japan in the *Irish World* cartoons saw him as consistently smaller than John Bull, who was styled in various cartoons as his "mentor" in war,[72] his "trainer" in fighting,[73] and his "teacher" in the "school" of imperialist policy.[74] The primacy of Britain in the evil canon of imperialism as seen by the *Irish World* was still unsurpassed, and other countries new to the pursuit of imperial acquisitions were still learning the trade perfected by Britain.

Looking for Trouble.

9.7. *Irish World*, October 7, 1905.

These cartoons echo those published in 1899 and in 1901 when McKinley stood accused by the *Irish World* of aping British imperialism in the Philippines. While McKinley himself was condemned in a cartoon published in February 1899 of throwing out all the key documents of the United States—including the Declaration of Independence, the Monroe Doctrine, and the Constitution, which he kicked into a fire—he was surrounded by objects reminiscent of the Roman Empire including a wastebasket shaped like the coliseum and

9.8. *Irish World*, May 4, 1901.

a crown on a cushion with the title "Guliemus Primus Imperator." Senator Hoar of Connecticut asked in January 1899 who would "haul down the flag" in the unconstitutional war, and the *Irish World* asked the same question as the country appeared to be drunk on "Imperial sec."[75] But the paper explicitly placed the United States as following Britain's imperial trajectory in its front-page cartoon of May 4, 1901.

Uncle Sam waited in "Dr. Mars's" waiting room, which sported framed pictures of land and sea battles on its walls, holding his ailment, the "Philippines." John Bull emerged with a million-dollar bottle of medicine to cure his ailment, the "Boer War." The text of the cartoon suggested that money was the only medicine to cure John Bull's "robber constitution" and that it also might cure Uncle Sam, who was going the same route in the Philippines.[76] This modeling of British imperialism, communicated by placing the figure of John Bull in recurring cartoons, invited condemnation of any country or leader who followed Britain's lead and example, and this was a reliable trope in the cartoons published in the *Irish World* and drawn by a variety of cartoonists.

But there was more to the anti-Japanese viewpoint of the *Irish World* than Japan's association with Britain. Although Cian McMahon maintains that the cartoons in the *Irish World* between 1870 and 1880 showed support for other nonwhite people around the world, this cannot be said for either the Japanese or the Chinese in the cartoons published in the paper at the beginning of the twentieth century.[77] Anti-Japanese sentiment had been centered on California, where the majority of Japanese immigrants lived and the formation of the Japanese and Korean Exclusion League there in 1905 sought to emulate the successful Chinese Exclusion Acts of 1882 and 1892. Renamed the Asiatic Exclusion League in 1907, it campaigned to exclude Asian immigrants on the West Coast of America in order to protect white labor.[78] Because of this hostility in the United States, Japanese immigrants began arriving in Canada, and by 1907, there were ten thousand immigrants in British Columbia. Aided by American labor activists, a new exclusion league was formed in Vancouver, and riots occurred there in September 1907.[79] On September 21, 1907, the *Irish World* published a front-page cartoon featuring a Canadian carrying an exclusion flag in one hand and a club in the other, chasing a Japanese immigrant back into a rowboat. He is halted by John Bull with the Anglo-Japanese Alliance in his pocket, who protests that he is Japan's friend.[80] While the use of John Bull in this cartoon does convey the fact that Britain was the mother country of Canada, and Canada duly acted in accordance with British demands and wishes, it also encouraged condemnation for the British and Japanese position and support for the Canadian rioters and the exclusion league more broadly. The attitude of the paper to this supposed threat of Asian labor was further reinforced by a cartoon published on the eve of the 1912 presidential election when, once again, the *Irish World* supported Theodore Roosevelt, this time over the Democrat Woodrow Wilson.[81] Because of its opposition to Wilson, the *Irish World* focused on Wilson's support for the repeal of the Chinese Exclusion Act and printed a cartoon of the candidate outside a set of factories patting a small, stereotypical Chinese worker on the head paternalistically as an equally sized white worker to Wilson looked on.[82] In spite of Wilson's good record on labor, the *Irish World* evoked anti-Asian sentiment and racial bias in this cartoon to stoke the fear of labor competition among its readers. Wilson won the election.[83]

Conclusions

The rhetorical and visual strategy of the *Irish World* during the period 1890–1913 played to the notion that the United States was out in front, advanced industrially and economically, and that it could maintain and improve that position but only if it remained true to its core principles, ideals, and beliefs. Two of these core principles were isolationism and economic nationalism. Regarding itself as the "national" newspaper of Irish America in the United States, and carrying its editorial position squarely on the front page in the form of a political cartoon, the *Irish World* offered to its readers a "symbolic construction" of political and national identity.[84] By presenting its political preferences for president, it sought to influence national political discourse and election outcomes by mobilizing its readers, not just in an ethnic network, but as a politically smart and effectual collective. Its visual commentary on national issues—whether the election of a president, the pursuit of imperialism, or the maintenance of protective tariffs—became part of a shared visual culture among Irish Americans that familiarized them with American political imperatives and communicated to its readers a significant lesson in American democracy—that their vote counted.

The support for the Republican Party, particularly on a national stage, is an interesting aspect of these cartoons. Colin Seymour-Ure, in his discussion of British cartoonists' views of American politics, suggests that American politics are not primarily about ideology but about people, and that "presidential candidates (to oversimplify) put together electoral coalitions based on who they are, where they come from and what they have done."[85] The *Irish World* regarded the Democratic Party as too loose on the question of economic nationalism and as antilabor; although while that was true in Cleveland's case, it was not in Wilson's. They were both portrayed as Anglophiles. Its cartoons castigated William McKinley for his imperialist policy in spite of his good record on protection and the tariff that actually bore his name in 1900. Yet Theodore R. Roosevelt, who personified the "manly" arts of war, who had personally fought in Cuba, and who was undoubtedly imperialist, was supported on two occasions for the presidency by the paper, lauded as a supporter of labor, and feted as a separatist from Britain in spite of evidence of closer relations between the countries during his tenure. The possibility that personality politics was at play here rather than purely ideological considerations cannot be discounted. There were undoubtedly issues with McKinley's imperialism and Cleveland's free-trade policies that swayed the editorial position of the paper. But the generous leeway given to Roosevelt does suggest that he was liked as a person, whatever some of his beliefs. He was also from Manhattan, one of "their own," and this might also be considered as appealing to the editor and the readers of the newspaper alike. The alignment of the paper with Republican Party planks more generally in the context of national policy marks a noteworthy and thought-provoking aspect of Irish American political affiliation.

There are elements of these political cartoons that capture contemporary convictions about race and the manner in which racial bias was expressed at the time. While the stereotypical caricatures of the Japanese were clearly drawn and readily identifiable in the cartoons, their alignment with the British through the iconic association with John Bull conflated the old Irish enemy and the possible new American one. Either way, the cartoons suggested, the Asians generally were internal competitors and external foes. The prevalence of these images on the front pages of the *Irish World* during this period suggests the utilization of the contemporary prejudices of Irish Americans in an American setting to inflect political outcomes. The environment of a rising America of innovation and progress is conveyed particularly effectively through taken-for-granted symbols such as the gramophone. The use of these contemporary, cultural references spoke to the idea of a rising, advanced America in comparison to the old world and the effort not to be contaminated especially by the British Empire. Condensing these prevailing perceptions into visual metaphors gives us an insight into readers' biases and beliefs during this period.

Cartoons, according to Martin Rowson, are "serious journalism."[86] For the *Irish World* and its readers during 1890 to 1913, they provided a visual space where Irish Americans, who although potentially a powerful voting bloc, may still have been wary of the consequences of making their voices heard. But they could collude with the editor in challenging prevailing orthodoxies in a way that did not antagonize or confront native-born Americans or threaten their position within the status quo.[87]

10

"Readiness and Range"

Margaret Sullivan: Irish Nationalist, American Journalist

Gillian O'Brien

Margaret Buchanan Sullivan was one of the foremost journalists of her generation. Her motto was "Readiness and Range," and her ability to produce fast, erudite copy on an astonishing variety of subjects, including politics, finance, editorials, art, education, and architecture, was the secret of her success.[1] In her private life, she had three key interests—Irish nationalism, the Catholic Church, and education—and while her journalism, books, and poetry reflect all three, she also used her pen to promote a range of causes including the rights of women, black Americans, and tenant farmers.[2] Over the course of a thirty-year career, she more than held her own in a man's world, avoiding the limelight (unlike her famous contemporary Nellie Bly), and letting her words speak for themselves. But it was her association with one particular man—her husband—that thrust her repeatedly into the glare of public scrutiny and ultimately threatened to destroy her career.

In her lifetime, Sullivan was highly regarded. The range of topics on which she wrote knowledgably meant she was constantly in demand. One journalist observed that "versatility, inexorable logic and rare beauty of diction" were her "distinguishing traits," another thought her "without superior or even an equal in literature or journalism," while John R. Walsh, the owner of the *Chicago Herald*, described her as "the best living writer of English."[3] Yet, after her death she was almost entirely forgotten, partly because, in an era in which bylines were rarely used, most of her work was unattributed, and she left no archive behind. But within her profession she was well known, and, from the 1870s until close to her death in 1903, she maintained a stellar career. She deserves to be recognized both as a pioneering journalist and as a woman who paved the way for other women to enter the profession.

A Pioneering Woman

When Margaret Sullivan started out as a journalist she was part of a rare breed. Women had been newspaper owners, editors, and journalists from the early eighteenth century, but they were few and far between.[4] Sullivan was certainly part of a pioneering cohort of women, including Margaret E. Sangster, Nellie Bly, Ida Tarbell, Ida B. Wells, Kathleen Conway, and Jennie L. Hopkins, who raised the profile of women in journalism in the late nineteenth century.

In *Occupations for Women*, published in 1897, the educationalist and temperance campaigner Frances E. Willard identified more than sixty suitable occupations ranging from photographer to interior designer to teacher and nurse. Though there were still very few women in journalism, Willard thought it "one of the best professions in the world" for women for "it catches and holds the enthusiasm of the workers as nothing else does. It opens possibilities of attainment that are undreamed of when the first steps are taken."[5] But for those women who secured positions at newspapers, the work was often a precarious and poorly paid career. There were many reports of women being paid "compliments, not cash" for their stories; others complained that men were paid twice the amount for the same work, and a significant proportion did piecework.[6]

At the turn of the twentieth century, it was estimated that women journalists earned between $8 and $100 a week, with the majority earning below $20 a week.[7] In 1895 Margaret E. Sangster, editor of *Harper's Bazaar*, estimated that the top salary for women editors was $5,000, but few earned above $3,000 a year.[8] Margaret Sullivan was commanding an annual salary of $5,200 as principal editorial writer for the *Chicago Herald* in 1893, which made her one of the most highly paid journalists of her era.[9]

By the 1890s Margaret Sullivan was a successful and wealthy woman, but her journey to the top of her profession was not easy. While Sullivan certainly did not lack for enthusiasm and ability, the world she entered could be hostile. Women journalists were largely confined to writing for the society and literature pages, with very few involved in editorial, political, or financial matters.[10] Those who ventured into such male-dominated fields had much to prove. As late as 1901, articles criticizing women journalists were being published. Edward Bok, the editor of *Ladies' Home Journal*, claimed that "a newspaper office certainly tends to make a woman too independent, too free, too broad. It establishes her on a footing with men that is not wise; it gives her opportunities of freedom that are not uplifting."[11] Margaret E. Sangster disagreed with this assessment. She, unsurprisingly, believed women had the ideal skills required to be journalists: "invincible patience, continued attention to details, tireless self-sacrifice, an intuitive vicarious consciousness, power of synthesis, power of analysis, tranquil impartiality, keen discrimination, a habit of surveying both sides of a question."[12] Margaret Sullivan certainly had many of these attributes.

Brief Biography

Margaret Frances Buchanan, the youngest of nine children, was born in County Tyrone in 1847. Soon after Margaret's birth her mother was widowed, and in 1851, the remaining family members moved to Detroit, Michigan, where some of her elder siblings already lived.[13]

She was educated both in a Catholic school run by the nuns of the Society of the Sacred Heart (RSCJ) and at Detroit High School.[14] Following her graduation in 1863, she taught for several years in the Detroit public schools.[15] While teaching, she dipped her toes into journalism, writing for the *Detroit Advertiser and Tribune*, then the leading Republican paper of Michigan.[16]

In the mid-1860s she met Alexander Sullivan, an ambitious young Irish American who would later become her husband. He was the owner of a shoe store that was destroyed in a suspicious fire in 1868, and when several witnesses came forward claiming that the fire was arson and that Sullivan had been seen leaving the shop just before it began, he was arrested. However, Margaret Buchanan provided an alibi, maintaining that Sullivan had been in a church with her at the time of the fire: 11 p.m. Perhaps fearful that the story was implausible, Alexander Sullivan skipped town and headed for Santa Fe, New Mexico. Following Sullivan's hasty departure, Margaret Buchanan moved to Chicago—the first, but not the last, time her association with Alexander Sullivan would result in upheaval. But despite their geographical distance, the couple remained close. In the spring of 1873, Sullivan joined Buchanan in Chicago, and in November 1874, they were married.[17]

Changing Professions

Following her move to Chicago, Margaret Sullivan changed professions, trading the classroom for the world of journalism and daily deadlines. Within a few years she had established herself not only as one of the finest journalists in the Midwest, but in the United States. There are a number of versions of the story of Margaret Sullivan's big break into journalism. The most plausible story is the one where she secured a position with the *Chicago Evening Post* in 1869. The paper's editor, C. H. Ray, recalled that soon after her arrival in Chicago, she appeared at his desk "dressed in plain, but neat attire, with a modest, but reliant and self-possessed manner" and informed him that she was seeking employment.

> I asked her what position she thought she could fill, when she replied in [an] easy confident manner, "I think almost any." . . . Then I said I would like to see what she could do, when,—to my surprise . . . —she quietly removed her coat and hat, and . . . seated herself at a table, which had a supply of writing materials, and with great rapidity dashed off "Copy." After completing her work . . . said she would return the next day.—I picked up the "Copy" with considerable curiosity and was not less surprised at the subject, than at the masterly manner in which it was handled—it was on 'Finance!' . . . She returned the next day, and in the same business-like way . . . she seated herself at a table and again rapidly produced copy, and after

> completing it left in the same manner as on the previous morning. This proved to be a political article of interest, ably handled, and thus for several days she continued taking up a new but live subject each time, and treating each and all in a clear, forcible and masterly manner, and to my great surprise and increasing satisfaction, demonstrated that she fully appreciated what she said at our first interview as to her ability to fill any position on the staff.[18]

This facility to turn her hand to almost any subject was Sullivan's great strength, and by 1873, she was an associate editor on the *Evening Post*.[19] Later she moved to Wilbur F. Storey's *Chicago Times*. Storey was notoriously difficult to work for. His motto was "to print news and to raise hell," and under him the *Times* was, as David Paul Nord put it, "sensational, irreverent, diverse in content, and quick in news coverage."[20] But despite her "calm-faced, kind-eyed, nun-like figure," Sullivan was well able to cope with the feistiness of the newsroom, and Storey allowed "her pen unchecked scope."[21]

Her robust style was often commented on, and she was regularly compared (favorably) to her male counterparts: "Though the most womanly of women in all things that are lovely in women, Margaret Sullivan is a man in resolution, courage, insight, mental force and faculty."[22] The *New York Herald* praised Sullivan for wielding "a strong masculine pen."[23] In a world in which the qualities required for good journalism were regarded as inherently "masculine," praising women for being like men was a regular occurrence. The journalist Jennie L. Hopkins was regarded as the "best newspaper man in Colorado," while Kathleen Conway was described by her editor, John Boyle O'Reilly, as having "the heart of a woman and the brains of a man."[24] Far than being insulted by this, Conway used these very words when praising Margaret Sullivan in an article she wrote after Sullivan's death.[25]

Sullivan was also prolific. In addition to her work as a journalist, she wrote for a range of periodicals while also producing poetry and books. Her nonjournalistic writing is often easily identifiable because, for the most part, it was signed. Much of her journalism was published without a byline, as was the practice at the time.[26] This helped

Sullivan maintain her anonymity, though she was also partly responsible herself.

The poet, editor, and journalist Harriet Monroe bemoaned the fact that "Mrs. Sullivan profoundly respected the anonymity of journalism—in fact the inborn modesty of her character caused her to respect it too much, so that it is difficult to trace and follow the influence of her pen."[27] In this, as in many other aspects of Margaret Sullivan's life and career, she appears contradictory. While she was ambitious, determined, and prepared to stand up for herself (and her husband) when necessary, she had little desire to be famous. Sullivan never cultivated a public persona, preferring her words on the page to represent her. She generally shunned the limelight, rarely agreeing to give speeches or make public appearances. However, on two occasions, in 1876 and in 1889, she found herself in a maelstrom of news stories connected with her husband, whose talent for attracting publicity was not always to his—or her—advantage.

Alexander Sullivan and His Ambitions

In August 1876 Alexander Sullivan shot and killed a school principal, Francis Hanford. In an anonymous letter to the Chicago City Council, Hanford had implied that Margaret Sullivan had had an improper relationship with the mayor, Harvey Colvin.[28] He claimed that she had used her influence not only to secure her husband the position of secretary of the Board of Public Works but also to hamper the public school system on behalf of the Catholic Church, which wanted Church-led (rather than state-led) schools.[29]

Sullivan was incensed and confronted Hanford at his home. When Hanford refused to retract his allegations, Sullivan shot and killed him. After two trials in October 1876 and March 1877, both before the same judge, Sullivan was acquitted, though the evidence clearly showed that he had gone to Hanford's house armed with a pistol and that Hanford himself was unarmed.[30] There were allegations of corruption on the bench and in the jury—the judge had repeatedly taken the side of the defense and allowed Sullivan's supporters to applaud and cheer the defendant throughout the case.[31] Yet, despite widespread negative publicity, neither Margaret nor Alexander Sullivan's careers were severely hampered. Sullivan retained his job with the Board of Public Works, though he had set his sights on a legal career and, by 1879, had been admitted to the Illinois bar.[32]

The primary focus of Sullivan's life lay not within the law courts of Chicago, however. He had larger ambitions, both in domestic politics, where he saw himself as a potential vice president, and across the Atlantic Ocean, where he was determined to play a key role in securing Ireland's independence from Britain.[33] Alexander Sullivan was a member of Clan na Gael, an oath-bound Irish American organization dedicated to achieving Irish freedom from Britain through the use of force. He was politically astute and personally charming, and through the 1870s, he established himself as a central figure in the Irish American republican movement. By 1880 he was a leader of the organization and determined to pursue a policy of attacking high profile targets in Britain. While Margaret Sullivan never explicitly supported her husband's "Dynamite War" in print, she certainly shared his ambition for an Irish republic, and it seems more than likely that she approved of the campaign. As one contemporary observed, "Alexander Sullivan never takes an important step without first consulting his wife."[34]

A "Power" Couple in Chicago

By 1880 the Sullivans were an influential couple in Chicago. Alexander Sullivan dominated the Clan in the city, and the Sullivans counted leading legal, political, and Catholic figures among their friends.[35] In February 1880 they were key figures when the city hosted Charles Stewart Parnell on his fundraising tour of America.[36] Parnell was a member of the British Parliament, president of the Land League, and a man many believed could establish an independent Irish Parliament (a cause better known as "Home Rule"). Parnell's trip was a whirlwind tour of forty cities in fifteen states, but he received the most support in Chicago. While seven thousand came out to greet him in New York, a crowd of between fifteen thousand and twenty thousand assembled in the Interstate Exposition Building in Chicago to see Parnell receive the Freedom of the City on the night of February 23, 1880.[37] As Michael Davitt, the founder of the Land League and close friend of the Sullivans, later recalled: "The hall was full of a vast audience, restive and impatient, full of eagerness to hear the envoys. . . . Among the items on the program which preceded the . . . speakers, was the recitation of a long poem of welcome . . . and this task was performed by a dramatic artiste, a young lady . . . who with other striking attractions, stood over six feet high. . . . The handsome young giantess poured into them and over them for nearly half an hour an elocutionary torrent of praise and worship."[38] Margaret Sullivan wrote a "long poem of welcome" titled "The Irish Famine of 1880." The poem made her political views abundantly clear. Through eight stanzas, she castigated Britain's abuse of Ireland and implored other nations to see that Ireland is "a land of graves."

> Philanthropist and missioner lives on St George's Channel—
> Sends Bibles—to the Pope of Rome, and to the tropics—flannel!
> Prays godly prayers for *foreign* sin before her holy altar,
> The while her hands twist at her back for Ireland's neck a halter!
> In *foreign* lands protects the weak, with treaties—or with cannon!
> And thrusts the dagger to the heart of her sister on the Shannon!
> So generous to her foreign foes they praise her to the sky—
> And leaves her Irish subjects *one* privilege—to die![39]

Coruscating though the poem was, Sullivan's writing generally steered clear of her personal politics.[40] She wrote regularly for a broad range of journals including *Harper's Bazaar*, *Catholic World*, the *Century*, the *Dial*, and the *Catholic Review*. The articles she wrote for Catholic periodicals generally reflected her interest in Irish history and politics rather than religion (though invariably they did touch on the poor treatment of Catholics in Ireland), while those for a broader audience focused on American topics and art and theater reviews.[41] Where her articles considered Irish politics, she sought to give current debates a historical context. She criticized those who spoke of a *restoration* of a national parliament in Ireland for, as she observed, "a parliament which contained no [Catholic] representative can scarcely be designated a national parliament."[42] While dismissing Oliver Cromwell as "that splendid ruffian," she commented that "all through Ireland the American traveller feels [that] the island is pinned down with a bayonet, lest, were the opportunity given, it would slip out to sea or run up the hills and hide itself."[43]

Irish nationalism was just one of Margaret Sullivan's interests. She also wrote passionately on Catholicism.[44] Faith remained a key touchstone throughout her life. Her friend Katherine Conway observed "too many of our Catholic women, once they have attained wealth or intellectual distinction, withdraw themselves as far as possible from all association with their fellow-believers." But Sullivan remained devoted to Catholicism, including Catholic schools and convents.[45]

In 1875 "Chiefly among Women" was published, first anonymously and later under Sullivan's name, in the *Catholic World*. The article was inspired by the British prime minister William Gladstone, who noted that there had been a growth in numbers of Catholics in England and that "the conquests have been chiefly, as might have been expected, among women."[46] Sullivan regarded this as an insult to women, an assumption that they were weak and foolish and susceptible to acts of folly. Her article refuted Gladstone's observation and drew heavily on examples of women in the past from Ariadne to St. Bridget in her discussion of "the power of women in propagating religion."[47] She observed that "women have shared in the establishment of educational institutions from the earliest period. . . . Their resources have founded schools, their talents have conducted them. Whenever, from the days of St. Catherine to those of Nano Nagle, special efforts have been made to teach the people, women have furnished their full share of energy and brains."[48] She concluded that "a religion which makes conquests enough among women . . . is the religion which must conquer the world."[49]

In her journal articles, she wrote on topics as diverse as Bohemian philosophers and revolutions in farm life. One of her particular passions was for libraries. She noted "a mental desert without books has blossomed into the travelling library. The despair of fine art is turned into rapturous glimpses by the travelling picture library. The portable school-house and chapel on wheels are factors in a radical and irreversible change."[50] In the aftermath of the Chicago Fire of 1871, Sullivan wrote editorials championing the creation of a public library. The idea commanded huge public support and on January 1, 1873, the Chicago Public Library reopened its doors.

In the early 1890s, she wrote a series of articles for the *Chicago Herald* that advocated higher education for women. She observed that women had provided large sums of money to support men's colleges while women's colleges were in need. In response, the Chicago Women's Club in 1893 raised $280,000 to build two dormitory halls for women at the "new" University of Chicago.[51]

Supporting the Irish Republican Cause

Sullivan's personal politics might have mirrored those of her husband, but their approaches to the cause were very different. In the early 1880s, while Alexander Sullivan was organizing a series of bomb attacks on Britain, Margaret Sullivan was using her pen to generate support for the cause of Irish freedom. While in her journalism she tended to steer clear of Irish politics, as an author Sullivan had a free hand to write about subjects close to her heart, and in 1881 her book, *Ireland of To-day: Causes and Aims of Irish Agitation*, was published. In *Ireland of To-day,* Sullivan focused on Irish land issues. The book was written for an Irish American audience, for, as T. P. O'Connor, member of Parliament and Home Rule campaigner, pointed out in his introduction to the book, "it is one of the disadvantages of the Irish people in this struggle that their history is told to the world by their enemies, for the English newspaper . . . is the authority which the mass of mankind accepts."[52]

Much of the book was preoccupied with the Land League, an organization established in 1879 by her close friend Michael Davitt. The League, which was focused on improving tenants' rights to the land they lived on and farmed, was largely controlled by Davitt, though Parnell was its president. Between 1879 and 1881 the "Land War" took place in Ireland as the Land League sought to secure the "3 Fs—'Fair Rent, Free Sale and Fixity of Tenure'" for tenants. Sullivan robustly defended the League, which she argued was "organized for a moral, human and righteous purpose; led by men of the highest personal character; directed by methods strictly constitutional . . . the Irish National Land League was proclaimed illegal by the English government in Ireland and suppressed by force. Its foremost men are imprisoned, unaccused, untried. . . . All liberty in Ireland is dead."[53] Sullivan was determined that Irish Americans (indeed all Americans) understood the Irish Question, which she summed up succinctly:

> England and Ireland are members of the British empire. They are supposed to enjoy alike the benefits of the British constitution; . . . But England is the richest, Ireland the poorest, country in the empire. . . . Irishmen prefer to live in their native country, yet there are four times as many of them in foreign countries as in their own: with them emigration has been a chronic national necessity. England hums with manifold industries; Ireland's vast waterpower, capable of turning the machinery of the world is silent. England's wharves are forests of masts; Ireland's beautiful harbors are empty except when the English ship carries away the products of her soil. . . . England governs Ireland by her enemies and in hatred.[54]

Sullivan was certain that the Irish diaspora would ensure Irish freedom: "Five millions of the Irish people in Ireland may be deprived of constitutional rights; twenty millions of the Irish people in the United States, in Australia and in Canada are free. They know that there can never be happiness or prosperity in their motherland until her laws are made by her own people on her own soil."[55] This call to arms was not explicitly encouraging men to follow her husband's path, but it certainly did not discourage them, and there is no evidence that she rejected the idea of using violence rather than parliamentary efforts to secure Irish independence. While she was not a member of Clan na Gael (as membership was restricted to men), it was believed by some that Margaret Sullivan was just as devoted as her husband to a radical solution to Ireland's connection with Britain. Indeed, by the mid-1880s Parnell's relationship with radical Irish America (and the Sullivans) had soured, and when Parnell saw her in the Ladies Gallery of the House of Commons, his reaction was not to think she was writing a newspaper article, but that she had joined her husband's "Dynamite War" and was there to throw a bomb into the house.[56] There is no evidence to suggest that this was ever her intention.

Unsurprisingly, *Ireland of To-Day* found favor among Irish and Irish American nationalists and republicans. Michael Davitt praised it as a "brilliant survey of the Irish movement from the earliest times. . . . [Sullivan] brought the salient facts of Ireland's history with great literary skill before the wide circle of her readers." James Redpath, a journalist and antislavery campaigner, thought her book was "the best statement of the case of Ireland that has ever been made."[57] The book was a commercial success, selling over thirty thousand copies.[58]

More Savvy Than Her Husband

Alexander Sullivan harbored ambitions to enter American domestic politics, but some regarded Margaret as much more savvy than her husband. Indeed, Secretary of State James G. Blaine reportedly said that "if she were a man he would like to send her as minister to one of the capitals of Europe."[59]

Margaret Sullivan never embarked on a glittering diplomatic career, but she did get to travel to Europe as a journalist. Her overseas reporting was not for one Chicago paper but for the Associated Press (AP). From the mid-1880s Sullivan wrote regularly for the AP, which syndicated her work across the United States.[60] She may not have sought fame for herself, but she was undoubtedly gratified to have her words read across the continent, for she boasted to the Irish poet and novelist Katharine Tynan that "she represented ten thousand American newspapers."[61]

In the summer of 1886, as the AP's London correspondent, she wrote a series of color articles about the current state of British politics. Given her firmly held beliefs regarding Britain and Ireland, these articles were surprisingly evenhanded. Indeed, she described the prime minster William Gladstone as "the most beneficent, the noblest, the most illustrious career in modern statesmanship. . . . He has not hesitated to confess error." Reflecting optimism that Ireland would be granted Home Rule, she concluded that "no one doubts that an overwhelming Liberal majority will confirm the great Minister's determination to plant the germ of Home Rule in Ireland."[62]

Her greatest journalistic coup took place in Paris in 1889 when she represented the AP at the Paris Exposition. The AP general manager expressly requested that the *Chicago Tribune* release Margaret Sullivan for three months so she could report on the exposition. Sullivan had been selected as the AP correspondent by some of the most influential newspapermen of the day, including Charles A. Dana of the *New York Sun*, Joseph Medill of the *Chicago Tribune*, and Whitelaw Reid of the *New York Tribune.* She was commissioned to write five thousand words on the exhibition and the opening ceremony plus four more three-thousand-word articles on fine arts, industrial arts, education, and manufacture, a commission reflecting both her polymathic qualities and her contemporaries' acknowledgement of them.[63] Nevertheless, when she arrived in Paris she discovered that she alone of all the journalists had not received a pass for the opening day ceremonies. Furious, she sent a series of letters to US Secretary of State Blaine, the president of the Associated Press, and the French president Marie François Sadi Carnot. Carnot replied that "the French Republic has never given official recognition to a lady." The indignant Sullivan retorted, "Your Excellency, it is time the French Republic created a precedent." A pass was provided, and she became the only woman to have access to the opening ceremony.[64]

Sullivan clearly reveled in her Parisian stay: "To-night Paris is ablaze with illumination. . . . The city is the people's . . . a vast unified picture, alive with color, its great avenues, colossal arches, numerous and massive bridges, spacious parks and squares, majestic monuments and pillars, clean thoroughfares, dazzling atmosphere, reflecting the sunlight upon the limestone."[65] Her account of a glittering Paris made the front page of many US newspapers including the *New York Tribune*, as did her series of articles on the content of the exposition.[66] Her star had never been brighter. However, just as she reached the peak of her fame, and her (signed) work was being syndicated across the United States, a fresh crisis engulfed the Sullivans.

Fresh Accusations

On May 4, 1889, while Margaret Sullivan was in Paris, Dr. Patrick Cronin, a Chicago physician, disappeared. Until recently, he had been a member of Clan na Gael, but he had fallen out with Alexander Sullivan, claiming he was a "professional patriot" only interested in Irish freedom to further his own career. Their dispute came to a head when Cronin accused Sullivan of embezzling $100,000 of Clan funds. Cronin was expelled from the Clan, but the disagreement rumbled on. The Clan split, with one side following Sullivan while another (led by John Devoy and Cronin) continued to insist that Sullivan was corrupt. When Cronin went missing, fingers (and newspaper columns) began to point at Sullivan. Two weeks after he disappeared, Cronin's naked and beaten body was pulled from a sewer in North Chicago. Sullivan was the prime suspect, and on June 11, he was arrested on suspicion of murder.[67]

The first Margaret Sullivan knew of his arrest was a telegraph from her husband urging her to stay away from Chicago: "Don't be alarmed . . . Arrested . . . Don't think of coming." As instructed she did not hasten home, cabling her husband: "Judgment against immediate return. Am with friends. All send assurance, affection. Be firm. Real nature of attack on you understood. It will be completely exploded. Your vindication will compensate for temporary injustice."[68]

At least outwardly, Margaret Sullivan appeared unperturbed by the storm engulfing her husband. From Paris she traveled to London, where she spent time with Michael Davitt and other figures in Irish political life, attended the Parnell Commission, and mixed with poets and artists such as the young W. B. Yeats, Sydney Prior Hall, and Sarah Purser. Yeats was quite taken with her and wrote to his friend Katharine Tynan, "I have seen a good deal of Mrs Alexander Sullivan. She is looking much better than when I wrote last and seems to have quite recovered her spirits."[69] Tynan, on the other hand, was skeptical of Margaret Sullivan's behavior, noting that upon hearing of her husband's predicament "we were all sympathetic and set out to be very conciliatory but . . . she brightened up so much that we concluded she knew everything and believed that he would soon be released, which he was. I think she had the deliberate intention at that time of appearing everywhere she could and meeting as many people—of facing the music, so to speak, and confuting by her presence those who might have believed her husband guilty."[70]

It was perhaps an indication of the fame of the Sullivans, and the attention paid across the United States to Alexander Sullivan's arrest, that, while in London, Margaret Sullivan issued a statement about the murder. She claimed to be "deeply pained at the falsehood of the imputation implied in associating her husband's name with the Cronin mystery," but the "knowledge of her husband's absolute ignorance of the crime sustains her." She railed against "Chicago newspaper rot" and "malignant aspersions of personal or political enemies."[71] Sullivan's statement was carried in newspapers across the country and for the second time in her career, much against her will, Margaret Sullivan had become the story.

While in London Sullivan made a rare incursion into reporting on Irish affairs.[72] The Parnell Commission had been established to investigate alleged links between Parnell and radical Irish republicanism. If such links were proven, Parnell's political career would be destroyed. Sullivan had a personal as well as professional interest in the commission as the revelations emerging from it about Parnell's links to radical republicanism potentially had repercussions for her husband. In the wake of his arrest, Alexander Sullivan's role in Clan na Gael and his relationship with Parnell were under scrutiny.[73]

In July 1889 Margaret Sullivan returned to Chicago. She found the atmosphere in the city highly charged. The Cronin murder, together with the subsequent trial, dominated the newspapers in the city from May to December, and despite Margaret Sullivan's close connection to many of the editors, she could do nothing to save her husband's reputation. Although Alexander Sullivan was neither a witness nor a defendant at the trial, he was regularly referred to by both prosecution and defense, and newspapers continually linked him to the murder, prompting an exasperated Margaret Sullivan to exclaim, "We have a fine assortment of stupids writing now for the Chicago press."[74]

Indeed, despite Margaret Sullivan's long relationship with the *Chicago Tribune*, it was that paper that functioned most consistently as a mouthpiece for the Cronin faction of Clan na Gael as Cronin's friends fed their version of the feud to James Sullivan (no relation of Alexander Sullivan), a reporter on the paper. Margaret Sullivan complained vigorously that the paper and others were biased against her husband. She was so incensed that she returned an advance the *Tribune* had given her, insisting that "until it makes some reparation for its brutality I will not write a line for it." She claimed that no paper was fair to her husband, and the best they could hope for was that some of the papers were "not offensive."[75]

In December 1889 four of the five men accused of Cronin's murder were found guilty, with three sentenced to life imprisonment. All had connections to Clan na Gael and Alexander Sullivan and, despite the lack of significant evidence, the public consensus was that he must have ordered the attack. The coverage of the Cronin murder and subsequent trial ruined Alexander Sullivan's career and clearly embittered Sullivan toward her chosen profession. In 1893 she described journalism as "the literary form of commerce that collects, corrupts and diffuses misinformation," yet despite her cynicism, she continued to use that literary form (and others) to promote causes she believed in.[76]

In many ways she had no choice. In the wake of the Cronin trial her husband was persona non grata within radical Irish America, and the couple had accrued significant debts. Alexander Sullivan's law practice suffered heavily, and his partner left. Certainly in the years immediately after the Cronin murder, Margaret Sullivan was the principal earner. Wisely, she steered clear of Irish politics in her journalism and did not return to the *Chicago Tribune*. By 1892 she was principal editorial writer on the *Chicago Herald*.[77]

Conclusion

In September 1896 Margaret Sullivan suffered a severe stroke, and it was feared she would not survive.[78] She recovered and resumed her journalism. She left the *Herald* and took a position as editorial writer with the *Chicago Chronicle* and continued to write for other publications, including *Harper's Bazaar* and the *Dial.* However, in December 1903, she suffered a second catastrophic stroke and died on December 28 at the age of fifty-six. John Finerty's Chicago-based Irish American newspaper the *Citizen* announced her death by declaring "the most brilliant woman of the Irish race is dead." Many eulogies followed. The *New World* noted that "it will always be a source of lasting regret . . . that she left no original work in book form truly representative of her phenomenal ability. As an editorial writer she had no superior on the American press, but alas all who know editorial writing know also that it is ephemeral, so far as fame of the writer is concerned. . . . The public is content to be stirred without caring to remember the name of the one who so moved public opinion."[79]

In an obituary, Harriet Monroe praised Sullivan's "combination of powers: the union of masculine strength and range with feminine delicacy and tenderness of precision. . . . She did a man's work in the great world and yet lived with singular intensity a woman's life."[80] She may have done "a man's work in a man's world," but she was mindful of the position of women. Indeed, championing the underdog was a constant theme throughout her life. She advocated for the establishment of free public libraries, perhaps reflecting the fact that she did not come from a wealthy background. She used her skills as teacher to pass on advice and knowledge to a new generation of women, whether mentoring them in newsrooms or inviting them to join her Dante Club—where young women read Dante in Italian—or her Foreign Book Club to discuss foreign literature.[81] She actively demanded that women be more visible in the arts and advocated greater legal rights for women, particular in relation to divorce.[82]

To a large extent Margaret Sullivan remains an enigma. She was talented, ambitious, and successful. She was one of the most prolific women journalists of her generation, yet she never courted publicity, and much of her newspaper work remains to be identified. A passionate campaigner, she committed herself to a variety of causes some of which, such as Catholicism and Irish nationalism, were far from universally popular. Perhaps the greatest mystery surrounds her decision to marry Alexander Sullivan, a suspected arsonist (and later murderer) whose thirst for power sometimes cast them both in a very unfavorable light. But what can be said is that Margaret Sullivan was a standard bearer for women in journalism, a profession that, casting off her bitterness in later years, she praised for mirroring the world "with a precision and sweep unequalled by any other branch of human industry."[83]

At the beginning of her career, a mere thirty-five women identified themselves as journalists, amounting to just 0.6 percent of US journalists.[84] Over the course of the next thirty years, in which Margaret Sullivan became one of the highest paid and most respected journalists of her generation, the number of women journalists in the United States swelled to 2,190 (7 percent of 30,098 journalists).[85] Though she was not single-handedly responsible for this increase, there is no doubt that her role as a consistent and enthusiastic mentor of women in journalism played a significant part.

1900s

11

"Manufactured News" and Michael Davitt's Journalism in South Africa and Russia for William Randolph Hearst

Colum Kenny

In 1900 and again between 1903 and 1905 Michael Davitt, radical Irish nationalist and journalist, was commissioned as a foreign correspondent for the "yellow-journalism" US newspapers of William Randolph Hearst. Davitt (1846–1906) was a prolific writer.[1] In addition to books, political tracts, and essays he wrote very many articles for newspapers in Ireland and elsewhere. He even launched and edited briefly his own labor weekly in England.[2]

But what of his style and purpose as a journalist? Davitt's passionate reporting from the Russian empire for Hearst won him the gratitude of Jews internationally. His pieces on a pogrom in Kishineff (also Kishinev, today Chişinaŭ, Moldova) are said to have had a lasting impact on international perceptions of Jewish history. Yet, Davitt's own position on anti-Semitism was somewhat ambivalent, and his journalism did not always reveal either this or other of his contradictions and conflicts of interest. This chapter explores Davitt's assignments as a foreign correspondent in the context of his personal attitudes and motivations and with reference to journalism's professional standards.

A Working Journalist and Politician

Many who know of Davitt see him as a Fenian and founder of the Land League, an association that promoted the interests of Irish tenant farmers. However, from the 1880s, he was also a correspondent for papers that included the *New York Daily News*, the *Melbourne Advocate*, London's *Pall Mall Gazette*, and Dublin's *Evening Telegraph*.[3] His ambition to succeed Edmund Dwyer Gray as editor of the Irish *Freeman's Journal* when the latter died in 1888 was dashed after Charles Stewart Parnell intervened in favor of a less radical choice, and so Davitt turned, for a while, to politics.[4]

In 1893, upon his election to the United Kingdom Parliament for Cork North-East, the standard parliamentary reference book described Davitt as "a journalist and political lecturer."[5] He had first trained as a printer. Although he had lost his right arm working in a Lancashire cotton mill at the age of eleven, Davitt managed somehow to become a skilled apprentice, deftly typesetting, as his astonished English employer attested publicly in 1863.[6] As was often the case in the nineteenth century, Davitt used his training in printing to move over to the editorial side of journalism.

Davitt had particular expectations of professionalism. When he sailed to cover the Boer War in 1900, Davitt took a dim view of one drunken English correspondent on his ship. Davitt wrote that, "This war will tend to extinguish genuine war correspondents. The amateurs now in South Africa . . . will cover this branch of the journalistic profession with ridicule."[7] Later, in Russia, he condemned the English press for its "carnival of falsehoods."[8] As regards his own professional standards, one recent biographer has claimed that "there is no evidence to suggest that in his various journalistic commissions, Davitt was ever guilty of self-censorship, or of having tailored his reports to conform to the line taken by a particular paper."[9] But does he, in fact, merit quite such lavish praise?

Davitt seems to have been relatively well remunerated for some articles, but in general his journalism did not provide him with a substantial income. Moody refers to him "earning a modest and precarious livelihood by his exertions as a journalist and a public speaker."[10] His socialist friend Henry Hyndman wrote that "Davitt was always struggling against poverty and was very badly paid for the journalistic and lecturing work which he did, [but] he rarely or never complained of his lot."[11] Still, Davitt's journalism was in demand and W. T. Stead, editor of the renowned British *Review of Reviews*, praised his dispatches from South Africa. Davitt's pieces from Russia would win him international acclaim.

Nevertheless, Davitt's articles for newspapers were generally excluded from that collection of his writings published in eight volumes in 2001. They were excluded because "Davitt was a working journalist. . . . The sheer volume of his journalism could not have been encompassed in this collection. Moreover, some of his journalism dealt with ephemeral issues, and other themes he reworked in his books."[12] Yet, journalism is not necessarily less accurate or less significant politically and intellectually than are other forms of observation, or less valuable as a source for historians. Memory or ideology may even render later "reworked" accounts of events less accurate or reliable than the proverbial "first draft of history" that is written for an imminent deadline.

South Africa 1900

In 1899 Davitt resigned his seat in Parliament in protest over the Anglo-Boer War. Like most Irish Catholic nationalists, he supported the Boers, notwithstanding their Protestant faith and the plight of native African populations in areas where the Boers settled. Irish nationalists regarded England's continuing expansion into Boer South Africa, which was due in part to the discovery of valuable diamond mines there, as somehow analogous to its conquest of Ireland many centuries before.

Davitt wanted to see for himself how the Boers were faring and persuaded the *Freeman's Journal* in Dublin to commission him to write some articles on the war. Boarding a ship at Marseilles, he received a cable from W. T. Stead telling him that William Randolph Hearst's

New York Journal (soon to be retitled the *New York American*) would also take pieces from him.[13] Stead was already a correspondent for Hearst, and he and Davitt were old friends. They were among the first to demand that Charles Stewart Parnell resign once the O'Shea scandal broke. In 1900 each would urge the other to stand for Parliament.[14]

One of Davitt's greatest challenges in reporting on the Boer War was British censorship. The British effectively insisted on licensing any journalists within their sphere of influence, embedding them with British forces and censoring their copy.[15] More recently, Potter has acknowledged that, during the war, Reuters "suppressed items of news . . . [that it] deemed would damage British interests if released."[16] Further, McCracken has documented that the British military intelligence service used journalists in its campaign to spread pro-British propaganda then. He has also given a brief account of Irish journalists who between 1827 and 1922 went to South Africa, writing that more than seventy journals employed more than 260 foreign journalists during the Boer War. Davitt, he noted, "the most famous Irish war correspondent was very different from the hacks who followed the [British commander, Frederick] Roberts' media circus up through the Orange Free State into the Transvaal. . . . He . . . sent home strongly worded pro-Boer reports."[17]

Davitt worried about being arrested later in London.[18] He had, after all, actively attempted to raise military support in Europe for the Boer cause. His stories now were calculated to further the Boer struggle in accordance with the anti-British disposition of his readers. He showed little interest in how the Boers treated indigenous people, or "kaffirs" and "savages," as he called them, but claimed that they did so better than the English did.

Davitt approved of censorship for military reasons. In his diary, he records a sleepy Sunday in Pretoria (April 8, 1900), where the Boer's post office was only open for one hour despite the fact that a war was being waged. He gave his copy for the *Freeman's Journal* to the postmaster, a "genial fellow" and "a good storyteller." Davitt wrote, "Handed my letters to the Postmaster general today to be

11.1. Michael Davitt in the Orange Free State, 1900. Frontispiece of his *Boer Fight for Freedom* (New York: Funk & Wagnalls, 1902).

censored. . . . All letters going from here to British territories are read and rightly so. Otherwise men could send information and plans to the enemy of this state."[19] For its news from the Boer War more generally the *Freeman's Journal* had little choice but to depend largely on the Press Association, Reuters, and English papers such as the *Times* and *Daily Mail.*

The *Freeman's Journal* was in decline by 1900.[20] It did not usually engage its own correspondents abroad, so Davitt's arrangement is striking. However, due to delays perhaps caused by British authorities, pieces that Davitt wrote in South Africa from the end of March 1900 onward did not begin to appear in the paper in Dublin until more than two months later, and Hearst's New York newspaper did not prominently display pieces by him from Africa as it later did his dispatches from Russia. His dozen substantial pieces in the *Freeman's Journal,* each about three columns long on average, usually appeared on page five or six, but were repeated on the front page of successive editions of the *Weekly Freeman's Journal* during June, July, and August 1900, with some of the articles also repeated along with added images in the Irish *Evening Telegraph.*[21]

On July 9, 1900, the *Freeman's Journal* boasted that, after Davitt had written about events at Magersfontein, some of the English correspondents going over the same ground as him "are forced to substantiate the details." The editor added, "It is most amusing, if not at times nauseating, to go back six or seven months on the files of the Jingo papers and compare the news supplied then with the facts which now stand revealed."

Davitt described the pieces he wrote for the *Freeman's Journal* as a "series of sketches of Boer camps, battles, officers, men and matters." In a standard refrain of his, he claimed that the Boer people had been "foully calumniated by the Jingo Press of Cape Town and London in order to manufacture some justification for the deliberate robbery and wilful murder of a small nation for the possession of great mineral wealth."[22]

Davitt himself was accused of censorship by Arthur Griffith, a leader of advanced nationalist opinion in Ireland. Griffith was an enthusiastic admirer of Parnell, whom Davitt had quickly abandoned when the O'Shea scandal broke. After Davitt resigned his seat in Parliament, Griffith and others nominated John MacBride as an independent candidate for the South Mayo vacancy in early 1900. MacBride was then fighting on the Boer side, with an Irish Transvaal brigade of up to three hundred men that he had organized against the British. Davitt declined to back MacBride, and a more conservative nationalist won the seat. Griffith's *United Irishman* later claimed that Davitt, "a man of warped mind rather than of bad heart," failed to give MacBride the credit due for his contribution to some Boer victories.[23]

Davitt used the interview technique to bolster his reports, this being a popular feature of the "new journalism" that had been pioneered in Britain by his friend W. T. Stead among others. Marley writes that, "Given his reputation as a Boer sympathiser, Davitt had no difficulty in securing interviews with the Boer leaders."[24] Stead thought that Davitt's letters for the *Freeman's Journal* were "the first really serious attempts that have been made to describe the Burghers' War of Independence from the Boers' point of view."[25] Such reports no doubt appealed to William Randolph Hearst who is said to have had a "monumental anti-British bias," going back to 1899 when British bankers obstructed his family's mining ambitions in Peru. Indeed, Hearst publicly supported the liberation of Ireland.[26] As his media and political ambitions grew, he also had commercial reasons to cultivate Irish American readers who lived in large numbers in New York and other cities in which he sold papers: "A patchwork of supporters gathered around him, including Irish, German, and liberalistic reformers duped by blarney about municipal ownership." He even stands accused of fixing a race around the world that he sponsored for high school boys, so that the winner would be not only Irish but also from Chicago—where his paper's circulation was in need of a boost.[27] Hearst also poached a cartoon character, "Mickey Dugan," from the New York newspaper of his chief competitor, Joseph Pulitzer. This young character, depicted among Irish immigrants in the New York slums, wore a distinctive cut-off, yellow nightdress and so was nicknamed "The Yellow Kid."[28]

Because much information about the Boer conflict was filtered through a British lens, Hearst would clearly welcome the opportunity to have a famous Irish patriot write from the other side of the conflict. Hearst's policy was "to engage brains as well as to get the news,"[29] and he was inclined to employ public figures to write about current affairs. Hearst angered his regular foreign correspondent, Julian Ralph, when he gave greater prominence to *The Red Badge of Courage* author Stephen Crane's accounts of the Greco-Turkish War and sent Mark Twain to cover Queen Victoria's Diamond Jubilee.[30]

Davitt was already known to some extent in the United States, not merely because of press reports of his role in Irish and British politics, but more specifically because he made a number of visits to America and had written articles for papers there. He might be expected to have an informed idea of what appealed to American readers, and not least to Irish Americans who also imbibed pro-Boer sentiments from the New York weekly *Irish World*.[31] Later in 1900, Hearst also commissioned Davitt to go to Marseilles and Paris to write about the reception of Boer president Paul Kruger there. Davitt understood that Hearst was pleased with his work then.[32]

Cables and the Correspondent

The evolution of cables as a communications medium complicated Davitt's relationship with editors. Telegraph technology permitted journalists to get news back to their newspaper offices quickly, in marked contrast to the earlier methods of overland and overseas mailing. However, long cables were costly and cumbersome to send, and so this new technology encouraged a more staccato style of writing as well as crisp judgments. Wire services such as Reuters and Associated Press took advantage of the telegraph to offer relatively neutral news swiftly from around the world.[33] While the agencies might have their own ideological or business biases,[34] the speed with which their stories moved could quickly render dispatches from individual correspondents in the field out of date, even when the latter eschewed the mail and sent back long cables.[35] The cable thus presented Davitt with a problem. He was conscious of its value to newspapers, noting inside the cover of his South African travel diary in 1900 that there were "170 telegraph offices in two republics [Orange Free State and Transvaal]."[36] However, short factual cables did not suit Davitt's style or purpose, for he was accustomed to mixing facts with both speculation and opinion in pieces that he wrote.

While Davitt was still in South Africa, he had written to John Dillion, "Tell T. P. not to put too much of his earnings in Rand mines. *Thiggin thu* [Irish for 'you understand']." Davitt in the 1890s had acted as an investment agent for mining ventures in Australia, South Africa, and the United States. This "T. P." was presumably "T. P. O'Connor," the journalist and politician who now put work Davitt's way on the latter's return from South Africa. O'Connor had been asked to write an occasional "Irish letter" for syndication in the United States, letters that Julius Chambers, commissioning editor of *Cosmographic*, wanted to be "aggressive and saucy" and "hot." O'Connor replied that he was too busy but arranged for Davitt to do it, at a rate of five guineas for twelve hundred words twice a month. Davitt supplied about eight letters, but the Americans felt that his pieces on Irish-British developments were not "hot" enough to have avoided being "anticipated by the cable." *Cosmographic* ended the arrangement early in 1901.[37] About this time Davitt also wrote to a Mr. Bryan offering to serve as a correspondent in Ireland "for the paper which he is to edit."[38] This was presumably the anti-imperialist Democrat William Jennings Bryan, who had lost the US presidential election of 1900 and who thereupon founded a progressive weekly magazine in Nebraska entitled the *Commoner*. Davitt is known to have met Bryan. If Davitt did write for the *Commoner* then, his words were not deemed to merit inclusion in a volume condensing its first year.[39]

In January 1903 the famous editor of the *Manchester Guardian*, C. P. Scott, quite curtly rebuffed Davitt's offer to be its Irish correspondent, writing that "we have already made arrangements which will suffice for the present for Irish correspondence."[40] However, that same year, Hearst's manager in London, "the well-known journalist" E. F. Flynn, commissioned Davitt to supply copy on the national convention in Dublin convened by the United Irish League to consider the

Irish ("Wyndham") Land Bill.[41] Redmond chaired that convention on April 16 and 17, 1903. Davitt, a critic of the bill, also participated from the platform. E. F. Flynn told Davitt that he should provide analysis and not news: "News agencies will report the routine happenings. . . . Deal with the spirit of the sessions, and the meanings and results of the action taken." Flynn described Davitt's work on this occasion as "excellent" and "very illuminating," and held out the prospect of further commissions.[42] Due to events in the Russian empire the following weekend, a new commission soon came.

Russia 1903

At the Easter holidays in 1903, from April 19 to April 21, residents of Kishineff assaulted and murdered local Jews. Kishineff (also Kishinev, today Chişinaŭ in Moldova) was then in Bessarabia, part of the Russian empire. The world soon learned of this violence, reminiscent of notorious atrocities committed against Jews in Russia between 1880 and 1881 that had resulted in a great exodus to North America. On April 24, 1903, the *Cork Examiner* and the *New York Times* were among newspapers that ran a brief first report from Reuters stating that twenty-five Jews had been killed and many injured. It soon became clear that the violence was worse than that.[43] In the United States, where many Jews from eastern Europe now lived and where inspectors at Ellis Island were processing an unprecedented number of immigrants, meetings and sermons and resolutions about the pogrom quickly helped to mobilize public opinion.[44]

On May 10, 1903, Flynn cabled Davitt at home in Dalkey, County Dublin, with a request: "Can you go Russia for us to investigate recent massacres Kishineff [in] Besarabia [*sic*] and recrudence [of] anti-Semitism Russia. Reply prepaid. Like answer early." He sent another cable the next day: "We would pay £20 week and all expenses, interpreter's as of course yours. I think mission is easily finished within month. Answer quick reply."[45] The payment promised to Davitt for the month (about £90 in total) was no less than what British correspondents retained abroad by a newspaper during wartime might then expect.[46] Davitt's socialist friend Henry Mayers Hyndman thought him "none too well paid, considering the arduous and distressing character of the work to be done" for Hearst in Russia.[47] On his way to Odessa from Paris, through Budapest, Davitt would bump into Hyndman. The latter recalled later, "He was in very good spirits, but assured me it was quite a mistake to imagine, as some took it for granted, that he had married an heiress, and was now well off." Davitt told him, "It is all we can do to keep a comfortable roof over our heads, and give our children a decent education. That is why I am off on this trip." Davitt's wife, Mary Yore of St. Joseph, Michigan, would eventually come into a substantial inheritance of £80,000. The fact that his wife was American and his parents were buried there after emigrating reportedly made him feel closely tied to the United States.[48]

Having dedicated very little space to breaking news from Kishineff before May 8, Hearst's *New York American* suddenly began to give it prominent coverage. On May 12 the paper splashed across its front page that it was sending an agent to Kishineff "for facts." The next day, in another banner headline, the paper named that "agent" and "special commissioner" as Michael Davitt. "No man is better fitted than this famous liberty-loving Irishman to give to the world a true story of the butchery" proclaimed the editor, who also told readers that[49]

> Mr. Davitt is a trained newspaper man . . . by his long journalistic training and extensive knowledge acquired by years of travel, admirably fitted for the task at hand. . . . His graphic descriptions of conditions in the Transvaal, printed in the *American* during the Boer War, are a sufficient guarantee of his ability to deal graphically with the Russian situation. . . . Starting as a printer's devil in one of the London newspaper printing offices, he learned to be a compositor, and then branched out as a reporter. He worked on several of the London dailies, and gained a thorough insight into human nature.[50]

Davitt was to serve in Russia not only as a correspondent but also as an agent for the relief fund that Hearst promoted through his papers.[51] Davitt had hoped to keep his involvement quiet until he got to Russia, the better to facilitate arrangements, he believed. Hearst's papers were

HELP WANTED THIS MORNING SEE PAGES 12 AND 13

New York American

AMERICAN PAPER FOR THE AMERICAN HOME

FRIDAY —NEW YORK, MAY 15, 1903.—14 PAGES. FRIDAY PRICE ONE CENT

"I AM GOING, RESOLVED TO FIND THE TRUTH."—DAVITT.

FROM MICHAEL DAVITT, SPECIAL COMMISSIONER FOR THE NEW YORK AMERICAN TO THE SCENE OF THE JEWISH MASSACRES IN SOUTHERN RUSSIA.

Special Cable to the New York American.

Paris, May 14.

TO THE EDITOR N. Y. AMERICAN:

"I HOPE to reach Kishineff next week. I feel confident that I can by an impartial investigation discover the real origin of the recent outrages in that town, their true character, extent and probable consequences.

MICHAEL DAVITT.

"I am going with an open mind, resolved to find the truth and, when that is found, transmit it to the 'AMERICAN' for the information of the world.

"I am confident that I can obtain statements and evidence from both sides which will throw some light upon occurrences that must be deplored and condemned as a violation of the elementary rights of civilized society, no matter what motive may have actuated the perpetrators or what provocation, real or alleged, may be advanced in explanation of the outbreak."

MICHAEL DAVITT.

DYNAMITE SCARE IN CHICAGO.

MLLE. EMMA CALVE.

STARVING MAN FALLS AND IS FED IN THE STREET.

Ravenously Devours Crumbs from the Sidewalk—Will Die It Is Feared—May Have Been Locked Up in a Freight Car

Why It Is Called Darkest Russia!

THE MASSACRE, BY ONE WHO SAW IT!

Jacob Freedman, the First Refugee from the Horror of Kishineff, Tells the "American" His Story

11.2. "I am going, resolved to find the truth," proclaimed Davitt on the front page of the *New York American* on May 15, 1903.

not inclined, however, to hide a light under a bushel. One of Hearst's New York City lieutenants, the heavy-drinking Sam Chamberlain, claimed that there had been a misunderstanding and instructed Flynn to apologize to Davitt for the prompt announcement of the Hearst correspondent's identity.

Davitt made the long journey by way of Odessa only to find himself dealing with Russian censorship. Readers had to wait before any substantial article by him actually appeared in the paper. Flynn seems to have grown uneasy, cabling Davitt on May 15 that, "If Kishineff doesn't 'pan out' a ripping good interview with Tolstoy on obligations of wealth, progress of socialism, religion, etc.—a peculiarly Tolstoyesque talk would be fine." He also warned Davitt that the *New York World*'s correspondent had arrived ahead of him and urged him to "try to get story out quick."[52]

In response, Davitt filed some discursive copy and indicated that he could not be rushed ("impossible [to] send anything Sunday"). Hearst's man in London made his feelings clear in a cable sent on May 31:

New York American

NEW YORK, FRIDAY, MAY 22, 1903.

ICHAEL DAVITT SENDS HIS FIRST REPORT FROM RUSSIA.

Help Needed, He Says, if Kishineff Victims Are to Be Saved from Starvation.

The Great Irish Patriot and Writer Cables to the "AMERICAN" a Stirring and Preliminary Array of Facts.

By MICHAEL DAVITT, the "American's" Commissioner to the Scene of the Kishineff Massacres.

Special Cable to the New York American.

ODESSA, RUSSIA, MAY 21.—A first survey of the situation convinces me that there is no likelihood of any other outbreak in Bessarabia. The military precautions are adequate, but notwithstanding these the Jews are still terrorized and fear a renewed attack.

All high-class Russians whom I have met condemn the atrocious deeds of the Kishineff mobs strongly. The origin of the massacres in that town was due to combined racial and economic influences, added to by the ruffianly incitements of the anti-Semitic press.

An accurate list of the casualties so far as I can make it up shows: Forty-two killed, eighty-three dangerously injured, five hundred seriously injured, 700 houses damaged or destroyed, 600 shops looted, 2,000 families homeless and 10,000 of the poor people ruined.

The local Jews have subscribed $45.000, and the German, French, American and English Jews have sent, combined, $30,000 up to date, BUT A GREAT DEAL MORE HELP IS REQUIRED IF THE VICTIMS OF THIS HIDEOUS OUTRAGE ARE TO BE SAVED FROM STARVATION.

—MICHAEL DAVITT.

Michael Davitt.

E RELIEF FUND FOR KISHINEFF SUFFERERS NOW AMOUNTS TO $8,434

The Note That Accompanied Mr. Schwab's Check.

OTHER HUNDREDS ADDED TO THE HEARST KISHINEFF FUND.

FOLLOWING is the list of contributions received at the office of the New York "AMERICAN" yesterday for

This Is the Full Text of Russia's Official Story of the Massacre.

11.3. *New York American*, May 22, 1903.

New York first wants facts [about] real conditions Kishineff, afterward explanations presenting Russian explanations; please telegraph Monday graphic summary [of the] facts [of the] massacre and present conditions placing responsibility massacres where they belong. Having this then we can publish explanations. Please telegraph good story Monday. Your second letter not available for cabling because filled [with] generalities. Kindly give us good story Monday. Tolstoy [and] Gorki's letters published Berlin [and] London long ago. Notify me early Monday what you will send.[53]

In the meantime, some short cables from him had been given great prominence (see illustrations 11.2 and 11.3), theatrically sustaining the ostensible significance of his mission.[54]

On June 4, 1903, the *New York American* published on its front page the report by Davitt that was to win him international acclaim. It was headed "Davitt Reveals Inside Facts of Kishineff Massacre." Just this one long and graphic piece, which due to censorship was cabled not from Kishineff but from Berlin after he left Russia, and two more sent later from London, appear to have been the sum of substantial investigative articles Davitt returned on Hearst's investment.[55] However, these longer pieces, together with Davitt's earlier short cables, solidly underpinned what by then had been prominently alleged and reported from other sources in Hearst's papers. By the time that Davitt managed to make his way overland to Kishineff and subsequently file copy, Hearst's papers had published pieces from the Associated Press as well as cabled eyewitness reports and photographs and some commentary from Russia.

To describe Hearst's commissioning of Davitt as a showy publicity stunt would not be entirely fair, nor is it true to say that Hearst simply accepted Davitt's judgment. Where the *New York American* made clear editorially that it blamed Russia for the pogrom, a position that was consistent with its hostility to Russia's government,[56] Davitt blamed events in Kishineff on local Russian officials in Bessarabia and only mildly scolded senior authorities in St. Petersburg for not intervening promptly or well. Indeed, that the pogrom was not concocted by the tsar's highest officials is also the judgment of history.[57] That also seems to have been the view of US ambassador to Russia Robert S. McCormick, whom Davitt met a number of times in St. Petersburg in 1903. McCormick even went further, being chided by the *New York American* for reportedly declaring that the condition of Russian Jews had been "never better."[58] Davitt may not have entirely agreed with McCormick, but his friend Hyndman noted the former's hostility toward Jews engaged in economic activities of which the Irishman disapproved, a hostility that I have discussed elsewhere.[59] Hyndman remarked that, "Undoubtedly, Davitt in private, while not excusing the Russian authorities, felt that Russia would be much better off if she had no Jews at all within her boundaries. . . . Perhaps the Irish feeling against the gombeen-man [a local trader who loaned money] made Davitt less bitter than he would otherwise have been against the slaughterers of Jews."[60]

DIRECTORY OF HELP WANTED THIS MORNING SEE PAGES 14 AND 15

New York American

EDITION FOR GREATER NEW YORK

AN AMERICAN PAPER FOR THE AMERICAN HOME

THURSDAY — NEW YORK, JUNE 4, 1903 — 16 PAGES — THURSDAY — PRICE ONE CENT

DAVITT REVEALS INSIDE FACTS OF KISHINEFF MASSACRE.

Whole Horror Planned by Russian Officials; Hired Assassins Imported for the Work; Rioters Led by Students on Bicycles; Victims Mutilated While Alive and Girls Driven to the Mob by Police.

GROUP OF MAIMED WOMEN AND CHILDREN IN FRONT OF THE HOSPITAL IN KISHINEFF.

All those in this group were struck down by the rioting Russians on the day of the awful massacre. Two of the children seen above bear sabre gashes. One of the women was cut across the head with a belt knife. All were beaten and left for dead in the streets. After the massacre the helpless women and little ones were carried to the hospital, where, after their convalescence, the picture was taken.

THE HIDEOUS PLOT LAID BARE BY THE 'AMERICAN'S' AGENT

Programme of Riot and Outrage Was Planned by Anti-Semite Leaders and Bloodthirsty Editor Kroushvan.

RESPONSIBILITY IS FINALLY FIXED.

Bishop of Kishineff Distributes His Blessing to the Inhuman Crowds—Atrocities Reported Whose Frightful Details Can Only Be Hinted At.

When the "AMERICAN" determined to get the absolute truth as to the massacre of the Jews in Kishineff, great care was taken in securing a proper commissioner. Prominent Hebrews requested that a Gentile be selected. Michael Davitt, a man of cool judgment, a lover of liberty and a lover of his kind, and trained in the accurate school of journalism, was asked to go to Russia, get the facts of the massacre and report them to this paper. Through the "AMERICAN" this morning Mr. Davitt gives to the world a story of pillage, rapine and death, whose unspeakable horror is without a parallel in all the bloody annals of religious or racial persecutions. Just as Davitt has written his story, the "AMERICAN" prints it. Davitt is not emotional. Read his story and you will see that no previous reports of the horrors of the slaughter of the Jews of Kishineff have been exaggerated.

The "AMERICAN" promised to reveal the whole truth of the Kishineff massacre. Here it is from Michael Davitt.

BERLIN, June 3.—Finding it impossible on account of Russian censorship, to send the truth from Kishineff, I do so from this point.

I have completed an investigation as to the origin, authors and extent of the recent massacre and looting of Kishineff.

I have traversed almost the whole

11.4. *New York American*, June 4, 1903.

Davitt's presence in Russia helped to galvanize public opinion in America. He cabled that in his travels across "almost [the] whole territory [of the] Jewish Pale settlement from Odessa [to] Warsaw," he found "violently anti-Semitic" attitudes among community leaders. He wrote that the Moldovan editor of a Kishineff paper had "systematically inflamed popular feeling against Jews," and that the local police chief had told him that it "would serve Jews right if driven from [the] city." Both the editor and police chief claimed that Jews preached socialism. Davitt thought that Moldovans were a "most ignorant, brutal populace."[61] Davitt was quoted at meetings in America protesting the pogrom.[62]

Davitt recommended "sending an eminent American to see the czar to state the case and secure an amelioration of the Jews' condition." This idea "made a hit in New York," Flynn told him, but Davitt's suggestion that the former US president Grover Cleveland be that American did not. Flynn told him, "We didn't fancy Cleveland as an emissary." Instead, a trip by Hearst was contemplated.[63] There was precedent for such an intervention. Hearst had, after all, sailed his yacht down to Cuba in 1898 during the Spanish-American War and had even taken some shipwrecked Spanish sailors prisoner. However, Hearst did not go to Russia then.

On June 5, Hearst's *American* publicly commended to President Theodore Roosevelt and to the US secretary of state Davitt's reports from Russia. The Irishman was, wrote its editor, "an impartial witness, whose standing is such as to compel respect and credence. He shows that official Russia was deeply concerned in this outbreak of anti-Semitism which has so shocked and stirred civilized mankind."[64] However, it is a stretch to read Davitt's report as "deeply" involving Russian officials outside Kishineff in the pogrom. He had, in fact, cabled that there was "no evidence produced for me [that] implicated [the] government [in] St. Petersburg [in] any way [as having had] responsibility [for the] outbreak which has covered [the] name Russia [in] shame." He merely conceded that its interior minister "must have known that [an] outbreak was contemplated," albeit not imagining that the affair would "culminate in massacres."[65]

As Russian authorities struggled to respond to criticism, Davitt had difficulty filing his stories. For example, his story about a Russian claim that a Jewish proprietor of a carousel machine had sparked riots by striking a Christian woman had to be "cabled from Berlin because he found it impossible on account of the Russian censorship to send the truth from Kishineff." In his piece he rejected the Russian version of the carousel incident. He had investigated it thoroughly, and wrote, "There is no truth in the story. I found the owner of the merry-go-round. He is a German named Reinhold Mergert, and is a Christian. He assured me that no woman was insulted or hurt on that occasion."[66]

Hayyim Nahman Bialik, who wrote an influential poem about the pogrom ("In the City of Slaughter") and who is regarded today as Israel's national poet, was in Kishineff at the same time as Davitt and used the same translator. Both men, no doubt with the best of intentions, appear to have repressed details of Jewish reaction to the pogrom that did not suit their purposes. Zipperstein observes that Davitt "chose for reasons never explained to sequester his criticisms" of Jewish passivity in the face of mob violence and argues that this "raises intriguing questions, not only with regard to Davitt's motivations, but also about how it is that complex, unsettling stories tend to be narrated, reproduced, and also, at times, obliterated."[67]

Among Davitt's photographs from Kishineff, the *New York American* published one of the Irishman standing in the Jewish cemetery next to two inscribed headstones and forty-four mounds that the editor described as "the newly made graves of the massacre."[68] Some of his writings on that pogrom are said to have made Davitt "a folk hero among Jews."[69]

By the end of 1903, Davitt had finished a book on the Kishineff pogrom in which he explained that Hearst had not published all of his dispatches from Russia, "for reasons which govern the exigencies of journals that are concerned much more with a record of daily events in the United States than with history."[70] This was, perhaps, Davitt's way of acknowledging that while Hearst was happy with his reporting "facts," the publisher was less interested in Davitt's interpretations where these did not align with Hearst's editorial position on Russia.

In the same book Davitt explained the newsgathering methodology that he had used in Russia—and his process reflects well on him. However, he also excused the Russian government, to some extent, for what happened; and remarkably, given that an American Jewish society published the book, he took the opportunity to justify selective anti-Semitism.[71]

Hearst's satisfaction with Davitt's Russian service is reflected in the publisher's efforts to get him to go to Bulgaria and Macedonia in September of that same year. "Thank you, could name your own

NEW YORK AMERICAN AND JOURNAL, SUNDAY, JUNE 14, 1903.

HERE IS PHOTOGRAPHIC EVIDENCE OF RUSSIAN MOB OUTRAGES ON THE JEWS

MICHAEL DAVITT IN THE JEWISH CEMETERY —THE 44 MOUNDS ARE THE NEWLY MADE GRAVES OF THE MASSACRED.

Proofs of Massacres More Eloquent Than Words

$14,529.07 MORE IS CABLED TO KISHINEFF.

Michael Davitt Explains the Causes of Anti-Jewish Outrages at Kishineff.

11.5. *New York American*, June 14, 1903.

terms," wrote E. F. Flynn to him. He told Davitt that Hearst believed he would "be the best man for the job" and asked, "Can't [your] break wait?"[72] By December 1903 Flynn was also urging Davitt to return to Kishineff.[73]

Russia 1904–1905

On February 9, 1904, Japan and Russia went to war, each jostling for control in Manchuria. Davitt tried to persuade Hearst to send him to the front, but Hearst rejected this idea, perhaps because of the possible dangers involved.[74] However, Davitt did return to Russia in May and June 1904, interviewing Leo Tolstoy at his country home for the *Freeman's Journal*.[75] Davitt also then met Howard Thompson of the Associated Press, and the two discussed what the Irishman termed "manufactured news." Davitt dismissed the London *Standard*'s report of mass executions by Russian forces in Warsaw as "absolutely without foundation."[76] In his Sherbourne Reporter's Note Book, Davitt recorded what he considered to be the "aristignorance" and bias of English correspondents in St. Petersburg. He thought that the Reuters man there was "a pretentious prig."[77] Davitt also met again the highly respected US ambassador Robert S. McCormick who, as Davitt wrote, "regrets [the] attitude [of the] American press over [the] war."[78]

Davitt went to Russia with letters of introduction from prominent men such as William Stead and Charles R. Crane, a wealthy businessman and friend of Hearst.[79] Crane, who fostered Russian studies in America but who was no admirer of Jews, personally penned notes in which he commended Davitt as "going to Russia to make a study of," variously, "the working people" or "the industrial classes" or "the working classes."[80]

The Russo-Japanese War was not to end until September 1905. In the meantime, social unrest grew in western Russia. On January 22, 1905, Russian soldiers opened fire on workers outside the Winter Palace in St. Petersburg, an event that came to be known as Bloody Sunday or Red Sunday. On January 23 Flynn cabled Davitt that Hearst desired him to start at once for Moscow, which he did. Passing through London, Davitt learnt from Flynn that Hearst wanted him to "interview Tolstoy. Then 'exploit' any and all sources for copy." He was off again (Davitt himself proudly noted) on a "special mission for Hearst's papers . . . in New York, Boston, Chicago, Indianapolis, San Francisco and Los Angeles, California."[81]

Arriving in St. Petersburg, Davitt quickly "gathered up [a] pretty accurate account of how things stand" and cabled his 153-word account to New York.[82] His notes suggest a conclusion earlier reached. Referring to "official sources," he reported claims that the Japanese and their financial allies in London and Paris had funded revolutionaries "to create disturbances and to embarrass Russia." Davitt declared this was likely true and "corresponds with my own belief."[83] He played down the events of January 22 at the Winter Palace, reporting that workers "wanted better conditions . . . not revolution" and blaming their leader, Father Georgy Gapon, for leading an unarmed mob into "almost certain" conflict with soldiers.[84] He noted that Ambassador McCormick considered London papers to be exaggerating the situation "beyond belief" and had hinted to Davitt that Gapon was a scoundrel who had "ruined girls, and possibly an agent provocateur."[85] Davitt appears to have justified soldiers indiscriminately shooting into crowds when necessary to restore order.[86]

Davitt underestimated the extent of growing discontent, writing scornfully that revolution was more likely in Germany or Colorado than in Russia.[87] He likewise cabled that the movement to dethrone the tsar was as unpopular with the Russian people as removing the pope would be with Catholics. He added, "Actual revolution out of question."[88] The London correspondent for the *Freeman's Journal* predicted quite differently that, "It seems to be deemed as certain as if sentence of death were passed on him by a regularly constituted tribunal that the Tsar's fate personally is sealed."[89]

Six days after Red Sunday, on behalf of "several leading American newspapers," Davitt requested an interview with Tsar Nicholas II, "in the confident belief that a brief statement from your majesty on the present situation in Russia would have a most beneficial effect upon public opinion in the United States." He described himself as being "in a humble way, a supporter of Russia in the press of the United States, England and Ireland since Japan declared war" and noted his belief that, "the real origin of the recent troubles in St. Petersburg can be traced to foreign influences operating through the press of London and Paris, against the financial credit of Your Majesty's government in the hope of injuring the prospects of the next Russian loan. In this way the financial friends of Japan are trying to force Your Majesty's hand in the direction of peace with England's ally in the Far East."[90] Davitt declared, "May I live until I am accorded this interview anyhow!"[91] He was not accorded it. Russian regulations required foreigners to go through their embassies to obtain an audience with the tsar. For Davitt, that would have required his availing of the services of the United Kingdom's ambassador, and he allowed politics to prevail over journalism. He exclaimed that he "would see fifty New York Journals in [flames?] before [I] would seek a favour from a British ambassador here or elsewhere."[92] In a further display of principle, he risked letting Pulitzer's *New York World* scoop Hearst's *Journal* when he again interviewed Tolstoy in the country,[93] for he took with him Stephen McKenna (Paris bureau chief of Pulitzer's paper and a friend of the Irish playwright John Millington Synge) because it was clear that McKenna could not otherwise get there and back in time to meet his deadline. Davitt wondered how the *Journal* editors would react if they knew he had aided a competitor. Fortunately, McKenna delayed sending copy and so did not scoop Davitt.[94]

From St. Petersburg, Davitt went to what were then the Russian provinces of Finland and Poland. In Warsaw on February 12, 1905, he noted "not alone a gross but a deliberate exaggeration" of strike troubles and casualties in those provinces by English, French, and German correspondents. He claimed that the European press, particularly those papers "owned and controlled by stock-exchange influences, and especially by Jews," were responsible for "the wildest exaggerations of Russia's internal troubles. . . . This is not fair journalism."[95] He wrote to Ernest Judet, director of *L'Éclair*, condemning "the atrocious campaign of falsehood against Russia . . . by the London press assisted by a few Paris journals." He added that never "as a public man and as a journalist have I had experience of such a carnival of falsehoods as that in which the London *Times* and all the other English papers have wallowed during the last three weeks over Russian internal troubles."[96]

Davitt's efforts to provide "balance" within the international media's coverage of Russia were not going unnoticed. On February 7, 1905, in Oakland, California, (where Davitt had met his future wife in 1880), the editor of a local newspaper penned a fierce editorial about him, headed "How the Mighty Are Fallen." The editor accused Davitt of smoothing matters over "for the court circle in St. Petersburg," and he noted that the Irishman's letters from Russia were not nearly as indignant as his "denunciation of British oppression in Ireland, India and elsewhere. His reports put a pleasant complexion on the policy and conduct of the despotic government of the tsar."[97]

Conclusion

Michael Davitt was an experienced and prolific journalist, writing for English-language papers in Ireland, Britain, the United States, and elsewhere. He mixed facts with opinions as was common for correspondents in his day. He intended his reports from South Africa and Russia to balance what he regarded as inaccurate, hostile, and jingoistic accounts in British and other newspapers that published what he called then not "fake news" but "manufactured news." His reports were sometimes both graphic and gripping as he sought to engage readers by providing alternative facts as a form of balance rather than always attempting to present both sides of a story.

Davitt did not neatly tailor his reports from Russia to conform to the editorial line taken by Hearst that was very critical of the Russian government, but moderated criticism at a time when Irish nationalists sympathized with Russia as England's foe in international affairs. His reports from Kishineff helped to shape international opinion and won him respect among Jews abroad, notwithstanding Davitt's hostility toward some rich and pro-British Jews internationally and his reservations about the behavior of some Jews in Kishineff.

Because of the political bias of what he wrote, as well as the fact that he understated the plight both of indigenous peoples in South Africa and of the workers in Russia who fought its government for radical reforms, one cannot with confidence claim that Davitt was never guilty of self-censorship.

12

Dr. Dillon in North America

Kevin Rafter

Some considered Emile Joseph Dillon, whose journalism career spanned the early 1880s to the mid-1920s, one of the top journalists of his day. Irish-born (1854–1933), Dillon reported primarily for the London *Daily Telegraph* from his base in St. Petersburg, although as special correspondent for that newspaper, he traveled widely covering stories such as the Turkish massacres in Armenia in 1894–95, the second Dreyfus trial in 1899, the Boxer Uprising in China in 1900, the collapse of Tsarist Russia, World War I, and the subsequent international peace treaty negotiations.[1] He contributed regularly to a variety of publications on international affairs and also on matters of religion—he had a doctorate in philosophy from the University of Leipzig. His employers included the *Contemporary Review*, *Pall Mall Gazette*, and *Review of Reviews*. His status and standing was testified to by many of his contemporaries including W. T. Stead, who nominated him as "the most brilliant living journalist,"[2] while one obituary after his death in 1933 noted the passing of "a famous foreign correspondent."[3]

Despite assessments such as Stead's, Dillon is a relatively obscure figure in the history of journalism. Moreover, his work in book and newspaper form tends to appear as mere footnotes in the histories of the various episodes in which he had an involvement. He, as yet, has not been the subject of a biography, nor was he accorded an entry in a dictionary of nineteenth-century British journalism.[4] In effect, Dillon has become—to borrow a phrase used by British academic Michael Bromley—"a missing person" of journalism's history. Bromley has explored how leading journalists can transition from being a "noted phenomenon to missing person"; he argues that journalists have been poorly served by historians, who have a tendency to "neglect" members of the profession, treating them as "bit-part actors in grand political dramas."[5]

An absence of documentary evidence is undoubtedly one explanation why individuals disappear from journalism history. Contextualizing and accessing a career is difficult when no personal papers are left behind. In the case of Emile Joseph Dillon, this issue has been lessened by the recent emergence into the public domain of a significant volume of his personal papers, now held at the National Library of Scotland and the Green Library at Stanford University.[6] These papers allow Dillon to be rescued from obscurity—and scholarly footnotes—so that he can be repositioned in the historiography of journalists in those important transition decades at the end of the nineteenth century and the start of the twentieth century.

This chapter focuses on visits made by Dillon to the United States, first in 1905 and later in 1919–21. The coverage of the arrival of a distinguished European newspaperman reveals something about the nature of journalism in those years, and fits with Joel H. Weiner's description of how on both sides of the Atlantic "human interest" had become a feature of press coverage.[7] This chapter helps to illustrate how news that was "humanly interesting" emerged as a distinctive component of newspaper coverage.[8]

The rise of celebrity news with newspapers "drawn increasingly into details of individuals' lives" has been linked to increased print commercialization in the nineteenth-century press.[9] The early years of the twentieth century brought the "journalism of revelation, exposure and muckraking" to the city press in the United States when editors wanted "success stories" on page one and sent reporters out to conduct interviews.[10]

Proprietors such as Joseph Pulitzer were clear about the type of journalism they wanted to dominate their newspapers. Pulitzer said of his target audience: "I want to talk to the nation, not to a select committee."[11] Reporting staff were instructed to give color on the personal lives of the well-known men they interviewed, including wives, children, and pets: "these are the things that will bring him more closely home to the average reader."[12] In putting a spotlight on one aspect of E. J. Dillon's life and career—his journeys to the United States in 1905 and again in 1919–21—it becomes clear that Pulitzer's instructions were being carried out across the American newspaper industry.

Dillon and the United States

The United States impinged upon Dillon's life long before he set foot in North America. An uncle—his father's brother—emigrated to the United States in the mid-nineteenth century. This was a familiar escape route for many Irish people who left famine and poverty behind in their native land. In an unpublished memoir, Dillon later wrote that his father kept "faded letters from relatives in America" in a trunk in the family's home in Dublin city center.[13] In the case of this particular uncle, however, he was "lost sight of completely"—such severing of family connections was undoubtedly a bleak reality of nineteenth-century transatlantic migration.

Having moved from rural Ireland, Dillon's parents managed a hardware shop from the family house in Dublin city. It was an austere environment. "The main purpose of the building was the warehousing and display of the goods, the lodging of the owners was secondary . . . our house was gloomy, uncomfortable and scantily furnished."[14] Dillon's father wanted his son to become a Catholic priest. This parental ambition was not uncommon in nineteenth-century Ireland, where career options for lower class Catholics were limited in the face of pro-British Protestant supremacy. But his father presented a cruel choice to be "a priest or a pauper."[15]

Dillon's first trip to the United States in October 1873 was related to his training for the priesthood. He was nineteen years old and struggling with significant pressure from his father to take priestly vows.[16] By this time, he had already spent five years in preparation for the priesthood. In the further pursuit of his religious studies, the original plan was to travel to a Catholic college in Indiana, but the young Dillon opted to stay with the Congregation of St. Paul's in New

York. He had thoughts of tracking down his long-lost uncle, but the man had apparently changed his name, and he was not to be found.

Dillon spent five months in New York at the Paulist House on the corner of Fifty-Ninth Street and Ninth Avenue. It was a lonely period. "I never took very kindly to life in America, the ideas and strivings and habits being so different to my own," he wrote.[17] His state of mind was no doubt impacted by the personal realization that he had no vocation and also the domestic conflict this reality was likely to cause. His father had well aired the threat of withdrawing financial support for his studies if plans for the priesthood were abandoned.

Dillon departed New York for Paris on March 18, 1874. He slept by day and spent his nights in comparative solitude by reading. The crossing was so violent that there were fears the ship would founder. Dillon wrote, "My fellow-passengers were panic-stricken and came rushing helter-skelter out of their beds but the sight of me quietly continuing to read my book seemed to restore their confidence."[18]

Back in Europe he continued with his education—eventually receiving qualifications from several European universities—but, much to his father's disapproval, thoughts of taking holy vows were abandoned. By the mid-1880s, he was in Russia attempting to secure a professorial position while struggling to earn a living from teaching languages, translating work, and dabbling in journalism. The latter career eventually offered the best prospects. In the three decades from when he arrived in Russia in the 1880s, Dillon built a significant reputation for important reportage, not only for the *Daily Telegraph*, but also for a range of other international publications. He amplified the value of these reports by the influential contacts—senior political and government officials—he cultivated during this period. When he visited London, he met with leading figures in positions of power. On the Continent, in Berlin and Paris, he was on personal terms with the most powerful politicians.

When Dillon traveled to the United States, leading newspapers like the *New York World* and journals like *World's Week*, sought him out for the knowledge of the men and the issues that made him an invaluable interpreter of the tangled international politics in the years before the First World War. With the United States having begun to emerge as a world power in these years, many of the leading American newspapers were eager to inform their readers of overseas developments. In addition, American publishers found in Dillon's travels and exploits, evidence of a figure who fit what they knew to be the general public's long-standing interest in the personality and celebrity of foreign visitors to its shores.

The Portsmouth Peace Conference, 1905

At the turn of the twentieth century, there was considerable international interest in political developments in Tsarist Russia. Dillon, with his amazing ability to acquire influential contacts, was considered "by far and away the ablest and most trustworthy chronicler of events in Russia."[19] He was in demand by a range of international publications. For example, in February 1905, the editor of the *American Monthly Review of Reviews* paid a fee of $120 for an article—"The Doom of the Russian Autocracy"—describing it as "exceptionally timely and [one that] has pleased us all very much."[20]

Not long after his appointment as the *Daily Telegraph*'s correspondent in St. Petersburg, Dillon had become a confidante of Sergei Witte, a leading political figure in prerevolutionary Russia. Witte oversaw the construction of the Trans-Siberian Railway, having been appointed minister for finance by Tsar Alexander III in 1892, a position he would hold for the next eleven years. The acquaintance between Dillon and Witte benefited both parties in that it "supplied [Dillon] with an insider's perspective to sell Western journalism and Witte a mouthpiece to the West for his version of events."[21]

Witte and Dillon had very different views on what the future held for Russia. Dillon had long believed that the downfall of the tsarist regime was inevitable. Witte clung to the belief that a stable and prosperous post-tsarist Russia was a possibility. In *The Eclipse of Russia* (1918) Dillon recalled frequently telling Witte "that his hopes and aspirations were doomed to disappointment, and his natural sagacity made him aware of the fact."[22] There were some concerns at the *Daily Telegraph* about Dillon's closeness to his influential Russian government contact, and the fact that he was known to be operating as a quasi adviser to Witte. There is no doubt that Dillon's normally sharp critical faculties were numbed in his admiration for Witte as this passage illustrates:

> Belonging to the highest ranks of the Russian aristocracy, he is as democratic in his views and ways as an American from Maryland; and having been for ten years the most successful Minister of Russian Finances, he possesses such a modest fortune that if he were deprived of his salary as President of the Council he would have to imitate many an American ex-President and take to working elsewhere for a decent livelihood.[23]

While Witte's influence at the tsarist court had been significantly reduced in 1903 with his removal as minister for finance, two years later Nicholas II asked him to travel to the United States to lead a Russian delegation to negotiate an end to the Russo-Japanese War. The conflict between Russia and Japan commenced in February 1904, essentially arising from the territorial ambitions of the two nations over Manchuria and Korea. Eventually, the US administration under President Theodore Roosevelt offered to mediate, and American soil was offered as neutral ground to negotiate a peace deal.

Dillon traveled to the United States to report on the peace negotiations for the *Daily Telegraph*. In US press coverage of this trip during 1905, Dillion prepared at least two examples of the type of human-interest news popular in early twentieth-century newspaper reporting. These stories had a strong focus on personality and a tendency to project the newspaperman as a celebrity. The first story arose from Dillon's work as a journalist while journeying from Cherbourg across the Atlantic to New York on the *Wilhelm der Grosse*, the same Hamburg-American Line steamer that carried Witte and the Russian delegation.

During the voyage Dillon secured an interview with Witte. He wrote up one thousand words, which were transmitted by wireless telegraphy that involved several ships and land stations before eventually being received in the *Daily Telegraph* offices in London. It was the first occasion such a feat had been achieved. The historic transmission was almost as big a story for the international press as the actual content of the interview with Witte. For example, on August 6, 1905, the *World* reported:

> Dr. Emile J. Dillon's interview with M. Witte, the Russian peace envoy, sent by wireless telegraph from the deck of the Kaiser Wilhelm der Grosse at sea to the London Daily Telegraph and then cabled to every part of the world was one of the sensations of the voyage of Russia's representative to America. It was not only a great newspaper feat, but the transmission of nearly a thousand words by such means and under such circumstances startlingly suggests the future possibilities of the wireless telegraph.[24]

The historic wireless coup was widely reported. In a subsequent account of the 1905 peace negotiations, Witte himself recalled that "the interview appeared in all the European papers and contributed a great deal toward acquainting the world with my views on the nature of my task."[25] Under the headline "Man of the Hour," the *World* published an interview with the *Daily Telegraph* correspondent describing how he prepared his journalistic feat:

> I wrote all the interview out very carefully for there is great liability of error in wireless transmission. Then I divided it into parts, each containing about one hundred words, closing each part with the words, "End of Part 1, or 2, &c., and more to come." The reason for dividing the message in this way is that on a moving ship it is quite likely that one hundred words would be the limit possible to send to one receiving station before we passed out of range. We had already gone too far from shore to send a message direct to the nearest land station. The wireless apparatus on shipboard does not transmit nearly as far as is generally supposed. Two or three hundred miles? No, I would say less than that. So it was necessary to send this message from ship to ship as we and they were moving on the ocean.[26]

Part of the difficultly in relaying the material was that the wireless signal was lost as ships moved in and out of range, and it took time to transmit the material between receiving points. Having started transmission on Friday, the entire article was eventually relayed in its various parts to the *Daily Telegraph* by Sunday, in time for the next day's edition. As Dillon explained: "There were four steamers properly equipped with wireless apparatus bound westward on which we could count. . . . This process of sending a message in mid-ocean from ship to ship, and then to land is a long and uncertain one."

Dillon speculated that moving beyond this "experimental stage" with stronger batteries might eventually make it possible to send messages directly to land stations while at sea. The precarious nature of the technology was evident later on the same transatlantic journey when, two days out from New York, he failed to send a wireless note to an American land station (from where it would have been replayed to London) and was obliged to wait until he set foot in the United States. Nevertheless, the initial achievement was billed "a mid-ocean beat" by the *Daily Telegraph*.[27]

The talks between the Russians and the Japanese took place in Portsmouth, New Hampshire. A peace treaty was signed on September 5, 1905. Given Dillon's strongly held views on Witte, it was not surprising that the editorial line adopted by the *Daily Telegraph* was that the treaty was a genuine attempt to end conflict between Japan and Russia. Press coverage contained human-interest news and plenty of color. Four copies of the treaty were produced—two in French prepared by the Russians and two in English written by the Japanese; and once the texts had been compared and both sides were satisfied the signing ceremony proceeded: "The pen used by Mr. Witte in signing the treaty was a gold one. The other signers used ordinary steel pens. Mr. Witte gave his pen to Dr. E. J. Dillon, St. Petersburg correspondent of the London Telegraph. The other pens and blotting paper were given to other people who were present."[28]

The second human-interest story occurred just after Dillon had landed in the United States to report on the peace talks. The *Boston Herald* on August 18, 1905, published a story under the headline, "Notable Reunion Held," in which it reported that, "One of the interesting incidents of this peace conference was the reunion of Archbishop Quigley of Chicago and Emile Joseph Dillon."

The two men had met previously as students in Innsbruck, but as the *Boston Herald* noted, "Their paths in life diverged, and each won distinction." We learn from the news report that the archbishop was in Wentworth on a short holiday and that having been reacquainted, they were invited by a local dignitary "on an automobile ride to Hampton." What's more, the newspaper informs us that on the day trip, Dillon "was initiated into two novelties of American life—popcorn and birch beer—and fell quite in love with them."[29]

A Famous Journalist of Europe, 1919–21

Dillon continued to work for the *Daily Telegraph* during World War I, although he was very frustrated that the censor in London removed a great deal of his copy. These deletions were primarily due to the high accuracy of Dillon's reportage, based on his extensive range of influential contacts in governments across Europe. There were increasing strains in the relationship with his main employer—in part due to the high cost of maintaining Dillon on the payroll (Dillon demanded that the newspaper cover the cost of his secretary). But his services were still in demand. In July 1918 the *Philadelphia Ledger* proposed a cost-shared arrangement with the *Daily Telegraph* to send Dillon to report on the revolution in the Russia. To negotiate this deal, Dillon spent October and November 1918 in the United States, arriving in New York on October 12, 1918, on board the steamer *Olympic* after a nine-day voyage. Prior to departing for Philadelphia, there was time for the opera and sightseeing. There were social engagements and contract negotiations with the *Philadelphia Ledger* proprietor, although he also found time to arrange articles with other publications including the *New York Times* and the *Christian Science Monitor.*

Upon his return to Europe, Dillon found himself not bound for Russia but reporting on the post–World War I peace treaty talks. During the Paris Conference, Dillon was introduced to Edward L. Doheny, an American oil tycoon. Doheny was the founder and president of the Pan American Petroleum & Transport Company with offices in New York, Los Angeles, New Orleans, and Tampico in Mexico. His first fortune had been made in the 1880s from silver mines in New Mexico. He struck oil for the first time in 1892 in Los Angeles and is credited with starting the oil boom in the region.[30] Eight years later Doheny ventured into Mexico and, having seen the oil potential near Tampico, he started acquiring land. Oil flowed—making Doheny fantastically wealthy.

For Dillon, the timing of the introduction to Doheny was opportune. He was now sixty-three years old. He had lost significant investments in Russia after the revolution in 1917. Moreover, his long-term relationship with the *Daily Telegraph* had concluded, and possibility not on the best of terms. A diary entry on August 1, 1919, bluntly noted, "Got Le Sage telegram that salary ended in July."[31]

Dillon, and his wife Kathleen Dillon, set off from Southampton on the Cunard ocean liner, the *Mauretania*, on October 15, 1919.[32] The arrival of the famous journalist and his wife in North America was reported widely in leading newspapers over the following two months as they made their way from a starting point of New York to Los Angeles, their final destination.

Dillon's book on the Paris Conference had just been published in London, and some review copies were circulating in the United States when he landed in New York in late October 1919. He spent time in New York and Boston before traveling by train to Montreal and Vancouver, and eventually arriving in Los Angeles for Christmas. In every city he visited across North America, reporters sought his views on the peace conference, the League of Nations, and the leading international negotiators. For example, a short insert in one of his pocket diaries records arriving in Vancouver on December 10, 1919, where a suite had been reserved at the Vancouver Hotel. Dillon wrote, "Reporter from the 'Sun' was waiting for interview. Gave it."[33] Throughout November and December 1919, reporters eagerly awaited his arrival with newspaper headlines playing on his authority:

- "Peace Table Secrets Told by Dr. Dillon. Famous Journalist Gives Details of How Former Kaiser's Trial Was Decided; Japs' Action" (*Los Angeles Examiner*);

- "Dillon Comments on Wilson Error. Famous Journalist of Europe Discusses Failure of League Plan" (*Seattle Post-Intelligencer*);
- "Peace Treaty a Makeshift, Says Dr. Dillon. International Expert Declares Covenant Is Not the One Wilson Took Abroad" (*San Francisco Chronicle*).

The *Seattle Post-Intelligencer* reported that Dillon's stay in Seattle was part of a journey to California, "for a vacation following his arduous duties as a special correspondent to the peace conference."[34] His photograph accompanied a front-page article in the *San Francisco Chronicle* in which he was described as "one of the great authorities on international politics."[35] While several newspaper articles noted that Dillon's arrival in the United States was motivated by the need for rest, there was another somewhat underreported factor behind his departure from Europe. Following their initial meetings in Europe, Doheny saw use for Dillon's talents in chronicling the political scene in Mexico as a means of assisting in the development of his oil interests in that unsettled region. It was reported that Dillon and his wife—who, after their arrival in Los Angeles on December 18, 1919, were staying in a private bungalow at the Beverley Hills Hotel—were being "widely entertained" by Doheny and enjoyed time on the tycoon's ranch.

Dillon was less than forthcoming on the precise nature of the relationship, telling one newspaper: "I am delighted with Southern California, so much so that I cannot tell when I will leave, for I shall stay as long as circumstances will permit; it is a perfect region in which to loaf or to work."[36] He actually neglected to say that he had already signed a lucrative contract to act as a publicist of sorts for Doheny's interests in Mexico. The coverage of Dillon's 1919–21 American visit focused as much on Dillon himself as on his views. Color and personality were dominant themes. For example, the *Los Angeles Examiner* reported the arrival of

> a newspaper man who has attained the position of an unofficial universal diplomat, whose views are sought by Premiers and Parliaments, and who was the intimate friend of the Kings that were and is of the few that are, is necessarily a man of commanding potency.

> Such is Dr. E. J. Dillon, now staying at the Beverly Hotel. He is known as possibly the most notable journalist of the world; certainly the most notable diplomat-journalist.[37]

The *Vancouver Daily World* ran a story on Kathleen Dillon's autograph album, which was filled with signatures and well wishes from statesmen and royalty who she had met at various functions and events across European capitals. Included among these was Lloyd George who wrote, "We shall win if we put our best into the war—but not otherwise."[38]

Readers of the newspapers were informed that "the book is a meeting place of neutral ground for friends and foes," although the article focused largely on the owner of the "little unpretentious album." Newspaper readers also learned that "Mrs. Dillon is a charming little woman, whose English is tinged ever so slightly with a foreign tongue, perhaps French, which she uses almost exclusively when abroad, although she speaks four other languages." The reader also learns that "she has a love of travel, and being a roamer over nearly every part of the world." Pulitzer would have approved of this human-interest journalism.

As mentioned previously, the purpose of Dillon's move from Europe had been an offer of employment by Doheny. While the terms of his well-remunerated contract were somewhat unambiguous—and would ultimately see the two men fall out—Dillon was tasked with writing positively about developments in Mexico and assisting with the advancement of Doheny's business interests in the region. Dillon visited Mexico during the first three months of 1920. While staying in the city of Oaxaca, he experienced firsthand the lawlessness in Mexico as political instability besieged the country. Rebels who had captured a neighboring town and railway station proceeded to cut off light and water to Oaxaca. As Dillon observed, this action "caused a panic among intending passengers who, rather than run the risk of death or worse, prolonged their stay in the city."[39]

During these early months in 1920 Kathleen Dillon had remained at the Beverly Hills Hotel while her husband crisscrossed Mexico. His return to the United States once more attracted press interest. For example, the *Washington Post* on May 12, 1920, announced that "Dr. and Mrs. E. J. Dillon and Miss Katherine Van Shine have arrived in Washington and have taken an apartment at the Lafayette for several months." Dillon's engagement diary records that he had several lunches at the Senate while in Washington. It would seem he was briefing US politicians on his experiences in Mexico. Within weeks he traveled to New York, but by early August, he departed again for Mexico where he would remain until March 1921.

This period was nothing short of rip-roaring adventure at the tail end of Dillon's professional career. He was treated as a dignitary and had special access. As he left the United States in August 1920, he was met at the border by a representative of the Mexican government who had arranged a "special carriage" to take him to Mexico City, where he had an audience with President Álvaro Obregón in Mexico City. He formed a particularly close relationship with Obregón, traveling in the presidential train and, along with his wife Kathleen, enjoying the company of Obregón's immediate family on many social occasions.[40] The Dillons even went so far as discussing moving permanently to live in Mexico.

Dillon fulfilled his contract by writing about his travels and the politics of Mexico. On September 29, 1920, the *Globe and Commercial Advertiser* (New York) published what the newspaper announced as "the first in a series of articles by Dr. Dillon, noted journalist and author, who is now working in Mexico studying conditions there."[41] The headline of the article—"Great Changes in Mexico, Dr. E. J. Dillon Believes"—put as much focus on the personality of the writer as on the topic under discussion.

This trait of injecting personality into news was now an established newspaper norm. When publishing Dillon's syndicated articles, the *Baltimore News* observed, "One of the world's best known correspondents Dr. Dillon is now in Mexico and has been the travelling guest and unofficial adviser of General Obregón for some time."[42] Dillon believed Obregón's emergence as head of state offered Mexico renewed hope of political stability and economic prosperity. He was struck by the dramatic contrast with the destruction he had left behind in Europe. Mexico, he believed, was poised to leave behind strife and anarchy and about "to inaugurate an era of internal reconstruction."[43] Dillon's view on political developments in Mexico, and his independence in writing what he wanted, caused considerable friction with Doheny. The conflict between them turned near violent at a meeting in early 1922, and a parting was instigated.

Conclusion

Dillon retained his interest in Mexico until 1923. He found time to author two books—both favorably disposed toward Obregón. He eventually returned to Europe and settled into a retirement of sorts in Barcelona. He continued to write—but increasingly sporadically—although there was a trip to the Soviet Union in 1928 and another book publication. He suffered ill health through his later years and died in June 1933. News of his passing was reported on the BBC, and news stories and obituaries were published in all leading newspapers. And then Dillon was forgotten, a far cry from the celebrity status he received as a distinguished journalist arriving in the United States in 1905 and again in 1919–21.

More recent academic work discusses the tabloidization of news and trivialization of content. Commentators often consider the role of journalism in the "dumbing-down of the public sphere."[44] In its most salacious way, these trends are closely identified with the British tabloids but in reality, they feature across all news media. For better or for worse—and there are arguments on both sides—hard news now competes with human-interest stories while sensational gossip about celebrities is a normal feature of all editorial diets. But a historical look back—in this article in the case of E. J. Dillon—confirms that much that is considered new is actually part of a long-term historical trend that defies geographical boundaries.

13

The *Gaelic American* 1912–1922

A Case Study in Irish American Transnational Journalism

Michael Doorley

The *Gaelic American* represents a classic example of a transnational newspaper. It was founded in New York in 1903 and appealed to a mainly Irish American readership. Its editor, John Devoy (1842–1928), also led Clan na Gael, a secret revolutionary organization that played a key role in instigating the 1916 Irish Rebellion and had close links to its counterpart in Ireland, the Irish Republican Brotherhood (IRB).[1]

By 1913 the *Gaelic American* had established itself as one of the leading Irish American newspapers and had doubled its circulation from approximately fifteen thousand copies in 1907 to thirty thousand.[2] The *Gaelic American* was mainly sold in the New York metropolitan area but was also available throughout the United States via mail subscription. Its readership included both Irish-born migrants and first- or second-generation Irish Americans, conscious of their ethnic identity. While the paper provided local news from home, organized under Irish county headings, it also provided detailed reports on American and world events, especially with regard to those areas of the globe struggling against the British Empire.[3]

According to Devoy, the rationale for the newspaper was clear. As he later wrote in 1925: "The Clan needed a defender in the press, and a public voice to enunciate its principles."[4] In this context, the newspaper reported on the Irish revolutionary decade of 1912 to 1922 through a radical Irish nationalist lens. It advocated a revolutionary solution to the Irish question and, in line with the objectives of the IRB in Ireland, called for the establishment of an Irish Republic through "physical force" means. However, this chapter will argue that American concerns, interacting with flows of news from Ireland and elsewhere, also shaped the *Gaelic American*'s journalism on a host of issues ranging from the defense of Irish American ethnicity to opposition to American participation in World War I and the League of Nations. These American concerns influenced its coverage of the Irish revolution itself and, as we shall see, provoked bitter conflicts with the representatives of Irish nationalism in the United States, notably Éamon de Valera (1882–1975), during his tour of the United States in 1919 and 1920.[5]

The Transnational Nature of the *Gaelic American*

The full title of the *Gaelic American* reflected its transnational journalistic objectives. That is: *The Gaelic American: A Journal Devoted to the Cause of Irish Independence, Irish Literature and the Interests of the Irish Race.*[6] While the object of Irish independence could be seen as a purely Irish motivation, this objective also held an appeal for the Irish in America since it was assumed that an independent Irish state would enhance Irish American pride in the same way as independent statehood had enhanced the status of other ethnic groups. As Jim Finerty, the Irish editor of the *Chicago Citizen*, lamented: "All other foreign elements in this country, with perhaps the exception of the Poles, have strong governments behind them, and they have more respect than the Irish, who have no government of their own to boast of."[7] The nurturing of Irish literature and cultural activities in the United States also helped to perpetuate an Irish American identity which could be harnessed for Irish American political objectives.

Daniel Cohalan (1865–1946), an ambitious New York lawyer and a leading figure in the Clan, helped Devoy launch the *Gaelic American* as a public company. Cohalan came from a relatively privileged background and was born in Middletown, New York, to Irish parents from County Cork. After moving to New York City, he obtained a law degree from Manhattan College and set up a thriving legal practice, undoubtedly helped by his close connections to Tammany Hall, the Democratic Party in New York.[8] Cohalan's grandfather and father had left Ireland during the Famine, and his ambition to liberate Ireland was matched by a deep hatred for the British Empire, which he believed had restricted Irish social and economic development. In a 1919 pamphlet, appropriately entitled *The Indictment*, Cohalan argued that the British government was responsible for the Famine, and having "systematically broken down every effort made to develop its industries," had used Ireland as "a great dairy farm" for its own economic interests.[9] However, while Cohalan prided himself on his Irish nationalism, he also possessed a strong sense of American patriotism and sincerely believed that the British Empire posed as much of a threat to the United States as it did to Ireland.[10]

Cohalan is listed as the first principal director on the initial share certificates issued for the paper, and he did much to promote the newspaper among both Clan members and the wider Irish American community throughout the United States.[11] Due to his connections to Tammany Hall, he became a state Supreme Court judge in 1911. Though Cohalan resigned from the board of directors of the *Gaelic American* after his judicial appointment, he nevertheless continued to play a role in directing the newspaper, and, according to one contemporary observer, helped determine its "editorial attitude."[12]

A Clan circular to its members, promoting the launch of the *Gaelic American* in 1903, argued that, since the "majority of the Irish Race" was in the United States, it had "in its hands the ultimate settlement of the Irish question."[13] This was no idle boast. By 1900, according to the census of that year, 4,826,904 Americans were either Irish born or had Irish parents. This figure exceeded the Irish population of Ireland at this time.[14] Also, while political and cultural developments in Ireland received much coverage in the *Gaelic American*, both Devoy and Cohalan recognized that their readership lived in the United States and had other loyalties that extended beyond the geography of Ireland. In common with their Irish American readership, both men felt a deep loyalty to the United States and to the interests of the Irish "race" in America as reflected in the full title of the newspaper.

The use of the word "race" to describe the Irish in the United States was not unusual during this period. While Irish Catholics had made much social progress since the Famine period, they still faced discrimination and hostility.[15] In this regard, their reception in America was very different from British Protestant migrants who were often seen as "invisible immigrants in the sense that they had a comparatively rapid assimilation and were not seen as true foreigners."[16] Alison Kibler, in her work *Censoring Racial Ridicule* (2015), argues that the Irish, though legally white, "still occupied a middle ground in terms of popular culture" in the early decades of the twentieth century. She also describes how the Irish were frequently lampooned in vaudeville theater productions as prone to drunkenness and brawling.[17]

The *Gaelic American*, therefore, sought to defend "the interests of the Irish Race" against what it saw as a pervasive Anglo-Saxonism in American life that corrupted American foreign policy and discriminated against Irish ethnicity.[18] A Clan circular written by Cohalan, promoting the *Gaelic American* and encouraging members to purchase stock in the company, highlights the newspaper's determination to inculcate a sense of cultural pride among its Irish American readership: "We want to reach out to young men and women of Irish Race who are fast falling away from Irish ideals. We want to reach the children of Irish-American families so that they may be taught that they belong to a race that was great in war—in literature, in art, and in music before the barbarous Anglo-Saxons emerged from the primeval forests."[19]

As part of its mission to celebrate the contribution of the "Irish Race," the *Gaelic American* covered the Irish role in the colonial settlement and in the foundation of the United States, often in heroic terms. This served two purposes. First, it was designed to counter elite Anglo-Saxon claims that England was the motherland of America and that the Irish had only arrived after the Great Famine of the mid-nineteenth century. Second, such articles were designed to stimulate among its readership an appreciation of their Irish American heritage. As the *Gaelic American* declared in an editorial: "We are stimulating their patriotism and fitting them to become more loyal citizens of the country of their allegiance."[20] This goal tied in with the objectives of other Irish American organizations such as the American Irish Historical Society (AIHS), which aimed to "awaken an appreciation of their (the Irish) worth as citizens." Michael O'Brien, who wrote many of the articles for the AIHS journal, the *Recorder*, was also a regular contributor to the *Gaelic American*, and many of his articles celebrated the Irish contribution to America's own revolutionary war. In a January 1907 edition, O'Brien recounted the heroic story of the "brilliant capture of the British fort at Stony Point, in which Irishmen are shown to have played the most prominent part."[21]

The *Gaelic American*'s support for the ongoing Gaelic revival in Ireland can be seen in the context of how its journalism was shaped by cultural flows from Ireland, but this coverage can also be seen in the context of nurturing a sense of Irish American ethnic pride. The inclusion of the word "Gaelic" in the title of the newspaper, in ancient Celtic script, clearly indicates sympathy with the aims of this revival. A 1903 circular promoting the *Gaelic American* stressed that the paper would give special attention "to the Gaelic revival, which is the surest sign of the resurgence of the old race and the old spirit of Ireland."[22] This revival witnessed a renewed interest in the Irish language, literature, and cultural activities such as the ancient Celtic games of hurling and football. While these objectives were not political, movements associated with this revival such as the Gaelic League (1893) and the Gaelic Athletic Association (1884) vehemently opposed the anglicization of Ireland.[23]

The *Gaelic American* both championed Irish cultural events in its columns and endorsed fundraising efforts on behalf of the Gaelic League, an Irish-based organization devoted to the revitalization of the Irish language which was then in decline. In a later article, the older Devoy claimed that he had wanted to call the new newspaper the *Irish Nation*. However, he admitted that he had been overruled by the younger Daniel Cohalan who favored the title *Gaelic American*.[24] Although American born, Cohalan frequently visited Ireland and maintained a summer home in Glandore in County Cork. He therefore seemed more in tune with the increasing popularity of Irish cultural movements then taking place in Ireland compared to Devoy, who had not visited Ireland since 1879. The newspaper coverage of such cultural topics illustrates how Irish developments, combined with its own Irish American nationalist ideology, influenced the content of the paper.[25]

Not surprisingly, Irish nationalists from Ireland were not overly concerned with combating Anglo-Saxon intrigue in the United States. Instead, they looked to their Irish American cousins for funds and diplomatic influence to support their respective nationalist causes. The *Gaelic American*, representing the voice of the Clan na Gael, saw itself as representing the cause of revolutionary nationalism in Ireland. However, it is important to note that until 1914, this form of nationalism was very much a minority voice. In contrast, most Irish nationalists, both in Ireland and the United States, supported the then more popular constitutional nationalist cause of Home Rule, represented by John Redmond's Irish Parliamentary Party. Indeed, Redmond had his own support group in the United States known as the United Irish League of America, and he also enjoyed the enthusiastic support of the *Gaelic American*'s main Irish American newspaper rival, the *Irish World* (New York).[26]

Defining Irish Independence in the Face of World War

The *Gaelic American* espoused a very different interpretation of "Irish independence" compared to the *Irish World*. While criticizing Redmond, the paper sought to educate its readers about Ireland's historic revolutionary Irish tradition. Articles devoted to this topic often appeared on the front page of the newspaper and included coverage of the failed Irish rebellions of the United Irishmen of 1798, the Young Ireland movement of the 1840s, and the Fenian rising of 1867. An article that appeared in December 1913 recounted Devoy's own experience as a prisoner in England following his arrest for Fenian activities in the 1860s.[27]

While celebrating this heroic revolutionary tradition, the *Gaelic American* poured scorn on the prospect of Home Rule. From the *Gaelic American*'s perspective, Home Rule, even if it was secured, would mean continued Irish membership of the British Empire and British control over Ireland's economic and foreign policy.[28] In 1909 the paper declared: "A critical people now argue that the kind of Home Rule that England may by some chance grant would not be worth the having."[29]

By 1914, to Devoy's dismay, Redmond's goal of Home Rule for Ireland seemed finally to be within reach, despite growing opposition from the mainly Protestant unionist population of Northern Ireland. However, events in Europe and in Ireland itself soon transformed Irish American opinion in favor of Devoy's point of view.

Following Britain's entry into the European war in 1914, Redmond pledged his support for the British war effort and called on Irish nationalists to join the British Army in defence of Catholic Belgium. Since most commentators believed that the war would be a short one, Redmond gambled that Home Rule would be granted by a grateful British government after a short war, thus overcoming Unionist objections to the measure. Redmond's pro-British policy did not sit well with many Irish Americans. Because of their collective memory of the Great Famine as exile, and stimulated by a sense of exclusion by white Anglo-Saxon Protestant Americans in the United States, Irish American nationalists had traditionally been more anti-British than the Irish in Ireland. The *Gaelic American* seized on this Irish American unease and highlighted Redmond's "open betrayal of Ireland."[30] Interestingly, even the *Irish World* adopted the same position and argued that for Redmond to "fritter away any part of her [Ireland's] military resources would be treason of the blackest kind."[31]

Newspapers such as the *Gaelic American*, and now the *Irish World*, encouraged anti-Redmond sentiment among Irish Americans. In a reversal of the usual relationship between Irish America and Ireland, Redmond's support organization in the United States, the United Irish League of America, had to be supported by funds from Ireland. Meanwhile, in Ireland itself, Redmond and the Home Rule party still enjoyed the considerable support of mainstream nationalist newspapers such as Dublin's *Irish Independent* and *Freeman's Journal*. This divergence in newspaper opinion illustrates how the Irish American attitudes toward the war in Europe differed from that of the Irish in

Ireland at this particular time, though the *Gaelic American* certainly helped to fan this traditional anti-British isolationist tendency.

Before the United States entered the war in 1917, the *Gaelic American* consistently took a pro-German position toward the European conflict. It argued that a German victory over Britain and Russia would mean freedom for not only Ireland but also for Poland, Finland, India, and Egypt.[32] The sinking of the British Cunard liner *Lusitania* by a German U-boat off the Irish coast in May 1915, which led to the deaths of 128 Americans, caused outrage in the American press, but the *Gaelic American* excused the sinking and described the ship as a "floating arsenal" carrying munitions for the British war effort.[33] The offices of the *Gaelic American* also became the hub for Irish revolutionary activity in the United States where German agents, Irish revolutionaries, and Clan members mixed freely. Visiting Irish nationalists included the internationally known figure Roger Casement, who reported to its offices to meet with Devoy prior to his mission to Germany to enlist support for an Irish rebellion. One could, therefore, argue that the newspaper not only reported on the Irish revolution but also played a key role in instigating it.[34]

By 1916, such was the unity among Irish Americans in their opposition to Redmond and support for American neutrality that Devoy and Cohalan, with the help of the *Gaelic American*, could mobilize a massive Irish Race Convention in March 1916. The convention, composed of twenty-three hundred delegates from Irish societies across the United States, provided the springboard for the launch of a new open Irish American organization now representative of Irish American opinion. In a dramatic gesture that symbolized the role of Irish American newspapers in cementing this unity, Robert Ford, editor of the *Irish World*, proposed the name of the organization as the "Friends of Irish Freedom" (FOIF); this was seconded by John Devoy of the *Gaelic American*.

In extensive coverage of the convention, the *Gaelic American* highlighted the aims of the FOIF in upholding Irish independence but also stressed its goal to maintain American neutrality in the face of what it considered as insidious British attempts to enlist United States support for its life and death struggle against Germany.[35] This latter goal clearly reflected the concerns of Irish America rather than the Irish in Ireland.

Within six weeks of the New York convention, dramatic but often confused reports reached the *Gaelic American* about an uprising against British rule in Ireland. The paper had a head start on other newspapers in its coverage of the rebellion because for months, its editor, John Devoy, as leader of the Clan, had been in contact with both the IRB in Ireland and German officials in New York in efforts to organize an arms shipment to the rebels so as to coincide with the rebellion.[36] The reaction of the *Gaelic American* to the rising stood in stark contrast to the mainstream newspapers in the United States. While the *New York Times* compared the Irish rebels to "forward children, causing untold annoyance to others," the *Gaelic American*, in a front-page headline, most likely penned by Devoy, proclaimed "Ireland in Arms Fighting for Freedom."[37]

Despite the *Gaelic American*'s unqualified support for the rebellion, Devoy also recognized that it stood little chance of success. The British navy intercepted the German arms ship loaded with weapons which the Clan, through their German contacts, had done so much to organize. Meanwhile, the small force of poorly armed rebels, numbering no more than two thousand, stood little chance of success against the might of the British Empire. Within a week the revolt had been put down, with severe loss of life to the civilian population of Dublin. The *Gaelic American*, even in its initial reports of the Easter Rising, downplayed the prospect of military success but also noted the significance of the event in the overall context of the world war and stressed: "No matter what the immediate outcome may be, the revolt must exercise an important influence on the result of the war. . . . Ireland puts in her claim for recognition at the peace conference."[38]

Irish public opinion, especially in Dublin, was initially critical of the rebellion, but the British executions of the rebel leaders that followed the revolt led to a transformation in public sentiment. These actions also undermined John Redmond's already weak standing among Irish American nationalists. The *Gaelic American* reported on FOIF rallies throughout the country protesting against the "military massacre in Dublin" and Redmond's supposed complicity in these actions.[39] One such rally took place in Philadelphia on May 12, 1916, and drew a large crowd of thirty-five hundred people. According to the *Gaelic American*, an honor guard of Germans dressed "in the grey-green uniforms and the spiked helmets of the Kaiser's troops attended" and a local band played "Die Wacht am Rhein," "The Wearing of the Green," and "The Star-Spangled Banner." Meanwhile, the paper reported Cohalan's speech to the assembly, which not only condemned Redmond but also called for continued American neutrality in the conflict. As Cohalan stated: "The sober common sense of the American people will never permit us, in spite of all the efforts of England's friends here, to abandon our old traditions and enter this world war. . . . She [England] has made her bed and must now lie in it."[40]

Cohalan's prediction did not, of course, prove correct, and in April 1917 the United States entered the war on Britain's side. While this proved an obvious disappointment to Devoy, it also presented the *Gaelic American* with an opportunity to link the cause of Irish independence to President Woodrow Wilson's pledge that the war was being fought for the freedom of "small nationalities." Within days of the American declaration of war, the *Gaelic American* front-page headline reported on a large Irish meeting at Carnegie Hall, New York, which sent telegrams to both President Wilson and Champ Clark, speaker of the House of Representatives, pledging Irish American loyalty to the American flag but also calling for American support for Irish freedom. This would now become a constant theme in the pages of the *Gaelic American.* In June 1917 the *Gaelic American* reported approvingly an interview with John D. Moore, national secretary of the FOIF, who claimed that America had entered the war "for the rights of all nations great and small . . . and to make the world safe for democracy." Again, drawing on Wilson's principles, Moore claimed that "the American people expected England to apply the principles of real democracy to Ireland."[41]

While remaining loyal to the American flag, the *Gaelic American* still adopted an anti-British tone. This can be illustrated by its outraged reaction in August 1917 to the arrest of John D. Moore in New York during FOIF protests against Britain's continuing policy of repression in Ireland. The *Gaelic American* reported how Moore was arrested as soon as he criticized England, despite the fact that he was waving the Stars and Stripes. The paper launched a vigorous attack on Mayor John Mitchel, who had authorized New York police to break up the protest. In dramatic tones, it claimed: "Mitchel's war against the Irish race is on. The open-air meetings of the FOIF, held at Broadway and 37th Street, have aroused the ire of the New York pro-Britishers, who are making every effort to have them suppressed."[42] Such claims reflected the *Gaelic American*'s conviction that pro-British Americans had taken control over American foreign and domestic policy and that this would have a detrimental impact on both the interests of the Irish race and the United States itself.

Wilson's Pro-British Attitudes as a Threat to the *Gaelic American*

The *Gaelic American*'s policy of remaining loyal to the United States while attacking British policy at the same time proved a difficult maneuver to maintain in an increasingly oppressive wartime atmosphere. Any criticism of Britain could be construed as an attack on the United States itself. Even before American entry into the war, President Wilson, a self-proclaimed Anglophile, had warned in a speech in December 1915, that so-called "hyphenated Americans" had "poured the poison of disloyalty into the very arteries of our national life."[43] Once the war began, antihyphen sentiment intensified. The *Gaelic American* and other Irish American newspapers came under increasing pressure to curb their anti-British tone. Finally, in February 1918, both the *Gaelic American* and the *Irish World* were barred from the mails. This meant that these newspapers could no longer be sold via mail subscriptions.[44]

This policy hurt the newspaper's finances, and during the summer of 1918 the *Gaelic American* launched a fund to help rescue the paper.

Irish American societies and former subscribers responded enthusiastically, and according to a *Gaelic American* report in September 1918, over $10,000 was collected. In a September article, a delighted Devoy noted that the fund had closed but could not resist attacking the pro-British element in the United States at the same time: "It [the fund] has exceeded all expectations and it is the most effective answer to the tyrannical bureaucrats of the Post Office Department who sought to strangle the paper in the interests of England."[45]

The ending of the war in November 1918 removed a major source of tension that had weighed heavily on the *Gaelic American*'s efforts to put the Irish nationalist case before a pro-Allied public opinion. Within three months, the Post Office had lifted mailing restrictions on the *Gaelic American*.[46] Meanwhile, the paper also welcomed the destruction of John Redmond's Irish Parliamentary Party by Sinn Féin in the December 1918 Irish election. Sinn Féin, which shared the same Irish republican nationalism advocated by the *Gaelic American* and the Clan, now represented majority nationalism in Ireland. For the first time in decades, Irish nationalism on both sides of the Atlantic seemed united in a common purpose. Sinn Féin in Ireland also recognized that the US government would play a key role in the Paris Peace Conference and looked to Irish America to publicize the cause of Irish independence in the context of Wilson's pledge to provide justice for oppressed nationalities.[47]

Devoy believed, with some justification, that Wilson would prefer to wash his hands of the Irish question in the interests of greater cooperation with Britain in constructing a postwar international order. He was, therefore, determined to hold him to account. In December 1918 the *Gaelic American* reported on so-called "Self-Determination for Ireland" rallies across the United States.[48] One of the biggest took place in Madison Square Garden in New York and drew a massive crowd of twenty-five thousand people. Cohalan had persuaded the influential Cardinal William O'Connell of Boston to deliver the keynote speech, which called on President Wilson to apply his principle of self-determination to Ireland. According to the *Gaelic American*'s front-page report on the rally, a wireless message to this effect was sent to the president, who was then on his way to the Paris Peace Conference on board the steamer *George Washington*.[49]

De Valera's US Visit

In January 1919 the *Gaelic American* reported on an upcoming "Third Irish Race Convention" to be held in Philadelphia the following month. The paper announced that the first session of the convention would be appropriately held on George Washington's birthday, thus linking the cause of Irish freedom to America's own struggle for independence against the same empire. The convention duly went ahead and attracted over five thousand delegates, highlighting the Irish American unity that now existed across the United States. Cardinal James Gibbons of Baltimore, one of the most influential Catholic churchmen of his time, and a former supporter of John Redmond, spoke in favor of self-determination for Ireland. In a letter to Boston FOIF leader Matthew Cummings, Cohalan argued that the holding of such conventions would "bring the [Irish] question into the press and before the public."[50] The national and international press reported on the convention, but the *Gaelic American* also played its part and featured a photograph of a proud Cohalan flanked by Cardinal Gibbons on its front page.[51]

In June 1919 Éamon de Valera, president of the Irish Dáil or Parliament and leader of Sinn Féin, arrived in the United States and would remain there until November 1920. Ireland was at this point experiencing widespread civil unrest as the military wing of Sinn Féin, the Irish Republican Army, launched sporadic military attacks against British forces in Ireland.[52] The brutal reaction of British forces to these attacks received considerable coverage in the *Gaelic American*, which in turn increased FOIF membership. In stark headlines in August 1920, the *Gaelic American* reported, "The British Hun is loose in Munster. Murder, House-Burning, Raids on the houses of the people, Rioting and indiscriminate shooting by soldiers and constabulary are everyday occurrences in the south of Ireland."[53]

De Valera recognized the important role that Irish America could play in providing funds and diplomatic recognition for the Irish republican cause. In achieving these objectives, he expected to rely on the support of the rapidly growing FOIF and Devoy's *Gaelic American*, yet tensions soon emerged between de Valera and his assistant Harry Boland on the one side and Devoy and Cohalan on the other.[54]

A number of factors were behind these growing tensions, not least a personality clash between de Valera and Cohalan. Éamon de Valera's famous remark about Cohalan—"Big as the country is, it was not big enough to hold the Judge and myself"—is a testament to this rivalry.[55] However, there were other differences that went beyond personality. Shortly after his arrival, de Valera launched a so-called bond drive with the intention of selling bond certificates that could be exchanged for real bonds once an Irish Republic came into being. De Valera assumed full control over the management of the drive despite efforts by FOIF leaders to have Cohalan lead fundraising efforts.

A further source of tension arose over the FOIF's vociferous opposition to American participation in the League of Nations. The *Gaelic American* enthusiastically supported this anti-League campaign. In a March 1919 edition, it recorded a speech by Cohalan where he argued: "How clever the Englishman who devised the term, but oh, how much more strongly an appeal a 'League of Nation'" makes to mankind in general than a League for the preservation of the British empire." As Cohalan went on to point out, under article X of the League Covenant, League members would have to protect the territorial integrity of the empires that made up the League against external aggression.[56]

De Valera disagreed with the use of FOIF funds in this anti-League campaign and believed that such funds should be sent to Ireland. Furthermore, de Valera was also sympathetic to the idea of a "real League," which would protect the rights of small nations in a predatory world of great powers. As early as July 1919, just a few weeks after his arrival in the United States, de Valera informed Arthur Griffith, who was then acting Sinn Féin leader in Ireland, that he was trying to let Wilson know that "if he goes for his 14 points as they were and a true League of Nations, men and women of Irish blood will be behind him."[57]

Conclusion

Broadly, the various disputes that developed between de Valera and Cohalan related to who should determine the strategy of the Irish nationalist movement in the United States. Some leading members of the Clan, such as Joe McGarrity, sided with de Valera, and other Irish nationalists in the United States, such as Cork-man Diarmuid Lynch, who had fought in the 1916 Rising, supported Cohalan's American perspective on events.[58] However, one source of tension directly involved the actions of the *Gaelic American* and its critical reaction to de Valera's famous "Cuba interview." An analysis of this particular dispute is useful in that it highlights how the objectives of the *Gaelic American* were fundamentally shaped by American considerations rather than by the perceived needs of the Irish leader.

In February 1920 de Valera, in an interview with a reporter from the *Westminster Gazette*, a London-based newspaper, attempted to counter suggestions that British security would be compromised in the event of Irish independence. In his interview, de Valera cited the Platt Amendment, which governed relations between Cuba and the United States, as a possible model for relations between an independent Ireland and Britain. In line with the Monroe Doctrine, designed to protect US security interests in the Western Hemisphere, one of the amendment's provisions stipulated that Cuba could not make a treaty with any other foreign power that might impair its independence and imperil American security. De Valera indicated that he would have no objection if Britain adopted similar safeguards toward an independent Ireland. In his interview, de Valera argued: "Why doesn't Britain declare a Monroe Doctrine for her neighboring island? The people of Ireland, so far from objecting, would co-operate with their whole soul."[59]

De Valera's interview ignored other provisions of the Platt Amendment that gave the United States "the right to intervene for the preservation of Cuban independence."[60] The *Gaelic American* seized on this interview and throughout the next month published articles highly critical of de Valera. In one editorial, Devoy thundered: "You cannot cite the Platt Amendment without bringing in the whole text of it, which gives the United States rights in Cuba which it would be suicidal to give England in Ireland."[61]

In response to these attacks, de Valera took the unprecedented step of writing directly to Cohalan rather than Devoy to question the purpose behind these articles. This would suggest that de Valera believed that Cohalan had somehow manipulated Devoy into launching these attacks against him. As de Valera stated:

> I see added force being applied, day by day, to the power end of the great lever of American public opinion, with which I hope to accomplish my purpose. I must satisfy myself as to the temper of the other end of the lever. The articles in the "Gaelic American," and certain incidents that have resulted from them, give me grounds for the fear that, in a moment of stress, the point of the lever would fail me. I am led to believe that these articles in the "Gaelic American" have your consent and approval. Is this so?[62]

Cohalan's reply to de Valera highlights the American priorities that shaped his own American-Irish nationalism and that of the *Gaelic American*. Cohalan initially noted that he was "amazed" by the contents of de Valera's letter but "in spite of its tone, and because of the position which you occupy, I am responding to it." After first declaring that he had no control over the contents of the *Gaelic American*, he highlighted Devoy's right "to comment upon, or discuss your public utterances, or those of any man who speaks for a cause or a people."[63]

Far from refuting Devoy's allegations, Cohalan restated the main points made in the *Gaelic American* article, claiming that "a British Monroe Doctrine, that would make Ireland the ally of England, and thus buttress the falling British empire, so as to further oppress India and Egypt and other subject lands, would be so immoral, and so utterly at variance with the ideals and traditions of the Irish people." Cohalan also questioned de Valera's right, as a citizen of another country, to dictate policy to Americans and Irish Americans: "Do you think for a moment that American public opinion will permit any citizen of another country to interfere, as you suggest, in American affairs?

If so, I may assure you that you are woefully out of touch with the spirit of the country in which you are sojourning." In closing, Cohalan stressed that "it was always as an American, and for my countrymen, that I spoke."[64]

Remarkably, both men managed to patch up their differences after this testy exchange of letters. However, the truce did not last long, and after further tensions, an open breach took place between Cohalan and de Valera in November 1920. In a press release, Harry Boland, de Valera's close ally in the United States, formally severed the links between the IRB and the Clan, stating that "we have been reluctantly compelled to sever our connections between Clan na Gael and the parent body in Ireland [IRB] until such time as the will of the members of the executive become operative and not the will of Justice Cohalan."[65]

This action was a bitter blow to both Cohalan and Devoy, who had devoted so much of their lives to the Irish nationalist cause in America. The *Gaelic American* accused de Valera of trying to split the Irish nationalist cause in the United States through a "campaign of falsehood and defamation."[66] This bitter condemnation of de Valera intensified after a civil war broke out in Ireland in 1922 over the terms of a treaty that concluded the Anglo-Irish War. De Valera took the antitreaty side in this dispute, accusing the protreaty side of having betrayed the republic. Ignoring the complexities behind this conflict, the *Gaelic American* simply blamed de Valera for the conflict: "He is a monster who must be punished for his crimes. Eliminate him and the trouble will soon end. He is not fighting for the Republic but for his own personal advancement."[67]

Both Devoy and Cohalan had no doubt that de Valera was the real source of the discord that wracked Irish America in 1920. However, the *Gaelic American*'s difficulty with de Valera and other Irish nationalist leaders can be attributed to its own sense of Irish American nationalism, which differed fundamentally from that of Irish nationalism. In 1957 the eminent Irish historian F. S. L. Lyons noted the "dual allegiance" felt by many Irish Americans to both Ireland and the United States. Referring to the 1920 clash between Irish American leader Judge Daniel Cohalan and Irish nationalist leader Éamon de Valera, Lyons commented perceptively on Cohalan's angry protestations to de Valera that his "only allegiance is to America." Lyons argued that "perhaps it is not altogether fanciful to discern in these phrases something of the tragedy of the exile. However nostalgically he may look back to the mother-country, however generously he may respond to her needs, he cannot help from forming fresh attachments and striking deep roots in a new soil."[68]

A study of the *Gaelic American* in the period 1914–22 offers an illustration of how Irish American journalists such as John Devoy had indeed struck deep roots in American soil and were as much concerned about the position of the Irish ethnic group in America and American foreign-policy concerns as they were about Irish demands for nationhood. While the *Gaelic American* reflected a strongly Irish nationalist tone from the outset, it also defended Irish American and American interests from so-called pro-British elements within the United States and from the actions of the British Empire abroad. In the eyes of the *Gaelic American*, these American goals were perfectly compatible with its Irish objectives. A strengthening of the Irish race in the United States would help counter what they perceived as the growing Anglo-Saxon influence in America. Meanwhile, an America free from Anglo-Saxon influence and free from any entangling alliances with Britain would in turn help weaken the British Empire and strengthen the cause of Irish independence. In turn, Irish nationalists from Ireland, focused purely on Irish interests, did not fully appreciate how these American considerations shaped the *Gaelic American*'s transnational journalism.

14

"An American Newspaperman"

Transatlantic Influences at the Irish Press *in the 1930s*

Mark O'Brien

Having attained its independence from Britain via the Anglo-Irish Treaty in 1921, the Irish Free State engaged in a period of nation building to unify the nation after the independence conflict (1919–21) and the civil war (1922–23).[1] There emerged, in the words of one historian, "an absorption with abstractions such as Sovereignty, the Faith, Republicanism, the Language" wherein the press "contented itself with the reportage of events and the propagandist reiteration of the familiar terms of Irish political and cultural debate until these categories became mere counters and slogans often remote from any actualities."[2]

It had not always been this way: Irish journalism had initially led the way in investigative journalism in Europe. Prior to independence certain Irish newspapers embraced the "new journalism" techniques of interviews and investigative journalism to highlight what was viewed as the corrupt nature of British rule. In 1878 the *Freeman's Journal* (Dublin) published William O'Brien's series "Christmas on the Galtees" that exposed the plight of the rack-rent tenants of the Buckley estate in County Tipperary. By interviewing tenants and investigating their living conditions, O'Brien shone a light on the negative effects absentee landlordism had on tenants.[3] And, while the new journalism of the late nineteenth century in Britain and Ireland is inextricably linked with W. T. Stead, editor of the London *Pall Mall*

Gazette—whose pioneering 1885 investigation into childhood prostitution has achieved iconic status, as Margot Gayle Backus has pointed out—William O'Brien's exposé in *United Ireland* of the Dublin Castle sex scandal, which involved sexual impropriety among government officials, predates Stead's series. She also noted that the failed libel suits that arose from the series would have been closely monitored by editors and journalists in London. Their timing, argued Backus, "strongly implies a connection between . . . O'Brien's right to publish and the new mode of investigative scandal that Stead launched the following year." Prior to O'Brien's series Stead's actions "would have been unthinkable."[4]

But, while using the techniques of new journalism to expose the rack-renting and sexual peccadilloes of the colonizers was one thing, after independence, there occurred a sustained campaign waged by the Catholic Church against the new journalism that, in Ireland, made itself most visible in the form of imported British newspapers. The new journalism's emphasis on crime, scandal, investigative journalism, and campaigning journalism did not endear it to a religious hierarchy concerned with preserving the morality of the island of saints and scholars. In 1926 the Irish government agreed to a request from the Catholic hierarchy to initiate an inquiry into evil literature, the result of which was the Censorship of Publications Act in 1929. This law allowed the minister for justice to ban any newspaper that "devoted an unduly large proportion of space to the publication of matter relating to crime" and also curtailed reportage of certain court cases. There followed the banning of six British newspapers and the prosecution of an Irish regional newspaper for falling foul of the new law.[5] It was in such an environment that Irish newspapers operated in the Free State.

Owned by former Irish Party MP, William Martin Murphy, the *Irish Independent* (Dublin) adopted the elements of the new journalism that seemed safe—display advertising, condensed reportage, illustrations, and serializations—but studiously rejected any element—gossip, scandal, crime reportage and investigative journalism—that might cause controversy or condemnation. Politically, the *Independent*, having supported the Anglo-Irish Treaty of 1921, backed—though was never formally associated with—the protreaty party that formed the Free State's government from 1922 to 1932. Thus, the title represented the worldview of those who viewed the Anglo-Irish Treaty as the freedom to achieve greater freedom. In stark contrast stood the *Irish Press* (Dublin), which was established in 1931 to articulate the political views of the defeated antitreaty side, which, in the guise of Éamon de Valera and Fianna Fáil, took power in 1932. The role played by the *Irish Press* in bringing the party to power cannot be easily measured, but it played a key role in countering the negative and relentless criticism in other titles of de Valera's rejection of the treaty in 1921. As the organ of the political party that would, more than any other party, hold power in Ireland over the course of the twentieth century, the *Irish Press* articulated the party's views on Irish unity, the need to revive the Irish language, the primacy of rural living, antiurbanism, and economic self-sufficiency and established these tenets as the dominant orthodoxies of Irish political life to which all other political parties and newspapers had to respond. The third national title, the *Irish Times* (Dublin), was established in 1859 as a pro-union organ and the voice of the southern unionist minority. As the voice of that minority, the title took its responsibility seriously and sought to highlight and possibly mitigate any legislation that it viewed as impinging on the civil rights of the southern unionist, Protestant community. In the early decades of the Free State, the title supported the protreaty faction of Irish politics simply because supporting the alternative was unthinkable.

Given the primacy afforded to the Irish constitutional question in the press, and the deference in all matters to the Catholic Church, there was no realistic prospect of mainstream Irish journalism addressing topics such as the material conditions under which Irish people lived. However, in October 1936, the *Irish Press* engaged in a sustained investigation into the conditions endured by the inhabitants of Dublin's inner-city tenements. The brainchild of the paper's American general manager, John J. Harrington, the series ran for six weeks and utilized investigative reporting and human-interest angles to highlight the appalling conditions people endured in the slums of the Irish capital. The series promoted vigorous public discussion of the social problem that was tenement housing and helped launch a campaign to improve living conditions. But it also prompted allegations that this first attempt at investigative journalism in an independent Ireland embarrassed the Irish premier, Éamon de Valera, who had established the *Irish Press* to improve his electoral prospects—not to expose his government's failings. The episode illustrates the unease with which new journalism techniques were received in a conservative press environment and highlights the importance of the "outsider journalist" in casting a cold eye on social problems in the host society.

Dublin's Slums

As noted by historian Kevin C. Kearns, the "decline of Georgian Dublin from elegant abodes of the aristocracy to 'human piggeries' is one of Dublin's saddest sagas."[6] The Act of Union in 1801, which abolished the Irish Parliament, saw Dublin stripped of its status as a capital city with the attendant flight of wealthy and prominent citizens to London, where Irish parliamentarians would thereon sit at the houses of Parliament. Thus began the gradual decline of the once beautiful city-center Georgian mansions to a situation wherein "rack-renting landlords viewed their properties as little more than cattle sheds to be packed with humanity."[7] As subdivision of houses became ever more prevalent, the Great Famine of the mid-nineteenth century again increased the population of Dublin. By 1900 there were over six thousand tenement properties in which tenants lived in appalling conditions as the houses, some between 100 and 150 years old, displayed the toll of successive generations of tenants. Leaking roofs, sagging ceilings, rotting floorboards, broken windows, and rickety staircases were the norm as was severe overcrowding: "Some tenement areas had 800 people to the acre, as many as a hundred persons in one house and fifteen to twenty family members in a single tiny room. A primitive toilet and water tap in the rear yard had to serve all the inhabitants of a house."[8]

In 1901 a critical article in the *Irish Builder* demanded that the identity of all landlords be made public and noted that "many there would be found figuring in the list who are looked upon as eminently useful citizens and leaders of public opinion."[9] Following a public inquiry prompted by the collapse of two tenement buildings in September 1913, it was revealed that members of Dublin Corporation were owners of tenement buildings. The corporation, which was responsible for enforcing housing standards, did not enforce regulations pertaining to the sector on the basis that if it did then large-scale homelessness would follow.[10] As the impetus for Irish independence from Britain gained momentum, the slum tenements were portrayed by the independence movement as a symptom of British rule and neglect: the Dáil Éireann Loan prospectus published in Irish newspapers in 1919 calling for people to loan money to the independence movement made a direct reference to the slums by declaring that those who contributed could "abolish the slums."[11] Indeed, interviewed in the 1960s, one of the leading lights of the independence movement, Dublin Corporation member (1906–24), minister for local government (1932–39), and president of Ireland (1945–59) Seán T. O'Kelly recalled that "for many years the Corporation had endeavoured to improve matters. Scheme after scheme was presented to the [British] Government. But the Dublin Castle authorities blocked the efforts of those who worked for reform."[12]

Political independence in the early 1920s brought very little change. Surveying the tenement problem in 1925, the radical journal *Honesty* criticized the "unconscionable manner of exacting 'rents' from the victims of this soul and body destroying system of housing."[13] In a similar vein, the left-leaning *Republican Congress* newspaper highlighted the continued existence of the slums after independence and organized inner-city tenant leagues that sought, with some success, to bring about rent reductions with nonpayment campaigns. In places, this campaign saw significant reductions in inner-city rental rates.[14] It has been eloquently argued by Mary E. Daly that Fianna Fáil's promotion of rural life and the pessimistic portrayal of urban life by the Catholic Church meant that, in the early decades of independence, rural Ireland was viewed as the ideal. This meant that the housing crisis in Dublin, and other Irish cities, was not afforded the governmental urgency that it deserved.[15] There also existed hesitancy on the part of government to overly involve itself in an area of competence that it viewed as the preserve of local authorities. Writing to Premier Éamon de Valera in 1937, his minister for finance, Seán MacEntee, observed that it was "unwise to keep giving Dublin Corporation large sums of money" and that the corporation "must shoulder a large part of blame themselves for not being able to finance its housing programme."[16] It was within this environment that a trans-Atlantic influence, in the form of John J. Harrington, made itself visible in the pages of the *Irish Press.*

"An American Newspaperman"

The *Irish Press* was edited in its infancy by de Valera loyalist Frank Gallagher, who did much to instill the distinctive tone of party loyalty within the paper and keep it alive with meager resources. After expending much effort in getting the paper established, Gallagher eventually resigned on the grounds that he could no longer work with general manager John J. Harrington, who had arrived at the paper in 1933. Born in Bridgeport, Connecticut, to Brooklyn parents of Irish extraction, Harrington was a graduate of the University of Pennsylvania's Wharton School of Finance and Commerce.[17] To this day, it remains unclear how and why Harrington, a thirty-six-year-old business graduate from New York, ended up traveling to Dublin to work at the *Irish Press.* One newspaper account has it that he was appointed after the company chairman, Edmund Williams, went to America "in search of an American newspaperman and selected Mr Harrington."[18] Why the *Irish Press* required "an American newspaperman" remains a mystery, although one author has suggested that he was appointed to represent the sizable Irish American investment in the paper.[19]

Having secured experience at "re-organization work" at the Scripps-Howard newspaper organization, Harrington arrived at the *Irish Press* with the reputation of an "efficiency expert" before becoming general manager in succession to Robert Brennan, who was appointed the Free State's first minister to the United States in 1934. His presence very much grated on Gallagher, who, in a letter to de Valera, declared that Harrington was "the worst possible man to handle staffs [as he had] the American view of workers—that they must be shown who is the boss and the best way to show them this is to sack somebody important." In another letter, Gallagher informed de Valera that Harrington had been banned from the case room after his repositioning of the Linotype machines had resulted in two of them becoming unusable.[20] The end for Gallagher came in July 1934 when Harrington transferred a member of staff before eventually firing him. Gallagher served his six months' notice and then agreed to remain until his successor was appointed, eventually leaving in June 1935. When de Valera canvased his opinion on who would be best to replace him, Gallagher nominated the paper's chief leader writer, Bill Sweetman, whom he described as having "great strength of character."[21]

However, Gallagher was replaced not by Sweetman but by John Herlihy, a seventy-one-year-old journalist who had begun his career on the radical Irish newspapers of the late 1800s and had spent the latter part of his career working for the Press Association in London.[22] Whatever skills he brought as editor, Herlihy may have had difficulty controlling the enthusiastic Harrington. As recalled by one senior Fianna Fáil figure, it was "a tragedy not only for the paper but for the country when Gallagher ceased to be editor. From that time the whole tone of the paper gradually deteriorated. A new and undesirable streak crept into its columns."[23] This "undesirable streak" may well have been Harrington's enthusiasm for investigative and campaigning journalism—helped in no small part by another overseas journalist then working at the *Irish Press*, Chris O'Sullivan from Australia.[24] It was during Herlihy's short three-year editorial tenure that Harrington, supported by O'Sullivan, launched his Dublin slums investigation.

There was precedent for such an investigation: in 1889 Jacob A. Riis, a Danish-born immigrant, had published an eighteen-page photo article capturing the squalor and abject poverty of the tenements of Manhattan in *Scribner's Magazine*.[25] As a New Yorker, Harrington could not have helped but be aware of this groundbreaking journalistic feat. Coming from a newspaper environment steeped in the traditions of new journalism, the slums were like manna from heaven for Harrington. The *Irish Press* was a young newspaper trying to establish itself, and the slums represented a very visible social evil that needed rectifying. In effect they represented a crusade on which the paper could use the techniques of new journalism to make an impact journalistically and socially. Looking back on his motives for initiating the series, Harrington observed that "he knew something about slums before he came to this country . . . and he was only in the country a couple of weeks when he was ashamed of the land of his ancestors. Because of that he had tried to do something about it."[26] Thus, as Harrington saw it, the objectives of the series were clear:

> From the very first we invited the co-operation and support of all those who were in agreement with the object which we set before ourselves, because we recognised the problem was one of enormous dimensions and we were only too conscious that it could only by solved by something in the nature of a mass movement on the part of all the citizens, irrespective of religious or political affiliations. We made it our object to mobilise public opinion at the back of our campaign, as we felt that it was only an absolutely irresistible volume of support which could break down the barriers and obstacles of all kinds which will have to be overcome before the field would be clear for the legislative and administrative action which will be necessary to extirpate the slums and provide better houses for their present occupants.[27]

Thus, throughout August 1936, "in the heat of summer *Irish Press* representatives who were inquiring into this matter found by day and night, in the heart of the city, sickening corroboration of the worst descriptions that exist in the pages of reports dealing with Dublin slums over the last 150 years."[28] Beginning on October 1, 1936, the paper devoted one page every day for six weeks to investigating the slums and, in terms of using elements of new journalism theretofore ignored in Ireland, it framed the series of articles as a campaign, referred to its series as an investigation, referred to the journalists who contributed to the series as "investigators," and used new journalism's emphasis on human interest and personal testimony by highlighting the suffering of the slums' inhabitants through the use of photographs and by focusing on individual case studies of families trapped in the slums. The photographs used in the series bore a striking resemblance to those of the New York slums published in 1889 by *Scribner's Magazine*: subjects were framed within the appalling conditions in which they lived their lives, and the testimony, such as that from slum inhabitant Winifred O'Rourke, who, aged 35, had lost five of her eight children to slum diseases such as tuberculous, gave an air of realism to a subject that was often discussed in more abstract forms.[29] The headlines—"Take Us Out of This Terrible Place"; "Massacre of the Innocents"; "Five Children Her Slum Sacrifice"; "Slum Landlordism Extracts a Huge Tax from Human Anguish"—also framed the series as a campaign. Referring to previous coverage of the slums, the paper noted that "it is not the want of inquiry that can be complained of, rather want of action, of driving power of the determination at any cost to abolish an evil, the existence of which had been so abundantly demonstrated," and it was this lack of action that the paper was determined to challenge.[30]

"Dublin's Slum Evil"

The series began with a "call to arms" editorial. Describing the slums as "a discredit and a menace to the Irish capital," it observed that the slums were "a legacy of alien rule" and "the fruit of generations of neglect and civic blindness." Noting that the government had informed Dublin Corporation that it would refund the corporation two-thirds of any expenditure used to replace the slums, the paper nonetheless declared that, given the scale of the problem, resolving it was beyond the scope of the corporation alone. This conclusion had been reached "after a careful survey of what has been done in the past, of what is being done now, and of what will remain to be accomplished." Determined not to alienate any person or organization from its campaign, the paper declared that its series was based on "official statistics, medical officers' reports on the slum evil in particular localities, reports of Royal Commissions, and the testimony of many trustworthy bodies and persons." The series was not "an attack on any person, slum owner or otherwise, individually" but was rather "an exposure and an indictment of a system" and "an attempt so as to focus public opinion." The editorial also laid bare the scale of the slum problem. It revealed that thirty-three thousand families lived in tenement dwellings—of these twenty-seven thousand families lived in one-roomed tenement dwellings, and sixteen hundred families lived in basements prone to fumes from the city sewers—and estimated that 21 percent of Dublin citizens (ninety-three thousand people) lived in slums. It also contrasted the 1934 infant mortality rate of the most overcrowded slum area (119 per 1,000 births) with that of Dublin overall (79 per 1,000), London (67 per 1,000), the Free State (63 per 1,000), and England (59 per 1,000) and urged its readers to think of the children "who come into existence in these fetid, squalid haunts of horror for whom there is no chance of life as compared with the children born in the rest of the country." What was needed, it concluded, was "an enlightened and aroused public conscience" to demand a scheme of building to "wipe out the slum horror of Dublin."[31] Over the subsequent six weeks the paper devoted a page per day on articles that outlined the historical context to the slums, current statistics, slum infantile death rates, slum landlordism, and the lack of regulation enforcement by Dublin Corporation, which the paper maintained was "one of the biggest, if not the biggest, slum landlords in Dublin."[32] It also published an interview with the city's medical officer, Matthew J. Russell, in which he declared that he would condemn the slums as uninhabitable but for that fact that this action would result in huge numbers of people becoming homeless.[33]

In its attempt to build a consensus of public opinion that action needed to be taken, the series provided a platform for the leaders of all major religions to express their position. The head of the Roman Catholic Church in Ireland, Cardinal Joseph MacRory, "expressed his surprise at the revelations concerning Dublin's lack of housing facilities as published in the *Irish Press*." Curiously, the statements did not include one from Dublin's Catholic archbishop, Edward Byrne. This lack of engagement from the city's Catholic hierarchy is odd, though it was later alleged that the Catholic Church owned several tenement buildings. As recalled by Tim Pat Coogan, who joined the paper in the early 1960s, some of the journalists who had worked on the series told him that "many of the slum properties excoriated by the series were owned by 'important personages'; including those of the Church."[34] Other religions were not as mute, possibly to the chagrin of the Catholic hierarchy. The Church of Ireland archbishop of Dublin, Rev. John Gregg, declared that he agreed "with the *Irish Press* that the problem must be tackled courageously and comprehensively in our time and not left to posterity," while the chief rabbi of the Jewish community, Dr. Isaac Herzog, declared that if the public purse could fund the abolition of the slums, then an appeal should be made to Irish America to "contribute generously towards a fund which aims at removing so serious a blot from the capital of Ireland, which is, to all Irishmen, the historic symbol of the Irish spirit and whose historic and national glamour is dimmed in no small measure by these wretched slums."[35]

In terms of campaign journalism, the series pushed the boundaries of what was the norm for journalism at the time, and indeed, what was the norm at the *Irish Press*. On one occasion, the paper published an open letter to Dublin's lord mayor and corporation in which it declared that the Dublin Corporation's housing construction figures "published in reply to the *Irish Press* campaign for the elimination of the slums of Dublin are the best evidence we could produce in support of our case, namely that construction in Dublin is hopelessly behind the need." The city's residents were, it noted "forced to live amid heart-rendering scenes of squalor, suffering, and slow-tortured death" and concluded, "We need action not words." In a side column, under the headline "Record of Futility," the paper listed the various commissions of inquiry into the slums that had been convened between 1798 and 1936. On the same page, it published an open letter to the minister for local government, Seán T. O'Kelly, in which it noted that 35 percent of Dublin Corporation dwellings built since the foundation of the state in 1922 had occurred since the election of the Fianna Fáil government in 1932. While this "splendid record of achievement" demonstrated that the government understood "the need for ameliorating the lot of the national capital's tenement dwellers," the paper maintained that progress was far too slow and that "additional powers must be invoked and additional groups set up to handle the crisis."[36]

This, in essence, was Harrington's position: the problem was on such a scale that the corporation could not alone resolve the issue and, in a very unusual move for any newspaper's general manager,

Harrington himself took to the pages of the *Irish Press* to articulate his thinking. In another open letter, this time to the newly appointed housing inspector of the local housing department, Harrington declared "there is a New Deal in Ireland—one of open dealing, so that the citizens may know what steps are being taken to lift them from the depths to which they have descended as a result of indifference or worse."[37] In a subsequent, detailed article, Harrington noted that the national public works program that had been introduced in the United States had provided much public infrastructure, employment, and a move toward economic recovery and called for a similar program to be introduced in Ireland.[38] What Premier Éamon de Valera and Fianna Fáil made of all this can only be speculated on: toward the end of the series the paper published an open invitation to the delegates attending the party's national conference in Dublin to visit the slums. While it conceded that the slums were a legacy of British rule, it noted, in what could only be interpreted as a criticism of Irish independence, that the year 1936 represented "the fourteenth year of a self-governed state, when the babies of Easter 1916 are still, as men and women, crying for a happier life for their babies, crying for simple shelter." It also noted that seventy thousand children had been born in Ireland's slums since the state's creation in 1922.[39]

Given the sustained prominence afforded the slum problem by the paper, it is unsurprising that it observed that it had been inundated by "the receipt of letters containing suggestions on slum clearance and rehousing and many related questions, as well as offers of personal help by health and housing specialists" and that it was "co-ordinating all the enthusiasm and special knowledge available for this campaign of war on slumdom and rehousing of its people."[40] It also noted the support received for its campaign from competitor newspapers such as the *Irish Times*, the *Irish Independent*, the *Evening Herald*, and the *Evening Mail*.[41] In mid-November 1936, the paper announced the formation of the Citizens' Housing Council to continue the campaign. The council was chaired by John J. Harrington (described as publisher and general manager of the *Irish Press*), and among its members were Chris O'Sullivan (described as joint secretary); W. Lombard Murphy, proprietor of Independent Newspapers; H. F. Tivy, proprietor of the *Evening Mail*; and John Herlihy, editor of the *Irish Press.* The council also had a sizable religious presence, including the Rev. John Gregg, Church of Ireland archbishop of Dublin; Dr. Isaac Herzog, chief rabbi; and the Rev. M. Murphy, administrator of the Catholic Pro-Cathedral of Dublin, who presumably represented Dublin's Catholic archbishop.[42] In December 1936, a joint meeting of the Dublin Corporation and the council occurred after which the *Irish Press* again declared its belief that the slum problem was beyond the corporation's solving and that effective change could only occur "by treating the evil as a national one and by applying national resources, in conjunction with those of the Corporation, to its extirpation."[43] This was Harrington's core belief: he later reiterated his belief that "they should have three hard-hitting experts and give them all the authority they needed to get the job done—get rid of the red tape which had strangled many a good man—and then say 'either get results or get out.'"[44]

There then followed a series of editorials arising, presumably, from the editorial intrigue that centered on who would eventually succeed the elderly Herlihy as editor. One critical editorial, in December 1936, observed that "there must be a feeling of wonderment among the people of Dublin at the complete disappearance from public view of the Citizens' Housing Council which had taken under its control the question of finding the best methods of providing a solution of the slum problem in the metropolis." It noted that while the council had undertaken to compile a report on the problem, such a course of action "savours somewhat of the political amateur" and public opinion was "steadily cooling and evaporating."[45] Two months later the paper noted that the council had "not been heard of for months and we have no option but to come to the conclusion that it has vanished into space."[46] Given that the council was chaired by Harrington and that Herlihy was a council member, it is conceivable that the critical editorials were written by the paper's chief leader writer, Bill Sweetman, who would replace Herlihy as editor in 1938.

Nonetheless, when the council's report—which called for the creation of "a statutory board with the broadest powers" to deliver five thousand houses per annum for ten years and called for the government to provide finance—was published in May 1937, the paper praised it as containing "positive, practical recommendations that, in our judgment, go to the root of the matter and provide a basis for measures that will in due time extirpate this great social evil."[47] And while coverage of the slums issue continued—including coverage of the Dublin Corporation's consideration of the report—it was clear that the paper's campaign was over.[48] When, in February 1938, the corporation described the Citizens' Housing Council's report as "impracticable" and released its own plan to build twelve thousand homes over five years, the paper welcomed the plan as demonstrating that the corporation had "at last come to grips with the slum problem in the Irish metropolis."[49] Given that the corporation had built 8,601 dwellings between 1922 and 1936, this was a significant step-up in building activity, albeit not on the level that the slum series had called for.[50]

Fallout

While, in the words on one historian, the slum series "resulted in real improvements in the living conditions of the Dublin poor [and] gave a jolting insight into how people really lived," it was marred toward the end of 1937 by allegations that the paper was instructed by its political masters to drop the issue.[51] While the slum campaign series was radical, campaigning journalism that hit home with readers, it is arguable that the series, in terms of its content and presentation, did not sit well with Premier Éamon de Valera and his party, Fianna Fáil. The campaign's constant refrain—that Dublin's slum problem constituted a national rather than a local crisis and required a national rather than a local response—was at odds with Fianna Fáil's position that responsibility for resolving the slum issue rested solely with the local authority. Similarly, the creation of the Citizens' Housing Committee represented a parapolitical force that sought to convince public opinion that the government should play a greater role in resolving the problem—again at variance with the party's position. Also, the public platform given by the series to minority religions was at odds with the party's fidelity to the Catholic Church. And, the manner in which

Harrington took to the pages of the paper to outline the policies he believed the government should adopt hardly endeared him to Fianna Fáil politicians. Whether or not de Valera requested that the paper tone down its slum campaign may never be definitively answered, though there exists some vivid testimony that he did.

In late 1937 former *Irish Press* journalist and Harrington supporter, Chris O'Sullivan, alleged such interference had indeed occurred. O'Sullivan had been a strong supporter of the slum series and had served as secretary of the Citizens' Housing Council. Many decades later, O'Sullivan recalled that the Catholic Church had made life difficult for him in Ireland on the basis that he "was not a conformist, not a Catholic, wasn't seen going to church." According to O'Sullivan, the Catholic Church "was the biggest landlord in Ireland and rack-renter [and] put pressure on de Valera to get rid of me." Indeed, O'Sullivan's appointment as managing editor, while approved by the company's board of directors, was vetoed in late 1936 by de Valera, who ultimately dismissed him for sending a reporter abroad without first clearing the expenditure involved with senior management.[52] Having become editor of the Labour Party weekly paper, *Labour News* (Dublin), O'Sullivan published a full page of extracts from the slum series on its first anniversary. Headed "Winter Comes on Dublin: Ministers & Corporation Accuse Each Other While the Mass of the People Suffer," it claimed that the Fianna Fáil government had "silenced" the slum campaign "because it became too revealing and might compel courses that bureaucrats hate or fear to adopt."[53] This charge was rejected by the *Irish Press*, which declared that "the man who wrote those lines had the best reason to be aware that there was not a scintilla of foundation for what he alleged against the government." There was, it declared, "no intervention by the government in any shape or form." As the *Press* saw it, the campaign had been "thwarted and defeated—unconsciously and unintentionally we admit—by men [presumably Harrington and O'Sullivan] who did not understand Irish conditions, who had no conception of how political action for a great humanitarian object should be conducted, and who deliberately, and in the face of repeated warnings, chose to adopt a course that resulted in the futility and fiasco which had been predicted." Specifically, it blamed the Citizens' Housing Council's six months' absence from public view (while it prepared its report) for the collapse of the campaign: by the time of its release "public interest in the question was practically dead."[54]

O'Sullivan begged to differ. In the following week's *Labour News*, he noted that his article had "burned into the Government's political conscience" and outlined, in great detail, what he saw as having transpired:

> The *Irish Press* was responsible for the 1936 slum investigations and for bringing into existence the Citizens' Housing Council as an auxiliary in the fight. But from the moment the Council met official pressure was used towards bottling up the affairs of that body or canalising its stream of effort into a quarter that would pass a grand resolution at a public meeting and conveniently leave the whole matter into the hands of government. This was more than once openly and directly urged on the Council. When the Housing Council did not take that line but formed its own technical committees, it incurred the editorial disfavour of the *Irish Press*, which has thrice gratuitously attacked it. The parent found the child had ideas of its own. Even when the Department of Local Government was invited to appoint an observer, the Minister declined. At a certain stage of the campaign, when the Housing Council was still quartered on Burgh Quay [headquarters of the *Irish Press*], when the campaign had brought the people to the height of expectation of government action and there were demands from all cities and towns for extension of the campaign, it was intimated to a leader of the Citizens' Council that in a certain government quarter the view was held that the campaign threated to bankrupt the country with its increased demands for housing. When that warning sign did not take effect, other action was promoted in the interest of dampening the campaign and getting it to cry off.

The *Irish Press* drive for slum clearance and rehousing had failed, O'Sullivan concluded, "simply because certain interests did not want it to go on. Too many vested interests were being disturbed by the demand for simple reforms necessary to accomplish the change. And the government was not seriously prepared to disturb those interests further."[55] Responding, the *Irish Press* described O'Sullivan's statement as "a gratuitous and malevolent invention" and announced that it had "no intention of playing his game by contradicting whatever he may write and shall for the future take no notice under any circumstances whatever of a scribe who is not ashamed to resort to such controversial methods."[56] Given that *Labour News* had a small circulation, it may be that the *Irish Press* decided that reacting to O'Sullivan's allegations simply gave them wider publicity.

An American Returns Home

Nonetheless, O'Sullivan's allegations did permit opposition politicians to criticize the manner in which the *Irish Press* had gone quiet on the slum problem. At a public meeting, Dublin councillor James Larkin observed how the paper's slum series had continued "until somebody came down with a hand . . . and said this thing has gone far enough"—an observation denied by Harrington at the same meeting. As recalled by Harrington, his intention was to "run the campaign for two weeks [but] we carried on for six, and then we stopped to see what . . . the members of the Corporation and the national government housing department were going to do about it."[57]

In June 1938 it was announced that, having invested in a New York newspaper, the *Brooklyn Daily Eagle*, Harrington had resigned from the *Irish Press*. His decision to return to New York prompted effusive praise from *Irish Press* company board chairman, Edmund Williams, who described the slum series as "the greatest single achievement of the *Irish Press*." As a result of Harrington's "pioneering work," Williams contended, Dublin Corporation had "been forced to launch a housing programme calling for the expenditure of £750,000."[58] For his part, Harrington, publicly at least, had no qualms with de Valera who was, he avowed, "the greatest statesman in Europe."[59]

Thereafter the issue of Dublin slums effectively disappeared from the mainstream press, though the *Bell* magazine (established by Seán Ó Faoláin and Peadar O'Donnell) published several articles on Dublin's slums, including one that starkly noted that political independence had changed little for those trapped in the tenements; the only difference the author could identify was that the names of the streets had been changed from English into Irish.[60] In the 1950s the slums were gradually replaced by high-rise apartment complexes in the city center and large-scale housing developments in suburban Dublin. It was at the *Irish Press* itself where the slums series had the most long-lasting impact—though as an example of the type of journalism that should be avoided. When appointed as the title's editor in 1968, Tim Pat Coogan met with the company's managing director, Vivion de Valera, who told him that the slum series, which had been published thirty-two years previously, was the type of journalism to avoid as it upset advertisers and created "a bad image, an impression of socialism."[61] The series was journalism's first engagement with investigative journalism in independent Ireland and involved outsiders casting a cold eye on Irish society. With the exception of the *Bell*, investigative journalism would not reoccur in Ireland until the 1960s, when a new generation of outsider journalists, including Mary Maher from Chicago and Michael Viney from England, would lead the charge in placing investigative journalism at the forefront of modern Irish journalism.[62]

15

First Impressions

A Bar Fight Introduces John Bull to an American Institution

Pamela E. Walck

American troops marching in formation through the streets of Belfast were a welcome sight to the war-weary citizens of Northern Ireland in late January 1942.[1] Newspapers that rarely ran photographs during the paper rationing of the war years suddenly dedicated dozens of column inches to images showing the arrival of the Yanks to Ulster.[2] In one photo, a cheeky white American stands on a ladder to the second floor of a home to woo a young woman leaning out the window. Belfast newspaper editors labeled him an "American 'Romeo,'" while another image featured the profile of a US soldier chomping on a fat cigar.[3]

Editorials breathlessly praised the speedy arrival of the Americans, whose president had pledged three weeks earlier, just after the Japanese bombing of Pearl Harbor on December 7, 1941, to send troops to aid his ally. The *Belfast News-Letter* noted: "No more striking demonstration of our great ally's earnestness could be desired than the presence of these fighting men in our midst."[4] It was as if the British Isles had taken a collective sigh of relief.

Six months later, however, British papers neither heralded the arrival of African American[5] troops in Northern Ireland, nor did Ulster newspapers photograph their arrival. Few mainstream American newspapers even reported the story. The *New York Times* only ran a photo at the top of page eight of its July 29, 1942, edition to mark the event.[6] The American black press, however, celebrated the news. The

Chicago Defender ran a page six photo documenting the deployment in its July 25, 1942, edition. Both the *Times*'s and the *Defender*'s images featured platoon-sized units of African American troops interacting with British soldiers. Names were omitted to avoid violating censorship regulations, but the similarities ended there.

The *Times*'s picture depicted a black platoon standing around a refreshments table looking frightened and uncertain after landing in Northern Ireland. Two white Ulster volunteers are pushed into the far-right corner. They are observers, not participants. This shot was a stark contrast to the photos of the white Americans who had arrived so triumphantly six months earlier. Meanwhile, in the *Defender*'s image, the troops are engaged in conversation with a corporal in the Royal Air Force. Everyone is smiling as the white airman shows off the spoils of war: a piece of German equipment. The image reaffirmed to *Defender* readers that the color bar was nonexistent in Britain and that African Americans deployed there enjoyed a life not possible back home. Few, if any, Ulster residents saw these images.

Those thousands of African American troops dispersed across Northern Ireland and England practically doubled the nation's minority population overnight.[7] For African Americans, especially those from Southern states, the deployment would be the first time they were in a society where Jim Crow laws did not dictate the boundaries of everyday life. White American soldiers became frustrated as they saw African Americans stepping out with British women and, in many instances, being treated better by their hosts.[8] Hostilities quickly developed among the segregated US camps. For Ulster citizens, particularly Irish Catholics, the arrival of African Americans represented an opportunity to defy the Crown by socially engaging with them—much to the dismay of British and American officials.[9]

This chapter examines the concerns British officials expressed about the effect of African American troops on their homogenously white society, how they braced for anticipated unrest among Americans, and how they put pressure on Northern Ireland newspaper editors to exercise discretion in reporting racial tensions. It will also explore how US military officials attempted to smooth over racial issues among deployed units—including a publicized tour of the British Isles by the US Army's only African American general officer with little success—and their eventual resort to an extension of Jim Crowism. Finally, this chapter uses reports from the British and American press to examine how predictions of racial problems were realized at a bar in Antrim, a village just north of Belfast.

While Antrim is a commonly cited example of places where high-profile racial tensions occurred among American troops stationed in Britain,[10] previous research has largely ignored media coverage of the incident that resulted in the death of one American soldier and the serious injury of another. A study of the news coverage will help create a better understanding of newsgathering routines the transnational press used to report on wartime racial tensions and paint a larger picture of race relations and press censorship during this period. Similarly, this chapter argues that because the Antrim incident occurred early in the war, both the British and American press demonstrated greater autonomy in terms of how it was reported—a freedom that diminished as the war continued and news organizations began to exercise greater self-censorship or experience increased government-imposed censorship. Primary sources included newspaper coverage[11] of the Antrim incident; US and British governmental documents, including correspondence among government leaders; and military reports concerning racial tensions among US troops.

Creating a "Considerable Flutter" in Ulster

"More American Troops in Ulster," the headline in the *Belfast News-Letter* blared across the front page on May 19, 1942.[12] Below the single-deck headline, sandwiched between stories about the war efforts in the China-Burma-India theater and Vichy talks in Rome, ran a photo of US troops walking down a gangway. Five months after the first arrival of Americans, the Ulster press was still reporting relief at the sight of more US forces.

The paper's correspondent noted: "It was heartening to see the tanks coming ashore"[13] in the largest contingent of American troops since the United States had joined the war. In the months that followed, the newspaper would print images of the Americans—US sailors saluting the American flag at a Londonderry naval base, US commanders participating in ceremonies with the lord mayor of Belfast, and servicemen playing games of baseball on local soccer pitches.[14] In each image, the Americans were white.

Indeed, in a summary of American forces and military activities in 1942, an Ulster cabinet official noted the general camaraderie between white American and British troops in early 1942. The report stated: "The first arrival on the 26th of January was a mere token force of some 4,000 men. . . . [T]heir coming caused a considerable flutter all over Ulster."[15] As Allied troops prepared for the Northern Africa campaign, the same cabinet member noted that cooperation and conviviality among the armies left positive feelings all around. The British found the Yanks to be less "assertive" than they had anticipated, and the Americans found the Brits to be less "unsociable and supercilious." The cabinet member wrote, "In fact, generally, the American was treated by the garrison and populace of Northern Ireland as a welcome guest."[16]

The official credited much of this to the fact that many of the first Americans to arrive in Ulster were from midwestern farms rather than major urban centers. These Yanks fit well into the rural surroundings of Northern Ireland. But the shiny veneer of the American invasion[17] did not last long in some quarters of British government. By June 1942, British officials in the Colonial, Foreign, and Home Offices were all voicing concerns. Of particular worry: the projected numbers of African American troops en route to Northern Ireland and the British Isles and how racial tensions among the Americans might influence British society.

A "Very Nasty Situation Brewing Up"

One Colonial Office official noted to a colleague on June 24, 1942: "I hear through a liaison officer with the Americans that they [white US soldiers] are taking a threatening attitude about the blacks and coloured people they find over here."[18] The official added there had also been growing talk among the Americans that they would lynch anyone of African descent seen dancing with white girls. He noted: "Allowance must be made for loose talk of course, but I fear there may be a very nasty situation brewing up."[19] The official concluded that as a matter of imperial policy, "We cannot encourage a colour bar or tolerate outrages on blacks."[20] It did not take long for more accounts of "nasty situations" to start popping up.[21]

Within a month, John L. Keith, a welfare officer in the Colonial Office, wrote to his superior, Sir Charles Jeffries, noting the large numbers of African American troops in the United Kingdom was "having repercussions on our work for coloured Colonial people, and the treatment the Americans mete out to their negroes is the subject of comment by coloured Colonials."[22] American commanders suggested presentations to British military staff explaining the complex race issue back home, prompting Keith to note:

> Any discriminatory treatment of coloured persons in this country is bound to react on the work we are trying to do to break down the colour bar and to help coloured people in this country to fit into the work and life of this country. I do not understand the reference to lectures to be given by Americans on the colour question. It would be very undesirable for the Americans to lecture British people on colour bar![23]

He concluded that any attempt by the Americans to segregate troops would result in British citizens developing resentments toward their allies.[24] A month earlier Keith said it was "rather a pity that the Americans cannot bring over some of their negro fighting men," which at the time he thought would help ease the lot for Colonials adjusting to British society.[25]

These mounting concerns were not limited to the Colonial Office. By July 1942 chief constables from across the country were writing to the Home Office with similar concerns about race relations. Oxfordshire's chief constable, T.E. St. Johnston, in a letter to Sir Frank Newsam, the British undersecretary of state in the Home Office, worried that while the eighteen hundred American troops in the county were thus far, all white, "it is expected that there will be a fair proportion of coloured troops among the incoming contingents, and the problems that will arise when this occurs, have been under active discussion in this County during the past few days."[26] St. Johnston pointed out the need for an established Home Office or War Office policy regarding African American troops in the United Kingdom, particularly when they were off duty. Otherwise, he feared "serious clashes" were likely.[27]

The Oxfordshire constable believed African American troops would be fine if left to themselves, but that "the American white troops will create trouble if it is found that the coloured troops are associating with white civilians, and in particular with white girls."[28] He suggested a propaganda campaign to explain the British position on the lack of a color bar in the country. St. Johnston also urged the Home Office to find a way to prevent British women from "misconducting" themselves with African American troops, "if for no other reason than that we do not desire to have a certain proportion of the population semi-coloured, in rural districts in this Country in the future."[29]

St. Johnston's latter request quickly gained traction among officials in the Home Office. By August 10, 1942, a confidential memo entitled "U.S.A. Coloured Troops" was circulating among the Home Office and the country's regional commissioners. Drafted by Harry Haig, regional commissioner for the Southern Regional Headquarters, the two-page report outlined how the presence of African American troops in the United Kingdom—and their interactions with British civilians—could stir up problems among American troops and urged a nationwide educational undertaking. He outlined a proposed "discreet" propaganda piece that included a "sympathetic historical statement" about how African Americans arrived in the United States, the experience US leaders had when attempting to "mix the races," and the general difficulties that resulted.[30] Haig's proposal noted: "This implies no inequality. But the races are different in character, in education, in outlook; and intimacy in the end means trouble. Do not treat them in any way as outcasts. Be helpful, be kind; but not intimate."[31] Further, Haig wrote that regional officials concurred that this propaganda campaign should be limited to word of mouth and strictly kept from the press.[32]

After reaching consensus among regional commissioners and Home Office staff, a circular was offered to the War Office, Ministry of Information, Foreign Office, and Colonial Office for comments. Newsam noted that the response had been positive and a draft could be shared with American military leaders in London.[33] Eleven days later, the circular was presented to Lieutenant General Dwight D. Eisenhower, commanding general of the US Army in the European Theater of Operations (ETO).

American Officials: Discrimination Should "Be Sedulously Avoided"

Frank Newsam's August 31, 1942, letter to Eisenhower, the highest-ranking US official in the ETO, was framed as a courtesy before the informational circular went to the country's constables and police departments. But rather than raising the worries over biracial births, the dangers of street fracases, or fears of building resentments among British civilians, Newsam instead used an incident in Liverpool among white American seamen, African American troops, and British women to explain why UK officials felt strongly about enforcing their country's policy of nondiscrimination in public places. He noted that police had separated the military men and the women, telling all three parties it was for their own good, particularly because of objections from white American troops. According to Newsam, "The coloured soldiers resented being spoken to on this matter by the British police, and one of them replied: 'It is not democracy if we cannot do what we like.'"[34] Newsam told Eisenhower he felt the general should know about the difficult position British police officers were facing and suggested that it would be helpful to know the US government's approach to matters between its service members and UK civilians so that an acceptable policy for British soldiers could be developed.[35]

Brigadier General John E. Dahlquist, Eisenhower's acting chief of staff, responded three days later. He wrote, "The Commanding general is in complete accord with the instructions the Home Office proposes to issue. This policy of non-discrimination is exactly the policy which has always been followed by the United States Army."[36] He also noted that US Army policy required that if a particular place was "out of bounds" for some US soldiers, it was "out of bounds" for all.[37]

Indeed, shortly after the arrival of African American troops to the British Isles, the US Army's Adjutant General's Office issued what it called a "Policy on Negroes"[38] that gave commanding officers responsibility for maintaining peaceful race relations among their troops. At Eisenhower's command, Lieutenant Colonel Fred A. Meyer, the assistant adjutant general, wrote: "It is the desire of this Headquarters that discrimination against the Negro troops be sedulously avoided."[39] Although Eisenhower and the Adjutant General's Office were aware that commanders of white and African American soldiers stationed near smaller towns might have trouble offering equal accommodations, particularly where social events were concerned, the commanders were expected to "use their best judgment" to avoid racial discrimination and to minimize friction between white and black soldiers.[40] Clearly, US Headquarters Command expected each commander to ensure that his troops behaved.

US military officials' concerns about race relations did not end with introductory pamphlets for troops to life in wartime Britain. European Theater of Operations, US Army (or ETOUSA) also issued a memorandum to commanders and leaders of African American troops explaining the sensitivity of the issue, noting that one in ten American soldiers were minorities and that discriminatory practices "have no place in our army life."[41] The memo argued that, in the name of military efficiency, team work would be required of everyone and noted that Eisenhower sincerely hoped that "every soldier returning to the homeland, will take back this comradeship, mutual respect, and the spirit of helpfulness developed during his service with us."[42] The memorandum concluded by announcing that Brigadier General Benjamin O. Davis Sr., who at the time was the US Army's only African American general officer, had been tasked with commanding a special section responsible for investigating and "adjusting problems which may arise in connection with the command and leadership of our colored troops."[43]

Citizens of Northern Ireland soon developed a preference among American troops. One Northern Ireland member of Parliament, Dame Dehra Parker, noted in a letter to Robert Gransden, the assistant secretary to the cabinet secretariat, that in her district of Moneymore "the coloured men are well looked after."[44] In fact, she stated, the African American troops were perhaps better looked after than their white compatriots in towns west of Belfast. She added: "Apart from the feelings of the troops concerned, the whole situation is bad. Our people do not understand and seem to prefer the black to the white. I am told that this applies particularly to the R.C. [Roman Catholic] population and of course—the lowest class of white girl."[45] Parker's comments reinforced some of the primary fears that British officials had expressed throughout the summer of 1942.

However, unlike officials in Whitehall who feared illegitimate biracial births and the social consequences of intimacy with African American troops, Parker's comments about the preferences for African American troops hinted at a more serious concern exclusive to Northern Ireland: the unwavering tension between Catholics and Protestants. Historian Simon Topping has argued it was the disparity in the treatment of Irish Catholics by their unionist government that prompted many citizens in Northern Ireland to defy Stormont and make friends with African American troops—knowing full well that officials in Westminster disapproved of such behavior.[46]

Exercising "Great Discretion"

On August 21, 1942, Belfast newspaper editors were called into a meeting with Stormont officials and British Troops Northern Ireland Lieutenant Colonel Turnham to discuss steps US commanders were taking to encourage a better understanding of the British troops and the differences in prevailing attitudes toward African Americans. Based on the meeting minutes, British officials were clearly convinced that it was more of a matter of when—and less of a question of if—something would happen among the Americans. According to Stormont's account of the meeting:

> Col. Turnham, addressing his remarks to the editors, asked for their aid in "playing down" incidents that may occur which were not serious in themselves, but which by undue publicity could be played up by their enemies in order to strain relationships between the two countries. He states that the incidents so far reported had been handled with great discretion by the newspapers and he hopes that the authorities could depend on the newspapers to use their influence to foster good relations between the two Forces.[47]

Turnham argued that since little was happening on the battlefront, Belfast readers would be more focused on inconsequential incidents that might spring up between Allied forces, but that "when the war activity became more marked" such attention would lessen.[48]

According to Mick Temple, British wartime censorship was more severe than America's.[49] Where American editors and publishers agreed to a "voluntary domestic censorship,"[50] the British press saw the war bring "a great self-abnegation of power by the Press."[51] It was common for British officials to ask newspapers to temper their news stories. Such was the case during the August 21, 1942, meeting. Stormont officials later reported that the journalists present agreed to do what they could to "encourage a better understanding between the two Forces," and agreed to be discreet with stories involving conflicts among the troops.[52] This resolve was tested a month later.

The First Casualty

US Private William C. Jenkins was the first casualty of racial unrest. He died of knife wounds on the evening of September 30, 1942, in Antrim. The incident involved all the hallmarks of future incidents between African American and white US troops in the United Kingdom: the deadly mixing of alcohol, prejudice, and white military police. On October 1 the *Belfast Telegraph* ran a nine-paragraph story on page three, sandwiched between articles about the Russians advancing to

Stalingrad and a shooting incident involving the Irish Republican Army in Belfast.[53]

The *Telegraph* noted that Jenkins, an African American, was "stabbed to death during a disturbance in the streets of Antrim about nine o'clock on Wednesday night."[54] An unnamed, white soldier was also injured. Jenkins was among a group of American soldiers who "came under the notice of a US military patrol." When the MPs ordered the men to return to camp, the newspaper reported, the soldiers refused, and a "disturbance ensued" that resulted in gunfire. Once calm was restored, Jenkins was discovered "lying in a pool of blood, knifed to death."[55] The *Telegraph* quoted an ETOUSA press release that admitted several shots had been fired but noted that Ulster civilians were not involved. The only time race was mentioned was in reporting who was injured. The story did not use racial identifiers for the other soldiers, neither those ordered back to their barracks nor the MPs.

A day later, the *Irish News* published a five-paragraph story on the bottom right-hand corner of the front page with an all-caps headline: "AMERICAN SOLDIER KILLED IN ANTRIM STREET FRACAS."[56] The *Irish News* led with a verbatim republishing of the US military's description. The Press Association had learned that "the U.S. soldier killed was a negro, while the wounded soldier is a white man."[57] The *Irish News* also reported the incident occurred outside an Antrim pub, which is where Jenkins and the group of men were approached by MPs. Again, racial descriptors were missing from the rest of the account.

The wires allowed the *Belfast News-Letter*'s report to be nearly identical. A subheadline, "Closing Time," indicated the incident occurred as the pub closed.[58] The extent of the white soldier's injuries remained unclear. The story did not state whether his wounds were from a knife or a gun. Neither soldier was named. In any case, no coroner's inquest was expected.[59] None of the Northern Ireland newspapers editorialized about the incident. Instead, their editorials focused on House of Commons debates over relaxing travel limitations between Britain and Northern Ireland,[60] and the latest from the Eighth Army's fight in Egypt against Rommel.[61]

Among mainland British newspapers, only the (London) *Times* reported the Antrim incident. The two-paragraph brief, headlined "U.S. Soldier Killed in Antrim," appeared on October 2, at the bottom of page two.[62] From the wording, the *Times* likely put the piece together from a wire story and the October 1 ETOUSA press release. Both noted that there had been a "disturbance in the streets of Antrim" between American MPs and soldiers.[63] The brief reported that shots were fired, one soldier died from knife wounds, and another was seriously injured. The incident was exclusive to US troops and no civilians were involved. There is no acknowledgement of race, nor any mention of the pub and the possible role that alcohol might have played. On the *Times*'s editorial page, writers pontificated on anxiety over coal supplies and disunity in India.[64]

News Crosses the Atlantic

News of the Antrim incident traveled quickly. The *New York Times*, *Washington Post*, and *Detroit Free Press* reported the incident on October 2—the same day as the (London) *Times*. The *Chicago Daily Tribune* reported it a week later. Among mainstream US newspapers examined, these four alone reported the first major racial incident among deployed US troops. Three of the four noted the racial identity of the men involved.

Under a headline declaring: "U.S. Soldier Killed in Brawl in Ireland," the *New York Times* noted in the subhead that an African American soldier was stabbed to death during an altercation where military police were involved.[65] The six-paragraph story ran down-page on page three. An African American soldier had been stabbed to death and a white US soldier seriously injured when MPs "had to use force to break up a brawl outside a pub in the village of Antrim."[66] Witnesses reported multiple shots fired, prompting residents to flee. The *Times* reported that several soldiers were arrested. "The argument was reported to have started as Negro troops left the pub. The military police rushed up, but the Negroes refused to disperse and the police were forced to draw their revolvers."[67] The story concluded with the ETOUSA statement, noting that civilians were not injured in the incident and that military officials did not acknowledge the races of soldiers involved—or the role race might have played. The *Times* did not identify either soldier.

That same day, the *Washington Post* ran only a two-paragraph brief on page four. The last brief in half a column of "War Sidelights," "Yank Killed in Ireland"[68] did not mention race, only that one US soldier was "stabbed to death and another shot seriously in an altercation with military police in the streets of Antrim."[69] The *Detroit Free Press* ran a page two brief, declaring: "Yankee Soldier Dies in Irish Brawl."[70] The lead sentence noted an African American soldier had died and a white American soldier was seriously injured after US military police "had to use force to break up a brawl" outside an Antrim pub.[71] The short story also noted that several American soldiers were arrested in connection with the incident but did not identify either the soldier who was killed or the one who was injured.

Around the time of the incident, the *Chicago Daily Tribune* reported how British girls between the ages of thirteen and sixteen were throwing themselves at US, Canadian, and "other overseas troops" stationed in Great Britain, but made no mention of the Antrim incident.[72] It would be a full week before the *Tribune* reported on it, and only in a single paragraph on page nineteen. The Associated Press was the first to publish the name of the dead soldier. "United States army headquarters disclosed today that the Negro soldier killed Sept. 30 in a street fight . . . was Pvt. William Jenkins."[73] The other new information: Jenkins was from Evansville, Indiana.

Same Story, Different Approach

The *Pittsburgh Courier*, *Chicago Defender*, and the (Baltimore) *Afro-American*, all weeklies, just missed getting the news into their papers the first weekend in October. The *Courier* and the *Defender* both reported the story on October 10; the *Afro-American* followed a week later. And while all three black presses used wire services—either the Associated Negro Press (ANP) or the National Negro Publishers

Association because the news organizations were banned from membership in mainstream wire services such as the AP—the manner in which the news was reported varied.[74]

For readers of the *Courier*, the headline: "Soldier Killed in Ireland," in extra bold font, dominated page twenty-two, despite being below the fold and only three paragraphs long.[75] Flanked at top and bottom with the *Courier*'s Double Victory campaign "VV," the unidentified wire report is nearly identical to the UP's wire story that appeared in the *New York Times*. But where the *Times* used the term "Negro,"[76] the *Courier* used "colored."[77] *Courier* editors also omitted the direct quote from ETOUSA. While the paper did include the fact that no civilians were injured, it did not identify which black press wire service provided the story.

The *Defender* relied on ANP for a page two brief with the bold headline: "Soldier Slain during Knife Fight in Eire."[78] But the story was vague. It stated: "One Negro soldier was stabbed to death Wednesday night and another sustained serious gunshot wounds after military police used force to quell a fight outside of a pub (tavern) in the village of Antrim."[79] The wire brief contained the same details published by other newspapers but omitted racial identifiers and names.

A week later, the *Defender* ran another ANP story, this time confirming the soldier's death by stabbing and naming him as Pvt. William Jenkins of Evansville, Indiana.[80] The story also offered more details: "Trouble is said to have started in a pub (tavern) between soldiers who had been drinking there. They moved out to the street and continued the argument."[81] When MPs attempted to break up the argument, violence broke out and "Jenkins was killed in the melee."[82]

The *Afro-American* was the last of the black newspapers examined for this study to report the incident. The October 17 page three story was nearly identical to the *Defender*'s but did not call the fight a melee. Instead, "Pvt. Jenkins was the victim of knife wounds."[83] The role of race was not mentioned, although the influence of alcohol as a potential accelerant was retained. The only other mention of the incident was an October 17 front page story by Ollie Stewart, who had attended a press conference by Brigadier General Benjamin O. Davis Sr. As the US

Army's only African American general officer, Davis had been tasked just a month earlier with overseeing race issues in the ETOUSA after conducting similar inspection tours of African American troop conditions in basic training camps and army installations across the United States during the first half of 1942.

Davis Gets "a Rather Tough Assignment"

General Davis arrived at ETOUSA Headquarters in late September 1942 to serve as an adviser to the army's Service of Supplies commander, Major General John C. H. Lee. Davis's appointment created a stir in both the American mainstream and black press alike. Newspapers that failed to report the Antrim incident were keen to publish stories about how the nation's only African American general was now in the United Kingdom and tasked with overseeing African American soldiers stationed there.[84] That Davis's appointment was news demonstrated the importance of his assignment, and the magnitude of the work was not lost on him. On September 30, Davis wrote his wife, Sadie: "I have received a rather tough assignment. I have had to be firm in several instances. I think my action is effective. Some of the folks in addition to being inexperienced appear to be afraid. . . . These troops, white and black of the Service of Supply have to work very hard. I am afraid that they are not sufficiently hardened and disciplined."[85]

Davis was in England only a matter of days when the Antrim incident prompted a personal visit to Northern Ireland, where he conducted the army's official investigation. Historian Marvin E. Fletcher noted:

> He talked with American soldiers and policemen and Irish civilians. The news of Davis's work quickly reached the American black press, whose members were able to reassure their readers that Davis was on the scene, investigating problems. After finishing his work, he left for England on the evening of 8 October . . . he submitted a report to General Lee on the murder of the black soldier. The SOS commander was impressed with the work and asked Davis to accompany him on another inspection tour.[86]

Davis's inspection tour of the Northern Ireland operations and subsequent investigation into the murder of Private Jenkins was significant because it, in part, demonstrated that US military leaders were aware of how volatile race relations were. It also revealed that Eisenhower and his staff were proactive, rather than reactive, regarding the Antrim matter.

The timeline of Davis's arrival counters historians such as Simon Topping and Graham Smith, who have argued that he was dispatched to Britain *because* of the incident.[87] Davis's high-profile position made him the de facto contact person for all things race-related during the war—both in the United States and on the British Isles.[88] While in Britain, Davis received numerous letters from American and British citizens regarding race and race relations. For example, one British woman expressed her perplexity on October 25, 1942, asking how white American soldiers could be so "unchristian" and "impertinent" as to dictate who their British hosts could and could not entertain.[89] Miss M. Lyall also asked Davis to explain his country's position on race relations. She wrote: "I have never been able to understand the American attitude to 'color.' Racial prejudice is an evil, wicked thing."[90] Lyall's letter is telling, in that it demonstrates and helps explain the growing frustration among British citizens, as early as October 1942, over the US Army's handling of African American soldiers. Lyall's frank correspondence also demonstrates how clearly America's ally understood and acknowledged the duplicity in what US leaders said versus the policies they implemented—even if Americans were blind to the problems such policies were causing.

Conclusion

Race, virtually from the onset of the US troops' deployment, was of great concern among both British and American officials. But the reasons for concern were different. For British officials, race relations were an added layer of nuance that began with general consternation over the differences between the two nations and their troops. American soldiers came to the British Isles better dressed, better paid, and better supplied in terms of food and war materiel. These facts—combined with the romantic notions fed to British society through Hollywood films—meant that jealousy on the part of British soldiers would inevitably spark conflicts.[91] Adding to the concern were men acting out of line merely because it was wartime and they were far from home. One British woman, in a letter to a friend, wrote: "Things are getting pretty bad in Bedford. The Yankees are molesting and beating up no end of girls, and getting a really bad name for themselves."[92]

Racial differences only added to British officials' worries, particularly where their womenfolk were concerned. Fears of a sudden influx of illegitimate, mixed-race war babies prompted the Home Office to launch a word-of-mouth campaign among women's groups urging British women to avoid intimate relationships with American troops—particularly African American soldiers. British officials also struggled to explain the American attitude toward race to a nation that had little exposure to people of African or Caribbean descent. This difficulty was only complicated by Britain's vast empire, where the overwhelming majority of inhabitants were people of color.

American officials were keenly aware of the potential problems. As early as 1940, President Roosevelt, hoping to appease the African American population and garner votes, appointed Judge William Hastie, the dean of Howard University's law school, as a civilian aide to Secretary of War Henry L. Stimson.[93] Two years later, Eisenhower appointed Davis commander of a special section in the Inspector General's Office tasked with investigating and "adjusting problems which may arise in connection with the command and leadership of our colored troops."[94]

Eisenhower, meanwhile, believed that military discipline enforced by a capable army officer corps could ensure that American soldiers would put their racial differences aside for the greater good. Further, he was naively convinced that "every soldier returning to the homeland" would bring with "this comradeship, mutual respect, and the spirit of helpfulness developed during his service with us."[95] But Eisenhower's dream was ahead of its time.[96] And it was an unachievable goal for Northern Ireland in 1942.

In terms of media reporting, several trends emerged. The *Belfast Telegraph* was the first publication to name the victim. It would be a full week before other newspapers did so—and only after ETOUSA released it in a statement. The *Telegraph* thereby demonstrated the most independence by investigating the incident. This was a bold move given Turnham's request to the Northern Ireland press just two weeks earlier urging editors to exercise discretion in news stories. The *Telegraph* essentially defied him by demonstrating the hallmarks of a free press. Meanwhile, the *Irish News*—which did not send editors to the Stormont meeting—only published the ETOUSA press release verbatim and, like other British papers, avoided racial identifiers.

In terms of the American black press, *Defender* correspondent George Padmore wrote a front-page column addressing his concerns about race relations among Americans troops. Padmore's censored dispatch reported: "More and more each day the entire question of race prejudice and U.S. pressure to extend discrimination to the British Isles is coming realistically to the fore here."[97] While his column was not unlike others in competing newspapers, Padmore was tongue in cheek when he noted: "While yet no official ruling has been made to lay off color bar difficulties, the trouble I have experienced in transmitting such information clearly indicates that the subject is disliked."[98] Padmore's commentary makes one wonder how much of the wire services' downplaying the racial tensions was a result of censorship, rather than ETOUSA controlling information.

Newspapers were at the mercy of censors and the military. Local newspapers demonstrated greater independence, including conducting investigations. Another lesson was that, unlike the American press, which was heavily divided along racial lines, British newspapers saw "American" *as* a racial identifier. To the British press the term American clearly meant both ethnicity and race.

Afterword

Marcel Broersma, Mark O'Brien,
and Debra Reddin van Tuyll

In his foreword to Ray O'Hanlon's 1998 book *The New Irish Americans*, noted journalist Pete Hamill addresses the differences between Irish émigrés to America at the new millennium and those who came before. He observes that, "for the Irish, the days of the American Wake are long over; nobody waves goodbye forever from the rocky shores of Donegal." It is, he concludes, easy enough to stay in touch with home via "telephone, fax, and e-mail."[1] Nothing surprising there—less so over twenty years later as social media keep people connected around the globe and around the clock.

Hamill, an American-born journalist whose parents emigrated from Belfast in the 1920s, did, however, make one startling observation, startling because, if he is correct, the role of Irish American journalists and newspapers has not changed much at all, at least since the end of the Washington presidency. In the foreword, Hamill concludes his analysis of how easy it is today for immigrants to stay in touch with home by observing that "several superb weekly newspapers complete the sense of remaining connected, preventing Ireland from becoming a permanent part of the past." And this might have become even easier now Irish newspapers are easily at hand on the internet. Virtually every chapter in this volume, regardless of the time period covered, at least implies the very same idea. Newspapers have always connected Irish immigrants to home. They have helped those immigrants adapt to their changed circumstances, but they have also kept "the Old Country" from becoming "some distant spot on a vast map."[2]

Hamill also notes that today's immigrants are not the immigrants of the late nineteenth or early twentieth century. "The new Irish immigrants . . . can . . . create their own American narratives, and with the help of technology, maintain a powerful connection to the old."[3] Journalism, and other forms of media, remains an important player in keeping that connection powerful. With the rise of social media, online newspapers, Facebook, and other means of digital communication, immigrants, and interested Americans, can easily keep up with the day's news in Ireland. True, media is only one factor—immigration laws, tourism campaigns, romanticism, and the fact that one-tenth of the American population refers to itself as Irish American, coupled with Americans' search for an identity within their vast pluralistic melting pot, have all played important roles in forging close relationships between not just Irish immigrants and Ireland but also between non-Irish Americans and Ireland. More than two million American passport holders visited Ireland in 2018, a 13.4 percent increase over 2017.[4] Jokes about Ireland being the fifty-first state are common on both sides of the Atlantic Ocean.[5] Even the irascible *Irish Times* columnist Fintan O'Toole has admitted that the Irish had much to do with creating American culture, but, he added, "Irish culture is inconceivable without America."[6]

As Ambassador Mulhall points out in his foreword to this volume, national identity does not arise out of the air, nor does diasporic identity. Both must be grounded in something, and both must have something to sustain them. As this book documents, print culture, particularly journalistic products, have played an important role in creating and maintaining Irish American identity—at least up until the mid-twentieth century. At the same time, American journalism itself has been influenced by Irish printers and journalists who immigrated to the New World and infused journalism with their knowledge, skills, and professional routines they were socialized in, as becomes clear from the contributions in this volume.

The ambassador also observes that the Irish-American relationship is today somewhat more remote than it was in the late nineteenth century and early twentieth century, the heyday of both Irish immigration and the transfer of journalists, news, news practices, and technologies between Ireland and the United States. In the early years of the twentieth century the ties between the Irish and the American Irish were extremely close, especially because so many of the latter vigorously supported Irish nationalism. The American perspective was often more anti-British than that of the native Irish. American Irish newspapers supported Irish freedom, although a tension existed between those who accepted the concept of "Home Rule," meaning domestic self-rule within the British Empire, and those who supported complete independence. This division was reflected in the editorial perspectives of the major American Irish newspapers. The Easter Rebellion of 1916 in Dublin inflamed Irish America: it played a key role in the subsequent Anglo-Irish conflict (1919–21) which culminated in a British withdrawal.

However, at that point, existing tensions boiled to the surface. When Ireland became (mostly) independent with the creation of the Irish Free State in 1922, there was rejoicing in America—but the Irish legislature had barely accepted the treaty with Britain before civil war broke out. This conflict puzzled and appalled the American Irish.[7] To them, Ireland had just succeeded in a centuries-old struggle for legislative freedom. They had neither understanding nor sympathy for the rebels who refused to accept the Anglo-Irish Treaty (1921) on the grounds that it required Irish parliamentarians to take an oath of allegiance to the British Crown.[8] It was not a question of misunderstanding; rather, it demonstrated that the two groups of Irish, despite their connections, looked at the world in very different ways. The American Irish did not lose their connection to Ireland, but it would never be the same. The "Irish Question" to them no longer existed.[9] The advent of the Great Depression also concentrated minds on issues closer to home.

Another factor in the changing Irish-American relationship is the greater ease with which those who do come to America can stay in touch with those back home in Ireland. Yet another factor is the lesser need for assimilation. America in the twenty-first century has plenty of problems associated with its pluralistic society, but many Americans embrace the diversity of their fellow citizens—hyphenated or otherwise. Few in America today would have the issue Joseph P. Kennedy faced in 1957 when he demanded to know, "What the hell do I have to do to be called an American," after a Boston newspaper referred to him as an Irishman. Kennedy pointed out that both he and his children had been born in America.[10] Three of those children would grow up to become, respectively, the first Irish Catholic American president, a US senator, and the attorney general of the United States. Yet, three years later when his second son, John Fitzgerald Kennedy, was elected president, his Irishness was taken for granted by most Americans who willingly accepted him as one of their own, regardless of their particular ethnic backgrounds. A century earlier, he would likely have been portrayed by newspapers as an illiterate simian drunkard.[11]

In many ways John Fitzgerald Kennedy's visit to Ireland during his presidency marked the emotional high point of Irish-American relations. His visit—the first time a serving US president visited Ireland—in the summer of 1963 was an affirmation of the emigrant experience and, as the *Irish Times* put it, the story of "a local boy who made good."[12] Kennedy's tour was broadcasted around the country by the national broadcaster (RTÉ), which had been established only eighteen months previously, and thousands of people—many with "Welcome Home Mr. President" banners—lined the streets wherever he went. His address to the Irish Parliament, his visit to the ancestral family homestead in County Wexford, and his evocative speech at the quayside in New Ross, from where his great-grandfather, Patrick Kennedy, had emigrated at the height of the Great Famine in 1848, received blanket coverage in the press and gave a fillip to a relatively new nation that was still finding its way in the world. His assassination in Dallas five months later stunned everyone: though even in death the Irish connection persevered. At his funeral a party of Irish Army cadets performed a military drill that had impressed Kennedy when he had laid a wreath at the Irish Garden of Remembrance in Dublin. This was the first—and remains the only—time in history that representatives of a foreign army have performed a ceremony at the burial of a US president.

In subsequent decades, other US presidents have visited—Richard Nixon in 1970; Ronald Reagan in 1984; Bill Clinton in 1995, 1998, and 2000; George W. Bush in 2004; and Barack Obama in 2011—all of whom have claimed Irish heritage. While each visit had its own characteristics, the visits of Clinton—at the height of the Northern Ireland Peace Process, which culminated in the Good Friday Agreement of 1998—and Obama came closest to generating the positive frenzy that greeted Kennedy's visit in 1963.[13]

In a real sense, the Irish-American relationship in the twenty-first century has evolved almost beyond recognition, and while Americans remain the second-largest tourism cohort to Ireland every year, in many ways the relationship is increasingly framed in economic rather than identity terms. Having positioned itself as "the gateway to Europe," Ireland is home to the European headquarters of a multitude of high-tech US firms. In 2020, US companies based in Ireland directly employed 160,000 people and indirectly employed a further 128,000 people. In the opposite direction, Irish companies employed 110,000 people in the United States.[14] As the relationship has changed, so too has the structure of the Irish American press. Its numbers now stand at fewer than twenty individual titles across the United States. That shrinkage is likely due in part to the greater assimilation of the Irish into the larger American society as well as to limits on Irish immigration that began in 1965, and came close to being expanded in 2018 before being defeated in the US House of Representatives.[15] Though there is a proud Irish diaspora in America, the Irish American community is smaller than it once was—many fewer immigrants are arriving on American shores because of limits on immigration. Consequently, the new "first generation" is smaller than it has been in the past, and those who have been here for several generations have slowly assimilated to the point that many only recall their Irishness on St. Patrick's Day.

The need for an Irish American press industry may have declined, as has the transfer of journalistic norms and practices from Ireland to the United States, but that has not stopped Irish American journalists from having influential positions at American media—just as they have done since the 1780s. Prominent Irish American and Irish journalists range from the ultraconservative talk-show hosts Bill O'Reilly and Sean Hannity to the more traditional political journalist Maureen Dowd, filmmaker Michael Moore, chat show host Conan O'Brien, President Regan's legendary speech writer Peggy Noonan, and Irish-born Alexander Cockburn. Each has made his or her mark on American public opinion: a process that, as this volume demonstrates, began centuries earlier in a very different media environment.

Notes

Bibliography

Contributor Biographies

Index

Notes

Foreword

1. US Census Bureau, "Facts for Features: Irish-American Heritage Month (March) and St. Patrick's Day (March 17): 2017," February 21, 2017, https://www.census.gov/newsroom/facts-for-features/2017/cb17-ff05.html.

2. Benedict Anderson, *Imagined Communities: Reflections on the Origin and Spread of Nationalism* (London: Verso, 2006), 31–36.

1. Seditionists and Revolutionaries

1. L. M. Cullen, *Europeans on the Move: European Migration, 1500–1800* (Oxford: Clarendon Press, 1994).

2. Patrick Fitzgerald, "The Scotch-Irish and the Eighteenth-Century Irish Diaspora," *History Ireland* 7, no. 3 (Autumn 1999): 37–41, https://www.historyireland.com/18th-19th-century-history/the-scotch-irish-the-eighteenth-century-irish-diaspora/.

3. Kevin Kenny, "The Irish Diaspora," *Aeon*, https://aeon.co/essays/the-irish-experience-and-the-meaning-of-modern-diaspora.

4. Christopher Shepard, "Irish Journalists in the Intellectual Diaspora: Edward Alexander Morphy and Henry David O'Shea in the Far East," *New Hibernia Review* 14, no. 3 (Autumn 2010): 75–90.

5. "The Printers' File at AAS," American Antiquarian Society, http://www.americanantiquarian.org/printers-file.

6. Mary Pollard, *A Dictionary of Members of the Dublin Book Trade, 1500–1800* (London: Biographical Society, 2000), 87; Allan C. Clark, "William Duane," *Records of the Columbia Historical Society, Washington, D.C.* 9 (1906): 18; James Morton Smith, "The Case of John Daly Burk and His New York 'Time Piece,'" *Journalism Quarterly* 30, no. 3 (1953): 23; Joseph I. Shulim, "John Daly Burk: Irish Revolutionist and American Patriot," *Transactions of the American Philosophical Society*, 54, no. 6 (1964): 7.

7. Shulim, "John Daly Burk," 5–6.

8. Thomas Jefferson to John Taylor, June 4, 1798, National Archives, Founders Online, http://founders.archives.gov/documents/Jefferson/01-30-02-0280.

9. Pollard, *A Dictionary*, 86–87; Maurice J. Bric, "The United Irishmen, International Republicanism and the Definition of Polity in the United States of America," *Proceedings of the Royal Irish Academy, Section C: Archaeology, Celtic Studies, History, Linguistics, Literature* 104C, no. 4 (2004): 81–106, 87; David A. Wilson, *United Irishmen, United States: Immigrant Radicals in the Early Republic* (Ithaca, NY: Cornell Univ. Press, 1998), 11, 43.

10. Wilson, *United Irishmen*, 15, 44.

11. James N. Green, *Mathew Carey: Publisher and Patriot* (Philadelphia: Library Company of Philadelphia, 1985), 3.

12. Green, *Mathew Carey*, 3; Henry Carey Baird, "Carey-Baird Centenary, 1885, Memoir of Mathew Carey, Founder of the House," *American Bookseller*, February 1, 1885, 59.

13. Green, *Mathew Carey*, 4; Wilson, *United Irishmen*, 17; Baird, "The Carey-Baird Centenary," 59; Maurice Bric, "Mathew Carey, Ireland and the 'Empire for Liberty' in America," *Early American Studies* 11, no. 3 (Fall 2013): 403–30, 406; Joseph M. Adelman, "Trans-Atlantic Migration and the Printing Trade in Revolutionary America," *Early American Studies* 11, no. 3 (Fall 2013): 516–44, 516–17; James N. Green, "'I Was Always Dispos'd to be Serviceable to You, Tho' It Seems I Was Once Unlucky': Mathew Carey's Relationship with Benjamin Franklin," *Early American Studies* 11, no. 3 (Fall 2013): 545–46; Edward C. Carter II, "Birth of a Political Economist: Mathew Carey and the Recharter Fight of 1810–1811," *Pennsylvania History: A Journal of Mid-Atlantic Studies* 33, no. 3 (1966): 274–88.

14. Carter, "Birth of a Political Economist," 274–88; Wilson, "United Irishmen," 18.

15. Green, *Mathew Carey*, 5; Cathy Matson and James N. Green, "Ireland, America, and Mathew Carey: Special Issue Introduction," *Early American Studies* 11, no. 3 (Fall 2013): 395–402, 397–98; Edward C. Carter II, "A 'Wild Irishman' Under Every Federalist's Bed: Naturalization in Philadelphia," *Pennsylvania Magazine of History and Biography* 94, no. 3 (July 1970): 332–33; Seth Cotlar, *Thomas Paine's America: The Rise and Fall of Transatlantic Radicalism in the Early Republic* (Charlottesville: Univ. of Virginia Press, 2011), 16, 24–25.

16. Bric, "United Irishmen," 83, 94.

17. Bric, "United Irishmen," 85–86, 88; Carter, "A 'Wild Irishman,'" 331.

18. Fred S. Siebert, *Freedom of the Press in England, 1476–1776: The Rise and Decline of Government Control* (Urbana-Champaign: Univ. of Illinois Press, 1965).

19. Mathew Carey, *The Olive Branch*, 10th ed. (Philadelphia: Carey and Son, 1818), 316–17; Bric, "United Irishmen," 91.

20. Shulim, "John Daly Burk," 5–6.

21. Shulim, "John Daly Burk," 9.

22. Shulim, "John Daly Burk," 7; Smith, "Case of John Daly Burk," 24; Kerby A. Miller, Arnold Schrier, Bruce D. Boling, and David N. Doyle, *Irish Immigrants in the Land of Canaan: Letters and Memoirs from Colonial and Revolutionary America, 1675–1815* (New York: Oxford Univ. Press, 2003), 586.

23. Shulim, "John Daly Burk," 9.

24. Charles Campbell, *Some Materials to Serve for a Brief Memoir of John Daly Burk* (Albany, NY: Joel Munsel, 1868), 20.

25. *Polar Star and Boston Daily Advertiser*, December 1, 1796; Smith, "Case of John Daly Burk," 24.

26. *Polar Star and Boston Daily Advertiser*, October 10 and 15, 1796.

27. *Polar Star and Boston Daily Advertiser*, October 20, 1796.

28. Shulim, "John Daly Burk," 12.

29. Shulim, "John Daly Burk," 19.

30. Smith, "Case of John Daly Burk," 24n5; Joseph T. Lawless, "Some Irish Settlers in Virginia," *Journal of the Irish American Historical Society* 2 (1899): 161–62.

31. Smith, "Case of John Daly Burk," 23.

32. Smith, "Case of John Daly Burk," 23; Shulim, "John Daly Burk," 22–23.

33. Shulim, "John Daly Burk," 23.

34. Shulim, 24.

35. Shulim, 23.

36. "United Irishmen," reprinted in the *New York Commercial Advertiser*, November 1, 1798, 2.

37. "United Irishmen," *New York Commercial Advertiser*, 2.

38. *New Hampshire Gazette* (Portsmouth), January 16, 1799, 3.

39. Shulim, "John Daly Burk," 24.

40. "For The Time Piece," *Time-Piece* (New York), June 22, 1798, 1.

41. "United Irishmen," *Time-Piece* (New York) August 23, 1798, 3.

42. *Time-Piece* (New York), July 6, 1798, 3.

43. Shulim, "John Daly Burk," 25.

44. *Time-Piece* (New York), June 27, 1798; Smith, "Case of John Daly Burk," 23, 28; Jeffrey L. Pasley, "*The Tyranny of Printers*": *Newspaper Politics in the Early American Republic* (Charlottesville: Univ. of Virginia Press, 2001), 125; Phillip I. Blumberg, *Repressive Jurisprudence in the Early American Republic: The First Amendment and the Legacy of English Law* (Cambridge: Cambridge Univ. Pres, 2010), 80; Geoffrey R. Stone, *Perilous Times: Free Speech in War Time from the Sedition Act of 1798 to the War on Terrorism* (New York: W. W. Norton, 2004), 48; Bruce A. Ragsdale, *Sedition Act Trials: Federal Trials and Great Debates in United States History* (Washington, DC: Federal Judicial Center/Federal Judicial History Office, 2005), 21.

45. Pasley, "*Tyranny of Printers*," 125.

46. Blumberg, *Repressive Jurisprudence*, 80; Shulim, "John Daly Burk," 33.

47. Rufus King to Alexander Hamilton, July 2, 1798, National Archives, Founders Online, https://founders.archives.gov/documents/Hamilton/01-21-02-0298; Rufus King to Timothy Pickering, July 19, 1798, in Charles R. King, *The Life and Correspondence of Rufus King, Comprising His Letters, Private and Official, His Public Documents and His Speeches* (New York: Putnam, 1895), 637–38; Nicole Anderson Yanoso, *The Irish and the American Presidency* (New Brunswick, NJ: Transaction, 2016); Richard Brookhiser, "The Politics of Immigration: Clashing Impulses," *American History* 48, no. 5 (2013): 17–18.

48. "To Farmers," *Russell's Commercial Gazette*, reprinted in *Springer's Weekly Oracle*, November 12, 1798, 1.

49. *Aurora General Advertiser* (Philadelphia), November 22, 1977, 2.

50. "Messrs. Brown and Relf," *Gazette and Universal Daily Advertiser* (Philadelphia), July 24, 1799, 3.

51. Ragsdale, *Sedition Act Trials.*

52. Michael Schudson, *The Sociology of the News* (New York: W. W. Norton, 2003), 159; James W. Carey, *Communication as Culture: Essays on Media and Society* (New York: Routledge, 1988), 18.

53. Benedict Anderson, *Imagined Communities: Reflections on the Origin and Spread of Nationalism*, rev. ed. (New York: Verso, 2006), 6–7.

54. Donald M. MacRaild, "Review of Anthony McNicholas, *Politics, Religion and the Press: Irish Journalism in Mid-Victorian England*," *Catholic Historical Review* 95, no. 1 (2009): 173–74.

2. William Duane

1. Timothy Pickering to John Adams, July 24, 1799, Timothy Pickering Papers XI, 487, Massachusetts Historical Society, Boston; Jeffrey L. Pasley, "*The Tyranny of Printers*": *Newspaper Politics in the Early American Republic* (Charlottesville: Univ. of Virginia Press, 2000), 189; Nigel Little, *Transoceanic Radical: William Duane, National Identity and Empire 1760–1835* (New York: Taylor & Francis, 2008), 123.

2. Little, *Transoceanic Radical*, 18.

3. Allen C. Clark, *William Duane*, *Records of the Columbia Historical Society* 9 (1906): 17–19; Marcus Daniel, *Scandal and Civility: Journalism and the Birth of American Democracy* (New York: Oxford Univ. Press, 2009), 234–35; Pasley, "*Tyranny of Printers*," 177; James Morton Smith, "The 'Aurora' and the Alien and Sedition Laws. Part 2: The Editorship of William Duane," *Pennsylvania Magazine of History and Biography* 77, no. 2 (February 1953): 123–24.

4. Little, *Transoceanic Radical*, 109; William John Duane, *Biographical Memoir of William John Duane* (Philadelphia: Claxton, Remsen, and Haffelfinger, 1868), 1; Daniel, *Scandal and Civility*, 235.

5. Little, *Transoceanic Radical*, 29; Daniel, *Scandal and Civility*, 235.

6. Daniel, *Scandal and Civility*, 235.

7. Colum Kenny, "Matthew Duane: A Prudent Irish Catholic Chamber Counsel in England," *Eighteenth-Century Ireland* 33 (2018), 88.

8. Daniel, *Scandal and Civility*, 235; T. B. Howell, "The Trial of John Almon," *Cobbett's Complete Collection of State Trials and Proceedings for High Treason and Other Crimes and Misdemeanors* (London: T. C. Hansard, 1814), 803–68; John Almon, *Another Letter to Mr. Almon: In Matter of Libel* (London: Printed for John Almon, 1770); Thomas Green, "The Jury, Seditious Libel and Criminal Law," in *Juries, Libel, and Justice: The Role of English Juries in Seventeenth- and Eighteenth-Century Trials for Libel and Slander; Papers Read at a Clark Library Seminar 28 February 1981*, ed. R. H. Helmholz and T. A. Green (Los Angeles: William Andrews Clark Memorial Library, Univ. of California, 1984), 43.

9. Pasley, "*Tyranny of Printers*," 178; Daniel, *Scandal and Civility*, 237–38.

10. Little, *Transoceanic Radical*, 6.

11. "India News," *Times* (London), February 28, 1792.

12. Little, *Transoceanic Radical*, 50.

13. Little, 56.

14. Little, 74.

15. Little, 78.

16. Little, 19.

17. Little, 90.

18. Pasley, "*Tyranny of Printers*," 180–81; Daniel, *Scandal and Civility*, 240–41.

19. Daniel, *Scandal and Civility*, 241–42; Little, *Transoceanic Radical*, 121–22.

20. Kim T. Phillips, "William Duane, Philadelphia's Democratic Republicans, and the Origin of Modern Politics," *Pennsylvania Magazine of History and Biography* 101, no. 3 (July 1977): 368.

21. Arthur Scherr, "'Vox Populi' Verses the Patriot President: Benjamin Franklin Bache's Philadelphia Aurora and John Adams (1797)," *Pennsylvania History: A Journal of Mid-Atlantic Studies* 62, no. 4 (Fall 1995): 503; Daniel, *Scandal and Civility*, 246.

22. The circulation of the *Aurora* under William Duane was about fifteen hundred, which made it approximately five times larger in circulation than his Indian newspapers. Little, *Transoceanic Radical*, 14.

23. Pasley, "*Tyranny of Printers*," 183; Daniel, *Scandal and Civility*, 252.

24. James Morton Smith, "The 'Aurora,'" 123; Daniel, *Scandal and Civility*, 254–55.

25. Edward C. Carter II, "A 'Wild Irishman' under Every Federalist's Bed: Naturalization in Philadelphia," *Pennsylvania Magazine of History and Biography* 94, no. 3 (July 1970): 333–34; Daniel, *Scandal and Civility*, 256.

26. Timothy Pickering to John Adams, Philadelphia, July 24, 1799.

27. William David Sloan, "The Party Press," in *The Media in America: A History*, ed. William David Sloan (Northport, AL: Vision Press, 2005), 80.

28. Sloan, 80.

29. Jeffery A. Smith, *War and Press Freedom: The Problem of Prerogative Power* (New York: Oxford Univ. Press, 1999), 85.

30. Bruce A. Ragsdale, "The Sedition Act Trials," in *Federal Trials and Great Debates in United States History* (Washington, DC: Federal Judicial Center, 2005), 1.

31. James Madison to Thomas Jefferson, May 3, 1811, in *Writings of James Madison, vol. 8 (Correspondence, 1808–1819)*, ed. Gaillard Hunt (New York: Putnam, 1908), 151.

32. Dwight L. Teeter Jr. and Don R. Le Duc, *Law of Mass Communications: Freedom and Control of Print and Broadcast Media* (Westbury, NY: Foundation Press, 1995), 22.

33. William Blackstone, *Commentaries on the Laws of England, Book the Fourth* (London: Strahan and Woodfall, 1791), 150.

34. Ragsdale, "Sedition Act Trials," 2.

35. Teeter and Le Duc, *Law of Mass Communications*, 28.

36. Gordon T. Belt, "The Sedition Act of 1798: A Brief History of Arrests, Indictments, Mistreat, and Abuse," First Amendment Center, Washington, DC, 2007, 2, https://www.freedomforuminstitute.org/wp-content/uploads/2016/10/Sedition_Act_cases.pdf.

37. Teeter and Le Duc, *Law of Mass Communications*, 28.

38. Jeffery A. Smith, *War and Press Freedom*, 75.

39. James Morton Smith, "'The Aurora' and the Alien and Sedition Laws: Part 1: The Editorship of Benjamin Franklin Bache," *Pennsylvania Magazine of History and Biography* 77, no. 1 (January 1953): 6–7.

40. James Morton Smith, "'The Aurora,'" pt. 1, 10.

41. Sloan, "The Party Press," 80.

42. Benjamin Franklin Bache and William J. Duane, *The Truth Will Out: The Foul Charges of the Tories against the Editor of the Aurora, Repelled by Positive Proof and Plain Truth, and His Base Calumniators Put to Shame* (Philadelphia: Bache, 1798), 3.

43. Richard N. Rosenfeld, *American Aurora: A Democratic-Republican Returns; The Suppressed History of Our Nation's Beginnings and the Heroic Newspaper That Tried to Report It* (New York: St. Martin's Press, 1997), 664.

44. Rosenfeld, 664.

45. Rosenfeld, 665.

46. "British Influence!" *Aurora* (Philadelphia), August 5, 1799.

47. Rosenfeld, *American Aurora*, 678.

48. "British Influence!" *Aurora* (Philadelphia), August 13, 1799.

49. Rosenfeld, *American Aurora*, 664.

50. Rosenfeld, 672–73.

51. "British Influence," *Aurora* (Philadelphia), July 24, 1799.

52. "British Influence."

53. Rosenfeld, *American Aurora*, 673–74.

54. Rosenfeld, 687.

55. Sloan, "The Party Press," 80.

56. Rosenfeld, *American Aurora*, 704.

57. "Federal Circuit Court," *Aurora* (Philadelphia), October 22, 1799.

58. Dumas Malone, *Jefferson and the Ordeal of Liberty* (Boston: Little, Brown, 1962), 463.

59. Rosenfeld, *American Aurora*, 776.

60. Malone, *Jefferson*, 464.

61. "Untitled," *Aurora* (Philadelphia), February 19, 1800.

62. Malone, *Jefferson*, 464.

63. Rosenfeld, *American Aurora*, 794.

64. Wendell Bird, *Press and Speech under Assault: The Early Supreme Court Justices, the Sedition Act of 1798, and the Campaign against Dissent* (New York: Oxford Univ. Press, 2016), 279.

65. Malone, *Jefferson*, 464.

66. Michael Kent Curtis, *Free Speech, "The People's Darling Privilege": Struggles for Freedom of Expression in American History* (Durham, NC: Duke Univ. Press, 2000), 93.

67. Malone, *Jefferson*, 465.

68. Malone, 465.

69. Bird, *Press and Speech*, 280.

70. Phillips, "William Duane," 368.

71. Curtis, *Free Speech*, 95.

72. Thomas Cooper, "Preface," in *Political Essays: A Treatise on the Law of Libel* (Philadelphia: Campbell, 1799).

73. Curtis, *Free Speech*, 75.

74. Ragsdale, "Sedition Act Trials," 5.

75. Malone, *Jefferson*, 468.

76. Rosenfeld, *American Aurora*, 795.

77. Thomas Cooper, "Preface," *Account of the Trial of Thomas Cooper of Northumberland* (Philadelphia: John Bioren, 1800).

78. Eugene Volokh, "Thomas Cooper, Early American Public Intellectual," *New York University Journal of Law and Liberty* 4 (2009): 377.

79. James Thomson Callender, *The Prospect before Us* (Richmond, VA: Jones, Pleasants, and Lyons, 1800), pt. 1, 179.

80. Thomas Jefferson to James Madison, May 26, 1800, in *The Papers of Thomas Jefferson*, ed. Barbara B. Oberg (Princeton, NJ: Princeton Univ. Press, 2004), 31:590.

81. Quoted in Fawn M. Brodie, *Thomas Jefferson: An Intimate History* (New York: W. W. Norton, 1974), 322.

82. "The Life of Representative Matthew Lyon of Vermont and Kentucky," US House of Representatives: History, Art & Archives, August 1, 1822, http://history.house.gov/Historical-Highlights/1800-1850/The-life-of-Representative-Matthew-Lyon-of-Vermont-and-Kentucky/.

83. Ragsdale, "Sedition Act Trials," 7.

84. Bird, *Press and Speech*, 274.

85. Bird, 275.

86. Ragsdale, "Sedition Act Trials," 8.

87. Richard Peterson, *The Public Statutes at Large of the United States of America*, vol. 6 (Boston: Little, Brown, 1846), 802.

88. "American Papers," *Cambridge Intelligencer* (UK), May 17, 1800.

89. "London," *Hampshire Chronicle* (Winchester, UK), August 17, 1801.

90. "The Editor of the Aurora Has Been Arrested at Philadelphia," *Times* (London), August 15, 1798.

91. "Congress of the United States," *Kentish Gazette* (Canterbury, Kent, UK), May 16, 1800.

92. "Editor of the Aurora."

93. "London," *Oxford Journal* (UK), May 17, 1800.

94. "William Duane," *Belfast Commercial Chronicle*, November 2, 1807.

95. "The United States of America," *Manchester Mercury* (UK), September 13, 1808.

3. A "Respectable Body of New Comers"

1. Writing in the *Press*, a United Irish newspaper, of March 3, 1798, O'Gorman asserted, "I glory in being an Irishman, and as an Irishman you will always find me ready to shed my blood, if requisite, or to sacrifice my existence."

2. Habermas's core concern is how, in eighteenth-century Europe, newspapers—together with public spaces, such as coffee shops, in which press content could be read and discussed—helped expand civil society, particularly among the bourgeoisie.

3. Benedict R. O'G. Anderson, *Imagined Communities: Reflections on the Origin and Spread of Nationalism*, rev. ed. (London: Verso, 2006), 224.

4. The author was the twenty-one-year-old John Kells Ingram, son of a Church of Ireland (Episcopalian) clergyman. Entitled "The Memory of the Dead," the ballad was, in 1845, set to music by John Edward Pigot, becoming thereafter a popular anthem.

5. *Savannah Morning News*, August 7, 1877.

6. According to David Gleeson's *The Irish in the South, 1815–1877* (Chapel Hill: Univ. of North Carolina Press, 2002), the Savannah Irish "made up less than 5 percent" of the "84,000" Irish resident, in 1860, in the eleven states that one year later

would join the Confederacy (2, 5). Gleeson recognizes that about 90 percent of the Irish who came to America settled north of the Mason-Dixon line (2).

7. Louis Althusser, "Ideology and Ideological State Apparatuses (Notes Towards and Investigation)," in *The Anthropology of the State: A Reader*, ed. Aradhana Sharma and Akhil Gupta (Malden, MA: Blackwell, 2006), 86–111; quoted in Charles Gavin Duffy, *Short Life of Thomas Davis* (London: T. Fisher Unwin, 1896), 66. The *Prospectus* identifies "Nationality" as the *Nation*'s "first great object."

8. Charles Gidden Haines, *Memoir of Thomas Addis Emmet* (New York: G. & C. & H. Carvill, 1829), 60. Thomas Addis Emmet was a member of and a legal advisor to the Society of the United Irishmen. In 1803, after his younger brother Robert's failed rebellion, he exiled himself to America, where, as a successful lawyer, he argued before the United States Supreme Court and also served, briefly, as the New York State attorney general. One of the earliest Savannah advertisements for Haines's *Memoir* appeared in the October 27, 1829, edition of the *Savannah Daily Republican*, placed there by a local bookseller, T. M. Driscoll.

9. In "The Rebellion of 1798 in South Leinster," in *1798: A Bicentenary Perspective*, ed. Thomas Bartlett (Dublin: Four Courts Press, 2003), 104–21, Daniel Gahan conveys the intensity of the rebellion in Wexford and a portion of the adjoining county of Wicklow, on Wexford's northern border. Respecting the three weeks through June 21, 1798, he writes, "The insurgents . . . realized that they were an isolated enclave in the southeast [of Ireland]" and, thus, "made extraordinary efforts to react to this reality in military terms and to construct a make-shift local republic" (115). In analyzing the insurrection in Wexford, one should note that different zones within the county had different experiences. Mid-nineteenth-century Wexford emigrants to Savannah originated from across the entire county.

10. In the opening two pages of his essay, "Wexford Remembered in Prince Edward Island," (in *The Past: The Organ of the Uí Cinsealaigh Historical Society*, 16 [1988]: 41–44), Brendan O'Grady observes that a "thousand or more Wexford immigrants" settled on the island "between 1800 and 1835," forming "clusters in dozens of villages dotting the 400-mile coast." During the 1820s, prior to Texas's secession from Mexico, a Wexford settlement developed in and around Refugio in rural southeastern Texas. Another Wexford community emerged on the Mississippi in northeastern Iowa, once emigrants, primarily from northern Wexford, were disappointed in a scheme whereby, in 1850, a Wexford priest, Father Thomas Hoare, recruited them to follow him and establish farms in Arkansas.

11. Adrian N. Mulligan, "A Forgotten 'Greater Ireland': The Transatlantic Development of Irish Nationalism," *Scottish Geographical Journal* 118, no. 3 (2002): 232.

12. While the authors of this chapter have not discovered passenger lists for Wexford vessels that carried emigrants to Savannah from the late 1840s through the

mid-1850s, the Chatham County, Georgia, section of the US Federal Census of 1860 constitutes a useful mechanism for enumerating Wexford-born residents of Savannah in the aftermath of that migration. The tenth data column on the census schedule sought "Place of Birth, Naming the State, Territory, or Country." Charles J. White, enumerator for the "City of Savannah, 1st District"—that is, the westernmost section of the city—recorded fifteen individuals present in the 606th dwelling, a boardinghouse, that he visited. Nine of them were from "Wexford, Ireland": the female boardinghouse keeper, a female domestic, and seven men (a tailor, a machinist, and five laborers).

13. Three County Wexford shipping firms—Graves & Son and Howlett & Co. of New Ross and R., M., & R. Allen of Wexford Town—maintained the service. Our examination of some surviving records from the defunct Graves & Son points to both Graves and Howlett vessels first departing for Savannah in 1845. From then until late in the decade, those two companies' primary interest in Savannah was not the delivery of emigrants from Wexford and its immediate hinterland but the purchase of Georgia goods, principally timber, for the Irish market. Thus, on October 19, 1847, the collector at the customhouse in New Ross issued a light-duty certificate to a Graves vessel, *Lady Bagot*, that notes its being "Bound to Savannah (Ballast)" (Grave & Sons Collection, National Archives of Ireland, box 97/48-2/10-3/087/10). Late in the 1840s, the Graves, Howlett, and Allen companies began actively pursuing the emigrant trade, likely in response to Ireland's Great Hunger, although a detailed study of the full range of precipitating factors remains to be carried out.

14. Edward M. Shoemaker, "Strangers and Citizens: The Irish Immigrant Community of Savannah, 1837–1861" (PhD diss., Emory Univ., 1990), 42.

15. Charles J. Kickham, *Knocknagow; or, The Homes of Tipperary*, 13th ed. (Dublin: Duffy, 1887), 201, 378.

16. Kickham, *Knocknagow*, 229.

17. Anderson, *Imagined Communities*, 34.

18. From the Preamble (1812) of the Hibernian Society of Savannah.

19. Timothy J. Lockley, *Lines in the Sand: Race and Class in Lowcountry Georgia, 1750–1860* (Athens: Univ. of Georgia Press, 2003), 36.

20. *Savannah Republican*, March 29, 1817.

21. *Georgian* (Savannah, GA), March 19, 1825. The piece acknowledges an additional toast invoking Tone and two invoking Emmet.

22. *Georgian* (Savannah, GA), March 19, 1825. In her biography, *Wolfe Tone* (Liverpool: Liverpool Univ. Press, 2012), Marianne Elliott discusses Tone's authorship of pamphlets that enjoined those sharing the island of Ireland "to merge religious identities into the common one of Irishman" (4).

23. Obviously, multiple factors informed the reception of Irish arrivals, not least capitalist employers' need for labor and the dominant population's racial bias in favor of white Europeans.

24. Shoemaker, *Strangers and Citizens*, 45.

25. Offered by Colonel T.U. Camak, the toast asserts, "The star of [Emmet's] greatness shines out from the midst of the past, untarnished in its brilliancy by the darkness of tyranny" (*Savannah Morning News*, March 20, 1850). As St. Patrick's Day 1850 fell on a Sunday, the Hibernian Society of Savannah held its anniversary dinner on the following day.

26. *Savannah Morning News*, March 20, 1850.

27. For a table of the five "main types of diaspora," see page 18 of Robin Cohen's *Global Diasporas: An Introduction* (Seattle: Univ. of Washington Press, 1997). Earlier in the book, Cohen identifies the Irish as a "victim diaspora," similar to "the Jewish, African, and Armenian diasporas"; he credits scholarship by Christine Kinealy with "adduc[ing]" that "there was much more deliberation in the British response to the potato blight" than had previously been identified (3). As he further develops his argument, Cohen emphasizes the rapidity of population decline: "The Irish lost 25 per cent of their homeland population between 1845 and 1851, the years of the potato famine" (162).

28. Daniel Gahan, "Wexford Emigrants and the Irish Experience in Canal Construction in Nineteenth-Century America: Evidence from the Wabash and Erie in Daviess and Huntington Counties, Indiana, 1850," *The Past: The Organ of the Uí Cinsealaigh Historical Society* 32 (2016): 15.

29. *Savannah Republican*, January 12, 1850.

30. Tempering the descriptive lyricism is additional prose of unsentimental character. The Wexford "girls," the newspaper observes, "went off briskly at four to five dollars a month, but toward ten o'clock as the stock became reduced, the article rose to seven and eight, at which the market closed firm."

31. Peter D. O'Neill, *Famine Irish and the American Racial State* (New York: Routledge, 2017), 33.

32. *Savannah Morning News*, December 6, 1859.

33. *Savannah Morning News*, December 10, 1850.

34. *Savannah Morning News*, August 18, 1880. In addition to Michael Cash (who endured some mental-health challenges), the litany of Savannah Wexfordians who gained distinction is impressive, as just two examples begin to illustrate. From the south Wexford townland (district) of Loughnageer, Peter Whelan, a Catholic priest and Confederate chaplain, gained the rank of vicar general of Savannah's Catholic diocese, becoming so beloved that his February 7, 1871, funeral was the longest Savannah had ever witnessed. A native of Mounthoward—a north Wexford townland and a United Irish redoubt—William Kehoe built up a nationally prominent ironworks and multiple other business interests in Savannah. Upon his demise on December 29, 1929, the flag on the gold-domed city hall was lowered to half-staff. Among other community functions, Kehoe served as a trustee of the Savannah

Branch No. 38 of the Catholic Knights of America, a benevolent society. In that capacity, he facilitated, in December 1880, a death-benefit payment of $2,000 to the family of the deceased Michael Cash, an example of social intercourse among Wexfordians in Savannah.

35. At a gathering to celebrate its first St. Patrick's Day, the Irish Union Society had "the memory of Emmett [*sic*], Tone, Fitzgerald, and their associates" as its third regular toast (*Savannah Georgian*, March 22, 1847). One notes that while Robert Emmet is likely being invoked here, the Irish in America also memorialized his brother, Thomas Addis Emmet.

36. Founded in Nashville, Tennessee, in 1877, the Catholic Knights of America established a Savannah branch in December of the following year. According to Gary W. McDonogh's *Black and Catholic in Savannah, Georgia* (Knoxville: Univ. of Tennessee Press, 1993), beginning in 1884, the city's Catholic cathedral sponsored an additional—and perhaps short lived—colored branch of the organization (232).

37. Not all Irish (or Irish-heavy) organizations accorded with or pleased the white establishment in Savannah. In 1857 Patrick Rossiter, an immigrant from Wexford, cofounded, primarily for the city's longshoremen, the Workingmen's Benevolent Association, which threatened strike action on the docks. See Monica Hunt, "Organized Labor along Savannah's Waterfront: Mutual Cooperation among Black and White Longshoremen, 1865–1894," *Georgia Historical Quarterly* 92, no. 2 (Summer 2008): 177–99.

38. *Savannah Morning News*, August 18, 1880. For a summary of Nast's treatment of Irish Americans, see Thomas J. Archdeacon, *Becoming American: An Ethnic History* (New York: Free Press, 1983), 100–101.

39. *Savannah Morning News*, February 13, 1884.

40. *Savannah Morning News*, February 16, 1887.

41. Bryan Giemza, *Irish Catholic Writers and the Invention of the American South* (Baton Rouge: Louisiana State Univ. Press, 2013), 159. O'Connor respected Parnell, taking a leading role in both the establishment of Savannah's Parnell Branch of the Irish National Land League and the Independence Day 1881 visit by Parnell's brother, John Howard Parnell, to Savannah.

42. Thomas F. McGrath, *History of the Ancient Order of Hibernians from the Earliest Period to the Joint National Convention at Trenton, New Jersey, June 27, 1898, with Biography of the Rt. Rev. James A. McFaul* (Cleveland, OH: J.S. Savage Press, 1898), 86.

43. David T. Gleeson and Brendan J. Buttimer, "'We Are Irish Everywhere': Irish Immigrant Networks in Charleston, South Carolina, and Savannah, Georgia," in *Irish Migration, Networks, and Ethnic Identities since 1750*, ed. Enda Delaney and Donald M. MacRaild (London: Routledge, 2007), 183–205, 39–61. A sense of the trauma experienced in Wexford may be obtained from a letter, dated July 30, 1798, in which John Colclough, nephew of a hanged rebel, wrote, "The cornfields are beaten

and trod down and the county [Wexford] is quite a desert. You might ride from one end to the other without seeing a single man" (Public Record Office of Northern Ireland, Belfast, McPeake Transcripts: T3048/C/18).

44. *Daily News and Herald* (Savannah, GA), December 13, 1866.

45. Henry James, *Partial Portraits* (New York: Macmillan, 1888), 50. James was critiquing George Eliot's "general attitude with regard to the novel," a genre he believed she saw as "the last word of a philosophy endeavoring to teach by example."

46. *Savannah Morning News*, March 5, 1879. The piece acknowledges that among the volunteer toasts offered was one to "The Savannah MORNING NEWS, the Banner Journal of the South."

47. *Savannah Morning News*, August 7, 1879.

48. This spelling reflects the Irish orthographic convention of writing the "long *a*" sound with an *a* followed by a silent *gh*.

49. From early in 1846, Savannah newspapers acknowledged shipments of much timber and some rice and cotton from Savannah on Wexford vessels, most bound for Wexford ports. However, the *Wexford Independent* did not cover that commercial connection.

50. *Wexford Independent*, September 18, 1852.

51. *Wexford Independent*, January 1, 1851.

52. *Wexford Independent*, March 29, 1851.

53. A "Ship News" entry in the *Wexford Independent* of March 12, 1851, emphasized that while the *Menapia*'s arrival in Savannah on February 13 followed "a boisterous passage," all on board "were in the best of health," making "the fourth time" that the vessel had "landed passengers in America within . . . thirteen months" without "a death on board."

54. *Wexford Independent*, March 29, 1851.

55. Kickham, *Knocknagow*, 170.

56. Anderson, *Imagined Communities*, 33n54.

4. "Good American Citizens"

1. Francis Robert Walsh, *The Boston Pilot: A Newspaper for the Irish Immigrant, 1829–1908* (unpublished PhD diss., Boston Univ., 1968), 11. See also Cian McMahon, "Ireland and the Birth of the Irish-American Press, 1842–61," *American Periodicals* 19, no. 1 (2009): 5–20.

2. Walsh, Pilot, 11.

3. *Jesuit* (Boston, MA), September 5, 1829.

4. *Jesuit* (Boston, MA), September 5, 1829.

5. *Pilot*, July 20, 1839.

6. For a detailed study of Donahoe's life and career see Sister Mary Alphonsine Frawley, *Patrick Donahoe* (Washington, DC: Catholic Univ. of America Press, 1946).

For his birth and early years in Ireland, see pages 4–12. See also Ian Kenneally, "Patrick Donahoe: An Irish-American Leader," *Breifne* 14, no. 52 (2017): 107–18.

7. Frawley, *Donahoe*, 14.

8. *Pilot*, December 22, 1838, and December 21, 1844.

9. Patrick Donahoe, "Reminiscences of an Old Time Journalist: A letter to Martin J. Griffin," *Records of the American Catholic Historical Society* 15 (1904): 314–17.

10. Today, the *Pilot* is perhaps best known through its "missing friends" column, which ran from 1831 until 1921. Irish immigrants placed advertisements in the column seeking information on family and friends who had traveled separately to the United States.

11. *Pilot*, June 8, 1844: editorial written by Thomas D'Arcy McGee, who edited the paper for a short period in the 1840s.

12. Walsh, *Pilot*, vii.

13. Walsh, 58.

14. Donahoe's Emigrant Savings Bank was a very successful business, although it had competitors within the Irish community; see the *Pilot*, April 30, 1870.

15. *New York Times*, April 6, 1876: according to the paper, Donahoe's annual profit from all his businesses may have been $100,000 per annum.

16. For a biography of John Boyle O'Reilly, see Ian Kenneally, *From the Earth, a Cry: The Story of John Boyle O'Reilly* (Cork: Collins Press, 2011).

17. The Irish Republican Brotherhood was founded in Dublin on March 17, 1858, with James Stephens and John O'Mahony taking the leading roles in the new organization. Although the term Fenian originated with O'Mahony, who claimed that it recalled the Fianna of Irish legend, it was not until 1863 that it became a part of popular parlance, when the New York *Mercury* newspaper printed a detailed feature on the "Fenian Brotherhood."

18. R. V. Comerford, *The Fenians in Context: Irish Politics and Society 1848–82* (Dublin: Wolfhound Press, 1998), 39.

19. Quotation taken from an oath taken by recruits to the Irish Republican Brotherhood.

20. *Pilot*, November 23, 1872. The paper described the scene after the fire had subsided: "Around the site of what was once the magnificent Pilot Building the whole street was nothing other than huge piles of cracked and powdered brick and stone."

21. Kenneally, *From the Earth*, 157–64.

22. Frawley, *Donahoe*, 217. Donahoe's insurance had been adequate to cover the losses incurred as a result of the fire of November 9, 1872. However, the claims resulting from this fire had subsequently bankrupted many insurers, and Donahoe did not recoup his losses for the fires of November 20, 1872, and the following May.

23. Frawley, *Donahoe*, 215.

24. *New York Times*, April 4, 1876. The decline in Donahoe's fortunes was covered in great detail in the Boston and New York press. Especially damaging to Donahoe was a loss of $170,000 that resulted from his endorsement of loans to Gustavus Finotti, a Boston-based businessman. Finotti, whom the *New York Times* described as "a dreamer and a theorist," had lost all the money in "experimenting and speculation" and had been unable to repay the loan, leaving the burden to fall on Donahoe.

25. Throughout February 1876 the *Pilot* covered the demise of Donahoe's business; see editions of February 5, 12, 1, and 26. See Frawley, *Donahoe*, 219–21 for details on these negotiations.

26. O'Reilly to Charles Hurd, January 27, 1876, John Boyle O'Reilly Papers, Boston Public Library, Boston, MA. O'Reilly claimed that his plan to take over the paper would benefit Donahoe. If his plan was successful, he told a friend, "the old man [Donahoe] will come saved."

27. Frawley, *Donahoe*, 222. See also *Boston Daily Globe*, April 17, 1876.

28. *Historical Statistics of the Unites States, Colonial Times to 1970*, vol. 1 (Washington, DC: United States Bureau of the Census, 1975), Labor Force, series D 1-682.

29. *Boston Daily Globe*, October 30, 1884: report of speech by O'Reilly.

30. Kerby Miller, *Emigrants and Exiles: Ireland and the Irish Exodus to North America*, (New York: Oxford Univ. Press, 1988), 329.

31. Thomas H. O'Connor, *The Boston Irish: A Political History* (Old Saybrook, CT: Konecky & Konecky, 1995), 141.

32. *Pilot*, October 20, 1877.

33. For an account of the *Pilot*'s stance on this issue, see Kenneally, *From the Earth*, 165–73 and 288–93.

34. *Pilot*, March 25, 1871.

35. *Pilot*, March 15, 1873.

36. *Pilot*, March 15, 1873.

37. O'Reilly had quit the Brotherhood after the failed Fenian raid on Canada, which took place in May 1870. This was a smaller version of the famous Fenian expedition of June 1866. O'Reilly took part in the 1870 raid, both as an officer and as a reporter for the *Pilot*. However, the Fenians were quickly repulsed by Canadian and British forces, and O'Reilly soon after left the Brotherhood, claiming that he was disgusted with the divisions within the organization.

38. *Pilot*, August 25, 1877.

39. *Pilot*, April 29, 1876.

40. *Pilot*, April 29, 1876.

41. *Pilot*, April 29, 1876.

42. *Pilot*, June 17, 1876.

43. *Pilot*, July 28, 1877; see also August 25, 1877.

44. Kevin Kenny, *Making Sense of the Molly Maguires* (New York: Oxford Univ. Press, 1998), 265.

45. Kenny, 240.

46. *Pilot*, February 28, 1880.

47. *Pilot*, August 10, 1878.

48. *Pilot*, January 18, 1879. The *Pilot* issued a rallying cry to its readers, dismissing commentators and politicians who claimed that any attempts to curtail the activities of large corporations would damage the economy: "It would not interfere with the return of 'good times' if the American people took advantage of their power and strangled a few monopolies."

49. Arthur Mann, *Yankee Reformers in the Urban Age* (Chicago: Univ. of Chicago Press, 1974), 35.

50. Francis G. McManamin, *The American Years of John Boyle O'Reilly, 1870–1890* (New York: Arno Press, 1976), 202–3.

51. *Pilot*, January 22, 1887.

52. *Pilot*, May 10, 1873.

53. Steven Bernard Leiken, *The Practical Utopians: American Workers and the Co-operative Movement in the Gilded Age* (Detroit, MI: Wayne State Univ. Press, 2005), 54.

54. *Pilot*, August 4, 1877.

55. *Pilot*, January 2, 1875.

56. James J. Kenneally, "Catholicism and Women Suffrage in Massachusetts," *Catholic Historical Review* 53, no. 1 (April 1967): 43.

57. *Pilot*, February 24, 1883.

58. Katherine E. Conway and Mabel Ward Cameron, *Charles Francis Donnelly: A Memoir* (New York: James T. White, 1909), 30–31.

59. Hasia Diner, *Erin's Daughters in America: Irish Immigrant Women in the Nineteenth Century* (Baltimore: John Hopkins Univ. Press, 1983), 139–53.

60. Rev. O. B. Frothingham, John Boyle O'Reilly, et al., *Woman Suffrage, Unnatural and Inexpedient* (Boston: [publisher not identified], 1886). O'Reilly's contribution to the pamphlet was dated February 11, 1886.

61. John Boyle O'Reilly, "What Has Ireland Gained by Agitation," *American Catholic Quarterly Review* 8 (October 1883): 715.

62. *Pilot*, April 18, 1885.

63. *Pilot*, April 18, 1885.

64. *Pilot*, April 18, 1885.

65. James Jeffrey Roche, *Life of John Boyle O'Reilly: Together with His Complete Poems and Speeches* (Philadelphia: John J. McVey, 1891), 227.

66. O'Reilly composed four volumes of poetry: *Songs from the Southern Seas and Other Poems*; *Songs, Legends and Ballads*; *The Statues in the Block and Other Poems*; and

In Bohemia. He also wrote one novel, *Moondyne*, and coauthored another, *The King's Men*. His final book was the nonfiction *Ethics of Boxing and Manly Sport*.

67. See *American Newspaper Directory* (New York: George P. Rowell, 1872), *American Newspaper Annual* (Philadelphia: N. W. Ayer & Sons, 1880), and *American Newspaper Annual* (Philadelphia: N. W. Ayer & Sons, 1889).

68. Kenneally, *From the Earth*, 296–311.

69. *Pilot*, January 3, 1891.

5. The Story without a Source

1. Pierre Nora, *Realms of Memory: Rethinking the French Past* (New York: Columbia Univ. Press, 1996), 3.

2. Janice Hume, "Memory Matters: The Evolution of Scholarship in Collective Memories and Mass Communications," *Review of Communication* 10, no. 3 (July 2010): 183.

3. Laura D. Kelley, *The Irish in New Orleans* (Lafayette: Univ. of Louisiana at Lafayette Press, 2014), 20.

4. Margaret Varnell Clark, *The Louisiana Irish: A Historical Collection* (New York: iUniverse, 2007), 38.

5. Clark, 38.

6. Kelley, *Irish in New Orleans*, 35.

7. Dennis Clark, *The Irish in Philadelphia: Ten Generations of Urban Experience* (Philadelphia: Temple Univ. Press, 1973), 66.

8. *Daily Orleanian*, October 20, 1850, quoted in Earl F. Niehaus, *The Irish in New Orleans, 1800–1860* (Baton Rouge: Louisiana State Univ. Press, 1965), 27.

9. *Louisiana Advertiser*, December 14, 1830, quoted in Niehaus, *Irish in New Orleans*, 27; Dennis Clark, *Irish in Philadelphia*, 66.

10. Tyrone Power, *Impressions of America: During the Years 1833, 1834, and 1835* (London: Richard Bentley, 1836), 138.

11. Power, 139.

12. Power, 141.

13. Power, 140.

14. *Daily Orleanian*, October 20, 1850, quoted in Niehaus, *Irish in New Orleans*, 27.

15. *Mercantile Advertiser* (New York), February 28, 1834, quoted in Niehaus, *Irish in New Orleans*, 46.

16. Edward H. Barton, *Account of the Epidemic Yellow Fever Which Prevailed in New Orleans during the Autumn of 1833* (Philadelphia: Joseph R. A. Skerrett, 1834).

17. Meigs O. Frost, *Times-Picayune* (New Orleans, LA), July 18, 1937, 2.

18. Frost, 33.

19. Frost, 2.

20. Frost, 33.

21. Frost, 33.

22. Diane Farrell, *Times-Picayune* (New Orleans, LA), February 12, 1950.

23. William E. Keith, *Times-Picayune* (New Orleans, LA), May 1, 1952.

24. Clarence Doucet, *Times-Picayune* (New Orleans, LA), July 30, 1965.

25. *Times-Picayune* (New Orleans, LA), August 28, 1967.

26. William Borders, "Ireland's Lynch Goes Home to Hear Sour Political Music," *New York Times*, November 18, 1979.

27. Joan I. Duffy, *Times-Picayune* (New Orleans, LA), November 11, 1979.

28. Damon Veach, *Times-Picayune* (New Orleans, LA), November 20, 1983.

29. Nell Nolan, "Social Scene," *Times-Picayune* (New Orleans, LA), May 31, 1988.

30. Mary Lou Widmer, "Death by the Lakes of Pontchartrain," *Irish America*, February 1988, quoted in *Times-Picayune* (New Orleans, LA), May 15, 1988.

31. Widmer, "Death by the Lakes."

32. Niehaus, *Irish in New Orleans*, 46.

33. Mary Lou Widmer, *Lace Curtain* (New York: Jove Books, 1985), 121.

34. Widmer, 282.

35. Widmer, 248.

36. Melinda Daffin, "Remembering O'Flaherty's, a Real Irish Pub in the French Quarter," March 16, 2019, https://www.nola.com/entertainment_life/article_e26cadb7-c3ba-5003-8fdb-3d9c5f5f6336.html.

37. Danny O'Flaherty, interview by the author, May 29, 2017.

38. O'Flaherty, interview.

39. It is not known how many were sold; no newspaper mentioned the poster again.

40. Mary Queen Donnelly, "Irish Descendants are Facing a Monumental Task," *Times-Picayune* (New Orleans, LA), March 15, 1988.

41. *Times-Picayune* (New Orleans, LA), March 23, 1988.

42. *Times-Picayune* (New Orleans, LA), March 23, 1988.

43. Adrian McGrath, "The New Basin Canal, 1832–1838," *Old NOLA Journal* (blog), July 3, 2012, http://oldnolajournal.blogspot.com/2012/07/new-basin-canal-1832-1838.html.

44. Kelley, *Irish in New Orleans*, 36.

45. Troy Gilbert, "Nearly Lost, but Not Forgotten," *Irish America*, December/January 2007, https://irishamerica.com/2007/01/nearly-lost-but-not-forgotten/.

46. Carolyn Scanlon, quoted in Gilbert, "Nearly Lost."

47. Irish Government News Service, "Minister Humphreys Travels to Atlanta and New Orleans and International Famine Commemoration," November 3, 2014.

48. Simon Carswell, "Feast and Famine as Minister Addresses Irish in New Orleans," *Irish Times*, November 10, 2014.

49. Mary Lou Widmer, *Margaret: Friend of Orphans* (New Orleans: Pelican, 1998), 53.

50. Widmer, 15–23.

51. Widmer, 121.

52. Widmer, 123.

53. Janice Hume, "Building an American Story: How Early American Historians Used Press Sources to Remember the Revolution," *Journalism History* 37, no. 3 (Fall 2011): 178.

6. Kindred Spirits

1. Yvonne C. Garrett, "From the Trail of Tears to the Famine Road: The Choctaw Nation's Gift to Irish Famine Relief," May 4, 2015, https://www.academia.edu/25302243/From_the_Trail_of_Tears_to_the_Famine_Road_The_Choctaw_Nations_Gift_to_Irish_Famine_Relief.

2. Garrett.

3. Garrett.

4. Donna L. Akers, *Living in the Land of Death: The Choctaw Nation, 1830–1860* (East Lansing: Michigan State Univ. Press, 2004).

5. Akers, 1.

6. Akers, 2.

7. Akers, 2.

8. Akers, 9.

9. Akers, 9.

10. "Irish Leader to Visit Oklahoma Tribe Who Sent Ireland Famine Aid," *Irish Central* (Dublin), March 9, 2018; Sean MacEachaidh, email interview by the author, October 4, 2018. Email in possession of the author. MacEachaidh is the curator at the Andrew Jackson House in Carrickfergus, Northern Ireland.

11. Akers, *Living in the Land of Death*, 11.

12. Akers, 88.

13. *Boston Recorder*, November 18, 1829.

14. *Boston Recorder*, November 18, 1829.

15. *Boston Recorder*, November 18, 1829.

16. *Cherokee Phoenix and Indians Advocate* (New Town, GA), April 7, 1830, 4.

17. *Cherokee Phoenix and Indians Advocate* (New Town, GA), April 7, 1830, 4.

18. Akers, *Living in the Land of Death*, 89.

19. *Statesmen and Gazette* (Natchez, MS), November 3, 1830.

20. *United States Telegraph* (Washington, DC) October 16, 1830.

21. Akers, *Living in the Land of Death*, 89.

22. Akers, 90.

23. Akers, 90.

24. Akers, 91.

25. Akers, 91.

26. Akers, 92.

27. *United States Telegraph* (Washington, DC), October 16, 1830.

28. *Farmers Cabinet* (Amherst, NH), April 2, 1831.

29. *Cherokee Phoenix and Indians Advocate* (New Town, GA), April 7, 1830, 4.

30. Gloria Jahoda, *The Trail of Tears* (New York: Wings Books, 1995), 74.

31. Akers, *Living in the Land of Death*, 94.

32. Akers, 112.

33. Akers, 112.

34. David M. Emmons, *Beyond the American Pale: The Irish in the West, 1845–1910* (Norman: Univ. of Oklahoma Press, 2010), 139.

35. Emmons, 144.

36. Emmons, 145.

37. Emmons, 145.

38. Emmons, 146.

39. Susan Campbell Bartoletti, *Black Potatoes: The Story of the Great Irish Famine, 1845–1850* (New York: Houghton Mifflin, 2001), 30.

40. *Belfast News Letter*, March 3, 1837.

41. *Belfast News Letter*, March 3, 1837.

42. Bartoletti, *Black Potatoes*, 30–31.

43. Bartoletti, 31.

44. Bartoletti, 31.

45. Bartoletti, 1.

46. Bartoletti, 1.

47. Bartoletti, 35.

48. *Kerry Evening Post* (Tralee, Ireland), October 22, 1845.

49. *Belfast Newsletter*, September 12, 1845.

50. *Nation* (Dublin), August 15, 1846.

51. *Nation* (Dublin), August 15, 1846.

52. *Tuam Herald*, November 28, 1846.

53. Bartoletti, *Black Potatoes*, 35.

54. Bartoletti, 35.

55. John Kelly, *The Graves Are Walking: The Great Famine and the Saga of the Irish People* (New York: Henry Holt, 2012), 255.

56. Kelly, 255–56.

57. Kelly, 255.

58. *Irish Examiner* (Cork), September 13, 1847.

59. *Irish Examiner* (Cork), September 13, 1847.

60. *Irish Examiner* (Cork), September 13, 1847.

61. *Wisconsin Democrat* (Madison, WI), May 1, 1847.

62. Arthur Gribben, *The Great Famine and the Irish Diaspora in America* (Amherst: Univ. of Massachusetts Press, 1999), 89.

63. Gribben, 89.

64. Gribben, 89.

65. Emmons, *Beyond the American Pale*, 149.

66. *Kerry Evening Post* (Tralee, Ireland), February 27, 1847.

67. *Wisconsin Democrat* (Madison, WI), May 1, 1847.

68. *Wisconsin Democrat* (Madison, WI), May 1, 1847.

69. *New England Puritan* (Boston, MA), March 4, 1847.

70. *Belfast Newsletter*, June 18, 1847.

71. Martin McGuiness, "Foreword" in *Touched by Thunder* by Waylon Gary White Deer (Walnut Creek, CA: Left Coast Press, 2013), 8.

72. McGuiness, 8.

73. "Sculpture Marks Choctaw Generosity to Irish Famine Victims," *British Broadcasting Network* (Europe), June 18, 2017, http://www.bbc.com/news/world-europe-40304645.

74. "Sculpture Marks."

75. "Sculpture Marks."

76. Cliodhna Russell, "Choctaw Chief to Visit Sculpture That Commemorates His Nation's Generosity during Irish Famine," *The Journal.ie*, https://www.thejournal.ie/choctaw-memorial-kindred-spirits-midleton-cork-3445847-Jun2017/.

77. Stanley Heller, "The Choctaw Gift to the Starving Irish," *Indian Country Today*, March 18, 2014, https://newsmaven.io/indiancountrytoday/archive/the-choctaw-gift-to-the-starving-irish-aenL15MWFkmarxUr0Q2gLw/.

78. "Sculpture in Ireland Honors Choctaw Nation," July 3, 2017, https://www.choctawnation.com/news-events/press-media/sculpture-ireland-honors-choctaw-nation.

79. "Sculpture in Ireland."

80. "Sculpture in Ireland."

81. "How Choctaw Indians Raised Money for Irish Great Hunger Relief," *Irish Central* (Dublin), October 13, 2015.

82. "Irish Prime Minister Visits Choctaw Nation," March 12, 2018, https://www.choctawnation.com/news-events/press-media/irish-prime-minister-visits-choctaw-nation.

83. "Irish Prime Minister."

84. "Irish Prime Minister." Note: "Taoiseach" means prime minister in Irish Gaelic.

85. White Deer, *Touched by Thunder*, 159.

7. John Mitchel

1. The author would like to thank the Office of Faculty Development and Teaching Excellence at Augusta University for funding a portion of this work.

2. "In Memory of John Mitchel," *Nation* (Dublin), May 8, 1875.

3. Kevin Grieves, *Journalism across Boundaries: The Promises and Challenges of Transnational and Transborder Journalism* (New York: Palgrave MacMillan, 2012), 24–25.

4. Gaye Tuchman, *Making News: A Study in the Construction of Reality* (New York: Free Press, 1978); Ulf Hannerz, *Transnational Connections: Culture, People, Places* (London: Routledge, 1996), 122.

5. Michael Schudson, "Four Approaches to the Sociology of News," in *Mass Media and Society*, ed. James Curran and Michael Gurevitch (London: Hodder Arnold, 2005), 187.

6. Marcel Broersma, "Transnational Journalism History: Balancing Global Universals and National Peculiarities," *Medien & Zeit* 25, no. 4 (2010): 11; Grieves, *Journalism across Boundaries*, 8.

7. Steven A. Channing, *Crisis of Fear: Secession in South Carolina* (New York: W. W. Norton, 1974), 20, 21, 24, 74, 76; Stefan Kieniewicz, "The Social Visage of Poland in 1848," *Slavonic and East European Review* 27, no. 68 (December 1948): 91.

8. Broersma, "Transnational Journalism History," 10.

9. "A Week Later from England," *Courier* (Boston, MA), June 12, 1848, 2; "Bold Talk—Treason in Ireland," *Daily Advertiser* (Newark, NJ), June 1, 1848, 2; "Later from Europe," *Republican Farmer* (Bridgeport, CT), June 13, 1848, 3; "One Day's Dirty Work," *New York Herald* June 20, 1848, 1; "Arrival of John Mitchel at Bermuda," *Times-Picayune* (New Orleans, LA), July 7, 1848, 2.

10. *Daily Journal* (Lafayette, IN), February 11, 1854, 2.

11. "Bold Talk," 2.

12. "The Irish and the Eastern War," *Baltimore Sun*, March 28, 1854, 2.

13. "News of the Day," *Alexandria Gazette* (VA), June 23, 1854, 2.

14. Glenn C. Altschuler and Stuart M. Blumin, *Rude Republic: Americans and Their Politics in the Nineteenth Century* (Princeton, NJ: Princeton Univ. Press, 2000), 3–4.

15. John R. McKivigan, *Abolitionism and American Politics and Government* (New York: Garland, 1999), 12.

16. Cong. Globe, 35th Cong., 1st Sess. 441 (1858); McKivigan, *Abolitionism*, 12.

17. Ian Delahanty, "'A Noble Empire in the West': Young Ireland, the United States and Slavery," *Britain and the World* 6, no. 2 (2013): 176–77.

18. "Mr. Haughton to Mr. Meagher Sends Greetings," *Irish Citizen* (New York), January 14, 1854.

19. Liam Hogan, "John Mitchel Was Hailed as a Totem for Irish Liberty . . . but He Was a White Supremacist," *Journal* (Dublin), January 18, 2014, http://www.thejournal.ie/readme/john-mitchel-was-hailed-as-a-totem-for-irish-liberty-but-he-was-a-white-supremacist-1266182-Jan2014/.

20. Bryan P. McGovern, *John Mitchel: Irish Nationalist, Southern Secessionist* (Knoxville: Univ. of Tennessee Press, 2009), 119, 129; Ann Tucker, "Newest Born of Nations: Southern Thought on European Nationalisms and the Creation of the Confederacy, 1820–1860," (PhD diss., Univ. of Southern California, 2014), 56; Anthony Russell, "Should Irish Slavery Supporter John Mitchel's Statue in Newry Be Taken Down?," *Irish Times*, February 7, 2018, https://www.irishtimes.com/culture/books/should-irish-slavery-supporter-john-mitchel-s-statue-in-newry-be-taken-down-1.3382077.

21. McGovern, *John Mitchel*, 119.

22. "Mr. Haughton to Mr. Meagher Sends Greetings."

23. "Affairs in Europe," *Charleston Mercury* (SC), December 25, 1860, 2.

24. "Interesting from Europe," *Charleston Mercury* (SC), December 23, 1861, 1; "Affairs in Europe," *Charleston Mercury* (SC), August 24, 1861, 1.

25. "Distinguished Arrival," *Semi-Weekly Raleigh Register* (NC), October 22, 1862, 2. Reprinted from the *Richmond Enquirer*.

26. "John Mitchel among the Rebels," *New York Herald*, April 18, 1863, 4; "Jeff Davis's Chief Defamer of the North," *New Haven Daily Palladium*, August 1, 1863, 1; McGovern, *John Mitchel*, 181.

27. McGovern, *John Mitchel*, 176; *Richmond Enquirer* (VA), March 17, July 25, September 5, and October 16, 1863.

28. "Fort Sumter Captured," *Vermont Watchman and State Journal* (Montpelier), August 28, 1863, 2.

29. "Letter from John Mitchel," *Semi-Weekly Raleigh Register* (NC), March 4, 1863, 1.

30. "Letter from John Mitchel."

31. "Letter from John Mitchel."

32. McGovern, *John Mitchel*, 184–85.

33. McGovern, 185–210, 216.

34. Brendan Ó Cathaoir, "An Irishman's Diary on John Mitchel, a Contentious Patriot," *Irish Times* (Dublin), November 3, 2015, https://www.irishtimes.com/opinion/an-irishman-s-diary-on-john-mitchel-a-contentious-patriot-1.2414491.

35. Anthony Russell, "John Mitchel: Flawed Hero," *History Ireland:* 24, no. 1 (January–February 2016): 30–33.

36. "John Mitchel: A Rebel with Two Causes Remembered," *Irish News* (Belfast), July 11, 2015.

37. *Nation* (Dublin), February 13 and 20, 1875.

38. Tucker, "Newest Born of Nations," 55–56, 65, 97, 102.

39. Tucker, 64–65.

40. "John Mitchel (1815–1875): Young Irelander, a Felon of our Land, Author, Publisher, Supporter of the Confederacy," Fenian Graves, posted August 24, 2010, http://feniangraves.net/Mitchel,%20John/Mitchel,%20John.htm; Ó Cathaoir, "An Irishman's Diary."

41. O'Connor, *John Mitchel*, 302.

42. John F. Kvach, *DeBow's Review: The Antebellum Vision of a New South* (Lexington: Univ. Press of Kentucky, 2013), 131.

43. "In Memory of John Mitchel."

44. John Quinn, "Southern Citizen: John Mitchel, the Confederacy and Slavery," *History Ireland* 15, no. 3 (2007): 30–35, http://www.historyireland.com/18th-19th-century-history/southern-citizen-john-mitchel-the-confederacy-and-slavery/.

45. Steven R. Knowlton, "The Politics of John Mitchel: A Reappraisal," *Éire-Ireland* 22, no. 2 (Summer 1987): 38–55, 40; Émile Montégut, *John Mitchel: A Study of Irish Nationalism*, translated and edited by J. M. Hone (Dublin: Maunsel, 1915), 27, 13; James Quinn, "John Mitchel and the Rejection of the 19th Century," *Éire-Ireland* 38, nos. 3/4 (2003): 95.

46. "John Martin," *Nation* (Dublin), April 3, 1875.

8. Gilded Age Humor as a Moral Force

1. "John Bull's Irish Relations," *Texas Siftings*, September 8, 1883. For background on the problem of absentee, Anglican landowners, the land-lease system in Ireland, and the burden that high rents placed on tenant farmers, see Jay P. Dolan, *The Irish Americans* (New York: Bloomsbury Press, 2008), 5–7.

2. For more on the types of caricatures and stereotypes common among American periodicals in the late 1800s, see Worth Robert Miller, *Populist Cartoons: An Illustrated History of the Third Party Movement in the 1890s* (Kirksville, MO: Truman State Univ. Press, 2001), 16–21.

3. Kerry Soper, "From Swarthy Ape to Sympathetic Everyman and Subversive Trickster: The Development of Irish Caricature in American Comic Strips between 1890 and 1920," *Journal of American Studies* 39, no. 2 (2005): 258.

4. Martha Banta, *Barbaric Intercourse: Caricature and Culture of Conduct, 1841–1936* (Chicago: Univ. of Chicago Press, 2003), 7; L. Perry Curtis, *Apes and Angels: The Irishman in Victorian Caricature* (Washington, DC: Smithsonian Institution Press, 1971).

5. Soper, "From Swarthy Ape," 264.

6. Kathleen Diane McGuire, "The Transatlantic Paddy: The Making of Transnational Irish Identity in Nineteenth-Century America," (PhD diss., Univ. of California, Riverside, 2009), 2; Dale Knobel, *Paddy and the Republic: Ethnicity and*

Nationality in Antebellum America (Middletown, CT: Wesleyan Univ. Press, 1986), 15–16.

7. Soper, "From Swarthy Ape," 260. The San Francisco humor magazine, the *Wasp*, was particularly vicious in its verbal and visual depictions of the Chinese during the late nineteenth century. For a scholarly assessment, see Nicholas Sean Hall, "*The Wasp*'s 'Troublesome Children,'" *California History* 90, no. 2 (January 2013): 42–63.

8. Joseph Boskin and Joseph Dorinson, "Ethnic Humor: Subversion and Survival," *American Quarterly* 37, no. 1 (1985): 81.

9. Leonard Dinnerstein and David M. Reimers, *Ethnic Americans: A History of Immigration*, 5th ed. (New York: Columbia Univ. Press, 2009), 2, 18, 24.

10. Boskin and Dorinson, "Ethnic Humor," 81.

11. Stephen A. Brighton, "Degrees of Alienation: The Material Evidence of the Irish and Irish American Experience, 1850–1910," *Historical Archaeology* 42, no. 4 (2007): 132–53, 133; Avtar Brah, *Cartographies of Diaspora: Contesting Identities* (London: Routledge, 1996), 190.

12. See Kevin Grieves on the definitions and implications of transnational journalism. Kevin Grieves, *Journalism across Boundaries: The Promises and Challenges of Transnational and Transborder Journalism* (New York: Palgrave Macmillan, 2012), 8.

13. Joseph Keppler, the German editor and cartoonist for *Puck* magazine, was similarly supportive of German immigrants in his publication, if they were not Jewish, but often was hostile to other immigrant groups. For more on Keppler, see Richard Samuel West, *Satire on Stone: The Political Cartoons of Joseph Keppler* (Urbana: Univ. of Illinois Press, 1988); Michael Alexander Kahn and Richard Samuel West, *Puck: What Fools These Mortals Be* (San Diego: IDW, 2014).

14. Walter Blair, "Traditions in Southern Humor," in *Essays on American Humor*, ed. Hamlin Hill (Madison: Univ. of Wisconsin Press, 1993), 15.

15. Robert K. Dodge, "The Irish Comic Stereotype in the Almanacs of the Early Republic," *Eire-Ireland* 19, no. 3 (1984): 112.

16. James L. Ford, "The Evolution of American Humor," *Collier's Illustrated Weekly* 30, no. 18 (1903): 21; Frank Luther Mott concurred, noting the period from 1885 to 1905 was "unique in having so many humorous journals of high quality." See Frank Luther Mott, *A History of American Magazines, 1885–1905*, vol. 4 (Cambridge, MA: Belknap Press, 1957), 383.

17. Ford, "Evolution of American Humor," 21; Mott, *History of American Magazines*, 383–85.

18. "New York's Comic Papers," *Hamilton Literary Monthly* 30 (April 1896): 284–85.

19. David Reed, *The Popular Magazine in Britain and the United States of America, 1880–1960* (Toronto: Univ. of Toronto Press, 1997), 50–51.

20. Ford, "Evolution of American Humor," 21.

21. Historian Frank Luther Mott's multivolume history of American magazines provides a solid accounting of the nation's national and regional humor magazines of the nineteenth century. For his analysis of *Texas Siftings*, see Frank Luther Mott, *A History of American Magazines 1885–1905*, vol. 4 (Cambridge, MA: Belknap Press, 1957), 385.

22. Leland Krauth, "Mark Twain: The Victorian of Southwestern Humor," in *Humor of the Old South*, ed. Thomas M. Inge and Edward J. Piacentino (Lexington: Univ. Press of Kentucky, 2001), 223; Carolyn S. Brown, *The Tall Tale in American Folklore and Literature* (Knoxville: Univ. of Tennessee Press, 1987), 5; Hennig Cohen and William B. Dillingham, *Humor of the Old Southwest*, 2nd ed. (Athens: Univ. of Georgia Press, 1975), xvii.

23. Virginia Eisenhour, *Alex Sweet's Texas: The Lighter Side of Lone Star History* (Austin: Univ. of Texas Press, 1986), 191. Americans' fascination with the West and its mythology led to the rise of such showman as William F. "Buffalo Bill" Cody and his stage show. For more, see Joy S. Kasson, *Buffalo Bill's Wild West: Celebrity, Memory, and Popular History* (New York: Hill and Wang, 2000), 62.

24. David Pickering, *Texas Siftings and Texas Journalism* (Austin: Univ. of Texas Press, 1976), v.

25. Pickering, 4. Unlike most of their fellow literary comedians, Sweet and Knox used their own personas in sketches rather than creating new characters and writing from those imagined perspectives. But, like their fellow journalist-humorists, Sweet's and Knox's sketches demonstrate the men were well traveled and well read. David B. Kesterson, "Those *Literary* Comedians," in *Critical Essays on American Humor*, ed. William Bedford Clark and W. Craig Turner (Boston: G. K. Hall, 1984), 167–83.

26. Mary M. Cronin, "Sifting Comic Wheat from Western Chaff: Alex E. Sweet, John Armoy Knox, and the Humor of the American West," in *The Funniest Pages: International Perspectives on Journalism and Humor*, ed. David Swick and Richard Lance Keeble (New York: Peter Lang, 2016), 53–66; Eisenhour, *Alex Sweet's Texas*; Pickering, *Texas Siftings and Texas Journalism*; Ernest B. Speck, "Alex Sweet: Comic Journalist from Texas," *Texas Press Messenger* 46 (1971): 6–8; William R. Linneman, "Colonel Bill Snort: A Texas Jack Downing," *Southwestern Historical Quarterly* 64, no. 1 (1961): 185–99.

27. Charles Henry Smith, Joshua Billings, Charles Farrar Browne, and Mark Twain all capitalized on their popularity and lectured to vast crowds. David B. Parker, *Alias Bill Arp: Charles Henry Smith and the South's Goodly Heritage* (Athens: Univ. of Georgia Press, 2009), 38.

28. Eisenhour, *Alex Sweet's Texas*, xvii; David Pickering notes that within one to two years of the publication's founding, *Texas Siftings* "was no longer the state paper

its editors had intended it to be, but a successful national journal that was engaging less and ever less in 'Texas Sifting.'" Pickering, *Texas Siftings and Texas Journalism*, 2.

29. James E. Caron, *Mark Twain, Unsanctified Newspaper Reporter* (Columbia: Univ. of Missouri Press, 2008), 52; Kesterson, "Those *Literary* Comedians," 167–83.

30. "Alex Edwin Sweet," *Vancouver Independent* (Vancouver, BC), December 20, 1883.

31. "Sweet, Alexander Edwin," *Appleton's Annual Cyclopaedia and Register of Important Events of the Year 1901*, vol. 6 (New York: D. Appleton, 1902), 470.

32. Eisenhour, *Alex Sweet's Texas*, xii–xiii; "Sweet, Alexander Edwin," *The National Cyclopedia of American Biography*, vol. 6 (New York: James T. White, 1896), 31.

33. John Fowler, *James P. Newcomb: Texas Journalist and Political Leader* (Austin: Department of Journalism Development Program, 1976), 82–83.

34. Speck, "Alex Sweet," 6.

35. "J. Armoy Knox," *Folio* 28, no. 4 (1885): 139.

36. "Death of a Distinguished Ulsterman," *Belfast Evening Telegram*, January 9, 1907. The obituary notes that a year of living in Texas "served completely to restore him to sound health again."

37. Harriett Smither, "Knox, John Armoy," *Handbook of Texas Online*, uploaded June 15, 2010, http://www.tshaonline.org/handbook/online/articles/fkn06. Knox's obituary also noted that he immigrated for a better climate; however, so little biographical material is available on Knox that it's unknown where he was from 1871 to 1874 when he arrived in Texas. Nor is there any information on why Knox did not want to follow his father into the family's grain business.

38. M. Mark Stolarik, *Forgotten Doors: The Other Ports of Entry to the United States* (Philadelphia: Balch Institute Press, 1988), 137. Numerous ferries ran regular routes between New Orleans and several Texas coastal cities.

39. Graham Davis, "Models of Migration: The Historiography of the Irish Pioneers in South Texas," *Southwestern Historical Quarterly* 99, no. 3 (1996): 326–49.

40. Phillip L. Fry, "Irish," *Handbook of Texas Online*, last modified April 10, 2019, http://www.tshaonline.org/handbook/online/articles/pii01.

41. Austin Texas Government, accessed August 24, 2019, https://www.austintexas.gov/sites/default/files/files/Planning/Demographics/population_history_pub.pdf. That population would grow to 11,013 by 1880.

42. In 1875 the census counted 757 inhabitants from Germany, 297 from Mexico, 215 from Ireland, and 138 from Sweden. For more information, see David C. Humphrey, "Austin, TX (Travis County)," *Handbook of Texas Online*, last modified October 23, 2018, http://www.tshaonline.org/handbook/online/articles/hda03.

43. "J. Armoy Knox," 139; *New York Clipper Annual for 1890* (New York: Frank Queen, 1890), 8.

44. Leon C. Metz, *John Wesley Hardin: Dark Angel of Texas* (Norman: Univ. of Oklahoma Press, 1998), 332. The brief sketch from *Folio* notes on page 139 that Knox met Sweet in 1880, but the accuracy of this statement can't be confirmed. Texas's journalistic circle was a relatively small one.

45. "Alexander Edwin Sweet," *Vancouver Independent* (Vancouver, BC), December 20, 1883, 6.

46. *N. W. Ayer & Son's American Newspaper Annual* (Philadelphia: N. W. Ayer & Son, 1888), 781.

47. *N. W. Ayer & Son's American Newspaper Annual* (Philadelphia: N. W. Ayer & Son, 1890), 515.

48. See the 1888 issue of *N. W. Ayer & Son's American Newspaper Annual*, pages 779–80, 508, and 512, for circulation figures for the above-mentioned magazines.

49. Ernest Speck, "Alex Sweet," 6.

50. Ernest B. Speck, "Texas Siftings," *Handbook of Texas Online*, last modified January 30, 2020, http://www.tshaonline.org/handbook/online/articles/edt16.

51. Throughout the nineteenth century, the American press engaged in an extensive normative practice of reprinting other writers' and publications' work, not always with credit. *Texas Siftings* always listed bylines for its authors or sources of its material, except for work produced by Sweet, Knox, and the periodical's other editors. For more on the origins of the culture of reprinting and its economic and literary controversies, see Meredith L. McGill, *American Literature and the Culture of Reprinting, 1834–1853* (Philadelphia: Univ. of Pennsylvania Press, 2003); Peter Baldwin, *The Copyright Wars: Three Centuries of Trans-Atlantic Battles* (Princeton, NJ: Princeton Univ. Press, 2014), 119–22. At a time when copyright laws were lax, Sweet's jokes, anecdotes, and comic sketches of the 1870s were reprinted by newspapers in the United States, Australia, and several European countries, which brought him to international popularity.

52. Kesterson, "Those *Literary* Comedians," 167–74; Edward J. Piacentino, "Sleepy Hollow" Comes South: Washington Irving's Influence on Old Southwestern Humor," in *Humor of the Old South*, ed. Thomas M. Inge and Edward J. Piacentino (Lexington: Univ. Press of Kentucky, 2001), 22–35.

53. Kesterson, "Those *Literary* Comedians," 168–74, 179.

54. Speck, "Alex Sweet," 7.

55. Eisenhour, *Alex Sweet's Texas*, xv.

56. US Census Bureau, "Nativity of the Population and Place of Birth of the Native Population: 1850 to 1990," internet release date March 9, 1999, http://www.census.gov/population/www/documentation/twps0029/tab01.html.

57. Noel Ignatiev notes that from 1815 until the first famine in the late 1840s, between eight hundred thousand and one million Irish sailed for America, up to two-thirds of whom were from Ulster. Noel Ignatiev, *How the Irish Became White* (New York: Routledge, 1995), 38.

58. Dolan, *Irish Americans*, 10.

59. Dinnerstein and Reimers, *Ethnic Americans*, 25; Brighton, "Degrees of Alienation," 134; John Higham, *Strangers in the Land*, 5–6.

60. D. Gregory Van Dussen, "An American Response to Irish Catholic Immigration: *The Methodist Quarterly Review*, 1830–1870," *Methodist History* 10, no. 1: 21–22.

61. Van Dussen, 25.

62. Higham, *Strangers in the Land*, 5–6.

63. Van Dussen, "An American Response," 22. Fear of Irish Catholic loyalties to the United States led to the establishment of a number of anti-Catholic groups, like the American Protective Association, a group that died by 1896. Also see Donald L. Kinzer, *An Episode in Anti-Catholicism: The American Protective Association* (Seattle: Univ. of Washington Press, 1964), 93–94.

64. James H. Dormon, "Ethnic Stereotyping in American Popular Culture: The Depiction of American Ethnics in the Cartoon Periodicals of the Gilded Age," *Amerikastudien* 30, no. 4 (1985): 489.

65. Michael de Nie, *The Eternal Paddy: Irish Identity and the British Press, 1798–1882* (Madison: Univ. of Wisconsin Press, 2004), 5.

66. Dodge, "Irish Comic Stereotype," 111.

67. Dodge, 114.

68. Dodge, 114.

69. Soper, "From Swarthy Ape," 259; William Murrel, *A History of American Graphic Humor* (New York: Cooper Square, 1967), 5; Curtis, *Apes or Angels*, xii; Miller, *Populist Cartoons*, 16; Banta, *Barbaric Intercourse*, 7; Dormon, "Ethnic Stereotyping," 490. Joshua Brown, a leading scholar on the nineteenth-century American pictorial press, notes that wood-engraved news imagery was a "social process." "Over time, it was altered and mediated by a rapidly changing social context and the demands of readers." Such stereotypes and depictions influenced reader's beliefs about minorities and immigrants. While *Harper's* magazine attracted a readership that was wealthier, *Frank Leslie's Illustrated Newspaper* attracted "the broad 'middle,' an elastic range of readers that, in the mid-nineteenth century, stretched from mechanics to merchants." Joshua Brown, "Reconstructing Representation: Social Types, Readers, and the Pictorial Press, 1865–1877," *Radical History Review* 66, no. 5 (1996): 6–7.

70. Robert L. Gambone, *Life on the Press: The Popular Art and Illustrations of George Benjamin Luks* (Jackson: Univ. Press of Mississippi, 2009), 64.

71. Brown, "Reconstructing Representation," 10; Elizabeth Johns, *American Genre Painting: The Politics of Everyday Life* (New Haven, CT: Yale Univ. Press, 1991), 1–23.

72. Dormon, "Ethnic Stereotyping," 494.

73. John J. Appel, "From Shanties to Lace Curtains: The Irish Image in *Puck*, 1876–1910," *Comparative Studies in Society and History* 13, no. 4 (1971): 367; Kathleen Donovan, "Good Old Pat: An Irish-American Stereotype in Decline," *Eire-Ireland* 15, no. 3 (1980): 6.

74. Appel, "From Shanties to Lace Curtains," 367.

75. Donovan, "Good Old Pat," 9; Gambone, *Life on the Press*, 65–67.

76. Dormon, "Ethnic Stereotyping," 492.

77. Brown, "Reconstructing Representation," 5–6.

78. For more on revolutionary Irish nationalists and violence in the 1880s in Ireland and England and their supporters in America, see Niall Whelehan, *Irish Nationalism and Political Violence in the Wider World, 1867–1900* (New York: Cambridge Univ. Press, 2012), 119; Deaglan O'Donghaile, *Blasted Literature: Victorian Political Fiction and the Shock of Modernism* (Edinburgh: Edinburgh Univ. Press, 2011), 3–4; Eileen Muccino, "Irish Filibusters and Know-Nothings in Cincinnati," *Ohio Valley History* 10, no. 3 (2010), 4.

79. "General Comment," *Texas Siftings*, March 29, 1884, 2.

80. Donal P. McCracken, *Inspector Mallon: Buying Irish Patriotism for a Five Pound Note* (Dublin: Irish Academic Press, 2009), 101–3.

81. "Editorial Brevities," *Texas Siftings*, December 16, 1882, 1.

82. *Texas Siftings*, June 16, 1883, 1.

83. "Justice to Ireland," *Texas Siftings*, January 23, 1886.

84. D. B. Knox, "The People of Ulster," *Texas Siftings*, June 6, 1885, 6.

85. "Editorial Brevities, 1."

86. Donovan, "Good Old Pat," 10.

87. Many of the articles, sketches, and so-called two-line dialogues were illustrated. Although *Texas Siftings* had several illustrators on staff who often, but not always, depicted the subjects of the articles in stereotypical fashion, the periodical's most famous illustrator was Thomas Worth, who, prior to his tenure at *Texas Siftings*, had penned illustrations for *Harper's* and *Frank Leslie*. For a biographical sketch of Worth, see "Siftings' Portrait Gallery," *Texas Siftings*, August 9, 1890, 12.

88. Donovan notes that on occasion some American humor magazines of the late nineteenth century portrayed the Irish as deserving of getting back at opponents in clever, verbal fashion. See Donovan, "Good Old Pat," 9, 11.

89. "Serving a Writ in Ireland," *Texas Siftings*, January 6, 1883, 3.

90. Donovan, "Good Old Pat," 10.

91. "A Pat Proverb," *Texas Siftings*, December 12, 1885, 1; in the July 16, 1887, issue, "Bridget" is shown as no one's fool. The two-line dialogue is as follows: Gypsy—"Give me fifty cents and I'll tell your fortune." Irishwoman—"Shure, an' if I had Fifty Sints that would be fortune enough."

92. "She Married a Lord," *Texas Siftings*, April 2, 1887, 7.

93. Soper, "From Swarthy Ape," 260. As Soper notes on page 261, the racist constructs implied "claims about biology and physiognomy."

94. "Not to Be Caught a Second Time," *Texas Siftings*, April 28, 1888, 3.

95. For example, see "Can't Stand Jealousy," *Texas Siftings*, December 22, 1888; "The New Year's Card Basket," *Texas Siftings*, December 29, 1888, 5.

96. "A Just Rebuke," *Texas Siftings*, December 29, 1888, 14.

97. An online search reveals four plays credited to Knox: a comedy titled *A Stuffed Dog* that he cowrote with Edwin Atwell; another play titled *Marcel*; an Irish musical titled *Shane-na-Law* cowritten with J. C. Roach and with music by William J Scanlan; and *A Comic Opera, in Three Acts, Entitled the False Prophet*, cowritten with Charles McCoy Snyder and Robert August Stoepel. For more information, see *New York Evening World*, October 1, 1889; *Philadelphia Times*, September 8, 1889; *New York Clipper Annual for 1890* (New York: Frank Queen, 1890); Smither, "Knox, John Armoy."

98. "Famous Texas Editor Dead," *New York Times*, December 20, 1906; "News and Notes," *Writer*, January 1907, 16.

9. Presidents, Protection, and Politics

1. J. P. Rodechko, *Patrick Ford and His Search for America: A Case Study of Irish American Journalism, 1870–1913* (New York: Arno Press, 1967), 49; Niall Whelehan, "Skirmishing, the Irish World, and Empire, 1876–86," *Éire-Ireland* 42, nos. 1–2 (Spring–Summer 2007): 180–200.

2. *Ayers Newspaper Annual and Directory* (Philadelphia: N. W. Ayers & Sons) 1904; 1914, https://www.loc.gov/rr/news/news_research_tools/ayersdirectory.html.

3. Cian T. McMahon, "Caricaturing Race and Nation in the Irish American Press, 1870–1880: A Transnational Perspective," *Journal of American Ethnic History* 33, no. 2 (Winter 2014): 36.

4. David Brundage, "'In Time of Peace, Prepare for War': Key Themes in the Social Thought of New York's Irish-American Nationalists, 1900–1916," in *The New York Irish*, ed. Ronald H. Bayor and Timothy J. Meagher (Baltimore: Johns Hopkins Univ. Press, 1996), 323.

5. Edward T. O'Donnell, "'Though Not an Irishman': Henry George and the American Irish," *American Journal of Economics and Sociology* 56, no. 4 (1997): 410.

6. Úna Ní Bhroiméil, "Political Cartoons as Visual Opinion Discourse: The Rise and Fall of John Redmond in the Irish World," in *Ireland and the New Journalism*, ed. Karen Steele and Michael de Nie (Basingstoke, UK: Palgrave Macmillan, 2014), 119–40.

7. Mick Mulcrone, "Those Miserable Little Hounds: World War I Postal Censorship of the Irish World," *Journalism History* 20, no. 1 (1994): 15–24.

8. *The Irish World and American Industrial Liberator* (*Irish World*), September 24, 1904.

9. Matthew J. Shaw, "Drawing on the Collections," *Journalism Studies* 8, no. 5 (2007): 747–48.

10. Shaw, 747–48. Also see Mark W. Summers, *Rum, Romanism, and Rebellion: The Making of a President, 1884* (Chapel Hill: Univ. of North Carolina Press, 2000) for a detailed account of the election.

11. Chris Lamb, "Drawing Power: The Limits of Editorial Cartoons in America," *Journalism Studies* 8, no. 5 (2007): 720.

12. I cannot find any background information for Charles Pickett. For Thomas Fleming, see Ní Bhroiméil, "Political Cartoons," 135n21.

13. Rachel Schreiber, "Before Their Makers and Their Judges: Prostitutes and White Slaves in the Political Cartoons of the 'Masses' (New York, 1911–1917)," *Feminist Studies* 33, no. 1 (Spring 2009): 167.

14. Janis L. Edwards and Laura Ware, "Representing the Public in Campaign Media: A Political Cartoon Perspective," *American Behavioral Scientist* 49, no. 3 (November 2005): 470.

15. William A. Gamson and David Stuart, "Media Discourse as a Symbolic Contest: The Bomb in Political Cartoons," *Sociological Forum* 7, no. 1 (1992): 64.

16. Elisabeth El Refaie, "Multiliteracies: How Readers Interpret Political Cartoons," *Visual Communication* 8, no. 2 (2009): 181.

17. Joel H. Wiener, "Get the News! Get the News!: Speed in Transatlantic Journalism, 1830–1914," in *Anglo-American Media Interactions, 1850–2000*, ed. Joel H. Wiener and Mark Hampton (London: Palgrave Macmillan, 2007), 54.

18. Ní Bhroiméil, "Political Cartoons," 120.

19. Schreiber, "Before Their Makers," 167.

20. Ria Wiid, Leyland F. Pitt, and Anne Engstrom, "Not So Sexy: Public Opinion of Political Sex Scandals as Reflected in Political Cartoons," *Journal of Public Affairs* 11, no. 3 (2011): 138.

21. Martin J. Medhurst and Michael A. DeSousa, "Political Cartoons as Rhetorical Form: A Taxonomy of Graphic Discourse," *Communication Monographs* 48 (1981): 205–13.

22. See, however, Roger Fischer for the perceived impact of Thomas Nast's cartoons on William Tweed's political career: Roger Fischer, *Them Damned Pictures: Explorations in American Political Cartoon Art* (North Haven, CT: Archon, 1996), 7.

23. Wiid, Pitt, and Engstrom, "Not So Sexy," 138.

24. Fischer, *Them Damned Pictures*, 15.

25. Fischer, 122.

26. See Margaret E. Duffy, "Web of Hate: A Fantasy Theme Analysis of the Rhetorical Vision of Hate Groups Online," *Journal of Communication Inquiry* 27, no.

3 (July 2003): 291–312. Cited in Fred Vultee, "Dr. FDR and Baby War: The World through Chicago Political Cartoons before and after Pearl Harbor," *Visual Communication Quarterly* 14 (2007): 161; Martin Conboy, *The Press and Popular Culture* (London: Sage, 2002), 59.

27. William M. Benoit and John P. McHale, "Presidential Candidates' Television Spots and Personal Qualities," *Southern Communication Journal* 68, no. 4 (November 2003): 323.

28. Charles Press, *The Political Cartoon* (Rutherford, NJ: Fairleigh Dickinson Univ. Press, 1981), 68.

29. John L. Offner, "McKinley and the Spanish-American War," *Presidential Studies Quarterly* 34, no. 1 (March 2004): 60.

30. Paul A. Kramer, "Decolonizing the History of the Philippine-American War," http://www.paulkrameronline.com/wp-content/uploads/2015/08/wolffintro.pdf. (Introduction to *Little Brown Brother: How the United States Purchased and Pacified The Philippine Islands at the Century's Turn* by Leon Wolff.)

31. Matthew J. Krogman, "Censorship: Spanish-American and Philippine-American Wars," in *The Encyclopedia of the Spanish-American and Philippine-American Wars: A Political, Social, and Military History*, ed. Spencer C. Tucker (Santa Barbara, CA: ABC Clio, 2009) 106–7; Jerry Kennan and Spencer C. Tucker, "Othis, Elwell S.," in *The Encyclopedia of the Spanish-American and Philippine-American Wars*, ed. Spencer C. Tucker, 457–58.

32. Stuart C. Miller, *Benevolent Assimilation: The American Conquest of the Philippines, 1899–1903* (New Haven, CT: Yale Univ. Press, 1982), 104–29.

33. Carnegie endorsed McKinley in 1896 and 1900. See Jeff Taylor, *Where Did the Party Go? William Jennings Bryan, Hubert Humphrey, and the Jeffersonian Legacy* (Columbia: Univ. of Missouri Press, 2006), 139.

34. Shakespeare's plays were on the curriculum of at least some public high schools in the United States. See, for example, Charles van Cleve, "The Teaching of Shakespeare in American Secondary Schools," *Peabody Journal of Education* 15, no. 6 (May 1938): 333–50. Macbeth opened on Broadway on February 26, 1900, Internet Broadway Database, accessed April 30, 2018, https://www.ibdb.com/broadway-production/macbeth-5316.

35. Kristin L. Hoganson, *Fighting for American Manhood: How Gender Politics Provoked the Spanish-American and Philippine-American Wars* (New Haven, CT: Yale Univ. Press, 2000), 158–59.

36. Hoganson, 88–93.

37. This cartoon was published after the signing of the Philippine Organic Act, July 1, 1902.

38. *Irish World* (New York), October 29, 1904; *Irish World* (New York), November 26, 1904.

39. *Irish World* (New York), March 25, 1905.

40. Ironically, this board was funded by Andrew Carnegie, who was a bête noire of the *Irish World* because of his Anglophone tendencies.

41. Janis L. Edwards, "Running in the Shadows in Campaign 2000: Candidate Metaphors in Editorial Cartoons," *American Behavioral Scientist* 44, no. 12 (2001): 2141.

42. Josh Greenberg, "Framing and Temporality in Political Cartoons: A Critical Analysis of Visual News Discourse," *Canadian Review of Sociology and Anthropology* 39, no. 2 (2002): 181–98.

43. See for example Steven P. Erie, *Rainbow's End: Irish-Americans and the Dilemmas of Urban Machine Politics, 1840–1985* (Berkeley: Univ. of California Press, 1990).

44. Summers, *Rum, Romanism, and Rebellion*, 217–19.

45. Marc-William Palen, "The Imperialism of Economic Nationalism, 1890–1913," *Diplomatic History* 39, no. 1 (2015): 161n17.

46. *Irish World* (New York), October 4, 1890.

47. For example, the Wilson Gorman Tariff, 1894, and the Dingley Tariff, 1897.

48. Palen, "Imperialism of Economic Nationalism," 29–31.

49. Interestingly, the use of the Democratic donkey symbol and the Republican elephant symbol are attributed mainly to the political cartoonist Thomas Nast. See "Why the Donkey vs. the Elephant?," Radio Free Europe / Radio Liberty, November 6, 2012, https://www.rferl.org/a/us-politics-why-donkey-vs-elephant/24762343.html.

50. *Irish World* (New York), February 17, 1894.

51. *Irish World* (New York), September 24, 1904.

52. *Irish World* (New York), October 22, 1904.

53. In a hotly contested convention at St. Louis, Parker had defeated Randolph Hearst for the Democratic nomination. The eight-hour day was a central labor demand throughout this period.

54. *Irish World* (New York), October 29, 1904.

55. *Irish World* (New York), April 3, 1909; *Irish World* (New York), February 11, 1911.

56. "Cherry Tree Myth," *Digital Encyclopedia of George Washington*, accessed April 24, 2018, http://www.mountvernon.org/digital-encyclopedia/article/cherry-tree-myth/.

57. *Irish World* (New York), April 22, 1905.

58. Stephen Tuffnell, "'Uncle Sam Is to Be Sacrificed': Anglophobia in Late Nineteenth-Century Politics and Culture," *American Nineteenth Century History* 12, no. 1 (2011): 77–99, 77.

59. See Paul A. Kramer, "Empires, Exceptions, and Anglo-Saxons: Race and Rule between the British and United States Empires, 1880–1910," *Journal of American History* 88, no. 4 (2002): 1315–53; Úna Ní Bhroiméil, "Anglo-American Rapprochement

and Irish America: John Bull in the *Irish World*, 1909–14," in *Culture and Society in Ireland since 1750: Essays in Honour of Gearóid Ó Tuathaigh*, ed. John Cunningham and Niall Ó Cíosáin (Dublin: Lilliput Press, 2015), 263–81; Úna Ní Bhroiméil, "'Up with the American Flag in All the Glory of Its Stainless Honor': Anti-Imperial Rhetoric in the *Chicago Citizen*, 1898–1902," in *Ireland in an Imperial World: Citizenship, Opportunism and Subversion*, ed. Timothy G. McMahon, Michael de Nie, and Paul Townend (Basingstoke, UK: Palgrave Macmillan, 2017), 245–65.

60. Tuffnell, "'Uncle Sam Is to Be Sacrificed,'" 81.

61. *Irish World* (New York), December 2, 1893.

62. Marc-William Palen, "Foreign Relations in the Gilded Age: A British Free-Trade Conspiracy?," *Diplomatic History* 37, no. 2 (2013): 235.

63. *Irish World* (New York), September 24, 1904.

64. *Irish World* (New York), October 22, 1904.

65. See Edmund Rogers, "The United States and the Fiscal Debate in Britain, 1873–1913," *Historical Journal* 50, no. 3 (2007): 593–622.

66. Andrew Gyory, *Closing the Gate: Race Politics and the Chinese Exclusion Act* (Chapel Hill: Univ. of North Carolina Press, 1998), 97–102, 115–30; Charles J. McLain, *In Search of Equality: The Chinese Struggle against Discrimination in Nineteenth-Century America* (Berkeley: Univ. of California Press, 1994), 9.

67. *Irish World* (New York), September 17, 1904.

68. *Irish World* (New York), September 16, 1905.

69. Marc G. DeSantis, "Laws of War: TR's 1905 Treaty of Portsmouth," HistoryNet, accessed April 29, 2018, http://www.historynet.com/laws-war-trs-1905-treaty-portsmouth.htm. Roosevelt won the Nobel Peace Prize in 1906 for the negotiation of this treaty.

70. *Irish World* (New York), October 7, 1905.

71. See Thomas H. Bivins, "The Body Politic: The Changing Shape of Uncle Sam," *Journalism Quarterly* 64, no. 1 (1987): 13–20; Medhurst and DeSousa, "Political Cartoons," 213.

72. *Irish World* (New York), April 14, 1906.

73. *Irish World* (New York), August 18, 1906.

74. *Irish World* (New York), December 15, 1906.

75. *Irish World* (New York), February 4, 1899.

76. *Irish World* (New York), May 4, 1901.

77. McMahon, *Caricaturing Race and Nation*, 44.

78. Raymond L. Buell, "The Development of the Anti-Japanese Agitation in the United States," *Political Science Quarterly* 37 (1992): 605–38.

79. Greg Robinson, "Quebec Newspaper Reactions to the 1907 Vancouver Riots: Humanitarianism, Nationalism, and Internationalism," *BC Studies* 192 (Winter 2016/17): 28.

80. *Irish World* (New York), September 21, 1907.

81. Woodrow Wilson was a Democrat; T. R. Roosevelt, a Progressive (in 1912); William H. Taft, a Republican; and Eugene Debs, a Socialist.

82. *Irish World* (New York), November 2, 1912.

83. See William M. Leary Jr., "Woodrow Wilson, Irish Americans, and the Election of 1916," *Journal of American History* 54, no. 1 (1967): 57–72.

84. Janis L. Edwards, "Visualizing Presidential Imperatives: Masculinity as an Interpretive Frame in Editorial Cartoons, 1988–2008," in *Gender and Political Communication in America: Rhetoric, Representation, and Display*, ed. J. L. Edwards (Lanham, MD: Lexington Books, 2009), 233–50.

85. Colin Seymour-Ure, "Farewell Camelot! British Cartoonists' Views of the United States since Watergate," *Journalism Studies* 8, no. 5 (2007): 737.

86. Cited in Mark Hampton, "The Political Cartoon as Educationalist Journalism: David Low's Portrayal of Mass Unemployment in Interwar Britain," *Journalism Studies* 14, no. 5 (2013): 681.

87. For this concept in a black context, see Windy Lawrence, Benjamin R. Bates, and Mark Cervenka, "Politics Drawn in Black and White: Henry J. Lewis's Visual Rhetoric in Late-1800s Black Editorial Cartoons," *Journalism History* 40, no. 3 (Fall 2014): 146.

10. "Readiness and Range"

1. *Tablet* (London), February 27, 1904; *Cincinnati Daily Gazette*, June 18, 1878; *Harper's Bazaar*, October 1901; *Dial*, June 16, 1901.

2. See for example: "Legal Injustice to Women," *Indianapolis Journal*, December 10, 1893; "Let It Die," *Chicago Times*, November 7, 1880; *Broad Ax* (Salt Lake City), January 2, 1904.

3. "Genius of Mrs. Sullivan," *Chicago Chronicle*, January 3, 1904; Isabella C. O'Keefe, "Catholic Women," *Intermountain Catholic*, November 18, 1899; *Gaelic American* (New York), February 21, 1925.

4. "Women in Newspapers," in *History of Woman Suffrage*, ed. Elizabeth Cody Stanton, Susan B. Anthony, Matilda Joslyn Gage, 2nd ed. (Rochester, NY: Susan B. Anthony, 1889); Maurine H. Beasley and Sheila J. Gibbons, *Taking Their Place: A Documentary History of Women and Journalism*, 2nd ed. (State College, PA: Strata, 2003).

5. Frances F. Willard, *Occupations for Women* (New York: Success, 1897), 284.

6. Agnes Hooper Gottlieb, "Grit Your Teeth, Then Learn to Swear: Women in Journalistic Careers 1850–1926," *American Journalism* 18, no. 1, (2013): 58. Helen M. Winslow, "The Confessions of a Newspaper Woman," *Atlantic*, February 1905.

7. Cynthia Westover Alden, *Women's Ways of Earning Money* (New York: University Society, 1904), 166.

8. Margaret E. Sangster, "Editorship as a Profession for Women," *Forum*, December 1895.

9. Lida Rose McCabe, "Margaret Sullivan: The Ablest Woman Journalist in the Country," *Los Angeles Times*, June 4, 1893. A US congressman or senator earned $5,000 per annum in 1889, while the average wage for a manufacturing worker was $427.

10. Gottlieb, "Grit Your Teeth," 63.

11. Edward Bok, "Is the Newspaper Office the Place for a Girl," *Ladies' Home Journal*, February 1901, quoted in Gottlieb, "Grit Your Teeth," 53.

12. Sangster, "Editorship as a Profession for Women."

13. Kathleen Sprows Cummings, *New Women of the Old Faith: Gender and American Catholicism in the Progressive Era* (Chapel Hill: Univ. of North Carolina Press, 2010), 20–21.

14. *Irish Standard* (Minneapolis, MN), January 2, 1904; *Evening Star* (Washington, DC), December 28, 1903.

15. Educated by the Religious of the Sacred Heart, she remained close to the nuns and was active in the Alumnae Society, and in 1866 she wrote a poem, "The Corridors of Memory," for the first general meeting of the Alumni Society. In 1868 she was the vice president of the Alumni Society and in 1870 she was on the committee organizing the annual reunion. In 1897 she was president of the alumnae association of Chicago. *Twelve Years of the Detroit High School Scholarship Fund, 1891–1903, with a Complete List of Officers of the Detroit High School Alumni Society* (Detroit: Detroit High School Scholarship Fund Association, 1903), 55–57. *New York Times*, "Noted Woman Writer Dead," August 29, 1903. I am grateful to Ellen Skerrett for information on Sullivan's presidency of the alumnae association.

16. James O'Brien, *Irish Celts: A Cyclopedia of Race History* (Detroit: L. F. Kilroy, 1884), 80–81.

17. Gillian O'Brien, *Blood Runs Green: The Murder That Transfixed Gilded Age Chicago* (Chicago: Univ. of Chicago Press, 2015).

18. James O'Brien, *Irish Celts*, 80–81; Harriet Monroe, "Margaret Sullivan's Meed," *Chicago Chronicle*, December 30, 1903; *Indiana State Sentinel*, May 9, 1894.

19. Federal Writers Project, *The Case of Dr. Cronin* (unpublished manuscript, probably 1936), Abraham Lincoln Presidential Library, Springfield, IL, 3; "Gifted Woman Dead," *Irish Standard* (Minneapolis, MN), January 2, 1904.

20. David Nord, *Communities of Journalism: A History of American Newspapers and Their Readers* (Urbana: Univ. of Illinois Press, 2001), 112.

21. "Margaret Sullivan: Some Facts about the Leading Woman Journalist of America," *Fort Worth Gazette*, July 30, 1889.

22. "Margaret Sullivan, "Some Facts."

23. *New York Herald*, March 6, 1882.

24. J.L.H., "A Woman's Experience of Newspaper Work," *Harper's Weekly*, January 25, 1890.

25. Quoted in Sprows Cummings, *New Women of the Old Faith*, 178.

26. Some writers' names appeared alongside their articles as early as the 1830s, but it did not become common until the end of the nineteenth century and indeed was not the default until well into the twentieth century. Such anonymity posed a problem for both sides in the American Civil War, and General Joseph Hooker, commander of the Army of the Potomac, issued General Order 48 in April 1863 to deal with the problems associated with anonymous reports of the war which Hooker believed were often either untrue or revealed crucial details to the Confederates. Journalists were not pleased with Hooker's action, but quickly changed their opinion as many of them developed national reputations because of their identifiable war coverage. William E. Huntzicker, *The Popular Press, 1833–1865* (Westport, CT: Praeger, 1999), 149.

27. Monroe, "Margaret Sullivan Meed."

28. For detail on the Hanford murder see Charles H. Wood, "The Sullivan Trial," *American Law Register (1852–1891)* 25, no. 7 (July 1877): 385–92. The city council was then known as the common council.

29. On the Catholic Church and public schools see Timothy Walch, "Catholic Social Institutions and Urban Development: The View from Nineteenth-Century Chicago and Milwaukee," *Catholic Historical Review* 64, no. 1 (January 1978): 16–32; Timothy Walch, "The Catholic Press and the Campaign for Parish Schools: Chicago and Milwaukee 1850–1885," *U.S. Catholic Historian* 3, no. 4 (Spring 1984): 254–72.

30. In the first trial the jury failed to reach a unanimous verdict. Professor David Swing, a well-known preacher and friend of Mrs. Lincoln, was certain that the killing of Hanford would destroy Sullivan's life: "Let us pity tenderly the widow and the fatherless, and pity also the hearthstone of Alexander and Margaret Sullivan. The ruin of their home, founded only last spring, seems complete." "What Prof. Swing Thinks of the Homicide," *Chicago Tribune*, August 20, 1876.

31. Isaac E. Adams, *Life of Emery A. Storrs* (Chicago: G. L. Howe, 1886), 548–65; *Thirteenth Annual Report of the Board of Public Works to the Common Council of the City of Chicago for the Municipal Fiscal Year Ending March 31, 1874* (Chicago: Board of Public Works, 1874), 23.

32. *Thirteenth Annual Report.* At the time of the shooting Alexander Sullivan was enrolled at the Union College of Law, but was expelled. However, by 1879 he had been admitted to the Illinois bar on the recommendation of a Chicago judge. The college was a department of the now defunct Chicago University and the city's first law school. It was established in 1859 and in 1891 became part of Northwestern University. Federal Writers Project, *The Case of Dr. [Patrick] Cronin: A Manuscript from the Federal Writers Project Papers, Illinois State Historical Library Federal Writers*

Project (Springfield: Illinois State Historical Library, 1935?), 21, 46. Sullivan's probate record states that he was a lawyer from 1873 to 1913, which is untrue. Alexander Sullivan probate record, Cook County Archives, Chicago, IL.

33. Gillian O'Brien, *Blood Runs Green*, 51.

34. "Notes from the Capital," *Daily True American* (Trenton, NJ), June 12, 1889.

35. Margaret Sullivan was so well known that she appeared in the society pages. For example, *Daily Inter Ocean* (Chicago), August 13, 1881, noted that "Mrs. Margaret F. Sullivan left for the seashore Monday."

36. List of meetings that Parnell attended in the United States, January–March 1880, National Library of Ireland (NLI), Devoy Papers, MS 18,041(2).

37. Alexander Sullivan, "Parnell as a Leader," *North American Review* 144, no. 367 (June 1887): 613; Ely M. Janis, "Anointing the 'Uncrowned King of Ireland': Charles Stewart Parnell's 1880 American Tour and the Creation of a Transatlantic Land League Movement," *Supplement of the German Historical Institute Bulletin* 5 (2008): 23, 32. Federal Writers Project, *Case of Dr. Cronin*, 40. The Exposition Hall was built in 1872 on the site of the present-day Art Institute. It was demolished in 1892.

38. Michael Davitt, *The Fall of Feudalism in Ireland* (London: Harper, 1904), 208; Alexander Sullivan to John Devoy, March 5, 1880, NLI, Devoy Papers, MS 18,012 (17).

39. Typescript of Poem: *The Irish Famine of 1880*, NLI, Devoy Papers, MS 18,142 (11).

40. See, for example, "A Prayer of Doubt," *Catholic World* 36 (1882): 771, and "A Paper-Knife of Irish Oak," in *The Poetry and Song of Ireland*, ed. John Boyle O'Reilly (New York: Gay Brothers, 1889).

41. In October 1874 she resigned from the *Chicago Times* in order to take over *Ave Maria*, a Catholic periodical established in 1865 by the founder of Notre Dame University, Fr. Edward Sorin. However, this proved a short-lived endeavor, and within a month she was back in Chicago. "Suffrage Notes," *Cambridge Chronicle* (Cambridge, MA), October 3, 1874.

42. Margaret Sullivan, "How Cornwallis Consolidated the British Empire," *Catholic World* 34 (December 1881): 300. Author's emphasis.

43. Margaret Sullivan, "Concerning Sir Walter Raleigh," *Catholic World* 39 (August 1884): 628.

44. Her faith was important to her, personally and professionally. The Sullivans rented pew no. 14 in the center aisle of Immaculate Conception Church. My thanks to Ellen Skerrett for this information.

45. "A Lesson in Loyalty," *Sacred Heart Review*, March 12, 1904, 5. Katherine Conway, "Margaret F. Sullivan, Journalist and Author," *Donahoe's Magazine*, March 1904, 220–23.

46. W. E. Gladstone, *The Vatican Decrees in Their Bearing on Civil Allegiance: A Political Expostulation* (London: John Murray, 1874), 61.

47. [Margaret Sullivan], "Chiefly among Women," *Catholic World* 21 (June 1875): 324.

48. "Chiefly among Women," 335. For a detailed consideration of the "Chiefly among Women," see Sprows Cummings, *New Women of the Old Faith*, 17–21.

49. "Chiefly among Women," 339.

50. Margaret Sullivan, "A Philosopher in Bohemia," *Catholic World* 69, no. 409 (June 1899), 365–75; "A Revolution in Farm Life," *Harper's Bazaar*, 35, no. 1 (1901), 590; "Growth of Musical Taste in the United States," *Dial*, May 1882, 4–5.

51. Monroe, "Margaret Sullivan's Meed"; *Evening Dispatch* (Provo, UT), July 16, 1894; McCabe, "Margaret Sullivan." My thanks to Margaret Storey for supplying the *Los Angeles Times* reference.

52. M. F. Sullivan, *Ireland of To-day: Causes and Aims of Irish Agitation* (San Francisco: Bancroft, 1881), 20.

53. Sullivan, 449.

54. Sullivan, 27–28.

55. Sullivan, 449. Sullivan returned to the land issue later in the 1880s. In 1888 she and Mary Elizabeth Blake, a friend, fellow Irish American, and poet published *Mexico: Picturesque, Political, Progressive.* In this work Sullivan made several comparisons between Mexico and Ireland, particularly in relation to land: Mexican landlords, like those in Ireland, were largely absentee "and the money produced by the soil flows out of Mexico in exports of bullion for these absentees . . . precisely as the crops and money of Ireland are carried from her to replenish the purses of her landlords." Mary Elizabeth Burke and Margaret Sullivan, *Mexico: Picturesque, Political, Progressive* (Boston: Lee & Shepard, 1888), 182–83. Sections of Sullivan's part of the book had first appeared in the *Boston Journal* and the *Catholic World* in 1887.

56. William O'Brien, *Evening Memories* (Dublin: Maunsel, 1920), 124.

57. Davitt, *Fall of Feudalism*, 716; "Irish Grievances," Third Letter from James Redpath to the Editor of the *Tribune*, July 1, 1882, published in the *Irish Canadian* (Toronto), August 3, 1882.

58. Mother Seraphine Leonard, *Immortelles of Catholic Columbian Literature Compiled from the Works of American Catholic Women Writers by the Ursulines of New York* (Akron, OH: D. H. McBride, 1897), 380.

59. "Notes from the Capital," *Daily True American* (Trenton, NJ), June 12, 1889.

60. W. J. Abbot, "Chicago Newspapers and Their Makers," *Review of Reviews* 11 (1895): 664; "Library Leaflets," *Good Housekeeping* 7 (1888): 238. The Associated Press had been established in New York in 1846 as a news agency representing seven newspapers. A midwestern group developed, and there was much rivalry between the

two until in 1882 an agreement was made that divided control between New York and the Midwest.

61. Katharine Tynan, *Twenty-Five Years: Reminiscences* (London: Smith, Elder, 1913), 184.

62. Margaret Sullivan, "Observations on the Grand Old Man," written for the *New York Sun*, republished in *Reynold's Newspaper* (London), July 4, 1886.

63. "Mrs. Sullivan in Paris," *Harper's Bazaar*, April 21, 1900, 364.

64. Gillian O'Brien, *Blood Runs Green*; Monroe, "Margaret Sullivan's Meed"; McCabe, "Margaret Sullivan."

65. Margaret Sullivan, "Features of the Festival," *New York Tribune*, May 7, 1889.

66. Her articles appeared in many newspapers across the United States. Examples include Industrial Art, *Daily Globe* (St. Paul, MN), May 12, 1889; Fine Art, *Daily Globe* (St. Paul, MN), May 18, 1889; Manufacturing, *Indianapolis Journal*, May 20, 1889; Education, *Pittsburgh Dispatch*, June 10, 1889.

67. On the Cronin murder see Gillian O'Brien, *Blood Runs Green*.

68. [Alexander Sullivan] to Mrs. S[ullivan], Paris, May 24, 1889; [Alexander Sullivan] to Mrs. S[ullivan], May 28, 1889; [Alexander Sullivan] to Mrs. S[ullivan], June 11, 1889; Mrs. S[ullivan], London, to Alexander Sullivan, June 13, 1889; Schedule and Transcripts of Cablegrams and Telegrams passing between AS, his wife, Michael Davitt, etc., March–June 1889, NLI, Devoy Papers MS 18,058 (11).

69. W. B. Yeats, London, to Katharine Tynan, July 25, [1889], in W. B. Yeats and Katharine Tynan, *Letters to Katharine Tynan*, ed. Roger McHugh (New York: McMullen, 1953), 98. Sullivan was equally impressed, later recalling the young Yeats as "pale, slender, just entering then on manhood, he seemed, in his lustrous dark eyes, modest demeanor, sincerity, earnestness and unconscious air of abstraction, what a man must be who wrought in journalism form bread of the body, and for necessity of his soul wrote poetry as a luxury." Margaret F. Sullivan, "Triumph of the 'Literary Play,'" *Dial*, June 16, 1901, 391–93.

70. Tynan, *Twenty-Five Years*, 184, 293.

71. "Chicago Newspaper Rot," *Evening Star* (Washington, DC), June 17, 1889.

72. *Northampton Mercury* (UK), July 6, 1889.

73. Abbot, "Chicago Newspapers," 664; *Sheffield Independent* (UK), June 21, 1889; *Northampton Mercury* (UK), July 6, 1889.

74. Margaret Sullivan to Davitt, October 28, 1889, Davitt Papers, Trinity College Dublin (TCD), MS 932/2590.

75. Margaret Sullivan to Davitt, August 9, 1889, Davitt Papers, TCD, MS 9432.2589.

76. "Mrs. Sullivan on the Women's Congress," *Citizen* (Chicago, IL), May 27, 1893, quoted in Sprows Cumming, *New Women of the Old Faith*, 25.

77. *Oamaru Mail* (New Zealand), May 3, 1892. From the 1890s onward Sullivan wrote less about Ireland in her poetry and articles for periodicals, instead focusing more on Catholicism. Sprows Cummings, *New Women of the Old Faith*, 168.

78. *New York Tribune*, September 16, 1896.

79. *New World* editorial, quoted in *Sacred Heart Review*, January 9, 1904.

80. Monroe, "Margaret Sullivan's Meed."

81. McCabe, "Margaret Sullivan."

82. "Legal Injustice to Women," *Indianapolis Journal*, December 10, 1893; Monroe, "Margaret Sullivan's Meed"; McCabe, "Margaret Sullivan."

83. [Margaret Sullivan], "Readiness and Range," *Chicago Chronicle*, August 29, 1903.

84. Gottlieb, "Women in Journalistic Careers," 54.

85. Jan Whitt, *Women in American Journalism* (Urbana: Univ. of Illinois Press, 2008), 5.

11. "Manufactured News" and Michael Davitt's Journalism in South Africa and Russia for William Randolph Hearst

1. I wish to thank Aoife Murphy of DCU Library for helping me to track down a library willing to send to Ireland rare microfilms of the *New York American* for the period under consideration, and I also thank the US Library of Congress for lending me those reels.

2. See, for example, Carla King, "'Always with a Pen in His Hand': Michael Davitt and the Press," in *Visual, Material and Print Culture in Nineteenth-Century Ireland*, ed. Ciara Breathnach and Catherine Lawless (Dublin: Four Courts Press, 2010), 186–97; Carla King, *Michael Davitt after the Land League, 1882–1906* (Dublin: UCD Press, 2016), 285–97; Laurence Marley, *Michael Davitt: Freelance Radical and Frondeur* (Dublin: Four Courts Press, 2007), 99–118.

3. T. W. Moody, *Davitt and Irish Revolution, 1846–82* (New York: Univ. Press, 1981); page 587 states that from 1878 to 1906 Davitt wrote "a host of polemical contributions" for the *Freeman's Journal*, the *Irishman*, and the *Nation*, and lists for 1879 to 1895 fourteen other titles for which Davitt also wrote; *Michael Davitt: Collected Writings, 1868–1906*, ed. Carla King, 8 vols. (London: Thoemmes Press, 2001), ii, 303–4.

4. King, "Always with a Pen," 188–90.

5. *Dod's Parliamentary Companion* (London: Dod's, 1893), 228.

6. Henry Cockcroft, "A Persevering Printer's Devil," *Burnley Free Press*, March 14, 1863, cited in Moody, *Davitt*, 19–21.

7. Trinity College Dublin (TCD), Davitt MS 9572/1, Diary no. 1, 78.

8. TCD Davitt MS 9582, 21v–24.

9. Marley, *Davitt*, 257.

10. Moody, *Davitt*, 552.

11. Henry Myers Hyndman, *Further Reminiscences* (London: Macmillan, 1912), 40.

12. King, *Davitt: Collected Writings*, i, vii–viii. Even were one to set out to find all of Davitt's journalism, it would be easy to overlook some of it. Many newspaper articles in his day carried no byline.

13. TCD Davitt MS 9572/1, Diary no. 1, note inside front cover.

14. TCD Davitt MS 9450, 3622 (September 21, 1900).

15. Fred Arthur McKenzie, "English War-Correspondents in South Africa," *Harper's*, July 1900, 209–16.

16. Simon J. Potter, *News and the British World: The Emergence of the Imperial Press System, 1876–1922* (Oxford: Clarendon, 2003), 43–44.

17. D. P. McCracken, "The Relationship between British War Correspondents in the Field and British Military Intelligence during the Anglo-Boer War," *Scientia Militaria, South African Journal of Military Studies* 43, no. 1 (2015): 99–126; Donal P. McCracken, "Imperial Running Dogs or Wild Geese Reporters? Irish Journalists in South Africa," *Historia (Historical Association of South Africa)* 58, no. 1 (January 2013): 122–38.

18. TCD Davitt MS 9411, to John Dillon, 1805 and 1808.

19. TCD Davitt MS 9572 ("Jottings on a Journey from Dalkey to Pretoria and Back," 1900), Diary no. 1 (of 2, although second is numbered "3"), 127.

20. Felix M. Larkin, "The Dog in the Night-Time: The *Freeman's Journal*, the Irish Parliamentary Party and the Empire, 1875–1919," in *Newspapers and Empire in Ireland and Britain: Reporting the British Empire, c.1857–1921*, ed. Simon J. Potter (Dublin: Four Courts Press, 2004), 112, 116.

21. Although Davitt reached Pretoria on March 26, 1900, it was not until June 6 that the editor published his first report, promoting it as "special to the *Freeman's Journal*." It was prefaced by an editorial addendum that, "Mr. Davitt, in a private note accompanying this letter, states that this is the sixth of a series of letters addressed by him to the *Freeman's Journal* from South Africa. It is the first to be received by us, the previous five having been delayed or suppressed." That same post brought the editor three later letters from Davitt, "numbered by him the seventh, eighth and ninth," which the editor promised to publish as they were "vivid" and "truthful." See TCD Davitt MS 9572/1, 115–16, 127 (re nos. 1–5) and 129–31 (re nos. 6–10, with a note that, "Ten letters in all written up to date of departure this mail—five by each mail"), 131–32 (re nos. 11–12 but "postponed" and "not written").

22. *Freeman's Journal* (Dublin), July 10, 1900.

23. *United Irishman* (Dublin), October 6 and 27, 1900, and May 11, June 1 (twice), and June 8, 1901; King, *Michael Davitt after the Land League*, 480.

24. Marley, *Davitt*, 246.

25. *Review of Reviews* 22 (July–December 1900): 15 (July); *Freeman's Journal* (Dublin), July 17, 1900; Joseph O. Baylen, "Stead, William Thomas (1849–1912)," *Oxford Dictionary of National Biography* (Oxford: Oxford Univ. Press, 2004), notes that Stead's stances against the Boer War "incurred severe circulation losses and financial difficulties for the *Review of Reviews*."

26. Ferdinand Lundberg, *Imperial Hearst: A Social Biography* (New York: Random, 1936), 91. On the first US visit by a prime minister of the Irish Free State, W. T. Cosgrave reportedly told Hearst's "universal correspondent" in 1928 that, "Ireland will never forget William Randolph Hearst, who has always been one of her best and truest friends" (Colum Kenny, *An Irish-American Odyssey: The Remarkable Rise of the O'Shaughnessy Brothers* [Columbia: Univ. of Missouri Press, 2014], 198).

27. Lundberg, *Imperial Hearst*, 91, 93, 102–3, 141–42; Ian Mugridge, *The View from Xanadu: William Randolph Hearst and United States Foreign Policy* (Montreal: McGill-Queen's Univ. Press, 1995), 34–36.

28. This pioneering colored cartoon strip led to the term "yellow journalism" being coined for the populist newspapers of Hearst and Pulitzer (Colum Kenny, "An Irishman's Diary," *Irish Times*, March 4, 2017).

29. Editorial, *New York Journal*, November 8, 1896.

30. Donald A. Ritchie, *American Journalists: Getting the Story* (New York: Oxford Univ. Press, 1997), 129.

31. Úna Ní Bhroiméil, "The South African War, Empire and the *Irish World*, 1899–1902," in *Newspapers and Empire in Ireland and Britain: Reporting the British Empire, c.1857–1921*, ed. Simon J. Potter (Dublin: Four Courts Press, 2004), 195–216.

32. TCD Davitt MS 9411, 1823 (November 12, 1900), 1826 (December 4, 1900); "Paul Kruger's Mission to Europe," *Review of Reviews* 22 (July–December 1900): 520.

33. Donald L. Shaw, "News Bias and the Telegraph: A Study of Historical Change," *Journalism Quarterly* 4, no. 1 (Spring 1967): 3–31, 4.

34. Menahem Blondheim, *News over the Wires: The Telegraph and the Flow of Public Information in America, 1844–1897* (Cambridge, MA: Harvard Univ. Press, 1994); Alex Nalbach, "'Poisoned at the Source'? Telegraphic News Services and Big Business in the Nineteenth Century," *Business History Review* 77, no. 4 (2003): 577–610.

35. Anthony Smith, "The Long Road to Objectivity and Back Again: The Kinds of Truth We Get in Journalism," in *Newspaper History from the 17th Century to the Present Day*, ed. George Boyce, James Curran, and Pauline Windgate (London: Sage, 1978): 167–68; Shaw, "News Bias," 3–12, 31.

36. TCD Davitt MS 9572/1, Diary no. 1, 58.

37. TCD Davitt MS 9480, 4539–48 (October 31, 1900 to February 15, 1901).

38. TCD Davitt MS 9411, 1832 (December 23, 1900).

39. W. J. Bryan, *The Commoner Condensed* (New York: Press Publishers, 1901–2). Also see W. J. Bryan, *The Old World and Its Ways* (St. Louis, MO: Thompson, 1907),

498–503 (see "Ireland and Her Leaders" for a flattering reference to Davitt). Bryan included a speech by Davitt on the Irish Land League in volume 6 of a collection that he edited entitled *The World's Famous Orations* (New York: Funk and Wagnalls, 1906). On May 3, 1901, the *Commoner* noted that "the *Irish World* is printing a continued story by Michael Davitt on the Boer war. It contains many interesting documents bearing on the present struggle." On June 8, 1906, the *Commoner* noted Davitt's death.

40. TCD Davitt MS 9480, 4562, Scott to Davitt.

41. *Tablet* (London), December 19, 1903, 18.

42. TCD Davitt MS 9480, 4565–72 (April 13–21, 1903).

43. *Cork Examiner*, May 4, 1903, quoted the Russian *Novosti* to inform its readers that stores and shops had been sacked, scores of people killed, and several hundreds wounded: "The majority hid themselves or fled for their lives."

44. *New York American*, May 3, 1903; Cyrus Adler, ed., *The Voice of America on Kishineff* (Philadelphia: Jewish Publication Society of America, 1904); Philip E. Schoenberg, "The American Reaction to the Kishinev Pogrom of 1903," *Jewish Historical Quarterly* 63, no. 3 (March 1974): 262–83.

45. TCD Davitt MS 9480, 4565–72 (May 10–11, 1903).

46. McKenzie, "English War-Correspondents," 211.

47. Hyndman, *Further Reminiscences*, 52.

48. Hyndman, 51–52; *New York Herald*, January 15, 1898; Noel McLachlan, "Davitt, Michael (1846–1906)," *Dictionary of Irish Biography* (Cambridge: Cambridge Univ. Press, 2009).

49. *New York American*, May 12, 1903, front-page headline, "'American' Sends Agent to Russia for Facts"; *New York American*, May 13, 1903, front-page headline with photograph of Davitt, "Michael Davitt Will Go to Russia as the 'American's' Agent"; Adler, *America on Kishineff*, 32–33.

50. *New York American*, May 13, 1903. Irish papers that relayed this rationale for Hearst choosing Davitt included the *Cork Examiner* (May 23, 1903) and the *Kerry Weekly Reporter* (May 30, 1903).

51. *New York American*, May 12, 1903; Adler, *America on Kishineff*, 330–31.

52. TCD Davitt MS 9501, 5302 and 5308.

53. TCD Davitt MS 9501, 5308–12. Davitt had sent a long cable from Odessa to New York on May 25 reporting expressions of anti-Semitic attitudes among Russians and foreigners there but it remained unpublished (TCD Davitt MS 9503, 5418).

54. *New York American*, May 15, 1903 (from Paris), front-page headline, "I Am Going, Resolved to Find the Truth"; May 22, 1903 (from Odessa), front-page headline, "Michael Davitt Sends His First Report from Russia"; May 28, 1903 (from Kishineff), "Michael Davitt Appeals from Kishineff for Its Thousands of Poor Orphans."

55. *New York American*, June 4, 1903, front-page headline, "Davitt Reveals Inside Facts of Kishineff Massacre"; June 7, 1903, front-page headline, "Davitt Pleads for

Independent American Envoy to the Czar"; June 14, 1903, "Michael Davitt Explains the Causes of Anti-Jewish Outrages at Kishineff" (with five photographs taken in Kishineff).

56. Mugridge, *View from Xanadu*, 60–64.

57. Steven J. Zipperstein, "Inside Kishinev's Pogrom: Hayyim Nahman Bialik, Michael Davitt and the Burden of Truth," in *The Individual in History: Essays in Honor of Jehuda Reinharz*, ed. ChaeRan Y. Freeze, Sylvia Fuks Fried, and Eugene R. Sheppard (Waltham, MA: Brandeis Univ. Press, 2015) 65–83, 66.

58. *New York American*, June 3 and 10, 1903.

59. Michael Davitt, *Within the Pale: The True Story of Anti-Semitic Persecution in Russia* (New York: Barnes, 1903), ix; Colum Kenny, "Sinn Féin, Socialists and 'McSheeneys': Representations of Jews in Early Twentieth-Century Ireland," *Journal of Modern Jewish Studies* 16, no. 2 (2017): 198–218.

60. Hyndman, *Further Reminiscences*, 55.

61. TCD Davitt MS 9523, 6025, telegram from Berlin to London, June 2, 1903.

62. Adler, *America on Kishineff*, 175, 205.

63. TCD Davitt MS 9506, 5454, E. F. Flynn to Davitt, London, undated.

64. Adler, *America on Kishineff*, 343–44.

65. TCD Davitt MS 9523, 6025, cable from Berlin to London, June 2, 1903.

66. *New York American*, June 8, 1903, cited in Adler, *America on Kishineff*, 347–48.

67. Zipperstein, "Inside Kishinev's Pogrom," 368.

68. *New York American and Journal*, June 14, 1903.

69. Edward Judge, *Easter in Kishinev: Anatomy of a Pogrom* (New York: NYU Press, 1995), 88; Zipperstein, "Inside Kishinev's Pogrom," 368.

70. Davitt, *Within the Pale*, v. Also see TCD Davitt Papers 9501/5324, Flynn to Davitt, June 22, 1903.

71. Davitt, *Within the Pale*, ix; Kenny, "Sinn Féin, Socialists and 'McSheeneys'," 198–218. Also see Colum Kenny, "James Larkin and the Jew's Shilling: Irish Workers, Activists and Anti-Semitism before Independence," *Irish Economic and Social History* 44, no. 1 (2017): 1–19.

72. TCD Davitt MS 9480, 4577–83.

73. TCD Davitt MS 9480, 4585 (December 26, 1903).

74. TCD Davitt MS 9480, 4588, Hearst to Davitt, undated.

75. TCD Davitt MS 9580, 55–67; *Freeman's Journal* (Dublin), July 4, 1904.

76. TCD Davitt MS 9507, 5493 and 9580, 4; London *Standard*, May 26, 1904.

77. TCD Davitt MS 9580, 4, 29–33.

78. TCD Davitt MS 9580, 4, 29–33.

79. Norman E. Saul, *The Life and Times of Charles R. Crane, 1858–1939: American Businessman* (Lanham, MD: Lexington Books, 2013), 84, 94.

80. TCD Davitt MS 9507, 5471–74, 5480.

81. TCD Davitt MS 9582, 1.

82. TCD Davitt MS 9582, 2 (January 25, 1905).

83. TCD Davitt MS 9582, 2v.

84. TCD Davitt MS 9524, 1, transcript of telegram sent January 27, 1905; *New York American*, January 29 and 30, 1905; *Irish Independent* (Dublin), January 30 and 31, 1905.

85. TCD Davitt 9582, 26v (February 4, 1905).

86. TCD Davitt MS 9582, 39v, 41.

87. TCD Davitt MS 9582, 11v.

88. TCD Davitt MS 9524, 13.

89. *Freeman's Journal* (Dublin), January 26, 1905.

90. TCD Davitt MS 9524, 2–3.

91. TCD Davitt MS 9582, 2 (January 28, 1905).

92. TCD Davitt MS 9582, 26.

93. *New York American*, February 3, 1905; *Irish Independent* (Dublin), February 4, 1905; *Kerry Sentinel*, February 8, 1905.

94. TCD Davitt MS 9582, 14, 17; Denis Brien, *Pulitzer: A Life* (New York: Wiley, 2001), 300.

95. TCD Davitt MS 9508, 5506.

96. TCD Davitt MS 9582, 21v–24.

97. *Oakland Tribune* (California), February 7, 1905. A copy at TCD Davitt MS 9508, 5501. The president of the *Oakland Tribune* was identified within it as William E. Dargle.

12. Dr. Dillon in North America

1. For Dillon's biographical profile see Kevin Rafter, "E. J. Dillon: From Our Special Correspondent, in *Irish Journalism before Independence: More a Disease than a Profession*, ed. Kevin Rafter (Manchester: Manchester Univ. Press, 2011), 91–105.

2. William Latey, "Dr. Emile Joseph Dillon: A Great Irish Journalist," *Everyman*, September 19, 1913.

3. "Obituary: Dr. E. J. Dillon," *Times* (London), June 10, 1933.

4. See Laurel Brake and Marysa Demoor, *A Dictionary of Nineteenth Century Journalism* (London: British Library, 2009).

5. Michael Bromley, "From Noted 'Phenomenon' to 'Missing Person': A Case of the Historical Construction of the *Unter-Journalist*," *Journalism* 11, no. 3 (2010): 259–75.

6. See Green Library, Stanford Univ., Emile Joseph Dillon Collection no. M0935; National Library of Scotland (NLS), Emile Joseph Dillon Reference 12382.

7. Joel H. Wiener, *The Americanization of the British Press, 1830s–1914*. (London: Palgrave, 2011), 156.

8. Fred Inglis, *A Short History of Celebrity* (Princeton, NJ: Princeton Univ. Press, 2010).

9. Martin Conboy, "Celebrity Journalism—an Oxymoron? Forms and Functions of a Genre," *Journalism* 15, no. 2 (2014): 171–85.

10. Inglis, *A Short History*, 121–22.

11. Quoted in Weiner, *Americanization*, 159.

12. Quoted in Inglis, *A Short History*, 121–22.

13. "Draft Memoir," NLS 12382: 51.

14. "Draft Memoir."

15. "Draft Memoir."

16. Rafter, "E. J. Dillon," 91–105.

17. "Draft Memoir," NLS 12382: 51.

18. "Draft Memoir."

19. W. T. Stead, "The Russian Revolution from Various Points of View," *Review of Reviews* 32 (December 1905): 606.

20. *American Monthly Review of Reviews* to EJD February 24, 1905, Stanford, series 1, box 22, folder 2; 1:22(2).

21. Frank W. Wcislo, *Tales of Imperial Russia: The Life and Times of Sergei Witte, 1849–1915* (Oxford: Oxford Univ. Press, 2011), 252.

22. E. J. Dillon, *The Eclipse of Russia* (New York: Doran, 1918), 44–45.

23. "Witte as Known at Close Range," *New York World*, August 6, 1905.

24. "Man of the Hour," *New York World*, August 6, 1905.

25. "Count Witte's Memoirs," *World's Work*, March 1921.

26. "A Mid-Ocean 'Beat': How It Was Achieved," *Daily Telegraph* (London), August 17, 1905.

27. "A Mid-Ocean 'Beat.'"

28. "Goodbye to Portsmouth," *New York World*, September 6, 1905.

29. "Notable Reunion Held," *Boston Herald*, August 18, 1905.

30. Lionel V. Redpath, *Petroleum in California: A Concise and Reliable History of the Oil Industry of the State* (Los Angeles: Redpath, 1900).

31. "Diary entry, August 1, 1919," Stanford 2:3(1). John Le Sage was managing editor of the *Daily Telegraph*.

32. EJD letter to Doheny, September 15, 1919, Stanford 13:22 and 13:23.

33. "Diary entry, December 10, 1919," Stanford 2:3(1).

34. "Dillon Comments on Wilson Error," *Seattle Post Intelligencer*, December 16, 1919.

35. "Peace Treaty a Makeshift, Says Dr. Dillon," *San Francisco Chronicle*, December 20, 1919.

36. "Peace Table Secrets Told by Dr. Dillon," *Los Angeles Chronicle*, December 28, 1919.

37. "Peace Table Secrets."

38. "Interesting Messages by Famous People Found in Mrs. Dillon's Autograph Album," *Vancouver Daily World* (Vancouver, BC), December 13, 1919.

39. "Great Changes in Mexico Dr. E. J. Dillon Believes," *New York Globe and Advertiser*, September 29, 1920.

40. "Diary entry, January 3, 1921," Stanford 2:3(4).

41. "Great Changes in Mexico."

42. *Baltimore News*, October 5, 1920.

43. "Great Changes in Mexico."

44. Graeme Turner, *Understanding Celebrity* (London: Sage, 2014), 78.

13. The *Gaelic American* 1912–1922

1. Devoy (1842–1928) had been arrested in 1865 prior to the Fenian rebellion of 1867. Released in a British amnesty of Fenian prisoners in 1870, he made his way to the United States to later become the leader of Clan na Gael. For a comprehensive account of Devoy's life see Terry Golway, *Irish Rebel: John Devoy and America's Fight for Ireland's Freedom* (New York: St. Martin's Press, 1998).

2. Its readership extended beyond this since a single newspaper would undoubtedly have been read by more than one individual in the same household. J. P. Rodechko, *Patrick Ford and His Search for America: A Case Study of Irish-American Journalism, 1870–1913* (New York: Arno Press, 1976), 23–26. The *Gaelic American* continued publication until 1951, when it was taken over by its main rival, the *Irish World.*

3. For more on the foundation and early years of the *Gaelic American* see Michael Doorley, "The *Gaelic American* and the Shaping of Irish-American Opinion, 1903–1914," in *Probing the Past: Festschrift in Honor of Leo Schelbert*, ed. Wendy Everham (New York: Peter Lang, 2015), 63–72.

4. "The Story of Clan na Gael," *Gaelic American* (New York), June 6, 1925.

5. Éamon de Valera was born in New York but brought up in Ireland. Imprisoned for his part in the 1916 Rising, after his release he became president of Sinn Féin in October 1917. He toured the United States seeking funds and diplomatic recognition for an Irish Republic from June 1919 to November 1920. For an account of these disputes see Michael Doorley, *Irish American Diaspora Nationalism: The Friends of Irish Freedom, 1916–35* (Dublin: Four Courts Press, 2005).

6. *Gaelic American* (New York), September 19, 1903. This objective was outlined in banner headlines in Gaelic lettering under the title *Gaelic American.*

7. *Chicago Citizen*, February 18, 1890.

8. Cohalan became an advisor to the powerful Tammany Boss Charlie Murphy. Michael Doorley, "Judge Daniel Cohalan: American Irish Nationalist and Crusader against British Influence in American Life," *New Hibernia Review* 19, no. 2 (Summer

2015): 113–29. Cohalan also has an entry in the comprehensive online *Dictionary of Irish Biography*.

9. Daniel Cohalan, *The Indictment* (New York: Friends of Irish Freedom, 1919), 1.

10. See in particular Daniel Cohalan, *The Menace of Foreign Entanglements: Let Us Awaken Before It Is Too Late!* (New York: Friends of Irish Freedom, 1923).

11. One of these share certificates, listing Cohalan as president of the Gaelic American Publishing Company, is located in the National Library of Ireland (NLI), McGarrity Papers, MS 17660.

12. Patrick McCartan, *With de Valera in America* (Dublin: Fitzpatrick, 1932), 15; "The Story of Clan na Gael," *Gaelic American* (New York), June 6, 1925.

13. Clan circular, NLI, McGarrity Papers, MS 17660. McGarrity (1874–1940) was from County Tyrone and led the Clan in Philadelphia.

14. US Bureau of the Census, *Twelfth Census of the United States: 1900*; Population (Washington, DC: US Government Printing Office, 1902–6), clxx.

15. Kevin Kenny, *The American Irish: A History* (Edinburgh: Pearson, 2000), 112–20.

16. William E. Van Vugt, "British and British Americans (English, Scots, Scots Irish, and Welsh) to 1870," in *Immigrants in American History: Arrival, Adaptation, and Integration*, ed. Elliott Robert Barkan (Santa Barbara, CA: ABC-CLIO, 2013), 19.

17. Alison Kibler, *Censoring Racial Ridicule: Irish, Jewish and African American Struggles over Race and Representation, 1890–1930* (Chapel Hill: Univ. of North Carolina Press, 2015), 30.

18. Doorley, *Irish-American Diaspora Nationalism*, 23–25. For a comprehensive analysis of American foreign policy in this period see Robert E. Hannigan, *The Great War and American Foreign Policy, 1914–24* (Philadelphia: Univ. of Pennsylvania Press, 2017).

19. Clan circular, NLI McGarrity Papers, MS 17660.

20. *Gaelic American* (New York), November 5, 1904.

21. *Gaelic American* (New York), January 19, 1907.

22. Clan circular, NLI, McGarrity Papers, MS17660.

23. John Hutchinson, *The Dynamics of Cultural Nationalism* (London: Unwin Hyman, 1987), 283.

24. "The Story of Clan na Gael," *Gaelic American* (New York), June 6, 1925.

25. Cohalan was head of the Gaelic League's finance committee in the New York area and maintained close contact with the president of the league in Ireland, Douglas Hyde. Cohalan, along with fellow lawyer John Quinn, later played a key role in organizing Douglas Hyde's successful tour of the United States, which received much coverage in the pages of the *Gaelic American*. Úna Ní Bhroiméil, *Building Irish Identity in America, 1890–1915: The Gaelic Revival* (Dublin: Four Courts Press, 2003).

26. Francis M. Carroll, "The Collapse of Home Rule and the United Irish League of America, 1910–18," in *Ireland's Allies: America and the 1916 Rising*, ed. Miriam Nyhan Grey (Dublin: UCD Press, 2016), 31–42.

27. *Gaelic American* (New York), December 27, 1913.

28. "Treason of the Parliamentarians," *Gaelic American* (New York), October 15, 1910.

29. *Gaelic American* (New York), November 20, 1909. The Liberal government finally introduced a Home Rule bill in 1912, but due to the opposition of the Conservative House of Lords, it would not become law until 1914. The implementation of the measure was postponed following the outbreak of the war.

30. *Gaelic American* (New York), August 15, 1914.

31. *Irish World* (New York), August 15, 1917.

32. *Gaelic American* (New York), August 15, 1914.

33. *Gaelic American* (New York), May 15, 1915. After decades of denial, the British Foreign Office admitted in 1982 that the ship did in fact carry large quantities of munitions. *Guardian* (London), May 1, 2014.

34. See correspondence between Casement and Cohalan in the NLI where Casement refers to using the offices of the *Gaelic American*. NLI Cohalan Papers, MS 22,463.

35. *Gaelic American* (New York), March 11, 1916.

36. Golway, *Irish Rebel*, 197–229.

37. *New York Times*, May 3, 1916; *Gaelic American* (New York), April 29, 1916.

38. *Gaelic American* (New York), April 29, 1916.

39. The *Gaelic American* reported that "the traitor Redmond" had approved these "murders." *Gaelic American* (New York), May 13, 1916. In reality, Redmond had pleaded with the British government to stop the executions knowing full well the impact these would have on nationalist opinion.

40. *Gaelic American* (New York), May 13, 1916.

41. *Gaelic American* (New York), June 9, 1917

42. *Gaelic American* (New York), September 15, 1917.

43. Cited in David Kennedy, *Over Here: The First World War and American Society* (New York: Oxford Univ. Press, 1980), 24.

44. Alan J. Ward, *Ireland and Anglo-Irish Relations, 1899–1921* (Toronto: Univ. of Toronto Press, 1969), 144; *Gaelic American* (New York), February 2, 1918. The Irish publication *Bull* was banned for the duration of the war, as were many socialist and anarchist newspapers.

45. *Gaelic American* (New York), September 28, 1918.

46. *Gaelic American* (New York), February 8, 1919.

47. Doorley, *Irish-American Diaspora Nationalism*, 105–21.

48. *Gaelic American* (New York), December 14, 1918.

49. *Gaelic American* (New York), December 14, 1918.

50. Matthew Cummings to Daniel Cohalan, January 12, 1919, box 3, folder 19, Cohalan Papers, American Irish Historical Society (AIHS), New York.

51. *Gaelic American* (New York), March 1, 1919.

52. Arthur Mitchell, *Revolutionary Government in Ireland: Dáil Éireann 1919–22* (Dublin: Gill and Macmillan, 1995), 68–77.

53. *Gaelic American* (New York), August 18, 1920.

54. David McCullagh, *De Valera: Rise (1882–1932)*, vol. 1 (Dublin: Gill Books, 2017), 164–70. The FOIF had grown to 270,000 regular and associate members by the end of 1920. Doorley, *Irish American Diaspora Nationalism*, 200.

55. De Valera to Arthur Griffith, March 6, 1920. Cited in T. Ryle Dwyer, *De Valera: The Man and the Myths* (Dublin: Poolbeg, 1991), 35. Griffith was acting head of the Irish cabinet while de Valera was in the United States.

56. *Gaelic American* (New York), March 15, 1919.

57. De Valera to Griffith, July 9, 1919. Univ. College Dublin Archives (UCDA), de Valera Papers, P150/727.

58. McGarrity believed that Irish Americans needed to put the Irish cause ahead of any American interests. For an account of McGarrity's critical perspective on Devoy and the *Gaelic American* see Sean Cronin, *The McGarrity Papers: Revelations of the Irish Revolutionary Movement in Ireland and America, 1900–1940* (Tralee: Anvil Books, 1972). Diarmuid Lynch (1878–1950) from County Cork was a member of the IRB and had fought in the Irish Rebellion. He became national secretary of the Friends of Irish Freedom at the 1918 Irish Race Convention. Eileen McGough, *Diarmuid Lynch: A Forgotten Irish Patriot* (Cork: Mercier Press, 2013).

59. *Westminster Gazette* (UK), February 7, 1920. See also McCullagh, *Rise*, 175.

60. Cited in Howard Zinn, *A People's History of the United States* (New York: Perennial Classics, 2001), 311–12.

61. *Gaelic American* (New York), February 21, 1920.

62. De Valera to Cohalan, February 20, 1920; Cohalan to de Valera, February 22, 1920, de Valera papers, UCDA, P150/1134; see also box 4, folder 1, Cohalan papers, AIHS.

63. De Valera to Cohalan, February 20, 1920; Cohalan to de Valera, February 22, 1920.

64. De Valera to Cohalan, February 20, 1920; Cohalan to de Valera, February 22, 1920.

65. Press release, October 22, 1920, NLI McGarrity Papers, MS17445, NLI.

66. *Gaelic American* (New York), December 25, 1920.

67. *Gaelic American* (New York), December 2, 1922.

68. F. S. L. Lyons, "The Irish Americans, A Dual Allegiance," *Irish Times* (Dublin), December 3, 1957. Lyons was reviewing a book by Charles Tansill, *America and the Fight for Irish Freedom, 1866–1922* (New York: Devin Adair, 1957).

14. "An American Newspaperman"

1. Irish independence, which was accompanied by the partition of the island, was followed by a civil war in the Free State, which remained within the British Commonwealth until a republic was declared in 1949. The six counties of Northern Ireland remained under British jurisdiction.

2. Terence Brown, *Ireland: A Social and Cultural History* (London: Harper Perennial, 2004), 192–93.

3. Felix M. Larkin, "Green Shoots of the New Journalism in the *Freeman's Journal*, 1877–90," in *Ireland and the New Journalism*, ed. Karen Steele and Michael de Nie (New York: Palgrave Macmillan, 2014), 35–55.

4. Margot Gayle Backus, *Scandal Work: James Joyce, the New Journalism, and the Home Rule Newspaper Wars* (Notre Dame, IN: Univ. of Notre Dame Press, 2013), 62–63. For an account of the Dublin Castle scandal, see Myles Dungan, *Mr Parnell's Rottweiler: Censorship and the United Ireland Newspaper, 1881–91* (Dublin: Irish Academic Press, 2014).

5. See Mark O'Brien, *The Fourth Estate: Journalism in Twentieth-Century Ireland* (Manchester, UK: Manchester Univ. Press, 2017), 46–50.

6. Kevin C. Kearns, *Dublin Tenement Life: An Oral History* (Dublin: Gill & Macmillan, 1994), 1.

7. Kearns, 1.

8. Kearns, 2.

9. *Irish Builder* 43 (1901): 678, cited in Kearns, *Dublin Tenement Life*, 11.

10. Kearns, *Dublin Tenement Life*, 10–11.

11. *Cork Examiner*, September 12, 1919.

12. *Irish Press* (Dublin), July 7, 1961.

13. "Dublin's Slum Plague," *Honesty*, June 27, 1925, 8–10. For more on *Honesty* see Anthony Keating, "Killing Off the Competition," *Media History* 22, no. 1 (2016): 85–100.

14. Richard English, "Socialism and Republican Schism in Ireland: The Emergence of the Republican Congress in 1934," *Irish Historical Studies* 27, no. 105 (1990): 48–65. The republican congress was a breakaway group of IRA volunteers who wished to pursue left-wing politics. Its leadership included Peadar O'Donnell, who later helped establish the *Bell* magazine.

15. Mary E. Daly, *The Slow Failure: Population Decline and Independent Ireland, 1922–1973* (Madison: Univ. of Wisconsin Press, 2006), 30–32.

16. National Archives of Ireland (Dublin), file D/T, S3642 (memo dated April 4, 1937).

17. *Brooklyn Daily Eagle*, June 24, 1938 and July 2, 1938.

18. *Brooklyn Daily Eagle*, July 2, 1938.

19. See Tim Pat Coogan, *A Memoir* (London: Weidenfeld & Nicolson, 2008), 35–36. In a quirk of history, while general manager of the *Irish Press*, Harrington was involved in a serious altercation with a deputy police commissioner, Eamonn Coogan, whose son, Tim Pat Coogan, would edit the paper between 1968 and 1987.

20. National Library of Ireland, Frank Gallagher Papers, MS 18361.

21. Frank Gallagher Papers, MS 18361.

22. See *Irish Press*, January 4, 1941, for Herlihy's obituary. Gallagher and Herlihy would have known each other from the time they both worked together at the *Cork Free Press*.

23. Joseph Connolly, *Memoirs of Senator Joseph Connolly (1885–1961)*, ed. J. Anthony Gaughan (Dublin: Irish Academic Press, 1996), 283.

24. O'Sullivan, an Australian journalist of Irish parentage, visited Ireland during the Irish war of independence and returned to Dublin in 1932, where he secured a position on the *Irish Press*.

25. The article was subsequently expanded and published in book form as *How the Other Half Lives: Studies among the Tenements of New York* (New York: Scribner's, 1890).

26. *Irish Press* (Dublin), December 20, 1937.

27. *Irish Press* (Dublin), October 15, 1936.

28. *Irish Press* (Dublin), October 2, 1936.

29. *Irish Press* (Dublin), October 7, 1936.

30. *Irish Press* (Dublin), October 2, 1936.

31. *Irish Press* (Dublin), October 1, 1936. The paper later extended its series to other cities, but for reasons of space, this chapter is confined to its Dublin investigation.

32. *Irish Press* (Dublin), October 9, 1936.

33. *Irish Press* (Dublin), October 5, 1936.

34. Tim Pat Coogan, *Ireland in the Twentieth Century* (London: Hutchinson, 2003), 721.

35. *Irish Press* (Dublin), October 9, 1936.

36. *Irish Press* (Dublin), October 21, 1936.

37. *Irish Press* (Dublin), October 22, 1936.

38. *Irish Press* (Dublin), October 29, 1936.

39. *Irish Press* (Dublin), November 3, 1936.

40. *Irish Press* (Dublin), October 14, 1936.

41. *Irish Press* (Dublin), October 22, 1936.

42. *Irish Press* (Dublin), November 24, 1936.

43. *Irish Press* (Dublin), December 5, 1936.

44. *Irish Press* (Dublin), December 20, 1937.

45. *Irish Press* (Dublin), December 18, 1936.

46. *Irish Press* (Dublin), February 10, 1937.

47. *Irish Press* (Dublin), May 31 1937.

48. *Irish Press* (Dublin), June 1 and November 2, 1937.

49. *Irish Press* (Dublin), February 1, 1938.

50. Figures quoted in the *Irish Press* (Dublin), October 21, 1936.

51. Coogan, *Ireland in the Twentieth Century*, 719.

52. Interview of Chris O'Sullivan conducted by Andrew Reeves, July 26, 1978, National Library of Australia (Canberra, ACT), Oral History and Folklore Collection.

53. *Labour News* (Dublin), November 27, 1937.

54. *Irish Press* (Dublin), November 27, 1937.

55. *Labour News* (Dublin), December 4, 1937.

56. *Irish Press* (Dublin), December 4, 1937.

57. *Irish Press* (Dublin), December 20, 1937.

58. *Brooklyn Daily Eagle*, June 24, 1938.

59. *Brooklyn Daily Eagle*, July 2, 1938.

60. Sheila May, "Two Dublin Slums," *Bell* 7, no. 4 (January 1944): 351–56, 354. For more on the *Bell*'s investigative journalism see Mark O'Brien, "Other Voices: *The Bell* and Documentary Journalism," in *Periodicals and Journalism in Twentieth-Century Ireland*, ed. Mark O'Brien and Felix M. Larkin (Dublin: Four Courts Press, 2014), 158–72.

61. Coogan, *Ireland in the Twentieth Century*, 721.

62. See O'Brien, *The Fourth Estate*, 152–55.

15. First Impressions

1. In 1942, it had been only twenty years since Ireland was partitioned. The British often referred to their territory as Ulster. The arrival of US troops in Northern Ireland sparked anger among leaders of the republic, which remained neutral throughout World War II. See David Reynolds, *Rich Relations: The American Occupation of Britain, 1942–1945* (New York: Random House, 1995), 117.

2. See "American Troops Arrive in Northern Ireland," *Belfast News-Letter*, January 27, 1942, 3.

3. See "American Troops Arrive."

4. "Welcome!" *Belfast News-Letter*, January 27, 1942, 2.

5. I have chosen to use the term "African American" to describe US troops of African descent in an attempt to restore dignity to men and women whose military

service, in the words of historian James Campbell, "does not conform nicely with the celebrated stories of white heroism and sacrifice." See James Campbell, *The Color of War: How One Battle Broke Japan and Another Changed America* (New York: Random House, 2012), xiii. Terms more commonly used during this period, such as "black," "Negro," "colored," and "coloured" appear in this research only in direct quotes from government reports or news articles.

6. "In First Contingent of American Negro Troops Abroad," *New York Times*, July 29, 1942, 8.

7. British historians have estimated that before World War II, the number of British colonial citizens of African descent totaled around eight thousand with the majority settling in coastal port cities. For most Britons, the war was the first time they would see people of color outside of movies. See Reynolds, *Rich Relations*, 216; and Juliet Gardiner, *"Overpaid, Oversexed & Over Here": The American GI in World War II Britain* (New York: Canopy Books, 1992), 152.

8. See Dehra Parker, O.B.E., member of Parliament, Clonmore, Northern Ireland, to Robert Gransden, Assistant Secretary to the Cabinet, undated letter, Cabinet Secretariat (henceforth CAB), Record Group (henceforth RG) 9/CD/225/19, Public Records Office of Northern Ireland (henceforth PRONI), Belfast, Northern Ireland, United Kingdom.

9. See Simon Topping, "Laying Down the Law to the Irish and the Coons: Stormont's Response to American Racial Segregation in Northern Ireland during the Second World War," *Historical Research* 86, no. 234 (November 2013): 741–59, 775.

10. Historian Graham Smith noted the Antrim incident was the "first casualty" in the racial war brewing among US troops stationed in Northern Ireland. See Graham Smith, *When Jim Crow Met John Bull* (New York: St. Martin's Press, 1987), 140. Fellow British historian Reynolds also lists the incident as the first. See Reynolds, *Rich Relations*, 222.

11. This chapter examined news coverage from September 30 through October 10, 1942, in twenty-four newspapers, including local, regional, and national newspapers in Great Britain and the United States. This period was expanded into mid-October for the American black press due to weekly production deadlines. Among the British newspapers examined that reached local and regional audiences, were *Belfast News-Letter*, *Belfast Telegraph*, *Bristol Evening Post*, *Bristol Evening World*, the *Chorley Guardian*, the *Lancashire Daily Post*, and the *Western Daily Press & Bristol Mirror*. American newspapers representing local and regional newspapers included *Pittsburgh Post-Gazette*, *Boston Daily Globe*, the *Baltimore Sun*, *Detroit Free Press*, *San Francisco Examiner*, and the *Los Angeles Times*. National British newspapers included the *Daily Express* (London), the *Daily Mail* (London), *Irish News* (Belfast), *News of the World* (London), and the *Times* (London). National US newspapers included *Chicago Daily Tribune*, *Washington Post*, and the *New York Times*. Because these mainstream

US newspapers largely excluded African American life, three black newspapers were also examined: *Pittsburgh Courier*, *Chicago Defender*, and the *Afro-American* (Baltimore, MD). These newspapers, in addition to being the three largest-circulation black press publications, also had the most war correspondents assigned to Europe. See John D. Stevens, "From the Back of the Foxhole: Black Correspondents in World War II," Journalism Monographs 27 (Columbia, SC: Association for Education in Journalism and Mass Communication), 1973.

12. "More American Troops in Ulster," *Belfast News-Letter*, May 19, 1942, 1.

13. "Armoured Force Landed," *Belfast News-Letter*, May 19, 1942, 1.

14. See "Visit to United States Naval Operations Base at Londonderry," *Belfast News-Letter*, July 2, 1942; and "Baseball in Belfast," *Belfast News-Letter*, July 27, 1942.

15. "American Forces in Northern Ireland, 1942," report, CAB, RG 3a/46, PRONI, Belfast, Northern Ireland, UK.

16. "American Forces in Northern Ireland."

17. See, for example, Gardiner, *"Overpaid, Oversexed & Over Here,"* 6.

18. Welfare of Colonial People in the U.K.—Relations with American Forces in the U.K., letter dated June 24, 1942, Colonial Office (henceforth CO), RG 876/14, Public Records Office (henceforth PRO), Kew Gardens, United Kingdom.

19. Welfare of Colonial People.

20. Welfare of Colonial People.

21. John L. Keith, a welfare officer in the Colonial Office, noted just a few days later that a white American soldier had publicly insulted a former serviceman from West India—an incident that resulted in a police report. He further noted: "There is to my knowledge apprehension among coloured Colonial people in this country about the generally rude attitude the American soldiers take towards them, and it is clear to me that the presence of American troops in any Service hostel makes impossible the entry of Colonial Servicemen." See J. L. Keith file note, June 30, 1942, Welfare of Colonial People in the U.K.—Relations with American Forces in the U.K., CO, RG 876/14, PRO.

22. J. L. Keith to Sir Charles Jeffries, July 30, 1942, CO, RG 876/14, PRO.

23. Keith to Jeffries.

24. Keith to Jefferies. Also see Gardiner, "Overpaid, Oversexed & Overhere," 152.

25. Keith file note, June 30, 1942, CO, RG 876/14, PRO.

26. T.E. St. Johnston to F. Newsam, July 22, 1942, Home Office (henceforth HO), RG 45/25604, PRO.

27. Concerns about British policy on race and race relations were constant among the country's leaders and officials in the summer of 1942. Of similar concern: American autonomy, particularly when it came to dealing with misconduct among US troops. This prompted British officials to adopt the 1942 Act and Defence Regulations, which permitted the United States to handle all disciplinary matters involving

its troops—including incidents with British civilians—through US military courts. See Note on "United States of America Visiting Forces. Coloured Troops," to Mr. Newsam, August 7, 1942, HO, RG 45/25604, PRO.

28. Note on "United States of America Visiting Forces." In his memoir, Truman K. Gibson Jr., who replaced William Hastie as a civilian aide to the US War Department, noted that white American troops often "bristled at the absence of Jim Crow social norms and segregation in the British Isles." See Truman K. Gibson Jr., *Knocking Down Barriers: My Fight for Black America*, with Steve Huntley (Evanston, IL: Northwestern Univ. Press, 2005), 102.

29. "United States of America Visiting Forces," August 7, 1942.

30. Harry Haig, "Confidential: U.S.A. Coloured Troops," August 10, 1942, HO, RG 45/25604, PRO.

31. Haig. Underlined emphasis in original text.

32. Haig.

33. F. Newsam minutes notes, August 20, 1942, HO, RG 45/25604, PRO.

34. F. Newsam to General Eisenhower, August 31, 1942, HO, RG 45/25604, PRO.

35. Newsam to Eisenhower.

36. John E. Dahlquist to Mr. F. A. Newsam, September 3, 1942, HO, RG 45/25604, PRO.

37. Dahlquist to Newsam.

38. Fred A. Meyer, "Policy on Negroes," July 16, 1942, Report of investigation of racial relations in U.K., RG 498/UD372, series 291.1, box 1600, National Archives and Records Administration (henceforth NARA), College Park, MD.

39. Meyer.

40. Meyer.

41. "Command and Leadership of Colored Troops," to Base Section Commanders, Com Z, undated, Benjamin O. Davis Papers (henceforth BODP), box 5, folder 1, US Army Military History Institute (henceforth USAMHI), Carlisle, PA.

42. "Command and Leadership of Colored Troops."

43. "Command and Leadership of Colored Troops."

44. Parker to Gransden, CAB, RG 9/CD/225/19, PRONI.

45. Parker to Gransden.

46. Simon Topping, "'The Dusky Doughboys': Interaction between African-American Soldiers and the Population of Northern Ireland during the Second World War," *Journal of American Studies* 47, no. 4 (2013): 1135.

47. "American File," August 21, 1942, CAB, RG 9/CD/225/19, PRONI.

48. "American File."

49. By 1940 the "draconian" Regulation 2D, introduced by British home secretary Sir John Anderson, "gave government the right to ban publication of material or

publications 'prejudicial to national interest': those accused had no right of appeal in the law, and inevitably, comparisons with Nazi Germany were made by opponents." In addition to the right to shut down publications, British censors commonly cut articles out of publications arriving from the United States. See Mick Temple, *The British Press* (Berkshire, England: Open Univ. Press, 2008), 44. Temple also noted the British government regularly went after publications that were vocal against the war. For example, it shut down the communist *Daily Worker* in January 1941, reopening in August 1942, only after the Russians joined the Allied effort. Temple, 44–45.

50. See Michael S. Sweeney, *Secrets of Victory: The Office of Censorship and the American Press and Radio in World War II* (Chapel Hill: Univ. of North Carolina Press, 2001), 2.

51. Anthony Smith, *The British Press since the War* (Totowa, NJ: Rowman & Littlefield, 1974), 109.

52. "American File," August 21, 1942, CAB, RG 9/CD/225/19, PRONI.

53. See "Russians Advance Along West Bank of Don N.W. of Stalingrad," and "Belfast Shooting Affair," *Belfast Telegraph*, October 1, 1942, 3.

54. "U.S. Soldier Was Killed: Knifed in Rumpus," *Belfast Telegraph*, October 1, 1942, 3.

55. "U.S. Soldier Was Killed."

56. "American Soldier Killed in Antrim Street Fracas," *Irish News* (Belfast), October 2, 1942, 1.

57. "American Soldier Killed."

58. "U.S. Soldiers: One Killed in Brawl in Antrim," *Belfast News-Letter*, October 2, 1942, 5.

59. "U.S. Soldiers: One Killed."

60. See "When Patience Is Wearing Thin," *Irish News* (Belfast), October 2, 1942, 2.

61. See "Eyes on Egypt," *Belfast Telegraph*, October 2, 1942, 4.

62. "U.S. Soldier Killed in Antrim," *Times* (London), October 2, 1942, 2.

63. "U.S. Soldier Killed in Antrim."

64. At the very bottom of the *Times*'s editorial page, a letter to the editor carried the headline "Coloured Soldiers." D. Davie-Distin, a snack bar manager for an Oxford shop, wrote that the shop's employees felt compelled to comment on race relations in England. Davie-Distin's letter described how an African American soldier had come into the store the night before carrying a note from his commander. In the correspondence, the Yank officer begged shop owners to look after his soldier, who was responsible for running supplies across the country thus missing regular meals and was having difficulty securing food off-post. The letter writer noted: "Naturally, we 'looked after' him to the best of our ability, but I could not help feeling ashamed that in a country where even stray dogs are 'looked after' by special societies a citizen

of the world, who is fighting the world's battle for freedom and equality, should have found it necessary to place himself in this humiliating position." For the readers of the *Times*, that letter to the editor would be the only mention of race in the newspaper that day. See D. Davie-Distin, "Coloured Soldiers," *Times* (London), October 2, 1942, 3.

65. "U.S. Soldier Killed in Brawl in Ireland," *New York Times*, October 2, 1942, 3.

66. "U.S. Soldier Killed in Brawl."

67. "U.S. Soldier Killed in Brawl."

68. "Yank Killed in Ireland," *Washington Post*, October 2, 1942, 4.

69. "Yank Killed in Ireland."

70. "Yankee Soldier Dies in Irish Brawl," *Detroit Free Press*, October 1, 1942, 2.

71. "Yankee Soldier Dies in Irish Brawl."

72. See "Briton Says Teen Age Girls 'Throw Selves' at Overseas Troops," *Chicago Daily Tribune*, October 3, 1942, 7.

73. "Identify Soldier Killed in Ireland as Indiana Negro," *Chicago Daily Tribune*, October 8, 1942, 19.

74. Just prior to World War II, the *Courier* and *Defender* joined founding newspaper member, the *Afro-American* (Baltimore, MD), in subscribing to the ANP wire services. See Lawrence D. Hogan, *A Black National News Service: The Associated Negro Press and Claude Barnett, 1919–1945* (Cranbury, NJ: Associated Univ. Presses, 1984), 57.

75. "Soldier Killed in Ireland," *Pittsburgh Courier*, October 10, 1942, 22.

76. "U.S. Soldier Killed in Brawl in Ireland."

77. "Soldier Killed in Ireland." There was debate in the black press about how to identify race. In his memoir, Enoch P. Waters recalled the debate in the *Defender* newsroom over which adjective to use. He noted: "[Robert S.] Abbott didn't like the words 'Negro,' 'Colored,' 'black,' or 'Afro American.' He tried to force the adoption of 'The Race' as a capitalized adjective. . . . Even though other Negro publishers held Abbott in high esteem, not one was persuaded" (222). While the term Negro was most commonly used (although the *New York Times* did not start capitalizing Negro until the late 1930s), use of the term was not "unanimous." The publisher of the *Afro-American* preferred Afro-American while the *Courier* used colored. Eventually, the *Defender* editors returned to using Negro. See Enoch P. Waters, *American Diary: A Personal History of the Black Press* (Chicago: Path Press, 1987), 222.

78. "Soldier Slain during Knife Fight in Eire," *Chicago Defender*, October 10, 1942, 2.

79. "Soldier Slain."

80. "Soldier Dies of Knifing in Ireland," *Chicago Defender*, October 17, 1942, 12.

81. "Soldier Dies of Knifing." The parenthetical "tavern" was used in the original text by newspaper editors to help readers unfamiliar with the English term "pub."

82. "Soldier Dies of Knifing."

83. "Identify Soldier Slain in Fight in Ireland," *Afro-American* (Baltimore, MD), October 17, 1942, 3.

84. See "Negro General in England," *Baltimore Sun*, September 29, 1942, 8; "Only Negro General Arrives in Britain," *Pittsburgh Post-Gazette*, September 29, 1942, 3; "General B. O. Davis on Duty in Europe," *Afro-American*, October 3, 1942, 1; and "Gen. Davis Overseas With Troops," *Chicago Defender*, October 3, 1942, 1.

85. Brigadier General Benjamin O. Davis to Sadie Davis, September 30, 1942, BODP, box 8, folder 13, USAMHI.

86. Marvin E. Fletcher, *America's First Black General: Benjamin O. Davis Sr., 1880–1970* (Lawrence: Univ. Press of Kansas, 1989), 102–3.

87. Topping, "Laying Down the Law," 749; Smith, *British Press*, 153.

88. Fletcher, *America's First Black General*, 95–97.

89. Miss M. Lyall to Brigadier General Benjamin O. Davis, October 25, 1942, BODP, box 3, folder 7, USAMHI.

90. Lyall to Davis.

91. Gardiner, "*Overpaid, Oversexed & Over Here*," 111–13.

92. Extract from Army Mail Censorship Report, No. 57, December 11–31, 1942, Foreign Office, RG 371/34123, PRO.

93. Neil A. Wynn, *The African-American Experience during World War II* (Lanham, MD: Rowman & Littlefield, 2010), 29.

94. "Command and Leadership of Colored Troops," to Base Section Commanders, Com Z, undated, BODP, box 5, folder 1, USAMHI.

95. "Command and Leadership of Colored Troops."

96. President Harry S. Truman was the first to forge societal changes through the military when he signed Executive Order 9981: Desegregation of the Armed Forces in 1948. It took two decades before American society followed with the Civil Rights Act of 1964, signed into law by President Lyndon B. Johnson. See "Executive Order 9981," Harry S. Truman Library, accessed March 15, 2015, https://www.trumanlibrary.gov/library/executive-orders/9981/executive-order-9981; and "Civil Rights Act of 1964," NARA, accessed March 30, 2015, http://research.archives.gov/description/299891.

97. George Padmore, "Race Problem Cause of Great Concern in Britain, Padmore Says in Dispatch," *Chicago Defender*, October 3, 1942, 1.

98. Padmore, 2.

Afterword

1. Pete Hamill, "Foreword," in Ray O'Hanlon, *The New Irish Americans* (Niwot, CO: Roberts Rinehart, 1998), page unnumbered.

2. Hamill.

3. Hamill.

4. Michael Dorgan, "New Figures Show 2.4 Million North Americans Visited Ireland in 2018," *Irish Central*, January 30, 2019, https://www.irishcentral.com/travel/north-american-vistors-ireland-2018; "Higher Number of American Tourists Expected to Visit Ireland in 2018," *Irish Examiner* (Cork), January 18, 2018, https://www.irishexaminer.com/breakingnews/business/higher-number-of-american-tourists-expected-to-visit-ireland-in-2018-823708.html.

5. O'Hanlon, *New Irish Americans*, 12.

6. Fintan O'Toole, "The Irish American Cultural Swap Shop," *Irish Times* (Dublin), May 11, 2000; Maureen Dezell, *Irish America: Coming into Clover* (New York: Anchor Books, 2002), 206.

7. Timothy Meagher, "Irish America," in *The Cambridge Social History of Modern Ireland*, ed. Eugenio F. Biagini and Mary E. Daly (New York: Cambridge Univ. Press, 2017), 509.

8. The oath of allegiance was abolished when the antitreaty faction assumed power in 1932.

9. David T. Gleeson, ed. *The Irish in the Atlantic World* (Columbia: Univ. of South Carolina Press, 2010), 6.

10. *New York Times*, January 28, 1957, 26.

11. William Shannon, *The American Irish* (New York: McMillian, 1963), vii.

12. *Irish Times* (Dublin), June 26, 1963, 7.

13. It should be noted that JFK's sister Jean Kennedy Smith served as US ambassador to Ireland during the critical peace process years of the 1990s.

14. *US-Ireland Business 2020* (Dublin: American Chamber of Commerce), 16–17.

15. Emergency Supplemental Appropriations Act for Defense, the Global War on Terror, and Tsunami Relief, 2005, Pub. L. No. 109–13, 119 Stat. 231 (2005), https://www.govinfo.gov/content/pkg/PLAW-109publ13/pdf/PLAW-109publ13.pdf; Jerry Kammer, "The Hart-Celler Immigration Act of 1965: Political Figures and Historical Circumstances Produced Dramatic, Unintended Consequences," Center for Immigration Studies, September 30, 2015, https://cis.org/Report/Hart Celler-Immigration-Act-1965); Brian O'Donovan, "Irish Access to E3 Visas Suffers Setback in U.S. Senate," RTÉ News, updated January 3, 2019, https://www.rte.ie/news/ireland/2019/0103/1020061-us-e-3-visa/; Alan C. Tidwell, "The Special One: Australia, Ireland and the U.S. Working Visa Fight," *Interpreter*, January 9, 2019, https://www.lowyinstitute.org/the-interpreter/special-one-australia-ireland-US-working-visa-fight.

Bibliography

Newspapers and Periodicals

Afro-American (Baltimore, MD)
Alexandria Gazette (Virginia)
American Monthly Review of Reviews (New York)
Aurora General Advertiser (Philadelphia)
Baltimore News
Baltimore Sun
Belfast Commercial Chronicle
Belfast Evening Telegram
Belfast News-Letter
Belfast Telegraph
The Bell (Dublin, Ireland)
Boston Daily Globe
Boston Herald
Boston Recorder
The Broad Ax (Salt Lake City, UT)
Brooklyn Daily Eagle (New York)
Burnley Free Press (Lancashire, UK)
Cambridge Chronicle (Massachusetts)
Cambridge Intelligencer (UK)
Catholic World (New York)
Charleston Mercury (South Carolina)
Cherokee Phoenix and Indians Advocate (New Town, GA)
Chicago Chronicle
Chicago Daily Tribune
Chicago Defender
Chicago Times

Chicago Tribune
Cincinnati Daily Gazette (Ohio)
Cork Examiner
Cork Free Press
Courier (Boston)
Daily Advertiser (Newark, NJ)
Daily Globe (St. Paul, MN)
Daily Inter Ocean (Chicago)
Daily Morning News (Savannah, GA)
Daily Orleanian (New Orleans, LA)
Daily Telegraph (London)
Daily True American (Trenton, NJ)
Detroit Free Press
The Dial (Boston)
Donahoe's Magazine (Boston)
Dublin Evening Post
Evening Dispatch (Provo, UT)
Evening Star (Washington, DC)
Everyman (London)
Farmers Cabinet (Amherst, NH)
Fort Worth Gazette
Freeman's Journal (Dublin)
Gaelic American (New York)
Gazette and Universal Daily Advertiser (Philadelphia)
Georgian (Savannah, GA)
Globe and Commercial Advertiser (New York)
Hamilton Literary Monthly (New York)
Hampshire Chronicle (Winchester, UK)
Harper's Bazaar (New York)
Honesty (Dublin)
Indianapolis Journal (Indiana)
Indiana State Sentinel
Intermountain Catholic (Salt Lake City, UT)
Irish Canadian (Toronto)
Irish Citizen (New York)
Irish Examiner (Cork)

Irish Independent (Dublin)
Irish News (Belfast)
Irish Press (Dublin)
Irish Standard (Minneapolis, MN)
Irish Times (Dublin)
Irish World (New York)
Jesuit (Boston)
Journal (Dublin)
Kentish Gazette (Kent, UK)
Kerry Evening Post (Tralee)
Kerry Sentinel (Tralee)
Labour News (Dublin)
Ladies' Home Journal (Des Moines, IA)
Lafayette Daily Journal (Indiana)
Los Angeles Chronicle
Los Angeles Times
Louisiana Advertiser
Manchester Mercury (UK)
Mercantile Advertiser (New York)
Mercury (New York)
The Nation (Dublin)
New England Puritan (Boston)
New Hampshire Gazette (Portsmouth)
New Haven Daily Palladium (Connecticut)
New World (New York)
New York American
New York Evening World
New York Globe and Advertiser
New York Herald
New York Journal
New York Times
New York Tribune
New York World
North American Review (Boston)
Northampton Mercury (UK)
Oakland Tribune (California)

Oxford Journal (UK)
Philadelphia Times
The Pilot (Boston)
Pittsburgh Courier
Pittsburgh Dispatch
Polar Star and Boston Daily Advertiser
Republican Farmer (Bridgeport, CT)
Review of Reviews (London)
Richmond Enquirer (Virginia)
Richmond Examiner (Virginia)
Russell's Commercial Gazette (Boston)
Sacred Heart Review (Boston)
Savannah Daily Republican
Savannah Republican
Savannah Morning News
San Francisco Chronicle
Seattle Post Intelligencer
Semi-Weekly Raleigh Register (North Carolina)
Sheffield Independent (UK)
Southern Citizen (Knoxville, TN)
Springer's Weekly Oracle (New London, CT)
Statesmen and Gazette (Natchez, MS)
The Tablet (London)
The Telegraph (London)
Texas Siftings (Austin, TX)
The Times (London)
Times-Picayune (New Orleans, LA)
Time-Piece (New York)
The Tribune (New York)
Tuam Herald (Galway)
United Irishman (Dublin)
United States Telegraph (Washington, DC)
Vancouver Daily World (Vancouver, BC)
Vancouver Independent (Vancouver, BC)
Vermont Watchman and State Journal (Montpelier, VT)
Washington Post
The Wasp (San Francisco)

Wexford Independent
Wisconsin Democrat
World's Work (New York)
The Writer (Boston)

Books and Journal Articles

Abbot, W. J. "Chicago Newspapers and Their Makers." *Review of Reviews* 11 (1895): 664.

Adams, Isaac E. *Life of Emery A. Storrs*. Chicago. G. L. Howe, 1886.

Adelman, Joseph M. "Trans-Atlantic Migration and the Printing Trade in Revolutionary America." *Early American Studies* 11, no. 3 (Fall 2013): 516–44.

Adler, Cyrus, ed. *The Voice of America on Kishineff*. Philadelphia: Jewish Publication Society of America, 1904.

Akers, Donna L. *Living in the Land of Death: The Choctaw Nation 1830–1860*. East Lansing: Michigan State Univ. Press, 2004.

Alden, Cynthia Westover. *Women's Ways of Earning Money*. New York: University Society, 1904.

Almon, John. *Another Letter to Mr. Almon: In Matter of Libel*. London: Printed for John Almon, 1770.

Althusser, Louis. "Ideology and Ideological State Apparatuses (Notes Towards and Investigation)." In *The Anthropology of the State: A Reader*, edited by Aradhana Sharma and Akhil Gupta, 86–111. Malden, MA: Blackwell, 2006.

Altschuler, Glen C., and Stuart M. Blumin. *Rude Republic: Americans and Their Politics in the Nineteenth Century*. Princeton, NJ: Princeton Univ. Press, 2000.

Anderson, Benedict. *Imagined Communities: Reflections on the Origin and Spread of Nationalism*. Rev. ed. London: Verso, 2006.

Appel, John J. "From Shanties to Lace Curtains: The Irish Image in *Puck*, 1876–1910." *Comparative Studies in Society and History* 13, no. 4 (1971): 365–75.

Archdeacon, Thomas J. *Becoming American: An Ethnic History*. New York: Free Press, 1983.

Bache, Benjamin Franklin, and William J. Duane. *The Truth Will Out: The Foul Charges of the Tories against the Editor of the Aurora, Repelled by Positive Proof and Plain Truth, and His Base Calumniators Put to Shame*. Philadelphia: Bache, 1798.

Backus, Margot Gayle. *Scandal Work: James Joyce, the New Journalism, and the Home Rule Newspaper Wars*. Notre Dame, IN: Univ. of Notre Dame Press, 2013.

Baird, Henry Carey. "The Carey-Baird Centenary, 1885, Memoir of Mathew Carey, Founder of the House." *American Bookseller*, February 1, 1885, 59.

Baldwin, Peter. *The Copyright Wars: Three Centuries of Trans-Atlantic Battles*. Princeton, NJ: Princeton Univ. Press, 2014.

Banta, Martha. *Barbaric Intercourse: Caricature and Culture of Conduct, 1841–1936*. Chicago: Univ. of Chicago Press, 2003.

Bartoletti, Susan Campbell. *Black Potatoes: The Story of the Great Irish Famine, 1845–1850*. New York: Houghton Mifflin, 2001.

Barton, Edward H. *Account of the Epidemic Yellow Fever Which Prevailed in New Orleans during the Autumn of 1833*. Philadelphia: Joseph R. A. Skerrett, 1834.

Baylen, Joseph O. "Stead, William Thomas (1849–1912)." In *Oxford Dictionary of National Biography*. Oxford: Oxford Univ. Press, 2004, 52:331–33.

Beasley, Maurine H., and Sheila J. Gibbons. *Taking Their Place: A Documentary History of Women and Journalism*. State College, PA: Strata, 2003.

Benoit, William M., and John P. McHale. "Presidential Candidates' Television Spots and Personal Qualities." *Southern Communication Journal* 68, no. 4 (November 2003): 319–34.

Bird, Wendell. *Press and Speech under Assault: The Early Supreme Court Justices, the Sedition Act of 1798, and the Campaign against Dissent*. New York: Oxford Univ. Press, 2016.

Bivins, Thomas H. "The Body Politic: The Changing Shape of Uncle Sam." *Journalism Quarterly* 64, no. 1 (1987): 13–20.

Blackstone, William. *Commentaries on the Laws of England, Book the Fourth*. London: Strahan and Woodfall, 1791.

Blair, Walter. "Traditions in Southern Humor." In *Essays on American Humor*, edited by Hamlin Hill, 15–24. Madison: Univ. of Wisconsin Press, 1993.

Blondheim, Menahem. *News over the Wires: The Telegraph and the Flow of Public Information in America, 1844–1897*. Cambridge, MA: Harvard Univ. Press, 1994.

Blumberg, Phillip I. *Repressive Jurisprudence in the Early American Republic: The First Amendment and the Legacy of English Law*. Cambridge: Cambridge Univ. Press, 2010.

Boskin, Joseph, and Joseph Dorinson. "Ethnic Humor: Subversion and Survival." *American Quarterly* 37, no. 1 (1985): 81–97.

Brah, Avtar. *Cartographies of Diaspora: Contesting Identities*. London: Routledge, 1996.

Brake, Laurel, and Marysa Demoor. *A Dictionary of Nineteenth Century Journalism*. London: British Library, 2009.

Bric, Maurice J. "Mathew Carey, Ireland and the 'Empire for Liberty' in America." *Early American Studies* 11, no. 3 (Fall 2013): 403–30.

———. "The United Irishmen, International Republicanism and the Definition of Polity in the United States of America." *Proceedings of the Royal Irish Academy, Section C: Archaeology, Celtic Studies, History, Linguistics, Literature* 104C, no. 4 (2004): 81–106.

Brien, Denis. *Pulitzer: A Life*. New York: Wiley, 2001.

Brighton, Stephen A. "Degrees of Alienation: The Material Evidence of the Irish and Irish American Experience, 1850–1910." *Historical Archaeology* 42, no. 4 (2007): 132–53.

Brodie, Fawn M. *Thomas Jefferson: An Intimate History*. New York: W. W. Norton, 1974.

Broersma, Marcel. "Transnational Journalism History: Balancing Global Universals and National Peculiarities." *Medien & Zeit* 25, no. 4 (2010): 10–15.

Bromley, Michael. "From Noted 'Phenomenon' to 'Missing Person': A Case of the Historical Construction of the *Unter-Journalist*." *Journalism* 11, no. 3 (2010): 259–75.

Brookhiser, Richard. "The Politics of Immigration: Clashing Impulses." *American History* 48, no. 5 (2013): 17–18.

Brown, Carolyn S. *The Tall Tale in American Folklore and Literature*. Knoxville: Univ. of Tennessee Press, 1987.

Brown, Joshua. "Reconstructing Representation: Social Types, Readers, and the Pictorial Press, 1865–1877." *Radical History Review* 66, no. 5 (1996): 5–38.

Brown, Terence. *Ireland: A Social and Cultural History*. London: Harper Perennial, 2004.

Brundage, David. "In Time of Peace, Prepare for War: Key Themes in the Social Thought of New York's Irish-American Nationalists, 1900–1916." In *The New York Irish*, edited by Ronald H. Bayor and Timothy J. Meagher, 321–34. Baltimore: Johns Hopkins Univ. Press, 1996.

Bryan, W. J. *The Commoner Condensed*. New York: Press Publishers, 1901–2.

———. *The Old World and Its Ways*. St. Louis, MO: Thompson, 1907.

Buell, Raymond L. "The Development of the Anti-Japanese Agitation in the United States." *Political Science Quarterly* 37 (1992): 605–38.

Burke, Mary Elizabeth, and Margaret Sullivan. *Mexico: Picturesque, Political, Progressive*. Boston: Lee & Shepard, 1888.

Callender, James Thomson. *The Prospect before Us*. Richmond: Jones, Pleasants, and Lyons, 1800.

Campbell, Charles. *Some Materials to Serve for a Brief Memoir of John Daly Burk*. Albany, NY: Joel Munsel, 1868.

Campbell, James. *The Color of War: How One Battle Broke Japan and Another Changed America*. New York: Random House, 2012.

Carey, James W. *Communication as Culture: Essays on Media and Society*. New York: Routledge, 1988.

Carey, Mathew. *The Olive Branch*. 10th ed. Philadelphia: Carey and Son, 1818.

Caron, James E. *Mark Twain, Unsanctified Newspaper Reporter*. Columbia: Univ. of Missouri Press, 2008.

Carroll, Francis M. "The Collapse of Home Rule and the United Irish League of America, 1910–18." In *Ireland's Allies: America and the 1916 Rising*, edited by Miriam Nyhan Grey, 31–42. Dublin: UCD Press, 2016.

Carter, Edward C., II. "Birth of a Political Economist: Mathew Carey and the Recharter Fight of 1810–1811." *Pennsylvania History: A Journal of Mid-Atlantic Studies* 33, no. 3 (1966): 274–88.

———. "A 'Wild Irishman' under Every Federalist's Bed: Naturalization in Philadelphia." *Pennsylvania Magazine of History and Biography* 94, no. 3 (July 1970): 331–46.

Channing, Steven A. *Crisis of Fear: Secession in South Carolina*. New York: W. W. Norton, 1974.

Clark, Allan C. *William Duane, Records of the Columbia Historical Society* 9 (1906): 17–19.

Clark, Dennis. *The Irish in Philadelphia: Ten Generations of Urban Experience*. Philadelphia: Temple Univ. Press, 1973.

Clark, Margaret Varnell. *The Louisiana Irish: A Historical Collection*. New York: iUniverse, 2007.

Cohalan, Daniel. *The Indictment*. New York: Friends of Irish Freedom, 1919.

———. *The Menace of Foreign Entanglements: Let Us Awaken Before It Is Too Late!* New York: Friends of Irish Freedom, 1923.

Cohen, Hennig, and William B. Dillingham. *Humor of the Old Southwest.* 2nd ed. Athens: Univ. of Georgia Press, 1975.

Cohen, Robin. *Global Diasporas: An Introduction.* Seattle: Univ. of Washington Press, 1997.

Comerford, R. V. *The Fenians in Context: Irish Politics and Society 1848–82.* Dublin: Wolfhound Press, 1998.

Conboy, Martin. "Celebrity Journalism: An Oxymoron? Forms and Functions of a Genre." *Journalism* 15, no. 2 (2014): 171–85.

———. *The Press and Popular Culture.* London: Sage, 2002.

Connolly, Joseph. *Memoirs of Senator Joseph Connolly (1885–1961).* Edited by J. Anthony Gaughan. Dublin: Irish Academic Press, 1996.

Conway, Katherine E., and Mabel Ward Cameron. *Charles Francis Donnelly: A Memoir.* New York: James T. White, 1909.

Coogan, Tim Pat. *Ireland in the Twentieth Century.* London: Hutchinson, 2003.

———. *A Memoir.* London: Weidenfeld & Nicolson, 2008.

Cooper, Thomas. *Political Essays: A Treatise on the Law of Libel.* Philadelphia: Campbell, 1799.

———. "Preface." In *Account of the Trial of Thomas Cooper of Northumberland.* Philadelphia: John Bioren, 1800.

Cotlar, Seth. *Thomas Paine's America: The Rise and Fall of Transatlantic Radicalism in the Early Republic.* Charlottesville: Univ. of Virginia Press, 2011.

Cronin, Mary M. "Sifting Comic Wheat from Western Chaff: Alex E. Sweet, John Armoy Knox, and the Humor of the American West." In *The Funniest Pages: International Perspectives on Journalism and Humor,* edited by David Swick and Richard Lance Keeble, 53–66. New York: Peter Lang, 2016.

Cronin, Sean. *The McGarrity Papers: Revelations of the Irish Revolutionary Movement in Ireland and America, 1900–1940.* Tralee: Anvil Books, 1972.

Cullen, L. M. *Europeans on the Move: European Migration, 1500–1800.* Oxford: Clarendon Press, 1994.

Curtis, L. Perry. *Apes and Angels: The Irishman in Victorian Caricature.* Washington, DC: Smithsonian Institution Press, 1971.

Curtis, Michael Kent. *Free Speech, "The People's Darling Privilege": Struggles for Freedom of Expression in American History.* Durham, NC: Duke Univ. Press, 2000.

Daly, Mary E. *The Slow Failure: Population Decline and Independent Ireland, 1922–1973*. Madison: Univ. of Wisconsin Press, 2006.

Daniel, Marcus. *Scandal and Civility: Journalism and the Birth of American Democracy*. New York: Oxford Univ. Press, 2009.

Davis, Graham. "Models of Migration: The Historiography of the Irish Pioneers in South Texas." *Southwestern Historical Quarterly* 99, no. 3 (1996): 326–49.

Davitt, Michael. *The Fall of Feudalism in Ireland*. London: Harper, 1904.

———. *Within the Pale: The True Story of Anti-Semitic Persecution in Russia*. New York: Barnes, 1903.

Delahanty, Ian. "'A Noble Empire in the West': Young Ireland, the United States and Slavery." *Britain and the World* 6, no. 2 (2013): 171–91.

de Nie, Michael. *The Eternal Paddy: Irish Identity and the British Press, 1798–1882*. Madison: Univ. of Wisconsin Press, 2004.

Dezell, Maureen. *Irish America: Coming into Clover*. New York: Anchor Books, 2002.

Dillon, E. J. *The Eclipse of Russia*. New York: Doran, 1918.

Diner, Hasia. *Erin's Daughters in America: Irish Immigrant Women in the Nineteenth Century*. Baltimore: John Hopkins Univ. Press, 1983.

Dinnerstein, Leonard, and David M. Reimers. *Ethnic Americans: A History of Immigration*. 5th ed. New York: Columbia Univ. Press, 2009.

Dodge, Robert K. "The Irish Comic Stereotype in the Almanacs of the Early Republic." *Éire-Ireland* 19, no. 3 (1984): 111–20.

Dolan, Jay P. *The Irish Americans*. New York: Bloomsbury Press, 2008.

Donahoe, Patrick. "Reminiscences of an Old Time Journalist: A Letter to Martin J. Griffin." *Records of the American Catholic Historical Society* 15 (1904): 314–17.

Donovan, Kathleen. "Good Old Pat: An Irish-American Stereotype in Decline." *Éire-Ireland* 15, no. 3 (1980): 6–14.

Doorley, Michael. "The *Gaelic American* and the Shaping of Irish-American Opinion, 1903–1914." In *Probing the Past: Festschrift in Honor of Leo Schelbert*, edited by Wendy Everham, 63–72. New York: Peter Lang, 2015.

———. *Irish American Diaspora Nationalism: The Friends of Irish Freedom, 1916–35*. Dublin: Four Courts Press, 2005.

———. "Judge Daniel Cohalan: American Irish Nationalist and Crusader against British Influence in American Life." *New Hibernia Review* 19, no. 2 (Summer 2015): 113–29.

Dormon, James H. "Ethnic Stereotyping in American Popular Culture: The Depiction of American Ethnics in the Cartoon Periodicals of the Gilded Age." *Amerikastudien* 30, no. 4 (1985): 489–503.

Duane, William John. *Biographical Memoir of William John Duane*. Philadelphia: Claxton, Remsen, and Haffelfinger, 1868.

Duffy, Charles Gavin. *Short Life of Thomas Davis*. London: T. Fisher Unwin, 1896.

Duffy, Margaret E. "Web of Hate: A Fantasy Theme Analysis of the Rhetorical Vision of Hate Groups Online." *Journal of Communication Inquiry* 27, no. 3 (July 2003): 291–312.

Dungan, Myles. *Mr Parnell's Rottweiler: Censorship and the United Ireland Newspaper, 1881–91*. Dublin: Irish Academic Press, 2014.

Dwyer, T. Ryle. *De Valera: The Man and the Myths*. Dublin: Poolbeg, 1991.

Edwards, Janis L. "Running in the Shadows in Campaign 2000: Candidate Metaphors in Editorial Cartoons." *American Behavioral Scientist* 44, no. 12 (August 2001): 2140–51.

———. "Visualizing Presidential Imperatives: Masculinity as an Interpretive Frame in Editorial Cartoons, 1988–2008." In *Gender and Political Communication in America: Rhetoric, Representation, and Display*, edited by J. L. Edwards, 233–50. Lanham, MD: Lexington Books, 2009.

Edwards, Janis L., and Laura Ware. "Representing the Public in Campaign Media: A Political Cartoon Perspective." *American Behavioral Scientist* 49, no. 3 (November 2005): 466–78.

Eisenhour, Virginia. *Alex Sweet's Texas: The Lighter Side of Lone Star History*. Austin: Univ. of Texas Press, 1986.

Elliott, Marianne. *Wolfe Tone*. Liverpool: Liverpool Univ. Press, 2012.

El Refaie, Elizabeth. "Multiliteracies: How Readers Interpret Political Cartoons." *Visual Communication* 8, no. 2 (2009): 181–205.

Ely, Janis M. "Anointing the 'Uncrowned King of Ireland': Charles Stewart Parnell's 1880 American Tour and the Creation of a Transatlantic Land League Movement." *Supplement of the German Historical Institute Bulletin* 5 (2008): 23–39.

Emmons, David M. *Beyond the American Pale: The Irish in the West, 1845–1910*. Norman: Univ. of Oklahoma Press, 2010.

English, Richard. "Socialism and Republican Schism in Ireland: The Emergence of the Republican Congress in 1934." *Irish Historical Studies* 27, no. 105 (1990): 48–65.

Erie, Steven P. *Rainbow's End, Irish-Americans and the Dilemmas of Urban Machine Politics, 1840–1985*. Berkeley: Univ. of California Press, 1990.

Federal Writers Project. *The Case of Dr. [Patrick] Cronin: A Manuscript from the Federal Writers Project Papers, Illinois State Historical Library Federal Writers Project*. Springfield: Illinois State Historical Library, 1935.

Fischer, Roger. *Them Damned Pictures: Explorations in American Political Cartoon Art*. North Haven, CT: Archon, 1996.

Fitzgerald, Patrick. "The Scotch-Irish and the Eighteenth-Century Irish Diaspora." *History Ireland* 7, no. 3 (Autumn 1999): 37–41.

Fletcher, Marvin E. *America's First Black General: Benjamin O. Davis Sr., 1880–1970*. Lawrence: Univ. Press of Kansas, 1989.

Ford, James L. "The Evolution of American Humor." *Collier's Illustrated Weekly* 30, no. 18 (1903).

Fowler, John. *James P. Newcomb: Texas Journalist and Political Leader*. Austin: Department of Journalism Development Program, 1976.

Frawley, Mary Alphonsine. *Patrick Donahoe*. Washington, DC: Catholic Univ. of America Press, 1946.

Frothingham, Rev. O. B., John Boyle O'Reilly, et al. *Woman Suffrage, Unnatural and Inexpedient*. Boston: [publisher not identified], 1886.

Gabore, Robert L. *Life on the Press: The Popular Art and Illustrations of George Benjamin Luks*. Jackson: Univ. Press of Mississippi, 2009.

Gahan, Daniel. "The Rebellion of 1798 in South Leinster." In *1798: A Bicentenary Perspective*, edited by Thomas Bartlett, 104–21. Dublin: Four Courts Press, 2003.

———. "Wexford Emigrants and the Irish Experience in Canal Construction in Nineteenth-Century America: Evidence from the Wabash and Erie in Daviess and Huntington Counties, Indiana, 1850." *The Past: The Organ of the Uí Cinsealaigh Historical Society* 32 (2016): 14–32.

Gambone, Robert L. *Life on the Press: The Popular Art and Illustrations of George Benjamin Luks*. Jackson: Univ. Press of Mississippi, 2009.

Gamson, William A., and David Stuart. "Media Discourse as a Symbolic Contest: The Bomb in Political Cartoons." *Sociological Forum* 7, no. 1 (1992): 55–86.

Gardiner, Juliet. *"Overpaid, Oversexed & Over Here": The American GI in World War II Britain*. New York: Canopy Books, 1992.

Gaughan, Anthony J., ed. *Joseph Connolly: Memoirs of Senator Joseph Connolly (1885–1961)*. Dublin: Irish Academic Press, 1996.

Gibson, Truman K., Jr. *Knocking Down Barriers: My Fight for Black America.* With Steve Huntley. Evanston, IL: Northwestern Univ. Press, 2005.

Giemza, Bryan. *Irish Catholic Writers and the Invention of the American South.* Baton Rouge: Louisiana State Univ. Press, 2013.

Gladstone, W. E. *The Vatican Decrees in Their Bearing on Civil Allegiance: A Political Expostulation.* London: John Murray, 1874.

Gleeson, David T., ed. *The Irish in the Atlantic World.* Columbia: Univ. of South Carolina Press, 2010.

———. *The Irish in the South, 1815–1877.* Chapel Hill: Univ. of North Carolina Press, 2002.

Gleeson, David T., and Brendan J. Buttimer. "'We Are Irish Everywhere': Irish Immigrant Networks in Charleston, South Carolina, and Savannah, Georgia." In *Irish Migration, Networks, and Ethnic Identities Since 1750,* edited by Enda Delaney and Donald M. MacRaild, 183–205. London: Routledge, 2007.

Golway, Terry. *Irish Rebel: John Devoy and America's Fight for Ireland's Freedom.* New York: St. Martin's Press, 1998.

Gottlieb, Agnes Hooper. "Grit Your Teeth, Then Learn to Swear: Women in Journalistic Careers 1850–1926." *American Journalism* 18, no. 1 (2001): 53–72.

Green, James N. "'I Was Always Dispos'd to be Serviceable to You, Tho' It Seems I Was Once Unlucky': Mathew Carey's Relationship with Benjamin Franklin." *Early American Studies* 11, no. 3 (Fall 2013): 545–56.

———. *Mathew Carey: Publisher and Patriot.* Philadelphia: Library Company of Philadelphia, 1985.

Green, Thomas. "The Jury, Seditious Libel and Criminal Law." In *Juries, Libel, and Justice: The Role of English Juries in Seventeenth- and Eighteenth-Century Trials for Libel and Slander; Papers Read at a Clark Library Seminar 28 February 1981,* edited by R. H. Helmholz and T. A. Green, 39–91. Los Angeles: William Andrews Clark Memorial Library, Univ. of California, 1984.

Greenberg, Josh. "Framing and Temporality in Political Cartoons: A Critical Analysis of Visual News Discourse." *Canadian Review of Sociology and Anthropology* 39, no. 2 (2002): 181–98.

Gribben, Arthur. *The Great Famine and the Irish Diaspora in America.* Amherst: Univ. of Massachusetts Press, 1999.

Grieves, Kevin. *Journalism across Boundaries: The Promises and Challenges of Transnational and Transborder Journalism.* New York: Palgrave Macmillan, 2012.

Gyory, Andrew. *Closing the Gate: Race Politics and the Chinese Exclusion Act.* Chapel Hill: Univ. of North Carolina Press, 1998.

Haines, Charles Gidden. *Memoir of Thomas Addis Emmet.* New York: G. & C. & H. Carvill, 1829.

Hall, Nicholas Sean. "*The Wasp*'s 'Troublesome Children': Culture, Satire, and the Anti-Chinese Movement in the American West." *California History* 90, no. 2 (January 2013): 42–63.

Hamill, Pete. "Foreword." In *The New Irish Americans*, by Ray O'Hanlon. Niwot, CO: Roberts Rinehart, 1998.

Hampton, Mark. "The Political Cartoon as Educationalist Journalism: David Low's Portrayal of Mass Unemployment in Interwar Britain." *Journalism Studies* 14, no. 5 (2013): 681–97.

Hannerz, Ulf. *Transnational Connections: Culture, People, Places.* London: Routledge, 1996.

Hannigan, Robert E. *The Great War and American Foreign Policy, 1914–24.* Philadelphia: Univ. of Pennsylvania Press, 2017.

Higham, John. *Strangers in the Land: Patterns of American Nativism, 1860–1925.* New Brunswick, NJ: Rutgers Univ. Press, 2002.

Hoganson, Kristin L. *Fighting for American Manhood: How Gender Politics Provoked the Spanish-American and Philippine-American Wars.* New Haven, CT: Yale Univ. Press, 2000.

Howell, T. B. *Cobbett's Complete Collection of State Trials and Proceedings for High Treason and Other Crimes and Misdemeanors.* London: T. C. Hansard, 1814.

Hume, Janice. "Building an American Story: How Early American Historians Used Press Sources to Remember the Revolution." *Journalism History* 37, no. 3 (Fall 2011): 172–79.

———. "Memory Matters: The Evolution of Scholarship in Collective Memories and Mass Communications." *Review of Communication* 10, no. 3 (July 2010): 181–96.

Hunt, Monica "Organized Labor along Savannah's Waterfront: Mutual Cooperation among Black and White Longshoremen, 1865–1894." *Georgia Historical Quarterly* 92, no. 2 (Summer 2008): 177–99.

Huntzicker, William E. *The Popular Press, 1833–1865*. Westport, CT: Praeger, 1999.

Hutchinson, John. *The Dynamics of Cultural Nationalism*. London: Unwin Hyman, 1987.

Hyndman, Henry Myers. *Further Reminiscences*. London: Macmillan, 1912.

Ignatiev, Noel. *How the Irish Became White*. New York: Routledge, 1995.

Inglis, Fred. *A Short History of Celebrity*. Princeton, NJ: Princeton Univ. Press, 2010.

Jahoda, Gloria. *The Trail of Tears*. New York: Wings Books, 1995.

James, Henry. *Partial Portraits*. New York: Macmillan, 1888.

James Madison to Thomas Jefferson, May 3, 1811. In *Writings of James Madison, Vol. 8 (Correspondence, 1808–1819)*, edited by Gaillard Hunt, 51. New York: Putnam, 1908.

"J. Armoy Knox." *Folio* 28, no. 4 (1885): 139.

Johns, Elizabeth. *American Genre Painting: The Politics of Everyday Life*. New Haven, CT: Yale Univ. Press, 1991.

Judge, Edward. *Easter in Kishinev: Anatomy of a Pogrom*. New York: NYU Press, 1995.

Kahn, Michael Alexander, and Richard Samuel West. *Puck: What Fools These Mortals Be*. San Diego, CA: IDW, 2014.

Kasson, Joy S. *Buffalo Bill's Wild West: Celebrity, Memory, and Popular History*. New York: Hill and Wang, 2000.

Kearns, Kevin C. *Dublin Tenement Life: An Oral History*. Dublin: Gill & Macmillan, 1994.

Keating, Anthony. "Killing Off the Competition." *Media History* 22, no. 1 (2016): 85–100.

Kelley, Laura D. *The Irish in New Orleans*. Lafayette: Univ. of Louisiana at Lafayette Press, 2014.

Kelly, John. *The Graves Are Walking: The Great Famine and the Saga of the Irish People*. New York: Henry Holt, 2012.

Kennan, Jerry, and Spencer C. Tucker. "Othis, Elwell S." In *The Encyclopedia of the Spanish-American and Philippine-American Wars: A Political, Social, and Military History*, edited by Spencer C. Tucker, 457–58. Santa Barbara, CA: ABC-CLIO, 2009.

Kenneally, Ian. *From the Earth, a Cry: The Story of John Boyle O'Reilly*. Cork: Collins Press, 2011.

———. "Patrick Donahoe: An Irish-American Leader." *Breifne* 14, no. 52 (2017): 107–18.

Kenneally, James J. "Catholicism and Woman Suffrage in Massachusetts." *Catholic Historical Review* 53, no. 1 (April 1967): 43–57.

Kennedy, David. *Over Here: The First World War and American Society*. New York: Oxford Univ. Press, 1980.

Kenny, Colum. *An Irish-American Odyssey: The Remarkable Rise of the O'Shaughnessy Brothers*. Columbia: Univ. of Missouri Press, 2014.

———. "James Larkin and the Jew's Shilling: Irish Workers, Activists and Anti-Semitism before Independence." *Irish Economic and Social History* 44, no. 1 (2017): 1–19.

———. "Matthew Duane: A Prudent Irish Catholic Chamber Counsel in England." *Eighteenth-Century Ireland* 33 (2018): 87–112.

———. "Sinn Féin, Socialists and 'McSheeneys': Representations of Jews in Early Twentieth-Century Ireland." *Journal of Modern Jewish Studies* 16, no. 2 (2017): 198–218.

Kenny, Kevin. *The American Irish: A History*. Edinburgh: Pearson, 2000.

———. *Making Sense of the Molly Maguires*. New York: Oxford Univ. Press, 1998.

Kesterson, David B. "Those *Literary* Comedians." In *Critical Essays on American Humor*, edited by William Bedford Clark and W. Craig Turner, 167–83. Boston: G. K. Hall, 1984.

Kibler, Alison. *Censoring Racial Ridicule: Irish, Jewish and African American Struggles over Race and Representation, 1890–1930*. Chapel Hill: Univ. of North Carolina Press, 2015.

Kickham, Charles J. *Knocknagow; or, the Homes of Tipperary*. 13th ed. Dublin: Duffy, 1887.

Kieniewicz, Stefan. "The Social Visage of Poland in 1848." *Slavonic and East European Review* 27, no. 68 (December 1948): 91–105.

King, Carla. "'Always with a Pen in His Hand': Michael Davitt and the Press." In *Visual, Material and Print Culture in Nineteenth-Century Ireland*, edited by Ciara Breathnach and Catherine Lawless, 186–97. Dublin: Four Courts Press, 2010.

———. *Michael Davitt after the Land League, 1882–1906*. Dublin: UCD Press, 2016.

———, ed. *Michael Davitt: Collected Writings, 1868–1906*. 8 vols. London: Thoemmes Press, 2001.

King, Charles R., ed. *The Life and Correspondence of Rufus King, Comprising His Letters, Private and Official, His Public Documents and His Speeches.* New York: Putnam, 1895.

Kinzer, Donald L. *An Episode in Anti-Catholicism: The American Protective Association.* Seattle: Univ. of Washington Press, 1964.

Knobel, Dale. *Paddy and the Republic: Ethnicity and Nationality in Antebellum America.* Middletown, CT: Wesleyan Univ. Press, 1986.

Knowlton, Steven R. "The Politics of John Mitchel: A Reappraisal." *Éire-Ireland* 22, no. 2 (Summer 1987): 38–55.

Kramer, Paul A. "Empires, Exceptions, and Anglo-Saxons: Race and Rule between the British and United States Empires, 1880–1910." *Journal of American History* 88, no. 4 (2002): 1315–53.

Krauth, Leland. "Mark Twain: The Victorian of Southwestern Humor." In *Humor of the Old South*, edited by Thomas M. Inge and Edward J. Piacentino, 222–35. Lexington: Univ. Press of Kentucky, 2001.

Krogman, Matthew J. "Censorship: Spanish-American and Philippine-American Wars." In *The Encyclopedia of the Spanish-American and Philippine-American Wars: A Political, Social, and Military History*, edited by Spencer C. Tucker, 106–7. Santa Barbara, CA: ABC-CLIO, 2009.

Kvach, John F. *DeBow's Review: The Antebellum Vision of a New South.* Lexington: Univ. Press of Kentucky, 2013.

Lamb, Chris. "Drawing Power: The Limits of Editorial Cartoons in America." *Journalism Studies* 8, no. 5 (2007): 715–29.

Larkin, Felix M. "The Dog in the Night-Time: The *Freeman's Journal*, the Irish Parliamentary Party and the Empire, 1875–1919." In *Newspapers and Empire in Ireland and Britain: Reporting the British Empire, c.1857–1921*, edited by Simon J. Potter, 109–23. Dublin: Four Courts Press, 2004.

———. "Green Shoots of the New Journalism in the *Freeman's Journal*, 1877–90." In *Ireland and the New Journalism*, edited by Karen Steele and Michael de Nie, 35–55. New York: Palgrave Macmillan, 2014.

Lawless, Joseph T. "Some Irish Settlers in Virginia." *Journal of the Irish American Historical Society* 2 (1899): 161–62.

Lawrence, Windy, Benjamin R. Bates, and Mark Cervenka. "Politics Drawn in Black and White: Henry J. Lewis's Visual Rhetoric in Late-1800s Black Editorial Cartoons." *Journalism History* 40, no. 3 (Fall 2014): 138–47.

Leary, William M., Jr. "Woodrow Wilson, Irish Americans, and the Election of 1916." *Journal of American History* 54, no. 1 (1967): 57–72.

Leiken, Steven Bernard. *The Practical Utopians: American Workers and the Cooperative Movement in the Gilded Age*. Detroit, MI: Wayne State Univ. Press, 2005.

Leonard, Mother Seraphine. *Immortelles of Catholic Columbian Literature Compiled from the Works of American Catholic Women Writers by the Ursulines of New York*. Akron, OH: D. H. McBride, 1897.

Linneman, William R. "Colonel Bill Snort: A Texas Jack Downing." *Southwestern Historical Quarterly* 64, no. 1 (1961): 185–99.

Little, Nigel. *Transoceanic Radical: William Duane, National Identity and Empire 1760–1835*. New York: Taylor & Francis, 2008.

Lockley, Timothy J. *Lines in the Sand: Race and Class in Lowcountry Georgia, 1750–1860*. Athens: Univ. of Georgia Press, 2003.

Lundberg, Ferdinand. *Imperial Hearst: A Social Biography*. New York: Equinox Cooperative Press, 1936.

MacRaild, Donald M. "Review of Anthony McNicholas, *Politics, Religion and the Press: Irish Journalism in Mid-Victorian England*." *Catholic Historical Review* 95, no. 1 (2009): 173–74.

Malone, Dumas. *Jefferson and the Ordeal of Liberty*. Boston: Little, Brown, 1962.

Mann, Arthur. *Yankee Reformers in the Urban Age*. Chicago: Univ. of Chicago Press, 1974.

Marley, Laurence. *Michael Davitt: Freelance Radical and Frondeur*. Dublin: Four Courts Press, 2007.

Matson, Cathy, and James N. Green. "Ireland, America, and Mathew Carey: Special Issue Introduction." *Early American Studies* 11, no. 3 (Fall 2013): 395–402.

McCartan, Patrick. *With de Valera in America*. Dublin: Fitzpatrick, 1932.

McCracken, Donal P. "Imperial Running Dogs or Wild Geese Reporters? Irish Journalists in South Africa." *Historia (Historical Association of South Africa)* 58, no. 1 (January 2013): 122–38.

———. *Inspector Mallon: Buying Irish Patriotism for a Five Pound Note*. Dublin: Irish Academic Press, 2009.

———. "The Relationship between British War Correspondents in the Field and British Military Intelligence during the Anglo-Boer War." *Scientia Militaria, South African Journal of Military Studies* 43, no. 1 (2015): 99–126.

McCullagh, David. *De Valera: Rise (1882–1932)*. Dublin: Gill Books, 2017.

McDonogh, Gary W. *Black and Catholic in Savannah, Georgia*. Knoxville: Univ. of Tennessee Press, 1993.

McGill, Meredith L. *American Literature and the Culture of Reprinting, 1834–1853*. Philadelphia: Univ. of Pennsylvania Press, 2003.

McGough, Eileen. *Diarmuid Lynch: A Forgotten Irish Patriot*. Cork: Mercier Press, 2013.

McGovern, Bryan P. *John Mitchel: Irish Nationalist, Southern Secessionist*. Knoxville: Univ. of Tennessee Press, 2009.

McGrath, Thomas F. *History of the Ancient Order of Hibernians from the Earliest Period to the Joint National Convention at Trenton, New Jersey, June 27, 1898, with Biography of the Rt. Rev. James A. McFaul*. Cleveland, OH: J. S. Savage, 1898.

McGuiness, Martin. "Foreword." In *Touched by Thunder* by Waylon Gary White Deer. Walnut Creek, CA: Left Coast Press, 2013.

McGuire, Kathleen Diane. "The Transatlantic Paddy: The Making of Transnational Irish Identity in Nineteenth-Century America." PhD diss., Univ. of California, Riverside, 2009.

McKivigan, John R. *Abolitionism and American Politics and Government*. New York: Garland, 1999.

McLachlan, Noel. "Davitt, Michael (1846–1906)." In *Dictionary of Irish Biography*, 107–15. Cambridge: Cambridge Univ. Press, 2009.

McLain, Charles J. *In Search of Equality: The Chinese Struggle Against Discrimination in Nineteenth-Century America*. Berkeley: Univ. of California Press, 1994.

McMahon, Cian. "Caricaturing Race and Nation in the Irish American Press, 1870–1880: A Transnational Perspective." *Journal of American Ethnic History* 33, no. 2 (Winter 2014): 33–56.

———. "Ireland and the Birth of the Irish-American Press, 1842–61." *American Periodicals* 19, no. 1 (2009): 5–20.

McManamin, Francis G. *The American Years of John Boyle O'Reilly, 1870–1890*. New York: Arno Press, 1976.

Meagher, Timothy. "Irish America." In *The Cambridge Social History of Modern Ireland*, edited by Eugenio F. Biagini and Mary E. Daly, 497–514. New York: Cambridge Univ. Press, 2017.

Medhurst, Martin J., and Michael A. DeSousa. "Political Cartoons as Rhetorical Form: A Taxonomy of Graphic Discourse." *Communication Monographs* 48, no. 3 (1981): 205–13.

Metz, Leon C. *John Wesley Hardin: Dark Angel of Texas*. Norman: Univ. of Oklahoma Press, 1998.

Miller, Kerby A. *Emigrants and Exiles: Ireland and the Irish Exodus to North America*. New York: Oxford Univ. Press, 1988.

Miller, Kerby A, Arnold Schrier, Bruce D. Boling, and David N. Doyle. *Irish Immigrants in the Land of Canaan: Letters and Memoirs from Colonial and Revolutionary America, 1675–1815*. New York: Oxford Univ. Press, 2003.

Miller, Stuart C. *Benevolent Assimilation: The American Conquest of the Philippines, 1899–1903*. New Haven, CT: Yale Univ. Press, 1982.

Miller, Worth Robert. *Populist Cartoons: An Illustrated History of the Third Party Movement in the 1890s*. Kirksville, MO: Truman State Univ. Press, 2001.

Mitchell, Arthur. *Revolutionary Government in Ireland: Dáil Éireann 1919–22*. Dublin: Gill and Macmillan, 1995.

Montégut, Émile. *John Mitchel: A Study of Irish Nationalism*, translated and edited by J. M. Hone. Dublin: Maunsel, 1915.

Moody, T. W. *Davitt and Irish Revolution, 1846–82*. New York: Oxford Univ. Press, 1981.

Mott, Frank Luther. *A History of American Magazines, 1885–1905*. Vol. 4. Cambridge, MA: Belknap Press, 1957.

Muccino, Eileen. "Irish Filibusters and Know-Nothings in Cincinnati." *Ohio Valley History* 10, no. 3 (2010): 3–26.

Mugridge, Ian. *The View from Xanadu: William Randolph Hearst and United States Foreign Policy*. Montreal: McGill-Queen's Univ. Press, 1995.

Mulcrone, Mick. "Those Miserable Little Hounds: World War I Postal Censorship of the *Irish World*." *Journalism History* 20, no. 1 (1994): 15–24.

Mulligan, Adrian N. "A Forgotten 'Greater Ireland': The Transatlantic Development of Irish Nationalism." *Scottish Geographical Journal* 118, no. 3 (2002): 219–34.

Murrel, William. *A History of American Graphic Humor*. New York: Cooper Square, 1967.

Nalbach, Alex. "'Poisoned at the Source'? Telegraphic News Services and Big Business in the Nineteenth Century." *Business History Review* 77, no. 4 (2003): 577–610.

"New York's Comic Papers." *Hamilton Literary Monthly* 30 (April 1896): 284–89.

Ní Bhroiméil, Úna. "Anglo-American Rapprochement and Irish America: John Bull in the Irish World, 1909–14." In *Culture and Society in Ireland Since 1750: Essays in Honour of Gearóid Ó Tuathaigh*, edited by John Cunningham and Niall Ó Cíosáin, 263–81. Dublin: Lilliput Press, 2015.

———. *Building Irish Identity in America, 1890–1915: The Gaelic Revival.* Dublin: Four Courts Press, 2003.

———. "Political Cartoons as Visual Opinion Discourse: The Rise and Fall of John Redmond in the *Irish World*." In *Ireland and the New Journalism*, edited by Karen Steele and Michael de Nie, 119–40. Basingstoke, UK: Palgrave Macmillan, 2014.

———. "The South African War, Empire and the *Irish World*, 1899–1902." In *Newspapers and Empire in Ireland and Britain: Reporting the British Empire, c.1857–1921*, edited by Simon J. Potter, 195–216. Dublin: Four Courts Press, 2004.

———. "'Up with the American Flag in All the Glory of Its Stainless Honor': Anti-Imperial Rhetoric in the *Chicago Citizen*, 1898–1902." In *Ireland in an Imperial World: Citizenship, Opportunism and Subversion*, edited by Timothy G. McMahon, Michael de Nie, and Paul Townend, 245–65. Basingstoke, UK: Palgrave Macmillan, 2017.

Niehaus, Earl F. *The Irish in New Orleans, 1800–1860.* Baton Rouge: Louisiana State Univ. Press, 1965.

Nora, Pierre. *Realms of Memory: Rethinking the French Past.* New York: Columbia Univ. Press, 1996.

Nord, David. *Communities of Journalism: A History of American Newspapers and Their Readers.* Urbana: Univ. of Illinois Press, 2001.

Oberg, Barbara B., ed. *The Papers of Thomas Jefferson, Volume 31: 1 February 1799 to 31 May 1800.* Princeton, NJ: Princeton Univ. Press, 2004.

O'Brien, Gillian. *Blood Runs Green: The Murder That Transfixed Gilded Age Chicago.* Chicago: Univ. of Chicago Press, 2015.

O'Brien, James. *Irish Celts: A Cyclopedia of Race History.* Detroit: L. F. Kilroy, 1884.

O'Brien, Mark. *De Valera, Fianna Fáil and the Irish Press: The Truth in the News?* Dublin: Irish Academic Press, 2001.

———. *The Fourth Estate: Journalism in Twentieth-Century Ireland.* Manchester, UK: Manchester Univ. Press, 2017.

———. "Other Voices: *The Bell* and Documentary Journalism." In *Periodicals and Journalism in Twentieth-Century Ireland*, edited by Mark O'Brien and Felix M. Larkin, 158–72. Dublin: Four Courts Press, 2014.

O'Brien, William. *Evening Memories*. Dublin: Maunsel, 1920.

O'Connor, Thomas H. *The Boston Irish: A Political History*. Old Saybrook, CT: Konecky & Konecky, 1995.

O'Donghaile, Deaglan. *Blasted Literature: Victorian Political Fiction and the Shock of Modernism*. Edinburgh: Edinburgh Univ. Press, 2011.

O'Donnell, Edward T. "Though Not an Irishman: Henry George and the American Irish." *American Journal of Economics and Sociology* 56, no. 4 (1997): 407–19.

Offner, John L. "McKinley and the Spanish-American War." *Presidential Studies Quarterly* 34, no. 1 (March 2004): 50–61.

O'Grady, Brendan. "Wexford Remembered in Prince Edward Island." In *The Past: The Organ of the Uí Cinsealaigh Historical Society* 16 (1988): 41–44.

O'Hanlon, Ray. *The New Irish Americans*. Niwot, CO: Roberts Rinehart, 1998.

O'Neill, Peter D. *Famine Irish and the American Racial State*. New York: Routledge, 2017.

O'Reilly, John Boyle. "What Has Ireland Gained by Agitation." *American Catholic Quarterly Review* 8 (October 1883): 715.

Palen, Marc-William. "Foreign Relations in the Gilded Age: A British Free-Trade Conspiracy?" *Diplomatic History* 37, no. 2 (2013): 217–47.

———. "The Imperialism of Economic Nationalism, 1890–1913." *Diplomatic History* 39, no. 1 (2015): 157–85.

Parker, David B. *Alias Bill Arp: Charles Henry Smith and the South's Goodly Heritage*. Athens: Univ. of Georgia Press, 2009.

Pasley, Jeffrey L. *"The Tyranny of Printers": Newspaper Politics in the Early American Republic*. Charlottesville: Univ. of Virginia Press, 2001.

Peterson, Richard. *The Public Statutes at Large of the United States of America*. Vol. 6. Boston: Little and Brown, 1846.

Phillips, Kim T. "William Duane, Philadelphia's Democratic Republics, and the Origin of Modern Politics." *Pennsylvania Magazine of History and Biography* 101, no. 3 (July 1977): 365–87.

Piacentino, Edward J. "Sleepy Hollow" Comes South: Washington Irving's Influence on Old Southwestern Humor." In *Humor of the Old South*, edited by Thomas M. Inge and Edward J. Piacentino, 22–35. Lexington: Univ. Press of Kentucky, 2001.

Pickering, David. *Texas Siftings and Texas Journalism*. Austin: Univ. of Texas Press, 1976.

Pollard, Mary. *A Dictionary of Members of the Dublin Book Trade, 1500–1800*. London: Biographical Society, 2000.

Potter, Simon J. *News and the British World: The Emergence of the Imperial Press System, 1876–1922*. Oxford: Clarendon, 2003.

Power, Tyrone. *Impressions of America: During the Years 1833, 1834, and 1835*. London: Richard Bentley, 1836.

Press, Charles. *The Political Cartoon*. Rutherford, NJ: Fairleigh Dickinson Univ. Press, 1981.

Quinn, James. "John Mitchel and the Rejection of the 19th Century." *Éire-Ireland* 38, no. 3/4 (2003): 90–108.

Quinn, John. "Southern Citizen: John Mitchel, the Confederacy and Slavery." *History Ireland* 15, no. 3 (May–June 2007): 30–35.

Rafter, Kevin. "E. J. Dillon: From Our Special Correspondent." In *Irish Journalism before Independence: More a Disease Than a Profession*, edited by Kevin Rafter, 91–105. Manchester: Manchester Univ. Press, 2011.

Ragsdale, Bruce A. *The Sedition Act Trials: Federal Trials and Great Debates in United States History*. Washington, DC: Federal Judicial Center, 2005.

Redpath, Lionel V. *Petroleum in California: A Concise and Reliable History of the Oil Industry of the State*. Los Angeles: Redpath, 1900.

Reed, David. *The Popular Magazine in Britain and the United States of America, 1880–1960*. Toronto: Univ. of Toronto Press, 1997.

Reynolds, David. *Rich Relations: The American Occupation of Britain, 1942–1945*. New York: Random House, 1995.

Ritchie, Donald A. *American Journalists: Getting the Story*. New York: Oxford Univ. Press, 1997.

Robinson, Greg. "Quebec Newspaper Reactions to the 1907 Vancouver Riots: Humanitarianism, Nationalism, and Internationalism." *BC Studies* 192 (Winter 2016–17): 25–49.

Roche, James Jeffrey. *Life of John Boyle O'Reilly: Together with His Complete Poems and Speeches*. Philadelphia: John J. McVey, 1891.

Rodechko, J. P. *Patrick Ford and His Search for America: A Case Study of Irish-American Journalism, 1870–1913*. New York: Arno Press, 1976.

Rogers, Edmund. "The United States and the Fiscal Debate in Britain, 1873–1913." *Historical Journal* 50, no. 3 (2007): 593–622.

Rosenfeld, Richard N. *American Aurora: A Democratic-Republican Returns; The Suppressed History of Our Nation's Beginnings and the Heroic Newspaper That Tried to Report It.* New York: St. Martin's Press, 1997.

Russell, Anthony. "John Mitchel: Flawed Hero." *History Ireland* 24, no. 1 (January–February 2016): 30–33.

Saul, Norman E. *The Life and Times of Charles R. Crane, 1858–1939: American Businessman.* Lanham, MD: Lexington Books, 2013.

Scherr, Arthur. "'Vox Populi' Verses the Patriot President: Benjamin Franklin Bache's Philadelphia Aurora and John Adams (1797)." *Pennsylvania History: A Journal of Mid-Atlantic Studies* 62, no. 4 (Fall 1995): 503–31.

Schoenberg, Philip E. "The American Reaction to the Kishinev Pogrom of 1903." *Jewish Historical Quarterly* 63, no. 3 (March 1974): 262–83.

Schreiber, Rachel. "Before Their Makers and Their Judges: Prostitutes and White Slaves in the Political Cartoons of the 'Masses' (New York, 1911–1917)." *Feminist Studies* 33, no. 1 (Spring 2009): 161–93.

Schudson, Michael. "Four Approaches to the Sociology of News." In *Mass Media and Society*, edited by James Curran and Michael Gurevitch, 172–97. London: Hodder Arnold, 2005.

———. *The Sociology of the News.* New York: W. W. Norton, 2003.

Seymour-Ure, Colin. "Farewell Camelot! British Cartoonists' Views of the United States since Watergate." *Journalism Studies* 8, no. 5 (2007): 730–41.

Shannon, William. *The American Irish.* New York: McMillian, 1963.

Shaw, Donald L. "News Bias and the Telegraph: A Study of Historical Change." *Journalism Quarterly* 4, no. 1 (Spring 1967): 3–31.

Shaw, Matthew J. "Drawing on the Collections." *Journalism Studies* 8, no. 5 (2007): 742–54.

Shepard, Christopher. "Irish Journalists in the Intellectual Diaspora: Edward Alexander Morphy and Henry David O'Shea in the Far East." *New Hibernia Review* 14, no. 3 (Autumn 2010): 75–90.

Shoemaker, Edward M. "Strangers and Citizens: The Irish Immigrant Community of Savannah, 1837–1861." PhD diss., Emory Univ., 1990.

Shulim, Joseph I. "John Daly Burk: Irish Revolutionist and American Patriot." *Transactions of the American Philosophical Society* 54, no. 6 (1964): 1–60.

Siebert, Fred S. *Freedom of the Press in England, 1476–1776: The Rise and Decline of Government Control.* Urbana-Champaign: Univ. of Illinois Press, 1965.

Sloan, William David. "The Party Press." In *The Media in America: A History*, edited by William David Sloan, 69–94. Northport, AL: Vision Press, 2005.

Smith, Anthony. *The British Press since the War.* Totowa, NJ: Rowman & Littlefield, 1974.

———. "The Long Road to Objectivity and Back Again: The Kinds of Truth We Get in Journalism." In *Newspaper History from the 17th Century to the Present Day*, edited by George Boyce, James Curran, and Pauline Windgate, 153–71. London: Sage, 1978.

Smith, Graham. *When Jim Crow Met John Bull.* New York: St. Martin's Press, 1987.

Smith, James Morton. "The 'Aurora' and the Alien and Sedition Laws. Part 1: The Editorship of Benjamin Franklin Bache." *Pennsylvania Magazine of History and Biography* 77, no. 1 (January 1953): 3–23.

———. "The 'Aurora' and the Alien and Sedition Laws. Part 2: The Editorship of William Duane." *Pennsylvania Magazine of History and Biography* 77, no. 2 (February 1953): 123–55.

———. "The Case of John Daly Burk and His New York 'Time Piece.'" *Journalism Quarterly* 30, no. 3 (1953): 23–36.

Smith, Jeffery A. *War and Press Freedom: The Problem of Prerogative Power.* New York: Oxford Univ. Press, 1999.

Soper, Kerry. "From Swarthy Ape to Sympathetic Everyman and Subversive Trickster: The Development of Irish Caricature in American Comic Strips between 1890 and 1920." *Journal of American Studies* 39, no. 2 (2005): 257–96.

Speck, Ernest B. "Alex Sweet: Comic Journalist from Texas." *Texas Press Messenger* 46 (1971): 6–8.

Sprows Cummings, Kathleen. *New Women of the Old Faith: Gender and American Catholicism in the Progressive Era.* Chapel Hill: Univ. of North Carolina Press, 2010.

Stanton, Elizabeth Cody, Susan B. Anthony, and Matilda Joslyn Gage, eds. *History of Woman Suffrage.* New York: Susan B. Anthony, 1889.

Stevens, John D. *From the Back of the Foxhole: Black Correspondents in World War II.* Journalism Monographs 27. Columbia, SC: Association for Education in Journalism and Mass Communication, 1973.

Stolarik, M. Mark. *Forgotten Doors: The Other Ports of Entry to the United States*. Philadelphia: Balch Institute Press, 1988.

Stone, Geoffrey R. *Perilous Times: Free Speech in War Time from the Sedition Act of 1798 to the War on Terrorism*. New York: W. W. Norton, 2004.

Sullivan, Alexander. "Parnell as a Leader." *North American Review* 144, no. 367 (June 1887): 613.

Sullivan, Margaret. "A Paper-Knife of Irish Oak." In *The Poetry and Song of Ireland*, edited by John Boyle O'Reilly. New York: Gay Brothers, 1889.

Sullivan, M. F. *Ireland of To-day: Causes and Aims of Irish Agitation*. San Francisco: Bancroft, 1881.

Summers, Mark W. *Rum, Romanism, and Rebellion: The Making of a President 1884*. Chapel Hill: Univ. of North Carolina Press, 2000.

Sweeney, Michael S. *Secrets of Victory: The Office of Censorship and the American Press and Radio in World War II*. Chapel Hill: Univ. of North Carolina Press, 2001.

Taylor, Jeff. *Where Did the Party Go? William Jennings Bryan, Hubert Humphrey, and the Jeffersonian Legacy*. Columbia: Univ. of Missouri Press, 2006.

Teeter, Dwight L., and Ron R. Le Duc. *Law of Mass Communications: Freedom and Control of Print and Broadcast Media*. Westbury, NY: Foundation Press, 1995.

Temple, Mick. *The British Press*. Berkshire: Open Univ. Press, 2008.

Topping, Simon. "'The Dusky Doughboys': Interaction between African-American Soldiers and the Population of Northern Ireland during the Second World War." *Journal of American Studies* 47, no. 4 (2013): 1131–54.

———. "Laying Down the Law to the Irish and the Coons: Stormont's Response to American Racial Segregation in Northern Ireland during the Second World War." *Historical Research* 86, no. 234 (November 2013): 741–59.

Tuchman, Gaye. *Making News: A Study in the Construction of Reality*. New York: Free Press, 1978.

Tucker, Ann. "Newest Born of Nations: Southern Thought on European Nationalisms and the Creation of the Confederacy, 1820–1860." PhD diss., Univ. of Southern California, 2014.

Tuffnell, Stephen. "'Uncle Sam Is to Be Sacrificed': Anglophobia in Late Nineteenth-Century Politics and Culture." *American Nineteenth Century History* 12, no. 1 (2011): 77–99.

Turner, Graeme. *Understanding Celebrity.* London: Sage, 2014.

Tynan, Katharine. *Twenty-Five Years: Reminiscences.* London: Smith, Elder, 1913.

van Cleve, Charles. "The Teaching of Shakespeare in American Secondary Schools." *Peabody Journal of Education* 15, no. 6 (May 1938): 333–50.

Van Dussen, D. Gregory. "An American Response to Irish Catholic Immigration: The *Methodist Quarterly Review,* 1830–1870." *Methodist History* 10, no. 1 (1971): 21–36.

Van Vugt, William E. "British and British Americans (English, Scots, Scots Irish, and Welsh) to 1870." In *Immigrants in American History: Arrival, Adaptation, and Integration,* vol. 1, edited by Elliott Robert Barkan, 19–29. Santa Barbara, CA: ABC-CLIO, 2013.

Volokh, Eugene. "Thomas Cooper, Early American Public Intellectual," *New York University Journal of Law and Liberty* 4 (2009): 371–81.

Vultee, Fred. "Dr. FDR and Baby War: The World through Chicago Political Cartoons before and after Pearl Harbor." *Visual Communication Quarterly* 14 (2007): 158–75.

Walch, Timothy. "The Catholic Press and the Campaign for Parish Schools: Chicago and Milwaukee 1850–1885." *U.S. Catholic Historian* 3, no. 4 (Spring 1984): 254–72.

———. "Catholic Social Institutions and Urban Development: The View from Nineteenth-Century Chicago and Milwaukee." *Catholic Historical Review* 64, no. 1 (January 1978): 16–32.

Walsh, Francis Robert. "The Boston Pilot: A Newspaper for the Irish Immigrant, 1829–1908." PhD diss., Boston Univ., 1968.

Ward, Alan J. *Ireland and Anglo-Irish Relations, 1899–1921.* Toronto: Univ. of Toronto Press, 1969.

Waters, Enoch P. *American Diary: A Personal History of the Black Press.* Chicago: Path Press, 1987.

Wcislo, Frank W. *Tales of Imperial Russia: The Life and Times of Sergei Witte, 1849–1915.* Oxford: Oxford Univ. Press, 2011.

West, Richard Samuel. *Satire on Stone: The Political Cartoons of Joseph Keppler.* Urbana: Univ. of Illinois Press, 1988.

Whelehan, Niall. *Irish Nationalism and Political Violence in the Wider World, 1867–1900.* New York: Cambridge Univ. Press, 2012.

———. "Skirmishing, the Irish World, and Empire, 1876–86." *Éire-Ireland* 42, no. 1–2 (Spring–Summer 2007): 180–200.

White Deer, Waylon Gary. *Touched by Thunder*. Walnut Creek, CA: Left Coast Press, 2013.

Whitt, Jan. *Women in American Journalism: A New History*. Urbana: Univ. of Illinois Press, 2008.

Widmer, Mary Lou. *Lace Curtain*. New York: Jove Books, 1985.

———. *Margaret: Friend of Orphans*. New Orleans: Pelican, 1998.

Wiener, Joel H. *The Americanization of the British Press, 1830s–1914*. London: Palgrave, 2011.

———. "Get the News! Get the News!: Speed in Transatlantic Journalism, 1830–1914." In *Anglo-American Media Interactions, 1850–2000*, edited by Joel H. Wiener and Mark Hampton, 48–66. London: Palgrave Macmillan, 2007.

Wiid, Ria, Leyland F. Pitt, and Anne Engstrom. "Not So Sexy: Public Opinion of Political Sex Scandals as Reflected in Political Cartoons." *Journal of Public Affairs* 11, no. 3 (2011): 137–47.

Willard, Frances F. *Occupations for Women*. New York: Success, 1897.

Wilson, David A. *United Irishmen, United States: Immigrant Radicals in the Early Republic*. Ithaca, NY: Cornell Univ. Press, 1998.

Wood, Charles H. "The Sullivan Trial." *American Law Register (1852–1891)* 25, no. 7 (July 1877): 385–92.

Wynn, Neil A. *The African-American Experience during World War II*. Lanham, MD: Rowman & Littlefield, 2010.

Yanoso, Nicole Anderson. *The Irish and the American Presidency*. New Brunswick, NJ: Transaction, 2016.

Yeats, W. B., and Katharine Tynan. *Letters to Katharine Tynan*. Edited by Roger McHugh. New York: McMullen, 1953.

Zinn, Howard. *A People's History of the United States*. New York: Perennial Classics, 2001.

Zipperstein, Steven J. "Inside Kishinev's Pogrom: Hayyim Nahman Bialik, Michael Davitt and the Burden of Truth." In *The Individual in History: Essays in Honor of Jehuda Reinharz*, edited by ChaeRan Y. Freeze, Sylvia Fuks Fried, and Eugene R. Sheppard, 65–83. Waltham, MA: Brandeis Univ. Press, 2015.

Contributor Biographies

Marcel Broersma is professor of media and journalism studies at the University of Groningen and the director of its Centre for Media and Journalism Studies. His research focuses on the current and historical transformation of journalism, changing media use, social media, and digital humanities. He has published three monographs, numerous book chapters, and articles in peer-reviewed journals, and edited nine books and eight special journal issues on media history, social media, transformations in journalism, and political communication. He chairs the boards of the Dutch Research School for Media Studies (RMeS) and of eHumanities.nl, and sits on the editorial boards of seven international journals.

David W. Bulla serves as a professor of communication at Augusta University. Bulla focuses his research on the history of journalism, examining limitations on press performance. He is the author of five books, including two with Gregory A. Borchard. Their book, *Journalism in the Civil War Era*, was published by Peter Lang in 2010, and *Lincoln Mediated: The President and the Press through Nineteenth Century Media* was published by Transaction in 2015. Bulla is assistant editor of both *Journalism History* and the *Southeastern Review of Journalism History*. He earned his PhD in mass communication from the University of Florida.

Mary Lamonica (Mary M. Cronin) is a professor in the Department of Journalism and Media Studies at New Mexico State University. Her PhD is from Michigan State University and her BA and MA are from the University of Miami. Her research areas are media law and media history, with an emphasis on nineteenth- and early twentieth-century press performance. She publishes under the name Mary M. Cronin. She is the author of three books, as well as numerous book chapters and scholarly articles. Prior to entering academia, Lamonica worked as a reporter, assistant news editor, and copy editor at newspapers in Massachusetts, New Jersey, and Florida. She also has worked for public radio and has freelanced articles to national magazines.

Michael Doorley is an associate lecturer in history with the Open University in Ireland. He is a graduate of University College Dublin and earned his PhD at the University of Illinois at Chicago. He is the author of *Irish American Diaspora Nationalism: The Friends of Irish Freedom, 1916–35* (2005). He has published widely on the history of the Irish diaspora in the United States including chapters in the landmark volumes, *Ireland's Allies: America and the 1916 Easter Rising* (2016) and *The Atlas of the Irish Revolution* (2017). His latest work, *Justice Daniel Cohalan, 1865–1946: American Patriot and Irish-American Nationalist* (2019), was published by Cork University Press.

Steven T. Engel is associate professor of political science and director of the University Honors Program at Georgia Southern University. He is the author or coauthor of several articles and book chapters on nationalism, political identity, police reform in Northern Ireland, and honors education. Along with Howard Keeley, since 2014 he has been investigating the nineteenth-century migration pathway and the historic and lasting connections between Wexford, Ireland, and Savannah, Georgia, through the Wexford-Savannah Axis Project.

Howard J. Keeley is director of the Center for Irish Research and Teaching at Georgia Southern University. He earned his PhD from Princeton University, and his research interests include Irish and British literature. Along with Steven T. Engel, since 2014 he has been investigating the nineteenth-century migration pathway and the historic and lasting connections between Wexford, Ireland, and Savannah, Georgia, through the Wexford-Savannah Axis Project.

Ian Kenneally is an author and historian whose books include *The Paper Wall: Newspapers and Propaganda during the War of Independence* (2008) and *From the Earth, a Cry: The Story of John Boyle O'Reilly* (2011). He recently coedited, with James O'Donnell, *The Irish Regional Press, 1892–2018* (2018). Kenneally has contributed to many books, journals, and edited collections. He has also written and produced a range of radio documentaries and acted as editor for publications such as *The Revolution Papers*, a weekly history magazine.

Colum Kenny is professor emeritus at Dublin City University. A barrister, journalist, and historian, he has written widely for the Irish national media and in academic journals. His books include *An Irish-American Odyssey* (2014), which is a study of immigration, and *Moments That Changed Us: Ireland after 1973* (2005). An honorary bencher of King's Inns, he has been awarded the gold medal of the Irish Legal History Society and the DCU President's Award for Research. A founding board member of the EU Media Desk in Ireland, he served on the Broadcasting Authority of Ireland.

Nancy McKenzie Dupont is a professor of journalism at the School of Journalism and New Media at the University of Mississippi. She is the adviser to the daily TV newscast and teaches mostly broadcast journalism courses, but her research interests include Southern newspaper history. She is the author of more than a dozen book chapters and regularly presents her research at the Symposium of the Nineteenth Century Press, the Civil War, and Free Expression and the Transnational Journalism History conferences. She holds a PhD from the University of Southern Mississippi.

Daniel Mulhall has spent four decades as a member of Ireland's diplomatic service, filling a number of high-level posts, including as ambassador to Germany, the United Kingdom, and the United States. A historian by training, he has maintained a lifelong interest in Irish history and literature, about which he has written extensively, including in *A New Day Dawning: A Portrait of Ireland in 1900* (1999) and *The Shaping of Modern Ireland: A Centenary Assessment* (2016), which he coedited. Ambassador Mulhall provides daily updates about his work and interests on his Twitter account (@DanMulhall) and posts regular blogs on the embassy's website.

Úna Ní Bhroiméil lectures in American history at Mary Immaculate College, University of Limerick. She is a graduate of the National University of Ireland Galway and earned her PhD at Lehigh University, Pennsylvania. Úna is the author of *Building Irish Identity in America, 1870–1915* (2003) and has published articles on the Irish American press, the formation of female Catholic teachers, and using visual methods in historical research. She is currently writing a book on the Irish American lawyer and patron of the arts, John Quinn.

Gillian O'Brien is reader in modern Irish history at Liverpool John Moores University. She is author of *Blood Runs Green: The Murder That Transfixed Gilded Age Chicago* (2015) and has published work on Irish America, Irish republicanism, convents in Ireland, and the history of Irish primary education. She has also worked as a historical consultant on a number of major museum and heritage projects including Kilmainham Gaol and Courthouse, Dublin; Nano Nagle Place, Cork; and Spike Island, County Cork.

Mark O'Brien is associate professor of journalism history at the School of Communications, Dublin City University, and a former chair of the Newspaper and Periodical History Forum of Ireland. Former academic director of Boston University's Dublin Program, he is the author of *The Fourth Estate: Journalism in Twentieth-Century Ireland* (2017), *The Irish Times: A History* (2008), and *De Valera, Fianna Fáil and the Irish Press: The Truth in the News?* (2001). He is also coeditor of eight volumes on various aspects of press and journalism history.

Kevin Rafter is full professor of political communication and head of the School of Communications at Dublin City University. He is chair of the Arts Council of Ireland and also chairs the Compliance Committee of the Broadcasting Authority of Ireland. He is the author/editor of over a dozen books on Irish media and politics including *Resilient Reporting: Media Coverage of Irish Elections since 1969* (2019). Prior to 2008, Kevin worked as a senior political journalist including with the *Irish Times*, *Sunday Times*, *Sunday Tribune*, and RTÉ, the Irish national broadcaster, as well as editor of *Magill* magazine.

Debra Reddin van Tuyll is a professor of communication at Augusta University where she teaches journalism and public relations classes. Her PhD is from the University of South Carolina. She is the 2019 recipient of the American Journalism Historian's Association Kobre Award for lifetime achievement in journalism history and is editor of the *Southeastern Review of Journalism History*. She serves on the editorial boards of *Journalism History* and *American Journalism* and is president of the steering committee for the Symposium on the 19th Century Press, Civil War, and Free Expression.

Along with Mark O'Brien and Marcel Broersma, van Tuyll is an organizer of the annual Transnational Journalism History conference, of which this book is a product. Van Tuyll is the author and/or editor of six books, most of which deal with the role of the press in Southern culture during the American Civil War. One of those works, coedited with Patricia McNeely and Henry S. Schulte, *Knights of the Quill: Confederate Correspondents and Their Civil War Reporting*, was a finalist for the AEJMC Tankard Award for the best book on journalism in 2011.

Jordan Stenger graduated from Augusta University with a BA in communication in 2019. She has published papers as an undergraduate researcher in the *Southeastern Review of Journalism History*, and she has also served as an editorial assistant for the journal. Stenger has presented her work at the Southeastern Colloquium of the American Journalism Historians Association and the Transnational Journalism History Conference. She has received several awards for her work at the Southeastern Colloquium. Stenger works as an assistant park ranger at Redcliffe Plantation State Historic Site and plans to begin her master's degree within the next few years.

Pamela E. Walck is an assistant professor in the media department in the McAnulty College and Graduate School of Liberal Arts at Duquesne University. She received her PhD in mass communication from the E. W. Scripps School of Journalism at Ohio University and her MA in journalism and mass communication from Point Park University, Pittsburgh, Pennsylvania. Her research agenda focuses on historic journalism, the African American press during the twentieth century, and the innovation of social media and technology in modern newsrooms. She is currently working on a book about the *Pittsburgh Courier*.

Index

Page numbers in italics refer to illustrations.